MW00576743

Recollections
of a
Naval Officer

CLASSICS OF NAVAL LITERATURE
JACK SWEETMAN, SERIES EDITOR

The purpose of this series is to make available attractive new editions of classic works of naval history, biography, and fiction. In addition to the complete original text, each volume will feature an introduction and, when appropriate, notes by an expert in the field. The series will include, among others, the following titles:

My Fifty Years in the Navy by Admiral Charles E. Clark
The Sand Pebbles by Richard McKenna
The Commodores by Leonard F. Guttridge and Jay D. Smith
Recollections of a Naval Officer, 1841–1865 by Captain William Harwar Parker
Man-o'-War Life by Charles Nordhoff
Sailing Alone Around the World by Joshua Slocum
Recollections of a Naval Life by John M. Kell
Journal of a Cruise by Captain David Porter
Two Years Before the Mast by Richard Henry Dana
Autobiography by Admiral George Dewey
Under the Stars and Bars: Confederate Naval Narratives by various authors
Delilah by Marcus Goodrich

Recollections
of a
Naval Officer
1841–1865

By Captain William Harwar Parker
With an introduction and notes by Craig L. Symonds

NAVAL INSTITUTE PRESS
Annapolis, Maryland

This book was originally published in
1883 by Charles Scribners' Sons, New York, New York.

Copyright © 1985 on the introduction and notes
by the United States Naval Institute
Annapolis, Maryland

The original edition of *Recollections of a Naval Officer* contained neither maps nor
illustrations. All of those that appear here have been specially selected for this edition of
Classics of Naval Literature.

Library of Congress Cataloging in Publication Data
Parker, William Harwar, 1826–1896.
    Recollections of a naval officer, 1841–1865.

    (Classics of naval literature)
    Reprint. Originally published: New York, N.Y.:
Scribner, 1883.
    Includes bibliographical references.
    1. Parker, William Harwar, 1826–1896. 2. United
States. Navy—Officers—Biography. 3. Confederate
States of America. Navy—Officers—Biography.
4. United States—History—War with Mexico, 1845–1848—
Personal narratives, American. 5. United States—
History—Civil War, 1861–1865—Personal narratives,
Confederate. I. Symonds, Craig L. II. Title.
III. Series.
V63.P34A37   1985   359'.0092'4 [B]   84-22788
ISBN 0-87021-533-7

CONTENTS

LIST OF ILLUSTRATIONS

Lieutenant William Harwar Parker, CSN (From Scharf, *History of the Confederate Navy*)

INTRODUCTION

Memoirs and "recollections" of naval officers and professional travelers were a common and popular literary genre in the nineteenth century. Such memoirs served as a combination travelogue and adventure story for the reading public. Many survive today, but few of them possess the charm and wit of William H. Parker's *Recollections of a Naval Officer*. In part, this is because of the peculiar nature of Parker's naval career—he fought in two wars for two different navies and saw a great deal of active service wearing Confederate gray. But in the main, Parker's memoir succeeds because of his lively and engaging style.

William Harwar Parker was born in New York City on 8 October 1826, but his northern birth belied a heritage that was both southern and aristocratic. The Parker family traced its lineage back to 1650 when George Parker settled in tidewater Virginia. William's uncle, Richard E. Parker, was attorney general under Andrew Jackson and later a senator from Virginia before resigning to take a seat on the Virginia Supreme Court. (William's cousin, son of this famous jurist, would also become a judge and preside over the trial of John Brown in 1859.) Both these influences were important in Parker's career; his sense of aristocracy made his adjustment to the naval hierarchy easy, and his southern lineage was the source of his decision to resign from the U.S. Navy in 1861 to fight for the Confederacy.

Family tradition was also instrumental, if not decisive, in helping determine Parker's choice of career. His father, Foxhall A. Parker, was a career naval officer who served more than forty years on active duty and retired as a captain. William's older brother, also named Foxhall, entered the navy as a midshipman in 1839 at the age of seventeen. Eventually this Foxhall Parker would also serve forty years in the navy, rising to the rank of commodore and the superintendency of the U.S. Naval Academy. Another brother, Richard Bogardus Parker, chose to enter West Point, from which he graduated in 1842, but died only a few months after joining his regiment.

For his part, William Parker entered the U.S. Navy in October 1841 at the age of fifteen. At such an age William was confused, as he tells us, when he was addressed by the officer of the deck as "Mister Parker," and assumed that the man must be addressing his father. Walking back to the ship the next day, he felt no awkwardness in holding his father by the hand in public. But fifteen was not an unusual age at which to accept an appointment as a midshipman, which was, after all, only nominally a rank, and one that included the responsibilities of student as well as those of naval officer. Even though they were addressed as "Mister" by all hands, midshipmen were expected to study the arts of navigation and seamanship and also to perform a variety of ship's jobs. After several years of this school—the school of experience—they might hope to become "passed midshipmen," eligible for promotion to the exalted rank of lieutenant.

Parker's years as a midshipman took him to both the Mediterranean and the coast of Brazil. In the 1840s the U.S. Navy's principal responsibility was to maintain an American presence in those areas of the world frequented by American trade. The navy was therefore divided into half a dozen overseas "squadrons"—in the Mediterranean, the Caribbean, the northern Pacific, the Far East, and off the coasts of Africa and Brazil. Ships rotated in and out of these squadrons, but the American presence was maintained year round. The rationale for the existence of each squadron was different. In the Mediterranean and the Caribbean seas it was to protect American merchant ships from piracy; in the northern Pacific it was to guard the American whaling fleet; off Brazil and in the Far East it was to show the U.S. flag and look after American interests in unstable political climates; and the African squadron was there to interdict the slave trade, which had become illegal for Americans in 1808. At one time or another, Parker saw duty in all of these except the Far Eastern squadron.

Duty in the Mediterranean squadron was considered the most desirable. That squadron had been established in the early nineteenth century as a continuing reminder to the corsairs of the Barbary coast that America possessed the means to retaliate for acts of "piracy" committed against merchant ships flying the Stars and Stripes. But by the time Parker served there, in the 1840s, this mission had virtually ceased to exist. In 1816 separate American squadrons under Stephen Decatur and William Bainbridge had wrested favorable treaties and pledges of passivity from the potentates of Barbary, and later that same year Lord Exmouth (the Edward Pellew who appears in several of C.S. Forester's Hornblower novels) shelled Algiers into submission. Then in 1830 the French landed in force and made Algeria a French colony. There would be no more trouble from the Barbary corsairs after that. But the American Mediterranean squadron nevertheless continued to fly the national ensign in various European ports of call as a reminder to the European powers of America's naval might. Indeed, reminding Europeans of the existence of an American navy became the primary mission of the squadron. In 1826 an English visitor to the United States noted that it seemed to be American policy to "fit out one of the finest specimens of their ship-building" and send her to cruise the Mediterranean in order to leave the Europeans "impressed with exaggerated notions of the maritime

powers of the country which sent her forth."[1] Duty in the Mediterranean squadron, therefore, was a splendid opportunity for
young midshipmen like Parker to visit ports of call such as Genoa,
Toulon, and Port Mahon in Minorca (the principal American naval
base in the Mediterranean) as part of their practical education.
After wintering over at Genoa in his first year at sea, Parker was
sent to serve off the coast of South America in what was known as
the Brazil squadron. The contrast with sophisticated Europe could
not have been greater. Parker notes ruefully that "the worst part of
the Brazil station is that there are so few ports to visit. . . ."[2] Here
the U.S. Navy served as the evangel of civilization in a very volatile
political environment. Argentina in particular was politically
fragmented, and foreign warships guarded the interests of European and American citizens in much the same way that western
gunboats would in China a half century later. At the time of
Parker's visit, Buenos Aires was a city-state ruled as a virtual
dictatorship by Juan Manuel de Rosas, a man who was almost
constantly at war with his neighbors and occasionally with European powers as well. Parker was unimpressed with de Rosas, and
indeed with most of the continent, and blamed its backwardness
on the frequency of intermarriage between the whites, the blacks,
and the natives. "It is this," he writes, "which causes the degeneration of the white man."[3] In this respect, Parker reflected not only
the strong belief in Anglo-American superiority common to the
American naval officer corps of his day but his aristocratic Virginia
heritage as well.

Parker's third cruise, still as a midshipman, gave him his first
taste of combat. He was assigned to the frigate *Potomac*, flagship of
Commodore David Conner, and as Conner's aide he found himself
at the vortex of the war with Mexico, 1846–1848. He participated
in the occupation of Port Isabel, just north of the Rio Grande,

---

[1]Frederick Barley, "A British Sailor Looks at the United States Navy of the
Early Nineteenth Century," *American Neptune* (January 1961), pp. 57–69.
[2]See text, p. 35.
[3]See text, p. 194.

during the battles of Palo Alto and Resaca de la Palma, and later
had the unique opportunity to witness at close range the first
large-scale American amphibious operation in history, the landing
at Vera Cruz. He saw service ashore during the siege of Vera Cruz
and was assigned to the naval battery (designed by a young captain
on General Scott's staff named Robert E. Lee) that helped shell the
city into submission. The experience was valuable for the young
midshipman, not only because it exposed him to combat for the
first time, but also because he had an opportunity to meet or at
least see in action many of the officers who would later become
famous as army commanders during the Civil War.

The experience did not, however, improve his opinion of the
military prowess of Latin Americans.

> What *is* a Mexican? [he wrote] Is he a Spaniard, or an Indian,
> or does the fact of a man's being born in Mexico, be he white,
> red, or black, make him a Mexican? . . . The mixed race is
> the worst and unfortunately by far the most numerous; and
> this applies to every country south of the United States. The
> only regeneration of Mexico will be by throwing open the
> doors and introducing some millions of pure-blooded white
> men.[4]

Moral and physical decline, he argues, is "the natural result of the
intermixture of races."[5] Parker's racism is the one false note in a
memoir that is otherwise open and fair minded. He makes no other
reference in his memoir to race, and in particular he offers no clues
about his attitude toward slavery.

Only after these experiences overseas and on the battlefields of
Mexico did Parker, now a seasoned veteran, at last attend the U.S.
Naval Academy, which had been founded on the grounds of old
Fort Severn near Annapolis in 1845. Parker's portrait of life at the
academy in its first years is one of the best early accounts available.
Graduating after a short course of study in 1848, he finally became

[4]See text, p. 194.
[5]See text, p. 212.

a passed midshipman and was assigned to the frigate *Constitution* bound for the Mediterranean. But Parker had had enough of sitting below the salt in large wardrooms. He applied for a change of orders to the sloop *Yorktown* bound for the coast of Africa.

If the Mediterranean was the most desirable overseas duty, the African station was the least. The squadron's mission was to intercept slave traders, especially those who sought to protect themselves from British cruisers by flying the American flag. The slave trade had been made illegal by the United States in 1808, and the British, who had led world opposition to the slave trade since the eighteenth century, had succeeded in declaring it a violation of international law at the Congress of Vienna in 1815. But when British warships tried to capture slavers off the Ivory Coast, slave ship captains frequently ran up the Stars and Stripes and claimed immunity from British interference. The few times that British captains refused to respect that flag, seeing it for the ruse it was, American diplomats felt obliged to protest. After all, the United States had recently fought a war with Britain that had been at least in part about the rights of American vessels at sea, and the United States was reluctant to allow any precedent that violated those rights. As a compromise, the two nations included a clause in the Webster-Ashburton treaty of 1842 that each nation would keep a "sufficient and adequate squadron of naval forces" off the African coast. The American ships would intercept and inspect ships flying the American flag, and the British would be responsible for all others—British ships, and ships of other nations less sensitive about maritime rights.

For Americans, duty in the African squadron was undesirable primarily because of the humid and stifling weather so close to the equator and the sickness that seemed to float about the African coast like a miasma. This duty was made more frustrating by the fact that the American "squadron" (usually only one or two ships) had to protect legitimate American traders as well as chase slavers, and often the difference between the two was difficult to discern. Even if a slaver were caught *in flagrante* and forced to put its human cargo ashore, it was virtually certain that that same cargo would soon be reembarked on another slaver. Parker's African odyssey ended rather spectacularly with the shipwreck of the *Yorktown*, which ran herself onto a submerged reef. No one drowned, but the entire ship's company was marooned for over a month on a sparsely populated island where the crew entertained itself by organizing donkey races on the beach.

Following his African cruise, Parker returned to Annapolis to serve as an instructor at the Naval Academy. It was in this capacity, perhaps, that Parker made his greatest professional contribution to the U.S. Navy. He taught for four years (1853–57) and subsequently wrote two manuals that were used for many years as textbooks at the academy. Both William and his brother Foxhall wrote several professional books on gunnery and naval tactics. William produced *Instructions for Naval Light Artillery* (1862) and also translated a French work on naval tactics, both for use at Annapolis. Ironically, only a few years later he also wrote *Questions on Practical Seamanship* (1863) and *Elements of Seamanship* (1864) for use at the *Confederate* Naval Academy, of which he became superintendent.

The four years at Annapolis constituted Parker's first shore duty, and in December 1853, only a few months into his tour, he married the former Margaret Griffin. Parker says virtually nothing about his married life in this memoir or elsewhere. All that is known for certain is that he and his wife remained married until William's death in 1896—some 43 years—and that they had no children.

News of the firing on Fort Sumter and the secession of Virginia placed Parker, and southern officers throughout the service, in a difficult dilemma. Like hundreds of others, Parker had to decide whether to resign and follow his home state out of the union, or to remain loyal to the flag. Most army officers in 1861 chose to follow their state; Robert E. Lee is only the most famous of those Virginians who struggled with this question and then decided that loyalty to state had to take precedence. But among naval officers the tie to the national ensign was stronger. The nature of their service on foreign stations led them to think of themselves as

Americans first. Only a small percentage of southern-born naval officers chose to resign their commissions and go south. William H. Parker was one of them.

According to the memoirs of Rear Admiral Charles E. Clark (whose *My Fifty Years in the Navy* comprises one of the volumes in this series), William and his brother Foxhall met in Washington just prior to the secession crisis and discussed what they would do if it came to a fight. At that time, according to Clark, Foxhall stressed the importance of their family's southern heritage and strong ties with Virginia, while William argued the primacy of loyalty to the flag. So persuasively did each put his case that when the time came to decide, each followed the other's advice. Whatever the truth of this story, it is a fact that Foxhall remained in the Union navy while William resigned and subsequently accepted a commission as a lieutenant (eventually rising to captain) in the Confederate navy. They faced each other only once in the war, and that indirectly, during the siege of Charleston, South Carolina, in 1863, when William was executive officer of the Confederate ironclad *Palmetto State* and Foxhall commanded the USS *Wabash*. Many years later, after the war, William pointed out Foxhall to a friend and told him: "There goes Foxhall, the disloyal unionist, on full pay, and here stands William, the loyal secessionist, down on his uppers."[6]

Parker's service in the Confederate navy makes up the bulk of his narrative account in *Recollections* and is the most valuable aspect of the book historically. He was given command of the gunboat *Beaufort*, in which capacity he took part in the unsuccessful defense of Roanoke Island and Elizabeth City in February 1862. The *Beaufort* then returned to Hampton Roads in time to be involved in the famous sortie with the *Merrimack*, now re-christened the *Virginia*. Parker was present in the attack on the Union fleet in Hampton Roads that decided the fate of the U.S. frigates *Congress* and *Cumberland* and was a witness to the events surrounding the

[6]Charles E. Clark, *My Fifty Years in the Navy* (Boston, 1917; Annapolis, 1984), p. 11.

capitulation of the *Minnesota*, which subsequently retracted her surrender and continued the fight. He was also a knowledgeable eyewitness to the battle between the *Monitor* and *Merrimack* the next day on 9 March 1862. Indeed, his description of the action is one of the best and most complete first-hand accounts extant.

Years after the war the controversy about this battle was renewed when Commodore John L. Worden, who had commanded the *Monitor* in her duel with the *Merrimack* and after whom the Naval Academy parade ground is named, petitioned Congress for a million dollars in prize money on behalf of himself and his crew as a reward for their "victory." His claim was based on the assertion that the *Monitor* had so badly defeated the *Merrimack* that the Confederates were subsequently forced to destroy her. Parker involved himself in this discussion by writing several public letters in which he argued that the *Merrimack* had not been defeated, that later it had on several occasions offered battle, which the *Monitor* declined, and that it had been destroyed not because of the the beating it had taken from the *Monitor*, but because the advancing Federal army threatened to occupy its base of supply.[7] Parker's account has become the historically accepted version.

As if he had a clairvoyant sense of where the next important naval action would be, Parker requested and was granted duty in Charleston Harbor aboard the Confederate ironclad *Palmetto State*. Lacking the shipbuilding facilities to compete with the North in the construction of conventional warships, the Confederacy had to experiment and improvise. The use of mines (called torpedoes or "infernal machines"), submarines, and ironclads were all part of this effort. Parker's duty in Charleston put him in the forefront of this effort, and his assignment as executive officer aboard the *Palmetto State* gave him the opportunity to participate in one of the few, clear Confederate naval victories of the war.

On 31 January 1863, the *Palmetto State* and another Confederate ironclad, the *Chicora*, sortied from Charleston Harbor to attack the

[7]Thomas J. Scharf, *History of the Confederate States Navy* (New York, 1887), p. 204.

blockading fleet. Caught by surprise as the two rebel rams emerged from the early morning mist, the Federals suffered a serious defeat. Parker's vessel rammed the USS *Mercedita* and forced her surrender. At the same time, the *Chicora* attacked the *Keystone State* and so damaged her that her captain later reported he believed his vessel was sinking. The remaining Union warships bore away to deep water where the ironclads could not follow. It was clearly a Confederate naval victory, and indeed, Major General P.G.T. Beauregard, commanding at Charleston, announced that the Federal blockade had been broken and arranged a boating excursion for the European consuls so that they could see for themselves that no Federal warships were in sight.

The battle was not without controversy, however. Parker and his fellow officers were outraged by the behavior of the captains of the surrendered Union vessels who, once the rebel rams backed off to attack another victim, rehoisted their flags and limped away. Combined with the behavior of the *Minnesota* during the Battle of Hampton Roads, this action seemed to suggest that Federal capitulations could not be taken at face value—that Yankees had no honor. Nevertheless, Parker's account of the action is a balanced one, and he saves his invective for Navy Secretary Gideon Welles, whose annual reports on this and other naval engagements during the war were, to Parker's mind, fabricated propaganda. He is especially scornful of Welles's claim that Confederate Admiral Raphael Semmes acted dishonorably by throwing his sword into the sea after his vessel, the *Alabama*, was defeated by the USS *Kearsarge* off the coast of France. After the way the Federal captains behaved off Charleston, how could Welles make such a claim?

Following his duty aboard the *Palmetto State*, Parker was next appointed superintendent of the Confederate Naval Academy, an ironic assignment in light of the fact that his older brother Foxhall later became superintendent of the U.S. Naval Academy. The Confederate version was established aboard the *Patrick Henry* (formerly the *Yorktown*) on the James River at Drewry's (or Drury's) Bluff, seven miles below Richmond. The *Patrick Henry* was a former passenger and mail steamer on the Chesapeake Bay that had been seized by the State of Virginia upon the onset of hostilities. She was armed with 10 guns and carried a complement of 150. As her commanding officer, Parker had two responsibilities—to educate his young charges and, because the Confederacy was so desperately short of men, to assist in the defense of the capital as well. In that capacity Parker was witness to Grant's assault on Petersburg and Richmond in the spring of 1864.

Parker's last adventure as a Confederate naval officer was the most curious of all. When Grant finally cracked Lee's thinned lines south of Petersburg in April 1865, Parker found himself the commanding officer of one of the few remaining bodies of organized and disciplined soldiery not already fighting in Lee's army. In the crisis of near-panic that seized Richmond in those days, Parker was ordered to take charge of the Confederate treasury during the evacuation of that city. Parker and his officer cadets served as the escort for the Confederate treasury during the government's flight southward. Parker's poignant account of this sad odyssey provides a glimpse of the death of a nation and in particular of the crushing of Jefferson Davis's final vain hopes for carrying on the struggle.

Parker's memoir ends with his return to Virginia after the war. His active naval service was ended, and his book is, after all, a recollection of naval service. Former Confederates were not welcomed back into the ranks of the U.S. Navy's officer corps. But Parker had three more careers still ahead of him in 1865. For nine years (1865–73) he captained a Pacific Ocean mail steamer running between Panama City and San Francisco and wrote in consequence, *Remarks on the Navigation of the Coasts Between San Francisco and Panama* (1871).

His third career began in 1873 when he accepted an appointment as professor of engineering at the Maryland Agricultural College (later the University of Maryland). At the same time, the trustees appointed another former Confederate officer, Major General Samuel Jones, to the presidency of the college. Jones (a West Point graduate) and Parker were both interested in expanding the offerings of the college and particularly in emphasizing the science and math components of the curriculum. Traditionalists, however, opposed the relative downgrading of agriculture in the college program, and as a result Jones was driven from office in 1875. Surprisingly, the trustees chose Parker to replace him. It was during his tenure as president of the Maryland Agricultural College that Parker wrote *Recollections of a Naval Officer.*

According to the official historian of the University of Maryland, Parker was "one of the ablest of Maryland's presidents."[8] He was instrumental in establishing a new organization that divided the curriculum into seven distinct departments, including new departments in physics, chemistry, and civil engineering. Like Jones, Parker drew criticism from those who opposed his introduction of what was perceived as "spit-and-polish military training." Parker went so far as to advertise Maryland as a preparatory school for West Point and Annapolis, and referred in a public advertisement to the students as "cadets" who would march to class and recite lessons very much in the military fashion then prevalent at both service academies. He even managed to acquire a ship, which was to be used for summer cruises. Although Parker's new programs did attract some new students from out of state, they drove away at least as many from inside the state. Like Jones, Parker came under attack from many of the college's early supporters, who were distressed that the original emphasis on agriculture was being undermined, and, again like Jones, he finally resigned under pressure in September of 1882.[9]

Parker's fourth, last, very brief and altogether unsuccessful career was as a diplomat. With the election of Democrat Grover Cleveland to the presidency in 1884, the Republican stranglehold on public offices was finally broken. Cleveland came under a great deal of pressure to appoint southerners, who under the Republicans had been virtually barred from office, to important positions. Parker was a beneficiary of this pressure, and in early 1886 he found himself appointed U.S. Minister to Korea.

---

[8]George H. Callcott, *A History of the University of Maryland* (Baltimore, 1966), p. 183.
[9]Ibid., pp. 182–87.

Arriving in Korea in June 1886, Parker made a very bad impression on the man he was supposed to replace, George Clayton Foulk. In a report to Secretary of State Thomas F. Bayard, Foulk described Parker as a hopeless drunkard who was almost completely incapacitated by his addiction to the bottle. Needless to say, Foulk was very disturbed by this discovery. He had been working hard to counter the growing influence of China in the Korean court, and he was reluctant to turn his cause over to an inebriate. On the other hand, Foulk was anxious to leave Korea and had been waiting for a replacement for a year and a half. He therefore extracted a promise from Parker to stay off the bottle, and with some reservations, he accompanied Parker to his first audience with the King of Korea. Foulk later wrote to his family that he had the feeling that "with the contemptible old drunkard by me, all my earnest work and aims were to be scattered to the winds. . . ."[10]

The Cleveland administration was not willing to allow this to happen. In Japan, Foulk was intercepted by a message ordering him to return immediately to Seoul and relieve Parker of his assignment. So urgent was this demand that a U.S. cruiser was detailed to carry Foulk back to Korea. Thus, Parker served less than a year at his diplomatic post and returned in disgrace.

Just when Parker adopted what was apparently a strong addiction to drink is not clear. It is possible that he began to drink heavily only after his exile from the Maryland Agricultural College, for in all the public criticism of his programs as president of the college, drinking was never mentioned. In any case Foulk's reports mince no words about Parker's drinking in 1886, and Parker himself did not appeal or protest his recall.

Parker's brief duty in Korea was his last public service. He returned to Washington, D.C., and to his writing. He published *Familiar Talks on Astronomy* in 1889 and lived in quiet retirement until he died suddenly at age 70 on 30 December 1896.

[10]Foulk to family, 10 July 1886, Foulk Papers, Library of Congress. Quoted in Donald M. Bishop, "Policy and Personality in Early Korean-American Relations: The Case of George Clayton Foulk," a paper presented at Kalamazoo, Michigan, 4 November 1976 at the Sixth Conference on Korea.

The annotating of Parker's naval "recollections" posed several unique challenges. First of all his title is quite apt—the book is literally a "recollection." Though Parker referred to several articles and he quotes from the official records of the Civil War, he writes what he remembers as he remembered it—and his memory is not always accurate. He sometimes mixes up dates and names, or recalls events out of chronological order. He is not particularly bothered by this, for he did not intend to write history. To be sure, he wanted to set the record straight where he believed that someone had been ill treated by historians, but his book is a memoir, not a history, and its greatest value is the richness of the personal stories of sailors, shipmates, and life at sea in the years of the navy's transition from sail to steam. It is Parker's gift as a raconteur, and not as an historian, that makes the stories fresh and vital, and makes the book worth reading.

Parker's frequent references to literary characters are based on his assumption that his readers will be familiar with them. This may have been a safe guess in 1882, but not one hundred years later. I have succeeded in finding the origin of most of these, but many of them will have to stand without editorial citation. When Parker refers to characters by their last name only, I have provided first names in brackets. A few obvious typographical errors have been silently corrected, and in conformity with modern usage, the titles of books mentioned are printed in italics. Certain inconsistencies in spelling and punctuation have been preserved to retain the flavor of the original edition.

I owe special thanks to Alice Creighton and the staff of the Special Collections division of the Nimitz Library at the U.S. Naval Academy. Thanks are due also to Harriet Bergman, Jack Sweetman, Richard Abels, and to William J. Clipson who rendered the maps.

CRAIG L. SYMONDS

Recollections
of a
Naval Officer

PREFACE

During the war with Mexico, 1847–48, a friend of mine, J. Hogan Brown, was the sailing master of the United States steamship *Mississippi*. The *Mississippi* went from Vera Cruz in the squadron to attack Tampico, and had in tow the schooner *Bonita*— gunboat.

During the night a "norther" sprang up, and the officer of the deck let the *Bonita* go, and did not think it necessary to report the fact to the commodore.

In the morning the commodore, Matthew C. Perry, came on deck, and not seeing the *Bonita*, inquired where she was. The officer of the deck told him that in the night they had let her go in consequence of the weather. The commodore, who was not noted for his *suaviter in modo*, though strong in the *fortiter in re*, said: "Send the master to me." Upon his appearance he said, "Mr. Brown, where is that schooner?" Brown, who was never at a loss for an answer, instantly replied, "She is S. S. E., fifteen miles distant." "She is, eh?" said the commodore, and turning to the officer of the deck he said, "Steer S. S. E." The officers in the ward room, hearing of the occurrence, said, "Well! old Brown is caught at last." In about an hour the man at the mast-head called out: "Sail ho!" "Where away?" said the officer of the deck. "Right ahead," was the reply; and in a few minutes: "Can you make her out?" "Yes, sir, a schooner." "By George," said the officers in the ward room, "old Brown is right, after all!" After awhile the strange sail was reached, and proved to be a *merchant* schooner bound to Pensacola. The commodore, in a great rage, sent for Brown and said: "Did you not say the schooner *Bonita* bore S. S. E. fifteen miles off?" "Well, sir," said Brown, "the reckoning called for a *schooner; but it did not say it was the Bonita!"*

Now the moral of this is that *this reckoning* calls for a schooner, but no *particular schooner:* so if any fellow expects *his schooner* to be mentioned he may find himself mistaken.

I wish to say here, with Captain Kincaid of the rifle battalion: "That this is *my* book; and if any man wishes his name or services to be specially mentioned, let him write a book for himself."[1]

43 YORK ST.,
Norfolk, Va.

[1]These lines are paraphrased from Captain John Kincaid's *Adventures in the Rifle Brigade* (London, 1830), a personal narrative of the campaigns against the French, 1809–15, and one of the most popular military books of its day.

CHAPTER I

Entrance into the navy—join the "North Carolina 74," at New York—first impressions—hammocks versus cotton-bales—midshipmen's pranks—the U.S. brig *Somers*—the brig *Boxer*—melancholy suicide—the "by-no-meal" theorem—am ordered to the line-of-battle-ship *Columbus*—a poetical sailmaker

We are told that when Mr. Toots attempted to write an acrostic to Florence Dombey he carefully prepared the first letters of the lines, and then never got farther than "For when I gaze";[1] and I must confess that in commencing these recollections I feel somewhat in the same predicament; so I think it best to plunge at once *in medias res*[2] and say that I entered the U.S. navy as a midshipman on the 19th day of October, 1841, being then fourteen years of age. I was almost immediately ordered to the

[1] A reference to characters in Charles Dickens's *Dombey and Son* (1848).
[2] Literally "in the middle of things"—the practice of starting a tale in the middle.

U.S. ship *North Carolina*, and on the 27th day of the same month reported for duty to Commodore M. C. Perry, then commanding the station at New York.[3]

I well recollect my extreme surprise at being addressed as *Mr.* by the commodore, and being recalled to my senses by the sharp *William* of my father, who accompanied me to the Navy Yard.

Upon our arrival at New York we had put up at the City Hotel, the favorite resort of naval officers. The night of our arrival we took a Whitehall boat at Castle Garden and pulled off to a transport lying in the North River, to visit my eldest brother who was on board with other officers on their way to join their regiments in Florida. My brother had just graduated at West Point, and was attached to the Fourth Infantry. I never saw him again as he died within a year.[4]

I reported on board the receiving ship *North Carolina*, Captain Francis M. Gregory, on the morning of the 28th of October. She was at anchor in the North River, off the Battery; had a full complement of officers and men, and was kept in fine order. She was one of the largest of our line-of-battle ships, or 74's as they were generally called. One of the midshipmen informed me the next day that she was called a 74 because she carried 80 guns! When I got upon her quarter-deck the marines were drawn up for drill, the band was playing, a large party of ladies were promenading the poop-deck, and these sights taken in connection with unaccustomed *smells* (for this ship had always a curious odor of rum, tar, bean-soup and tobacco combined), tended to confuse me terribly. The one defined recollection I have is of a midshipman (whom I had met the day before in Commodore Perry's office)

---

[3]Matthew Calbraith Perry (1794–1858) was the captain of the *North Carolina*, a 74-gun ship of the line launched in 1820. Perry is best known for his 1853 voyage to Japan, during which he successfully negotiated a commercial treaty with that previously isolationist island empire. He was the younger brother of Oliver Hazard Perry (1785–1819), victor of the Battle of Lake Erie.

[4]Richard Bogardus Parker died in Philadelphia on 13 September 1842 after spending less than a year with his regiment.

passing us, and recognizing my father with a touch of the cap, so jaunty and *debonair*, that I thought that if I could ever attain to that perfection I would be a naval officer indeed.

My father soon left me and I was taken below to be introduced to my messmates, of whom I found about thirty, messing in the gun-room and sleeping on the orlop deck.[5] During the first day I was in a constant state of excitement; the frequent calling of all hands, and the running about caused me to think the ship was on fire, and I repaired to the quarter-deck many times to see what the matter was.

Several of the midshipmen hung about me, watching a chance to perpetrate their jokes; but a greenhorn, like myself, happening to complain to them that he "could not find Cheeks, the marine, anywhere," caused me to smile; for I was well up in Marryatt's novels—so they let me alone with the remark that they supposed my father and brother (both of whom were in the navy) had put me up to the usual navy jokes.[6]

About this time all hands were called to stand by the hammocks, and my surprise was great when I saw the hammocks taken out from the nettings; for I had previously supposed that naval officers, taking the hint from General Jackson's defences at New Orleans, had stuffed the ship's sides with bags of cotton, to resist shot! Fortunately I did not allow this to escape me, or I should have been called "cotton-bale Parker" to this day.

When I was taken down to the orlop deck and saw the hammocks swung I could not imagine how I was to sleep in, or rather *on* one; for, not knowing that it was not unlashed and that it contained inside a mattress and blankets, I naturally thought it was the way of sailors to sit a-straddle of it and repose in this

[5]The orlop deck is the lowest deck on a warship, generally used for the storage of cables and other seldom-used equipment.

[6]Cheeks was a major character in the stories of Frederick Marryat (1792–1848). Marryat wrote many famous sea novels, the most popular of which was *Mr. Midshipman Easy* (1836). Parker's father and elder brother (both named Foxhall A. Parker) were career naval officers.

unnatural attitude. It caused me much unhappiness that night in the gun-room, and I thought I had, perhaps, better resign and go home at once; but at two bells, nine o'clock, when we all went down to turn in, I was much relieved to see the hammocks spread out into a more reasonable shape.

Here another surprise awaited me: up to this time I had suffered much with ear-ache, and my mother had caused me to wear night-caps—there was nothing strange to me in this, as other boys wore them at my boarding-school—but it seems it was not a "way they had in the navy." My caps were of many colors: red, blue, green, etc., for they were made of remnants of my sisters' dresses. Now as I made my final preparations for repose I opened my trunk and put on a close-fitting night-cap. It was the signal for an indescribable scene of confusion. If I had put on a suit of mail it could not have caused greater astonishment among these light-hearted reefers. They rushed to my trunk, seized the caps, put them on, and joined in a wild dance on the orlop deck, in which were mingled red caps, blue caps, white caps—all colors of caps— in pleasing variety. I had to take mine off before turning in as it really did seem to be too much for their feelings; but I managed to smuggle it under my pillow, and when all was quiet I put it on again; but when the midshipman came down at midnight to call the relief he spied it, and we had another scene. This was the last I ever saw of my caps. I have never had one on since, and *consequently* have never had the ear-ache!

I do not propose to give a detailed account of my life on board this ship, but only to present a few scenes as they come to my recollection.

My first duty was to carry the daily dispatches to Commodore Perry at the Navy Yard, and this kept me in a boat pretty much all day, and involved a good deal of risk in passing the ferries; but after a few weeks I was, to my great joy, (for I was green then and didn't know any better) assigned to a watch.

About the latter part of November the ship was taken to the Navy Yard, laid alongside the wharf, and made comfortable for the winter, by building houses over the hatches, closing in the half-ports, etc. Our time was occupied in keeping our watches and learning navigation under Professor Ward.[7] I, for one, soon learned to work all the rules in Bowditch's *Navigator*; though, if the truth must be told, I did not exactly understand "what it was about:" nor did I learn until I got fairly to sea on my first cruise.[8] Few explanations were given as to "theory," as well as I remember.

The navy at that day was, as to the officers and men, very similar to the British navy, as described by Marryatt in his novels: the same jokes were perpetrated and the same characters existed.

We had on board the *North Carolina* some sailors who had been in the *Constitution* when she captured the *Guerriere*; some who were in the *United States* when she took the *Macedonian*, and others who had served under Commodores Perry and McDonough on the Lakes; and it was the custom to get them in the gun-room at night, to sing the old sailor ditties of "The Constitution and the Guerriere," "The Wasp and the Frolic," "The Enterprise and the Boxer," etc. Of course I looked upon these men as not only heroes, but Methusalehs as well![9]

Among my messmates was the ill-fated Spencer. He was a classmate of mine, and joined shortly after I did. I remember him as a tall, pale, delicate-looking young man of perhaps nineteen years of age. It will be remembered that Midshipman Spencer was accused of inciting a mutiny on board the United States brig *Somers*, in November, 1842. He was tried by a summary court-martial at sea, and hanged at the yardarm on the 1st of December following, in company with the boatswain's mate, Cromwell, and the gunner's mate, Small. This affair caused an immense sensation in the country, and the commander, Alex. Slidell Mackenzie,

---

[7]Probably this was Lieutenant James H. Ward, one of the seven original U.S. Naval Academy faculty members.

[8]*The New American Practical Navigator*, by Nathaniel Bowditch, was first published in 1802, went through 65 editions, and remained the standard for over half a century.

[9]The songs celebrated the victories of American warships over the British in the War of 1812.

asked for and obtained a Court of Inquiry. His course was sustained by it; though J. Fenimore Cooper, the novelist, took up the cudgels, and made a savage attack upon him. Officers of the navy in my time generally declined to discuss this affair.[10]

I saw the *Somers* launched at the New York Navy Yard in the spring of 1842.

During the winter the brig *Boxer* was fitted out for foreign service, and I was anxious to apply for her, but our judicious, and kind-hearted first lieutenant, Charles Armstrong, would not allow me to do so.

It was the luck in that day of the small, crowded, ill-ventilated vessels like the *Boxer* and *Dolphin* to be sent to the West Indies, coast of Africa, and other sickly stations: on the same principle I suppose, as Dickens says, that in serving out clothing the long men get into the short trousers, and the short men into the long ones. While the *Boxer* was fitting out our junior lieutenant was ordered to her, much against his will; he tried very hard to have his orders revoked, but without success. He was much loved by the midshipmen, and we often went to see him.

One afternoon while rowing about the dock for amusement, in company with another reefer, I saw a boat under the bows of the *Boxer* smuggling liquor to the men. We went on board and reported it to our friend, whom we found the senior officer—the captain and executive officer being on shore. I well remember his kindness to us, boys as we were, taking us below and treating us to cakes. The next morning shortly after 4 o'clock we were aroused by

[10]The U.S. brig *Somers* was a training vessel whose function was the development of young apprentices as navy petty officers. On a return voyage from Africa in 1842, Commander Alexander Slidell Mackenzie learned from a steward that some of the apprentices, led by Philip Spencer, were planning a mutiny. Mackenzie responded by ordering Spencer and two others hanged. His decision to act thusly while still at sea rather than wait for a duly assembled court-martial ashore, and the fact that Spencer was the son of the Secretary of War, made his decision highly controversial. The ensuing publicity helped to underscore the need for a shore-based training and educational institution, and a few years later, in 1845, the U.S. Naval Academy was established at Annapolis.

the news that the *Boxer's* men had mutinied and killed this lieutenant. Our marines were immediately sent on board, and I went in charge of the boat. It was a mistake about the mutiny. Our friend had gone on deck at 4 A.M. to keep the morning watch, and a few minutes after he blew his brains out. I saw his body lying cold and stiff upon the quarter-deck. No one ever knew the cause of the fatal act. Our fellows felt the death of this officer very much, and it was some days before we were up to our tricks and deviltries again.

The midshipmen were constantly changing during the six months I was on board this ship. As vessels were fitted out drafts of reefers were sent to them, and new ones were constantly arriving. In consequence of this our mess was kept in a disorganized condition, and in point of fact our money would give out before the end of the month and we would go for several days without regular meals. I have occasion to remember this fact. I joined on the 28th day of October, when the mess was in this condition. The caterer did not ask me for my mess bill, and I never thought of offering it; in fact, I did not know how the mess was supplied and had an idea that the government furnished it. The day after I joined, Friday, I was invited to breakfast with the lieutenants in the ward-room. I had not much appetite, and when I left the table Mr. Armstrong said: "Youngster, this will never do; you must learn to eat your ration." To my extreme surprise we had no dinner in the gun-room that day, and no supper! The table was not even set! It seems that during this *dies infaustus* [hectic] kind of a time the midshipmen lived upon the bum-boat and skirmished on the berth-deck for a living; but I knew nothing about that, and was too proud and bashful to make any inquiries, and, strange to say, no one thought of giving me information. All day Saturday it was the same *dies non*.[11] I frequently thought of the *ration* alluded to by Lieutenant Armstrong and wished I could see it! On Sunday after muster, Mr. Neville, the sailing master, told me my father wanted me to come ashore in the 1 o'clock boat, and said the first lieutenant would

---

[11]Literally "non day." A day on which no legal business may be transacted.

give me permission to go if I asked him. I was rather astonished to hear this, for I had supposed that I was to remain on board three years without going on shore, and had been wondering how long I could hold out without eating. I think that reading about Admiral Collingwood's long cruises had given me this idea.[12] I went on shore and hurried up to the City Hotel; the clerk informed me that my father had gone to Brooklyn to dine, and left word for me to follow him. I found I had left my purse on board and had no money to pay my ferriage: but there was a chance to overtake my father. I caught up with him on Fulton Street, just opposite the old Dutch Reformed church (I have never passed it since without recalling this incident), and getting some money from him went to a stand and purchased some pies and cakes, which I immediately commenced devouring. My father seemed surprised, and well he might be! He asked me how I liked it on board ship. I told him that I did not like it at all; that they had no meals there. He, thinking that the midshipmen lived, perhaps, on the ship's rations—salt beef and hard-tack—and that I did not like it, replied that I would get accustomed to it. I told him no; that I had never been used to going without meals and that I was too old to learn; it might do for other midshipmen, but I could not stand it; and finally, as to returning to that ship and trying to live without eating, I couldn't and I wouldn't.

My father naturally failed to entirely comprehend the actual condition of our mess, and we continued the conversation until we arrived at our destination. We had an excellent dinner, and I rather suspect my performance at it somewhat astonished our kind entertainers. We had tarts for dessert. I ate about twelve, and there was one remaining on the dish. Observing me to eye it rather hard, our kind hostess said: "William must have this, because he is a sailor boy." The sailor boy took it accordingly!

It was now time to set off for the Battery as I was ordered to

---

[12]Probably a reference to Admiral Lord Collingwood's achievement of maintaining a continuous blockade off Cádiz for nearly two-and-one-half years after the Battle of Trafalgar in October 1805.

return in the sunset boat. I unwillingly accompanied my father, and though I was dressed in a midshipman's jacket and trousers, with a smart dirk at my side, I was a little enough fellow to hold him by the hand. Upon our arrival at Castle Garden we found one of the older midshipmen who explained the condition of affairs to my father; he said that the next day, being the first of the month, everything would be all right, and meals would be served regularly. Upon this assurance I consented to return, but took the precaution to lay in pies and cakes enough to last me several days. Upon getting back to the gun-room, one of the older midshipmen surprised me by an invitation to an oyster supper that night at 9 o'clock. I cannot say I felt hungry, but I remembered Major Dalgetty's advice as to the laying in of *provance*, and accepted. The next morning we had a regular breakfast to my great gratification. We always had this to go through with as long as I was in the ship; it was "bite and cry" for the last three days of every month; but I "knew the ropes" then, and could skirmish with the best of them, and my experience taught me to look after the greenhorns on such occasions and see that they got enough to eat.

Towards the latter part of the spring of 1842 I was detached from the *North Carolina* and ordered to the line-of-battle ship *Columbus*, then fitting out at Boston for the Mediterranean.

I bade adieu to the old ship with many regrets; and with this shall close my first chapter, which I found so hard to commence. And, after all, when I come to think of it, this is not so much to be wondered at; for I once sailed with a fellow—a poetical sail-maker—who, after we had been only a few days at sea, remarked to me confidentially, that he would like to read me a piece of his poetry, "if I wouldn't laugh at it:" (the idea!)

I having duly promised, he read as follows:

Far o'er the billow the moonlight is streaming,
Dispelling the vapor and gloom of the night,

and then stopped, with the remark that "that was as far as he had got:" and though I continued with him for two years *he never got any farther! Basta.*

CHAPTER II

My first cruise—the *Columbus* 74—ghosts—cross the Atlantic—Gibraltar—Guarda Costa and smugglers—Port Mahon—
assassination of Mr. Patterson—Lieutenant Charles G. Hunter—squadron winters in Genoa—passed midshipmen Beale
and Murray—the brig *Somers*—a duel—return to Mahon—the
Delaware 74—Toulon—Cape de Gata—Gibraltar again—
Madeira—sail for the coast of Brazil—Saturday-night yarns—
target practice—improvements in gunnery—Captain Marryatt
and American thunder

The *Columbus* was an old-fashioned 74, built about the beginning of the century.[1] She carried long 32-pounders on her
main and lower gun decks, and 32-pounder carronades on her spar

---

[1]The *Columbus* was laid down in June 1816 in the Washington Navy Yard
and launched on 1 March 1819. She was 193′3″ in length with a beam of 52′
and displaced 2,480 tons. In April 1861 the old ship was among the vessels
burned by the Federals during the evacuation of the Norfolk Navy Yard.

deck. She had four 8-inch shell guns, or Paixhams as they were called from their inventor, on the main deck amidships, and the same number on the lower deck.[2] She had made but one short cruise in the Mediterranean, which was said to have been specially marked by two incidents: first, in crossing the Atlantic, she had "fetched a compass" around about a fly-speck on the chart which the Commodore took to be a rock; and secondly, her false keel getting slued athwartships she would neither tack, veer nor sail. She was called at that time an unlucky ship. It was furthermore said by the men that a woman and child had been murdered on her orlop deck while she was laid up in ordinary at the Navy Yard.

In company with many other midshipmen I reported for her early in the summer of 1842, and as she was not ready for her officers and men we took up our quarters at the old National Hotel in Charlestown. Here we remained but a short time in consequence of our mad horseback rides; for some twenty of us happening to gallop past the commodore's house on a Sunday, we were next day ordered on board the receiving ship *Ohio* for "safe keeping."

Some time in July, however, the *Columbus* was put in commission and we all went on board.

I suppose that a finer body of men than the *Columbus'* crew never trod a ship's deck. In all my experience I have never seen their equal. Some eight hundred strong they could, as the boatswain said, "tear the ship to pieces." She was commanded by Captain William H. Spencer, and had a full complement of officers, among whom were eight passed midshipmen, and about thirty midshipmen—mostly green.[3] In consequence of the ship having a bad name the men commenced to desert while lying in the stream and we were obliged to row guard around her at night to prevent it. In performing this duty I frequently heard the men in the boat declare that they heard a baby crying on the orlop deck—and (as the old

[2]The Paixhans (not Paixhams) gun, named for its designer, French General Henri-Joseph Paixhans, was the first naval gun to fire explosive shells.

[3]William A. (not H.) Spencer was on his last assignment as a naval officer; he resigned from the service in 1843.

sailor says) "being sailor-men, 'taint likely they lied about it;" but I never heard it myself. The orlop deck, which was below the water-line, and very dark and gloomy-looking even in the day-time, had a peculiarly ghostly appearance at night, and indeed a ghost *was* frequently seen descending the ladder of the fore-hatch in the "wee short hour ayont the twal," (whatever that may be) and disappearing through the gratings which covered the fore-hold. It was so fully believed that it became difficult at last to get a marine to walk that lonesome post; but after crossing the Atlantic the story died out, and we heard no more about ghosts; and now I come to think about it one of our passed midshipmen was detached about that time!

Speaking of ghosts reminds me of a singular circumstance which happened to a great-uncle of mine.

He had served in the Revolutionary war, and rose to be a brigadier-general in the U.S. Army. He was said to be a very brave man; but be that as it may, one night while sleeping, with his door wide open as was his habit, a ghost appeared to him and said, "Aleck, Aleck, get up!—Aleck, Aleck!" Just then he awakened and replied "Eh!" then instantly recollecting that *it was bad luck to answer a ghost*, he turned it off into, "Eh diddle dinkum dido," as though he was singing. At this—which showed his presence of mind at least—the ghost disappeared.

We sailed from Boston on the 29th day of August, 1842, and after a very smooth passage across the Atlantic arrived at Gibraltar, which I shall always especially remember as being the first foreign port I ever visited.

Gibraltar is a rocky promontory, some 1400 feet high, at the southern extremity of Spain. It is at the entrance to the Mediterranean sea, and the straits here are fifteen miles wide. It is strongly fortified on the western front, and its galleries, cut out of solid rock, are one of the sights of the world. The eastern face is entirely inaccessible to assault. The town is built at the foot of the promontory, and the bay is nine miles across. The name comes from the Arabic words *gibel al Tarif* (the rock of Tarif): the name of the general who took it in 711. The Spanish took it in 1302, and it fell into the hands of the English under Admiral Rooke in 1704. In 1779 the Spanish made a desperate effort to recover it. It was defended by General George Elliot. The siege lasted three years, and has been described by Drinkwater whose book is a model of its kind.[4] The rock is separated from the main by a low, sandy neck of land called the neutral ground. At St. Roche and Algeziras the Spaniards have erected extensive fortifications and a large garrison is kept. The English garrison Gibraltar with their best troops.

Gibraltar is generally said to *command* the straits; but this must be understood in a "Pickwickian sense" at the present day. There is nothing to prevent steamers going through at any time. It is valuable to the British as a depot for stores, and the harbor gives protection to their vessels, just as Malta does. The current runs *in* from the ocean at all times—a singular fact;—the surplus water is probably carried out by an under current.

A stay here of a few days is an excellent introduction to the Mediterranean; for, I believe, there are natives of most of the countries of Europe to be met with; as well as many inhabitants of Asia and Africa. I spent many hours in the captain's gig at the mole, and saw Englishmen, Spaniards, Frenchmen, Russians, Germans, Italians, Turks, Jews, Armenians, Egyptians, Arabs, Moors and Negroes intermingled. A novel sight to any one, but especially to a greenhorn!

We sailed from Gibraltar after a short stay for Port Mahon. The day after sailing we saw a Spanish *Guarda Costa* chasing a large smugglers' boat. The smugglers ran under our lee for protection, and as we were sailing only about four knots an hour they easily kept up with us with their oars. There were about twenty men in the boat, and fine, hearty-looking fellows they were, and their red caps gave them a most picturesque appearance. Our captain took no notice of them, and the *Guarda Costa* did not approach any nearer, but sailed along in company. After night fell the smugglers left us, and I presume made for the shore.

[4]John Drinkwater Bethume (1762–1844) was the author of *A History of the Late Siege of Gibraltar* (1786).

Gibraltar is a free port, and there was at that time much smuggling done between it and Algeziras and other Spanish ports.

Upon our arrival off Port Mahon we fell in with the U.S. frigate *Congress*, a new frigate on her first cruise.[5] She was built in Portsmouth, N. H., and at that time was said to be the largest frigate afloat. We were struck by a heavy squall that afternoon, the first I had ever seen. The *Columbus* came out of it all right; as she did out of all kinds of weather. Though an old-fashioned ship she was the finest sea-boat I have ever seen; moreover she sailed well and could be handled like a pilot boat. It would surprise some of the young officers who have never sailed in anything but the long, narrow ships of the present navy to see one of these old-time ships beating in a narrow channel. Upon our arrival at Mahon we found the entire squadron, consisting of the frigate *Congress* and sloops-of-war *Fairfield* and *Preble*, assembled there. Commodore Charles Morgan, who commanded the squadron, now hoisted his flag aboard our ship, and I was appointed his Aid.[6]

Port Mahon is on the island of Minorca. Its harbor is one of the best in the Mediterranean—a natural mole runs along the shore, and is occupied by shops with naval stores. At the time of our visit provisions and clothing were to be had very cheap and in great abundance.

It was off Mahon that Admiral John Byng had a partial engagement with the French squadron in May, 1756; for his conduct on this occasion he was shot on board the Monarch at Spithead, March 14, 1757. Voltaire says this was done *"pour encourager les autres!"*

The article of war under which Byng was tried, says: "If any person, through cowardice, disaffection or *negligence*, shall fail to put his ship in readiness for battle, etc., he shall suffer death." The

---

[5]The *Congress* (the fourth U.S. ship to bear that name) was a new 44-gun frigate launched in Portsmouth in 1841. She was subsequently rammed and sunk by the Confederate ironclad *Virginia* (*Merrimack*) on 8 March 1862. See chapter 22.

[6]Charles W. Morgan was commissioned a midshipman on 1 January 1808 and made captain on 21 February 1831. He died in 1853.

admiral was acquitted of cowardice and disaffection, but found guilty of *negligence*, which, under the articles of war, required a sentence of death. It is well known now, however, that he was shot to satisfy the clamors of a political party. Not the only man or woman so sacrificed. In point of fact it was the admiral's second-in-command who acted badly in not supporting him, and who richly deserved punishment, but got off scot free.[7]

Up to this time Mahon had been the wintering port of the American squadron and we were making our preparations for it when a melancholy event took place: the sailing-master of the *Congress*, Mr. Patterson, was assassinated!

He had been on shore and was returning to his ship very late at night—some time in the mid-watch in fact—and was descending the hill by the winding path which led to the landing-place of his boat. Following Mr. Patterson at some little distance were Lieutenant Charles G. Hunter and the surgeon of the *Fairfield*; they were startled at hearing Mr. Patterson cry out, and as they quickened their steps, he met them with the expression: "The villain has murdered me," and fell dead at their feet. He had two, or, perhaps three stabs directly through his heart, either of which, the doctor said, would have killed him; so that the assassin was no novice in the art. While the doctor knelt down by the side of the murdered officer, Hunter drew his pistol and started in pursuit of the murderer. He saw his shadow in the moonlight as he ran towards the *house of Blazes* (as the sailors called it), but could not get a shot at him, and he finally returned to the assistance of the doctor. I shall have something more to say of this Lieutenant Hunter when I come to relate some incidents of the Mexican war.

---

[7]At the Battle of Minorca (20 May 1756), Byng's second in command, Rear Admiral Temple West, was unable to comprehend his commander's innovative tactical plan due to a very limited signaling system. As a result, Byng's squadron suffered heavy damage from the enemy in a drawn battle. Byng was found culpable, not because of any failure by West, but because he did not subsequently renew the action. Voltaire satirized Byng's execution in *Candide*, which contains the famous line: "It is useful from time to time to kill one admiral in order to encourage the others."

There was a large number of Spanish troops in Mahon at this time, and it was thought that the murder was committed by a soldier; but the truth was never known—by us, at least. I think it was in consequence of this affair that the commodore decided not to winter in Mahon; and the American squadron has never wintered there since.

A few days after the burial of Mr. Patterson we sailed in company with the squadron for Spezia, it was said; but in passing near by Genoa it presented so inviting an appearance that the commodore was induced to go in, and finally decided to winter there. The vessels were moored head and stern under the lee of the mole, and we remained here in safety all the winter. We rode out several heavy gales and had plenty of exercise in housing topmasts and sending down lower yards. Take it all in all it was the best disciplined squadron I have ever served in, and it was a credit to the country.

Genoa being the birth-place of Columbus, our ship attracted particular attention, and we were crowded with visitors and overwhelmed with invitations. We in the steerage were kept under pretty taut discipline, and were only occasionally permitted to visit the shore. Our mornings were spent on the half-deck, under the professor of mathematics, and the rest of our time was taken up by our watches and writing our logbooks, or journals. For this reason I do not know much about Genoa, and therefore (contrary to the custom of some travelers) will not attempt to describe it.

One incident I will relate which occurred in the harbor: one dark, stormy night while a number of us were sitting in the bow port a cry of "man overboard" was heard from the *Congress*, lying half a cable's length inside of us. Passed Midshipman E. F. Beale sprung out of the port, swam to the man, and held him until a boat picked them both up. To say nothing of the gallantry of the act, it always struck me as most remarkable that on so dark a night he should have found the man, and that afterwards the boat should have found them both! This was not the first time that Mr. Beale had rescued a man from drowning. He resigned from the navy a few years after this cruise, and highly distinguished himself in

California during the war with Mexico. He is now General Beale, and resides in the city of Washington.[8]

Our ship was fortunate in having a remarkably fine set of passed midshipmen, and the midshipmen were still more fortunate from their close association with them. One can readily understand the influence they would naturally exert over a set of boys ranging from fourteen to eighteen years of age. The *tone* of the steerage was given by them. Among the number was Francis Key Murray, than whom a nobler spirit never served under the United States flag. Frank, generous, brave, and self-contained in a remarkable degree, he influenced all with whom he came in contact; he had "the heart to conceive, the understanding to direct, and the hand to execute." It was his fortune to be thrown early in life in responsible and critical situations. In a fight with the Seminole Indians at Indian Key, Florida, where he had only a few sick and convalescent men to aid him; in riding out a gale of wind off Cape Hatteras in the brig *Washington*, where his commander, Lieutenant George Bache, and a number of men were washed overboard and drowned; and in command of the Coast Survey steamer *Jefferson*, shipwrecked on the coast of Patagonia, he showed in these as in every other situation of his life the same heroic qualities. It was my good fortune to be honored by his friendship. He lived but a few years after the close of the civil war, and to borrow the words of General Harry Lee on a similar occasion (for my feeble pen is unequal to the task), he died "embalmed in the tears of his faithful comrades, and honored by the regret of the whole navy."[9]

While in Genoa we got the news of the unfortunate affair of the brig *Somers*, before alluded to. It caused much excitement on board our ship, as our captain was the uncle of Midshipman Spencer, and

[8]Edward Fitzgerald Beale (1822–1893) served as a scout alongside Kit Carson during General Kearney's campaigns in California. In the summer of 1848 be carried news of the California gold strike to Washington. Subsequently active as an Indian agent and railroad surveyor, he died in Washington, D.C., in 1893.

[9]The quotation is from Lee's eulogy for George Washington.

the captain's clerk was his brother. Knowing as I did most of the officers of the *Somers*, I always felt much interest in the matter. Different opinions have been held as to the action of Captain Mackenzie, but I do not propose to discuss it.

Only a few months ago I saw the death announced of Mr. [Adrian] Deslondes, who was a midshipman in the *Somers*. I expect he was the last survivor among the officers. It is a remarkable fact that the *Somers* sunk in a squall off Vera Cruz, (as I shall hereafter describe); and most of the officers who were in her at the time of the mutiny died sudden and tragic deaths.

During the winter here two of our midshipmen broke upon the monotony by fighting a duel, in which one was badly wounded in the knee, though he subsequently recovered. There was nothing singular in their fighting a duel, for midshipmen often took a shot at each other in that day; but in this case the principals and seconds all went out *in the same carriage*, and not getting into the country as soon as they expected, the seconds decided to post their men *in the street*, and let them fight there; this they did with the result mentioned; after which they all returned in the same carriage again in a very amicable manner. The Genoese marveled much at the strange conduct of these North Americans, and said it was not their *costumbre del pais*. No notice was taken of the matter by either the American or Genoese authorities.

In the spring of 1843 the squadron sailed for Mahon. Upon our arrival we went busily to work filling up our provisions and water for a long cruise up the Levant; for rumor said the *Delaware*, 74, bearing the flag of Commodore Charles Morris, was coming over from the coast of Brazil to relieve us, and we were to take her place on that station; which was not to our liking. We were to fill up and get off before the arrival of the *Delaware*, and would make a long summer cruise before we could be found, at least that was the "galley news." However, one fine morning the *Delaware* arrived with our orders to proceed to the coast of Brazil.

We sailed with the entire squadron, parted company the second day out, and went to Toulon. From Toulon we returned to Mahon, remained a few days and sailed for Gibraltar. We had the usual blow off Cape de Gata, celebrated in the old sailor song of "Off Cape de Gatte I lost my hat, and where do you think I found it?"

During the blockade of Toulon by the British squadron in the latter part of the last century vessels bound thence to Gibraltar for stores would frequently find themselves unable to beat round this cape, and would bear up for one of the Italian ports for supplies— here the sailors received instead of rum a kind of wine they did not like, and which they called *blackstrap*: from this they came to say on such occasions that they were *black-strapped* off the cape. We beat round in a few days and arrived at Gibraltar. Our commodore used to go on shore every evening about sunset, and I passed most of the nights waiting for him in the barge at the "ragged staff." We finally sailed for Rio Janeiro, touching *en route* at the delightful island of Madeira.

I recall with much pleasure the pleasant Saturday nights on this passage. I was a member of the passed midshipmen's mess, some members of which sang and played upon the guitar, and all spun a good yarn.

Among our best *raconteurs* were passed midshipman J. Hogan Brown and Mr. James Tilton. This latter gentleman had a varied experience; he entered the navy as a captain's clerk; went round the world in the U. S. brig *Perry*, as purser; served through General Scott's campaign in Mexico as captain of voltigeurs; became civil engineer, surveyor general of Washington territory, and finally died in Washington city. He was a gallant officer and a chivalric man.

One of his best stories, told to me in after years, was of Brown himself. Brown was the navigator of the brig *Perry*, and on a passage from China to Mexico he allowed the chronometers (by which they found the longitude) to run down. They were bound to San Blas, and running to make Cape St. Lucas, which is high and can be seen a long way off. The captain, Jot Stone Paine, was not told that the chronometers had run down and that they were depending on *dead reckoning* for the longitude. Brown got on the parallel of the Cape, and steering due east kept a good lookout ahead. He kept a foretopman at the masthead with orders to come

down and tell him *quietly* when he saw the land, and not otherwise
to announce it—promising him a bottle of whiskey in return.
Accordingly one day shortly before twelve o'clock the foretopman
came down and reported the land in sight from aloft. He was told
by Brown to return to the masthead, and when the bell struck *one*
to report it in the usual manner. A little after twelve o'clock the
captain came out of the cabin and said: "Well, Mr. Brown, when
do you think we will make the land?"

"We will make the land, sir," said Brown, "at half-past twelve
o'clock," (one bell).

"We will, eh?" said the captain. "Yes, sir," replied Brown in
his most pompous manner, "at half-past twelve precisely."

Just then the bell struck, and the man at the masthead roared
out in a stentorian voice, "Land ho!"

"By George," said Captain Jot, "that's the most remarkable
landfall I ever made!" and he afterwards told the first-lieutenant
that he considered Brown one of the most skilful navigators he had
ever met!

Tilton told me also that one night, in the *Perry*, (*Saturday* night
be it noted) the fellows insisted upon our looking over Brown's
journal, which they had noticed he wrote up every night. After
some resistance on Brown's part one of the mess opened it, and
began to read aloud. Tilton said the yarns in it all commenced in
this way: "being once in Berlin," or "happening to remain over-
night in St. Petersburg," etc. As Brown had never been in any of
the places referred to, he was taken to task, and finally said that
when he returned from a cruise and went to his home in Alabama,
he frequently dined out and was always expected to tell of his
travels; so he made it a practice to copy all the yarns he heard in the
mess in his journal for future reference.

One of Brown's stories was that when he was first appointed, he
reported for duty on board the schooner *Experiment*, at the navy
yard, Philadelphia; he was put in charge of the deck to keep the
first watch, from 8 P. M. to midnight, though he had never seen a
man-of-war before in his life. About 9 o'clock the captain put his
head out of the cabin door and said: "Quarter-master, how is the

hawse?" (this was simply to inquire into the state of the cables by which the vessel was anchored). "The hawse is all right, sir," answered the quarter-master. "Hello!" says Brown to himself, "they have a *horse* on board, it seems," and he went forward to take a look at him! Not finding him, he returned to the quarter-deck and asked the quarter-master whether the captain had not asked him as to the condition of the horse. "Yes, sir," he replied, "the hawse is all right!" "Well," says Brown, "I so understood you," and he passed the remainder of his watch looking for him!

Taking into consideration what I have said concerning Brown's journal, this *may* have happened to some other officer: especially as the records of the Navy Department show that Brown's first orders were to the sloop-of-war *Levant*, at Pensacola!

On the passage from Madeira to Rio Janeiro we had target practice for the first time. I well remember the preparations for it; it took so long to get ready for the great event that we seemed to require a resting spell of six months before we tried it again. Then, *shells* were a great bother to us; as they were kept in the shell-room, and no one was allowed even to look at them; it seemed to be a question with the division-officers whether the fuse went in first or the sabot; or whether the fuse should be ignited before putting the shell in the gun or not! However, we used to fire them off, though I cannot say I ever saw them hit anything.

We were great in running the guns in and out rapidly, but some parts of the "manual" would strike an officer of these days as very ridiculous; for instance, after the guns were pointed, the orders were, very slowly and deliberately, "handle your match and lock-string," "cock your lock," "blow your match," "stand by,"— "fire": and if the ship did not remain stationary all this time it was not our fault. We were great, too, in "boarding" and "repelling boarders" in those days, and to see the *Columbus'* officers and crew engaged in this business was a sight to behold.

The Mexican war taught us a good deal about gunnery, and what we did not learn then we picked up in the civil war, when greater advances were made in ordnance, rams, and torpedoes in four years than the European nations had made in centuries. But although the navy has made such gigantic strides in gunnery it has not improved in ships and seamen; indeed, I was told only the other day that an old growl of a boatswain was heard to say: "Formerly we had wooden ships and iron men; now we have iron ships and wooden men!"

As I have said before, the navy as it was in 1843 could not be better described, as to its *personnel*, than by Captain Marryatt in his novels.

Speaking of him reminds me of an anecdote I read which happened while he was travelling in this country. He was in a small town in New England, and his pompous manner did not tend to make him popular. A thunderstorm coming up, the captain said in a condescending manner to the landlord: "You have very heavy thunder in this country!" "Well! we *dew*, considerin' the number of inhabitants," was the reply.

CHAPTER III

Arrival at Rio de Janeiro—the East India Squadron—anecdotes of the War of 1812—the Brazil station—slavers—the harbor of Rio Janeiro—marriage of the emperor Dom Pedro—salutes—promotions in the squadron—Monte Video—the bishop of Honolulu—visit to Buenos Ayres—Rosas, the dictator—la senorita Manuelita—a day at Rosas' quinta—return to Rio—arrival of the frigate *Raritan*—Sandy Thompson's will—return to the United States

We arrived off Rio de Janeiro some time in July, 1843,[1] and were three days getting in the harbor; indeed, we had like to have never gotten into port, like the flying Dutchman, for our captain would stand *in* all day with the sea breeze, and stand *out* all night with the land breeze; then in the morning we would find ourselves becalmed like "Barney's brig with both main tacks aboard;" we began at last to think we should never get in until *the*

[1]The *Columbus* arrived off Rio de Janiero on 29 July 1843.

days were longer than the nights. However, on the third day towards sunset we succeeded in anchoring on the "rolling ground" just outside the harbor, and the most dangerous anchorage we could have selected. The next afternoon we went in with the sea breeze, and made a beautiful "come to" by running in with royals and stun'-sails set both sides, taking in everything together, and making a flying moor. It was not an uncommon sight to see a ship do this at that time.

We found in Rio the squadron intended for the East Indies, consisting of the frigate *Brandywine* and the sloop of war *St. Louis*, commanded by my father; and I remember no happier moment of my life than the visit to the *Brandywine* the night of our arrival.[2]

Upon his return from this cruise my father told me an interesting episode in his naval career. Immediately after the declaration of war against Great Britain in 1812, he sailed as junior lieutenant of the U. S. brig *Nautilus*, commanded by Captain Crane—the day after sailing from New York they found themselves enveloped in a thick fog, and upon its lifting discovered that they were close under the guns of the *Africa*, 74, the flag ship of the British squadron. Of course the brig was captured, and they were on board the *Africa* during the celebrated chase of the U. S. frigate *Constitution* by the English squadron.[3] My father told me that the officers of the *Africa* were very desirous that Captain Dacres, who was considered a very dashing officer, should get alongside her with the *Guerriere*. The *Guerriere did* get alongside her on the 19th of August

---

[2]Parker's syntax is confusing here. Foxhall A. Parker, Sr., commanded the *Brandywine*, not the *St. Louis*. As senior officer, he also served as commodore of the two-ship squadron.

[3]The *Nautilus* was captured off New York by HMS *Africa* and two other vessels on 17 July 1812. The American frigate *Constitution* ("Old Ironsides") encountered a vastly superior British squadron in July of 1812 and was forced to flee. In very light airs, with the ship's boats used to tow or kedge the frigate along, the chase lasted some two and a half days before the *Constitution* succeeded in escaping. A month later the *Constitution* encountered HMS *Guerrière* commanded by James Dacres and soundly defeated her.

of the same year, and the result is well known. But to my story: On the way to Halifax one of the *Africa*'s lieutenants observing my father to be very low-spirited inquired what the matter was; he replied that he felt badly at being taken prisoner, and moreover had no money. The Englishman told him that his father lived in Halifax and would cash any drafts he chose to draw upon his father in Virginia. This gentleman's family were exceedingly kind and hospitable to the officers of the *Nautilus* during their short stay in Halifax, and especially so to my father.

When the *Brandywine* arrived at Bombay on the cruise I have just alluded to, the British commodore, who commanded the squadron there, came on board to pay the customary visit of civility, and my father recognized him as his old friend of the *Africa*; they had not met since parting in Halifax in 1812, and were now both in command of their first squadrons.

The *Brandywine* and her consort, the *St. Louis*, sailed for the Cape of Good Hope shortly after our arrival. Some fifteen days afterwards we were surprised at seeing the *St. Louis* coming back alone, and my heart sank as we made out her "number." I could only think that the *Brandywine* had gone down with all hands. A boat soon came from her with the information that she [the *St. Louis*] had sprung a leak and returned for repairs. She sailed again in about ten days, and got safely to China, where her captain left her and was succeeded by a better man.[4]

The brig *Perry* came out from Norfolk, where she was built, about this time, bound to the East Indies; and so many of her officers left her that she was almost officered from our ship. Our acting commander, Edward C. Tilton, went as her captain; our junior lieutenant, Horace N. Harrison, as her first lieutenant; our sailing master, John C. Howell, as her junior lieutenant, and our captain's clerk, James M. Tilton, went as her purser.

These new brigs were not looked upon with favor in the navy,

---

[4]Captain Isaac McKeever succeeded Commander John M. Dale as captain of the *St. Louis* in 1844.

being thought unsafe. The *Perry*, however, made the cruise around the world and two cruises on the coast of Africa. She was finally lost off our coast during the civil war. I think she capsized and went down with all hands.

Commodore Charles Morgan left us here, and was succeeded by Commodore Daniel Turner: an officer who had distinguished himself in the command of the schooner *Caledonia* at the battle of lake Erie. He was an irascible old fellow, and suffered with the gout; but I soon found that his bark was worse than his bite. I was his aid and stood in dread of him at first, though I afterwards learned to love him for his great kindness to me. Being an "aid" during my entire service as a midshipman I was much thrown with the officers who had served in the war of 1812; and I heard many incidents relating to it, told by men who had been in the actions described.

I heard a commodore say that in the action between the *Chesapeake* and *Shannon*, off Boston, June 1st, 1813, the latter had suffered so much from the *Chesapeake*'s fire that she must have surrendered had she not run the *Chesapeake* on board. In proof of which he cited the fact that Captain Broke of the *Shannon* "headed his boarders," and that the regulations of the British navy at the time forbade a captain doing so, *unless his ship was in a critical condition!*[5]

Captain Broke of the *Shannon*, it will be remembered, was severely wounded in boarding the *Chesapeake* by a blow over the head with a cutlass in the hands of the *chaplain*, who was on deck and conspicuous for his gallantry. This gentleman was a Mr. Livermore of Kentucky. He was a friend of Captain Lawrence and being in Boston at the time he applied to him to go out and take a hand in the fight. The captain consented, and appointed him his

---

[5]During the War of 1812, James Lawrence, captain of the American frigate *Chesapeake*, accepted the implied challenge of Captain Philip Broke of HMS *Shannon* and sailed out to meet him outside Boston Harbor on 1 June 1813. During the brief battle, in which the *Chesapeake* was badly outgunned, Lawrence was mortally wounded and carried below where he is reputed to have muttered "Don't give up the ship," as his dying words.

chaplain as he had the power to do. Captain Marryatt in his novel of Midshipman Easy may have had him in mind when he sketched the character of Chaplain Hawkins.

The squadron on the coast of Brazil at this time consisted of the *Columbus*, the frigate *Columbia*, the sloop-of-war *John Adams* and the schooner *Enterprise*. The *Columbia* soon went to the Mediterranean, and our old consort, the *Congress* took her place in the squadron. The station was considered a very healthy one at that time; small-pox in Rio being the only disease to be feared. Yellow fever was not known in Rio until some years later. I think it broke out about 1849; it was probably introduced by some of the vessels engaged in bringing slaves from the coast of Africa. The custom of these vessels was to land their slaves somewhere on the coast, and then come to Rio to refit and prepare for another voyage.

One of our midshipmen, however, (an oldster) told me that the slaves *were* brought into Rio; but that *they could not be seen* in consequence of their being painted *air color*, which of course rendered them *invisible*! He said that the slaves were landed, and taken to a pond outside the city; and, the *air-colored paint* being washed off, they became *visible*; but, as a friend of mine is in the habit of saying, "I don't know anything about *that*!"

The harbor of Rio de Janeiro is without doubt the most beautiful one in the world. Other sheets of water I have seen as fine, but the *surroundings* of this bay cannot be equalled. Seen from the sea, the high range of mountains back (or rather in front, as seen from the sea) of the city first come in view. Their outline presents the effigy of a man lying on his back, and this is known as "Lord Hood's Nose"—one very remarkable peak is known as the "*corcovado*," (*humpback*, a favorite name with the old Spanish voyagers). Nearing the harbor, and just at the narrow entrance, a conspicuous hill called "The Sugar-Loaf," is seen.

The city, which is the largest and wealthiest in South America, lies at the foot of the mountains. The streets rise one above the other and as the houses are painted in bright colors the effect is very fine. At night the lights present an unusually brilliant appearance. I think the appearance of this harbor in the early morning with the first rays of the sun reflected from the mountain-sides is not to be surpassed. The place derives its name, signifying *river of January*, from the mistake of the first discoverer of the bay, who conceived it to be the mouth of a large river. It was founded by the Portuguese in 1565.

Rio has some handsome public buildings, a very fine aqueduct, and a well-kept botanical garden. The climate is warm and humid, and as in all tropical climates, there are but two seasons: the wet and the dry. The population consists of a mixture of all colors and nations. Of the natives I can only say, in the words of the old sea captain when required to describe the Chinese: "Manners they have none, and their customs are very beastly." They are hybrids, and will never improve; but I shall have more to say on this subject in another place.

The sea breeze which blows every afternoon tempers the heat and renders it more bearable; it dies out towards ten o'clock at night, and about two in the morning the land breeze springs up, and blows till about eight o'clock. In the intervals the heat is most oppressive. Vessels take advantage of these winds: leaving port with the land wind, and entering with the sea breeze some time in the afternoon. One of the great beauties of this bay is the large number of pretty coves, or smaller bays, communicating with it: such as "Boto Fogo," etc., and the picturesque villages on their shores. It was my fortune to make many boat expeditions with the commodore, and we used to explore all these nooks.

One of them, near Praya Grande, possessed a melancholy interest from the fact that on its shores and near the ruins of an old convent, the first lieutenant of the United States frigate *Hudson* killed the surgeon of the ship in a duel. They fought with ship's pistols, and the surgeon fell dead at the first fire. I have always heard he forced the duel upon the lieutenant.

The present emperor, Dom Pedro, was married while we were lying here in the fall of 1843.[6] His wife was the sister of the king of

---

[6]Dom Pedro II, Emperor of Brazil, married Therese, Princess of Bourbon-Sicily on 4 September 1843.

Naples. She was brought over in the Brazilian frigate *Constitution*, escorted by a Neapolitan squadron consisting of a line-of-battle ship and two frigates.

There being a very large number of men-of-war of all nations in port at the time the firing of salutes exceeded anything I have ever heard. It was kept up for a week, and we all got so accustomed to it that one morning at sunrise a salute of twenty-one guns was fired from our lower gun-deck, and it did not wake up the midshipmen who were sleeping on the deck directly under. I can scarcely believe this now, though I know it to be true from my personal experience. It goes to show that we had good consciences; though I *have* known a man to say (but he was a *passed* midshipman), "that he would as lieve have a *bad memory* as a good conscience."

Much rivalry existed among the ships in port, and some very pretty work was done with masts, sails and yards. We used to furl sails "from a bowline" in twenty-eight seconds, I recollect.

All of our passed midshipmen were promoted to be sailing masters, or navigators, to supply vacancies in the squadron; and I noticed that after a vessel with a new master sailed great anxiety was felt in our mess until we heard she had arrived safely at her destined port. We wanted to know what kind of a *landfall* the new master had made! Perhaps if her captain had known of the doubts of our fellows, and *the reasons for it*, he would not have slept so soundly.

In October we sailed from Rio to Monte Video, the capital of the republic of Monte Video, situated on the left bank of the Rio de la Plata, not many miles from its mouth. Here we were forced to anchor well off shore owing to our great draught of water; and the boat service, of which I had more than my share, was attended with much danger from the *pamperos*, which winds spring up very suddenly and blow with great violence. I passed many hours in the barge with Commodore Turner beating off to our ship under reefed sails, and learned more about sailing boats than I had ever known before.

Monte Video at that time was a rather pretty city, built on a gentle ascent. The streets are wide and straight, and the houses of one story, with flat roofs. It takes its name from a neighboring mountain—the climate is moist and the cold is severe in the winter months, June, July and August. Gales are frequent in summer. The city is fortified, and when we were there was in a state of siege, and had been for I don't know how many years; indeed that was its normal condition. What the war was about, and who were the parties to it I never knew; being in that respect like Lieutenant Denny of the British navy, who had been seriously wounded in a fight with the Japanese at Simoda or Simoneseki.[7] He once described the fight to me, which was a bloody one, and upon my asking him the *cause* of the war, replied that one of the Damios had given the admiral a lot of *cheek*; this was all he knew or cared to know as to the cause.

Speaking of the distance ships have to anchor from this city reminds me of an accident which happened to the English Bishop of Honolulu, and which he related to me some time about 1870, when I was commanding a Pacific mail steamer between Panama and San Francisco. The bishop was a passenger with me to San Francisco, being on his return, with his family, to Honolulu. He joined me at Panama, having come out from England *via* Rio de Janeiro, Monte Video and the Straits of Magellan. He told me that while going ashore at Monte Video, with his wife and children, in a small boat, they were run into by a Spanish schooner, and that he, in his fright caught hold of the schooner's bobstay (a rope leading from the stem to the end of the bowsprit). The boat was not upset, and got clear; and the schooner sailed away carrying off the bishop in his *upside-down* position! Those in the boat cried out to the captain of the schooner; but as he did not understand

---

[7]As part of an anti-foreigner campaign instigated by the Japanese in 1861, the Choshu chief of Shimonoseki, which guarded the entrance to the Inland Sea, fired upon French, Dutch, and American ships in the harbor in May and June 1863. In retaliation, the U.S. steam sloop *Wyoming* sank three of the chief's ships in July 1863, and a British squadron attacked Shimonoseki and virtually demolished the Japanese forts in September 1864. The long-term result of these events was to spur Japanese military modernization.

English, and as, moreover, the bishop could not be seen from the schooner's deck—being under the bowsprit, in fact—so that no one on board knew he was there, it was some time before the captain could be made to "heave-to," so that the boat might rescue the bishop. He said he was just ready to let go his hold and tumble backwards into the water.

As the good man always wore his uniform—gaiters and three-cornered cocked hat included—I could not help thinking at the time the story was told me what a picture it would have been for Punch!

At the time we were at Montevideo the notorious Juan Manuel de Rosas was the Dictator of Buenos Ayres.[8] He was descended from an old Spanish family, according to some: the others said he was a *gaucho*, born on the pampas; and was credited with many bloody acts before attaining the position he then held. It was, indeed, war to the knife between the two parties in the country, and our men-of-war lying off Buenos Ayres the year before had been crowded with women and children flying from Rosas' party.

News reaching us that an American merchant ship had been unjustly seized at Buenos Ayres, the commodore determined to visit the city; and as our ship could not go there, he went up in the schooner *Enterprise*, escorted by a large number of officers of which I was one.

We reached Buenos Ayres in due time, and even so small a vessel as the *Enterprise* had to anchor some miles off the land—the water shoals so gradually that even row-boats cannot approach the shore nearer than half a mile. Carts come out to them when they ground, and all passengers and freight are landed in these carts. This is so to this day.

---

[8]Juan Manuel de Rosas became virtual dictator of Buenos Aires in 1835. Though he brought greater stability to the Argentine government than had existed before, he nevertheless was often engaged in wars against his neighbors as well as with both Britain and France. In consequence, Buenos Aires was often under seige by foreign powers. Rosas was finally overthrown by a coalition of Brazilians, Uruguayans, and French in 1852.

I do not remember much about Buenos Ayres at this time; it struck me as a large, straggling town, the streets filled with savage-looking *gauchos* on horseback, and carts with solid wooden wheels drawn by oxen. On all the walls placards were posted with the inscription, "death to the savage Unitarians," and I believe that even then scarcely a day passed that Rosas did not put some one to death. He had only to "tip the wink" to one of his followers and the thing was done. No eastern potentate ever had greater power over his subjects than Rosas had over the wretched inhabitants of this city at this time. Buenos Ayres will live in the memory of the English, for it was here that their army suffered two defeats at the hands of the inhabitants; in 1806 under General Beresford, and in 1807 under General Whitelock. Gen. W. lost one-third of his army of 8000 men, and was glad to conclude a truce.[9]

Commodore Turner had an interview with Rosas, and the ship was immediately released and sent down the river to Monte Video to be restored to her owners.

We passed a week here very pleasantly, visiting the ladies, and riding over the pampas. One day we all spent at Rosas' *quinta* by special invitation; it was about four miles from the city and we went out there on horseback. We found there Rosas, his daughter Manuelita, and a large number of the ladies of the court. La Señorita Manuelita spoke English pretty well, and was said to be fascinating. She was a graceful girl, but not particularly pretty. Report said that the year before our visit she had been engaged to a U. S. lieutenant of marines; but happening to go down to receive him on one occasion with a number of *human ears strung on a string, in her hand*, the lieutenant fled the palace. I do not know the truth of this; it *may* have been prepared especially for the marines!

[9]During the Napoleonic Wars, Spain was a French ally until 1808 and both Argentina and Uruguay were Spanish possessions. As a result, the British occupied Buenos Aires in 1806 and 1807. British forces under General John Whitelocke (1757–1833) suffered very heavy casualties. The occupation helped breed new ideas in the Spanish colony and led indirectly to the independence movement of 1810–11.

On the occasion I speak of we rode all over the *quinta* with Rosas and his body-guard—a bloody-looking set of villains—one could see the blood in their eyes.

The country was then in so unsettled a condition that some of our officers actually feared treachery that day. They were armed and we were not. All the ladies were of the party, and they, and the guard of *gauchos* were continually leaping wide ditches and beckoning us to follow; the *padre*, who had his gown tucked up on his saddle, and who was the worst-looking villain of the lot, was conspicuous in this amusement.

We declined to follow these fellows, fine riders as we were: *being sailors!!* We excused ourselves on the plea that ours were livery horses and could not leap. I really believe that the commodore was on a horse for the first time in his life. Everybody knows what a *gaucho* is on horseback; and to see him on the pampas in his wild state lassoing cattle is a sight worth traveling for.

We attended a ball at the palace that night, and the next day returned to the *Enterprise*, and went in her back to our ship. Rosas finally fled the country in April 1852, and went to England where he died. His daughter married an Englishman and probably is still living.

In consequence of Monte Video being besieged we could obtain no fresh provisions in the city, and were forced to send the launch occasionally down to Maldonado, a village some fifty miles below us, at the mouth of the river. Here we obtained fresh beef and ostrich eggs; which latter I ate for the first time. We returned to Rio in February 1844, and remained there until the time came for us to sail for home.

The worst of the Brazil station is that there are so few ports to visit: Rio Janeiro, Monte Video, Buenos Ayres, Pernambuco and Bahia complete the list. The Cape of Good Hope was included in our command, but none of our ships went there while I was on the station.

In April 1844 the frigate *Raritan*, Captain Francis S. Gregory, arrived out to relieve us. Our gallant old commodore transferred his flag to her, and about the middle of the month our boatswain, with his eight mates standing in line with him on the main gun deck, piped that "call" which sends a thrill through every heart— old or young—"All hands up anchor for home!" While on the "Coast of Brazil," as the station is called, I frequently heard old "stagers" repeat what was known as "Sandy Thompson's Will." I give here such of it as I can recall, not so much for the merit of the lines, as on account of the mournful interest attached to them. It was said that Midshipman Sandy Thompson of the navy wrote them while lying on the mess table in the steerage of his ship, and that he died a few minutes after.

SANDY THOMPSON'S WILL

Dear Jack you know that on this river
Folks very rarely live forever;
This cursed climate and fresh water
Among our people make great slaughter.
Beside the Orinoco's flood,
And near a copse of tangled wood,
A reefer whom we all lament
And seven poor sailors home were sent.
May Heaven which all events controls,
Extend its mercies to our souls,
When at destruction's very portal:
For well you know we all are mortal!
So, now, my dear old messmate Jack,
Should sickness lay me on my back,
Or should it be the will of God
To lay me underneath the sod,
I pray some things that I may mention,
May claim from you some small attention.

The last of all my earthly cares
Is the bad fix of my affairs;
What causes most of my regrets
Is for the payment of my debts;
But whether they be great or small.
We'll see by looking at them all:

First, to the purser, much I owe,
The true amount I do not know;

But thirty dollars with my pay,
Would not clear me to this day.
The unpaid mess-bill in New York;
The money due for beef and pork;
To fifty dollars these amount,
As near as I can now account.
Confusion take these cursed bills
This catering is the worst of ills.

• • • • • •

My writing desk to Thomas give it;
Beg him from me that he'll receive it.
Present to Charles my shaving case
To help him scrape his dirty face.

• • • • • •

My journals, books and all such trash,
That are not worth one cent in cash,
These with my side-arms you will send
To Carolina to my friends:
To Beaufort in South Carolina,
And there you will obtain the rhino,
As much as will enable you
To give to each his proper due.

And, now, dear Jack, for one request,
Much more to me than all the rest,
If ever to New York you go,
In summer's heat or winter's snow,
You'll straight repair to Second Street,
And there Miss S. you'll surely meet;
Tell her that I, her faithful swain,
To her faithful did remain;
And with my last and dying breath,
When struggling with that traitor Death,
I called upon her worshipped name,
In life or death I'd be the same.

• • • • • •

When I am dead and body rotten,
And memory almost forgotten,
Then let the starboard messmates meet,

And every reefer take his seat
Let whiskey circulate around
And mirth, and wit, and joy abound.

• • • • • •

And wheresoever you may wander
Remember your old friend,

ALEXANDER.

We made a good passage home, having fine weather. After we struck the N. E. trades we averaged ten miles an hour for seven consecutive days, and I have logged the ship fifty miles in a watch of four hours—not bad for an old line-of-battle ship! The first vessel we spoke on the coast gave us the news of the bursting of Commodore Stockton's gun, the *Peacemaker*, on the steamer *Princeton*, at Washington; by this accident several distinguished gentlemen lost their lives, Hon. Abel P. Upshur, who had been secretary of the navy in 1841, among others. [10]

We arrived in New York late in May. We anchored inside of Sandy Hook, and I went up in the gig with our captain, Benjamin Cooper, to Brooklyn, where he lived. It being late when we arrived he told me not to return to the *Columbus*, but to go to the receiving ship *North Carolina* for the night. I did so; and as soon as I got down on her lower deck, I recognized the old smell of rum, tar, bean-soup and tobacco which I had noticed three years before. The next day the *Columbus* came up, and after lying a few days off the battery, went to the navy yard. The men were paid off and discharged, and the officers granted three months' leave of absence. So ended my first cruise.

---

[10]The sloop of war *Princeton*, launched in 1842, was the first steam warship driven by a screw propeller. During an exhibition firing in 1844, a 12-inch wrought-iron gun exploded killing the secretaries of state and of the navy, two congressmen, an officer, and four other persons.

CHAPTER IV

The frigate *Potomac*—the Millerite excitement—sail for Norfolk—leave Norfolk for the West Indies—the landfall of
Columbus—Gonaives—Port-au Prince—a San Domingo
game-cock—the yellow fever—Port Royal—Havana—tomb of
Columbus—Pensacola—Vera Cruz—rumors of war with Mexico—return to Pensacola—sharks—a leak in the bow—a coffer
dam—the U.S. ship *Princeton*—return home

I remained on shore but a few months, and in September was
ordered to the frigate *Potomac*, the flag-ship of Commodore
David Conner, commanding the West India, or Home Squadron.[1]
The *Potomac* was a vessel of 1750 tons; she carried fifty-two guns

---

[1]David Conner (1772–1856) was commissioned a midshipman on 16 January 1809. He won two medals for bravery during the War of 1812, and died as a
commodore in 1856. The Home Squadron was created in 1842 by renaming the
West India Squadron.

The frigate *Potomac*. Courtesy Naval History Division.

and was *consequently* called a "44!"[2] She carried thirty long 32-pounders on her main, and twenty-two 32-pounder carronades on her spar deck. These carronades were certainly the most ridiculous guns ever invented; they had neither range or penetration, and were never known to hit anything when fired. The *slides*, though, on which they were mounted were very convenient for *sitting down on*, and the midshipmen made good use of them in their long night watches. When I reported for duty the ship was lying off the navy yard. She had been some time in commission and had but lately returned from the West Indies. The appearance of a fine frigate, in full commission, was not usual in Philadelphia, and she was visited by persons from all parts of the State.

This was the time of what was known as the *Millerite* excitement.[3] One Miller had prophesied that the world would burn up on a certain day in October; and strange to say had found many to believe him. The papers said that on the night appointed the fields in the neighborhood of Philadelphia were thronged with believers in their ascension robes, ready to go up. In fact, I knew myself a distinguished "society-lady" who was all ready for the event which she fully believed in. There was so much said about it in the papers that I think a good many people felt *uncomfortable*, to say the least.

On the night appointed for the destruction of the world I had the mid-watch, and about 3 o'clock I heard a curious, rumbling noise which I could not account for, and which caused me much uneasiness. The discipline of the ship would not allow of my stepping across the deck and asking the lieutenant of the watch

---

[2] It was common for a warship to carry more guns than its official rating, but the U.S. Navy was notorious for this practice. The *Potomac* was rated as a 44-gun frigate but could—and did—carry as many as 60 guns.

[3] William Miller (1782–1849) was the father of a religious movement that professed belief in the imminent reappearance of Christ. Miller preached in the 1830s that the end of the world would come "about the year 1843." When that year passed without event, the date 22 October 1844 was named for the second coming of Christ. After 1844 interest in the movement dropped off rapidly.

what he thought about it; so I kept my weather eye open for any change in the weather. The noise continued, and when I called my relief at 4 the first thing he said when awake was: "What's that; is the world coming to an end?" It showed how completely men's minds were taken up with the prophecy when *even a midshipman* condescended to pay some attention to it. My relief told me afterwards that the noise was caused by a steamer blowing off steam under water.

We sailed from Philadelphia in November, 1844, and went to Norfolk, where we received on board Messrs. Crump of Virginia, and Bryan of Ohio who were to take passage with us to Port Royal, Jamaica; there they were to take the English mail packet for Chagres. There were no steamers running between New York and the Isthmus at that time, and the trip to California or the ports in South America was very long and tedious. Mr. Crump was appointed *Chargé d' Affaires* to Chili, and Mr. Bryan to Peru. We left Norfolk about December 1st and shaped a course to pass through the Turk's island passage. Our course took us along the eastern side of the Bahama islands, one of which is the first land discovered by Columbus in 1492. Concerning this same *landfall* there is much difference of opinion. All opinions are based upon that portion of Columbus' journal preserved by Las Casas.

When Washington Irving was writing the history of Columbus he got Captain Alexander Slidell Mackenzie of the U. S. navy to investigate this matter, and after an exhaustive analysis, which received the approbation of Humboldt, the captain decided that the first land discovered was Cat island. It was called by the natives Guanahani, and by the Spaniards San Salvador.[4]

In 1856 Captain A. B. Beecher, Royal navy, after another exhaustive analysis decided that the *landfall* was Watling's island, which is 41 miles S. E. from San Salvador, or Cat island.

Navarrete the Spanish historian, (and one might suppose a Spaniard should be the best informed), says it was Turk's island, 280 miles from Cat island.

[4]See Irving's *Columbus*, vol. 1. [Author's note]

Fr. Adolph de Varnhagen has published a book to prove that it was Mariguana island, distant from Cat island 160 miles: and finally, in 1882, the Hon. Gustavus V. Fox, who was the Assistant Secretary of the Navy during President Lincoln's administration, came out in an article published in the Coast Survey report, to prove that they were all wrong, and that the *landfall* was Samana or Atkins Kay! This is 100 miles distant from Cat island.

It appears to me that in this investigation it is impossible to determine the first land seen by Columbus by simply taking his journal which gives only the daily *course* and *distance* from the island of Gomera—(one of the Canaries). Let a ship *in this day* sail from Gomera and only give the same *data*, and what seaman will undertake to say what island she would first make in the space comprised between Cat and Turk's islands! He would want to know something more than the course and distance; such as the prevailing winds, the set of the currents, and not only the variation of the compass, but the *local deviation*. This latter point seems to have been overlooked by the investigators.

The compass in use in that day must have been of rude construction, and we do not know anything at all as to how it was mounted. Who knows but that the helmsman occasionally hung his steel helmut, (if he wore one) upon the binnacle, (if there was one)! Bringing into the discussion the *magnetic deviation*, or variation of the compass as it is called, is, in my humble opinion, *drawing it entirely too fine*; it is painting the lily, as it were.

We know that Columbus first observed the "variation" on the compass; but what means had he of determining it? All his instruments were imperfect. His improved Astrolabe did not hinder him from making many errors in the latitude—he never *did* know his longitude, and he never used the log-line; it was not known then.

It seems to me that the best way to determine the *landfall* is to start from a known point—such as Isabella, on the northern coast of the island of San Domingo, where Columbus built a fort—and "try back" as it were. This was the plan pursued by Mackenzie. But even here we meet with the same difficulties of winds, currents, and local attraction.

Having read much and thought more on this subject I shall continue to pin my faith on Guanahani, or San Salvador, or Cat island, as it is severally called. As Captain Mackenzie says: "Do not disturb the ancient landmarks."

It is worthy of note that in his voyage to the islands and back Columbus was forced by the N. E. trades and the Gulf stream to pursue precisely the route followed by navigators of the present day. On the voyage out he made a straight course for the Bahamas, and on his return was forced to go up to the parallel of 40° in order to get the west winds. He stopped on the voyage back to Spain at the Azores in latitude 39° north. Moreover he sailed from Palos in Spain on his voyage of discovery on a *Friday*, and he first made the island of Guanahani on a *Friday*!

The *Potomac* passed through the Turk's island passage and went first to Gonaives, a small port on the western coast of San Domingo island—from thence we went to Port-au-Prince which is situated at the bottom of a deep bay on the same island. The island of San Domingo was known as Hayti by the natives and called Hispaniola by the Spaniards. At present the eastern half of the island is called Dominica, and the western Hayti. It was taken by the French in 1677. In 1793 the negroes revolted and massacred nearly all the whites; since which date it has remained in their possession.[5]

Upon our arrival at Port-au-Prince we found the yellow fever raging and the commodore decided to remain but one day. Only the caterers of the messes were allowed to go on shore, and our caterer went with the others. Whether he had underestimated our

---

[5]The slave rebellion actually began in 1791, but it achieved success only after 1793 when Pierre-Dominique Toussaint L'Ouverture assumed leadership. Though Toussaint himself was captured by the French in 1803, the French armies were devastated by yellow fever, and in 1804 Haiti became virtually independent. The government was dominated by the mulatto elite and run by Jean Pierre Boyer, who ruled from 1818 to 1843. In 1843, the year it was visited by Parker, the Spanish half of the island succeeded in setting up a separate Dominican Republic.

powers, or not, I do not know; but our stores were exhausted, and we had been reduced to the By-no-meal theorem for some days. With much difficulty we raised ten dollars and sent him on shore. We did not expect much for that sum of money, but we had visions of *yam* and fruit at least. When our caterer returned he brought back a *one-eyed game cock*, for which he had spent all our money! We were inclined to grumble, but as he could *man-handle* any member of the mess we kept our complaints to ourselves. This caterer, who was one of those who go through the world with a "light heart and a thin pair of breeches," said to us: "it's no use to growl; this game cock will give you more satisfaction in the end than the fruit," and he did. We turned him loose upon the main deck where he lived upon the captain's chickenfeed as a kind of free lance; he became a great favorite with the men, and many were the fights he gained. He lived in this way many months and was eventually murdered by the captain's steward. His death caused much indignation in the steerage, and his epitaph was written by our mess poet. It was somewhat after the style of "Old Grimes is dead."

With all our care the yellow fever broke out soon after we sailed from Port-au-Prince; but we only had two cases. Since then I have seen more of this disease than most men, and have had it twice. The first time was at Pensacola in the summer of 1846. I was ashore at the navy yard one night in the gig waiting for the captain, and while there saw that a steamer at the wharf near us was on fire. I gave the alarm and went on board with the gig's crew. The men from our ship soon came to our assistance and we extinguished the fire; and when that was done, we midshipmen got to skylarking with the hose and were soon very wet. Our captain (God bless him) kept me waiting for him in my wet clothes until near midnight and I was chilled to the bone. When I got on board I found the starboard mess "keeping it up!" Tom Kinloch I remember was making an omelette in a tin cup over three candles. The caterer of the mess having to write orders for the steward to get the next day's marketing, and having kept it up *too high* himself, asked me to write for him. Upon taking the pen I found *I could not see*. I thought it hard times that the others were seeing double, and I not at all; but nevertheless in a few hours I was down with the yellow fever and I did not get to my duty again for a long, long time. As the ship had a spar-deck cabin in addition to one on the main deck, and our captain could not occupy both, (though he tried to) I was removed to it. Just as I had "turned the corner," though still very weak, one-half of our midshipmen were ordered home for their examination as passed-midshipmen. The night before leaving they came to bid me good-bye, and in the excitement of going home and joy at my probable recovery (I am happy to say), one of them, Harry Bluff by name, danced a horn-pipe on the centre-table with his boots on. The next day our captain—a *Tartar* if there ever was one—came in to see me, and on leaving the state-room he noticed the state of the table. "Why! what's all this?" he exclaimed: "Damme, it looks as though some one had been scratching this table with a nail!" I preserved a judicious silence; but I thought to myself, if you had seen Harry Bluff's performance last night you would not be so much surprised.

Less than a year after this, near the close of the war with Mexico, I was returning home in the frigate *Raritan* and again had the yellow fever. My symptoms were the same as in the first attack. We had many cases on board, but I had not feared it; indeed, I was under the impression that I could not have it a second time. I was walking the deck and went to look at the compass to see how the ship was heading, preparatory to turning in. *I could not see the compass* and a few hours after I was down again, and this attack was as bad as the first.

When we left Port-au-Prince one of our midshipmen was ill of the fever and I used to lie in his cot with him while nursing him, and so did some of the other midshipmen; but it did not spread. Altogether, I have seen enough to know that it is not contagious, though it may be infectious. I believe doctors are not certain of it, however. That it can be carried in ships admits of no doubt. In 1855 the steamer *Ben Franklin* conveyed the yellow fever to Norfolk—the men working on her first carried it to Gosport, and it crossed the river into Norfolk with them. This was as plain as a thing could be.[6]

There is much yet to be learned concerning this fearful scourge, and one difficulty, which I have myself observed, is that in one place it is of a mild type, and in another of a very bad one; and even in the same place the fever of one year differs from the fever of another. It prevails every summer on the east coast of Mexico, but is not known, I think, on the west coast. We had on this occasion but two cases; one proved fatal, and the other, being a midshipman, got well.

A few days after leaving Port-au-Prince we arrived at Port Royal, Jamaica, the seaport of Kingston. I have since been much in the tropics, but I have never seen any spot that came up so completely to my idea of "tropical scenery" as Port Royal, with its groves of cocoa-nut trees, thatched cottages and still life.

Our *Chargés* landed here, and in company with many of our officers, visited the governor, Lord Elgin, at his palace, situated somewhere up in the mountains.

This being our first convenient stopping place two of our midshipmen took advantage of it to fight a duel. Neither was hurt and the authorities knew nothing about it.

From Port Royal we sailed for Havana, touching at the beautiful port of Santiago de Cuba by the way. Off Havana we experienced a heavy "norther," which caused us to lie to under a close reefed main topsail for two days. At 12 o'clock on the third day the commodore determined to bear up for the harbor; I expect he did not happen to bear in mind what a heavy sea there would be off the port. In entering Havana you steer directly for the mouth of the

[6]Yellow fever is transmitted by several species of mosquitos. Parker is therefore correct in noting that it was infectious but not contagious. This was argued by Carlos Finlay of Havana, Cuba, as early as 1881, two years before Parker's book was published, but was not proven until 1900, the evidence being provided by the Yellow Fever Commission of the U.S. Army headed by Major Walter Reed.

harbor and then haul short round the Moro Castle, which stands on the left hand side. As we went flying before the wind and sea, under double reefed topsails, we commenced rolling our spar deck guns under water as we approached the port. The pilot could not come off, so our captain had to take the ship in; and he soon becoming confused, the commodore took charge of the deck; it was the best thing I ever saw him do. The ship was yawing four or five points, and four men at the wheel could hardly steer her. At one moment she would be heading for the Moro Castle as though she was about to run it down, and the next for the rocks off the *playa* on which the sea was breaking higher than our fore-top. It was an anxious moment with all hands; the braces were led along ready to be manned, and the men were hanging on to the belaying pins, guns, and everything else that would yield a support. On shore the *playa* was crowded with spectators, and as our ship would point her head in that direction as though determined to be among them, there would be an involuntary movement on their part to get out of the way. It must have been a most beautiful sight to them and no doubt they enjoyed it. I was hanging on to the spanker boom myself and could not help thinking at the time what a grand spectacle we must present, and how much I would enjoy it if *on shore*! As Ross Brown says in his description of his horse Saladin running away with him: "It would have been so funny to see somebody else mounted upon Saladin!"[7] As we got nearly abreast the Moro, the frigate gave a heavy roll to port, then to starboard, taking the water in over each bulwark in succession, and nearly dipping her lower yardarms in the water, pointed her bow toward the *playa* for one awful moment, and then with the helm hard a-starboard she slowly doubled round the castle, and in less than one minute was in smooth water, and nearly becalmed under the lee of the precipitous cliff on which it is situated. Those of us

[7]Parker's reference here is to John Ross Browne (1821–1875), whose book entitled *Yusef, or The Journey of the Frangi: A Crusade in the East* (1853) contains a chapter entitled "The History of My Horse Saladin."

who had been singing to ourselves the long metre doxology drew a long breath, and resumed our every day duties!

Havana was founded in 1511; it was taken by the English in 1762 and restored in 1763. The old town is surrounded by a wall and the streets are very narrow. In the new portion they are wide and there are many handsome public buildings. The Tacon theatre is one of the largest and prettiest I have ever seen. In the cathedral are deposited the remains of Columbus.

Columbus died in Spain on the 20th of May, 1506. His body was deposited in the Convent of St. Francisco, and his obsequies were celebrated at Valladolid. In 1513 his remains were transported to the Carthusian monastery of Las Cuevas of Seville. In 1536 the bodies of Columbus and his son Diego were removed to Hispaniola and interred in the principal chapel of the cathedral of the city of San Domingo. At the termination of the war between France and Spain in 1795, all the Spanish possessions in the island of Hispaniola were ceded to France, and in 1796 the remains were again removed to the cathedral in Havana.

A few years ago in consequence of some discoveries in the cathedral at San Domingo an attempt was made to throw some doubt as to whether the body removed to Havana was that of Columbus or not, but as Navarrete in his "collections" has given a circumstantial account of the proceedings, and has minutely described the precautions taken by the Spanish authorities upon the occasion of disinterring the body, I do not see that there could have been a mistake made or a reasonable doubt as to the authenticity of the narrative.[8]

In February we sailed from Havana and went to Pensacola where we found the other ships of our small squadron; they were the *Falmouth* and the brigs *Lawrence* and *Somers*. The 7th U. S. Infantry

---

[8]After the funeral in May 1506 in Valladolid, Columbus's remains were taken to the Monastery of Santa Maria de las Cuevas in Seville. His body was exhumed in 1542 and reinterred in the Cathedral of Santo Domingo. The question of his subsequent resting place is still a matter of some dispute. Both Santo Domingo and Cuba claim the distinction.

was at this time garrisoning Forts Pickens and Barrancas, and we became well acquainted with the officers. Pensacola was very gay at this time, and many were the balls given, alternately, on board ship, at Fort Pickens, at the navy yard, and in town. Affairs with Mexico were beginning to look squally. General Taylor was assembling a force at Corpus Christi in Texas, which the 7th Infantry soon joined, and Commodore Conner proceeded to Vera Cruz with his squadron.[9]

Upon our arrival there we anchored off Green island, which lies 4¼ miles east of Vera Cruz, and no one was permitted to visit the city. We had only occasional communication with the town—a boat coming off now and then with dispatches for the commodore, and taking his in return. I have always understood that Commodore Conner's dispatches at this time were regarded as models in their way, and were highly approved of at Washington.

We remained here for four months and had a hard time of it; there was no place to visit but Green island—a little spot formed of coral. We had frequent and long exercises at the guns, and worst of all a half allowance of water. It was an idiosyncrasy of the commodore's to keep his men on a short allowance of water. There was in this case no earthly necessity for it. We had only to go a few miles up or down the coast to find rivers where we could have gotten all we wanted. It became so unbearable at last that the lieutenants represented it to the Navy Department, and the Secretary issued an order that the allowance should not be reduced unless it was absolutely necessary. It was a joyful moment when we got under-way and returned to Pensacola, where we arrived in August, 1845.

In consequence of the advance of our army under General Taylor towards the Rio Grande and the threatening attitude of Mexico, it

[9]Texas had been annexed by joint resolution of Congress on 1 March 1845. Soon afterward Mexico broke off diplomatic relations with the United States because of a dispute over the precise location of the Mexican-Texas border. Eager for a conflict in order to lay claim to even more Mexican territory, Polk sent Taylor's army into the disputed area.

was thought necessary to make large additions to the squadron and we soon had quite a respectable fleet in Pensacola harbor.

Many sharks were seen in the harbor at this time—the pilots said it was because of the large number of ships in port, which they followed in. Among them I particularly remember the *Leopard shark*, a horrid spotted monster, about 14 feet long.

In the fall of this year a fishing party came over from Mobile and whilst they were hauling the seine on Santa Rosa island the leader, a large, corpulent man, was seized by a shark and carried off in spite of the shouts and splashings of his companions; I think they did not recover the body.

This is the only case that ever came under my observation where a shark actually took a man off. I believe that such cases are rare, and that a shark only attacks a man, in a crowd, when very hungry.

I recollect that a boat came alongside of us from the *Saratoga* one day with a man's ghastly head in a bucket, for recognition. They had caught a shark and found the head inside. It proved to be that of a man who had fallen overboard from the *Falmouth* the night before. In this case the man was probably drowned before the shark bit his head off.

While on our way from Vera Cruz to Pensacola we discovered a leak in the bow of the *Potomac,* and there being no dock at the navy yard it was thought the ship would be sent north. Mr. Brodie, the naval constructor on the station, however, thought he could get at it by means of a *coffer-dam,* as he had once succeeded in stopping a leak in the bottom of the *Delaware,* 74, in that way. Accordingly a false bow was built at the navy yard, and finally launched and brought to the ship. I believe we had commenced pumping it out and it would probably have proved a success, but a gale of wind springing up suddenly the other bower anchor was let go, and this with the wind and sea combined, caused the false bow to open and it was forced asunder on the ship's stem. This was a very badly managed affair throughout, and Mr. Brodie did not have the cordial co-operation of our officers; indeed, when the news came aft that the thing was done for, it was received with cheers. Poor Mr.

Brodie was seized with an apoplectic fit on the quarter deck, and died before he could be removed to his house.

The commodore transferred his flag to the *Falmouth* and early in December we sailed for Norfolk in company with the screw sloop-of-war *Princeton*, which vessel was sent with us as a matter of precaution.

The *Princeton* was the first screw steamer we had in the navy, and I sometimes think the *best*. She was commissioned in 1843, and during the entire war with Mexico was actively employed. I never served in her myself, but was in squadron with her for three years, and she was always ready for service. At the time of which I am writing screw ships were rare, and the appearance of the *Princeton*, with her sails furled, going along seven knots an hour—like the ship of the Ancient Mariner, "without or wave or wind"—used to excite much astonishment among the merchant craft.

We anchored on the 19th of December in Lynhaven Bay, just inside Cape Henry. The next day was too foggy to proceed up the bay. About noon a merchant schooner passed close to us, and I was sent in a boat to put some officers on board her. She had a fair wind and tide and it was some time before I caught her up. The captain told me he had not seen the land since leaving Boston, yet here he was in a thick fog steering directly for Norfolk.

I had some difficulty in finding the ship again and came near "losing the number of my mess." Fortunately the captain ordered guns to be fired and the ship's bell to be rung. When I heard the first gun I found I had passed the ship, and was pulling out to sea. It was nearly four o'clock when I got on board. We arrived at Norfolk on the 20th day of December and, contrary to our expectations, the ship was put out of commission and the crew discharged.

CHAPTER V

Return to the frigate *Potomac*—list of her officers—first impressions—sail for Vera Cruz—arrival—Sacrificios Island—San Juan de Ulloa—sail for Brazos Santiago—land a force at Point Isabel—battle of Palo Alto—battle of Resaca de la Palma—General Taylor and Commodore Conner—an alarm—Major Ringgold—Captain May—Lieutenant Ridgeley—boat expedition up the Rio Grande

The *Potomac* was put into dock and the leak soon stopped. She was immediately re-commissioned, a new set of officers ordered to her, and a new crew shipped. Feeling sure that war with Mexico was imminent, I applied to return to her; and after some difficulty received my orders. I reported on board in February 1846.

As the *Potomac*'s officers and men took part in all the naval operations in the Gulf of Mexico during the war, I give a list of the officers so far as my memory serves me: captain, J. H. Aulick; lieutenants, Lockwood, Jas. Rowan, Humphreys, North, Frailey and Doyle; sailing-master, Noland; purser, Bryan; surgeon, Dodd; assistant surgeons, Baxter and Hamilton; marine officer, Garland; chaplain, Lewis, passed midshipmen, Moore, Abbott, Tattnall and Hopkins; midshipmen, Monroe, Carmichael, Powell, Pembroke Jones, McLane, C. Hunter, Murdaugh and Somerville. The forward officers I do not recollect. There were many changes in the wardroom during the cruise, but none among the midshipmen.

My first impressions were not agreeable. I was the last officer to report, and when I arrived I found the ship in commission and nearly ready for sea. Full of zeal, I barely stopped to get my breakfast at the hotel, and then slipping on my uniform I hurried over to the navy yard to report. Our captain was known in the service as a *martinet* and I knew it would not do to delay.

After reporting I asked his permission to remain on shore a day or two to purchase my mattress, blankets, &c., and get my things together—it was quite usual to allow this—but the captain refused it; and indeed it was with some difficulty that I obtained permission to return to the hotel for my trunk.

Said he—after saying he would give me one hour to do this— "Sir, when I get a midshipman on board *my* ship I never let him go on shore until I know something about him,"—and I will do him the justice to say he was as good as his word: for I was with him sixteen months and was only allowed to go ashore on liberty *twice* in that time; and yet I was his aid and supposed to be a favorite!

I found the officers much discontented and all hands were prophesying an unpleasant cruise; but we had a set of midshipmen on board that even Captain Aulick could not put down. They were all on their second cruise and knew their duty well. Intelligent, gentlemanly and full of zeal it was hard for the captain to find fault with them. Then they were sworn friends, and all pulled together—indeed, the feeling among seven of them was more like that of brothers than friends, and to this day among the four who survive the tie continues as strong as in the days of our youth. Kept in three and sometimes even two watches; roused out at all hours of the night to take lunar observations; kept for hours in the tops; knocked about in boats, and "ridden down like a main tack" generally, all would be forgotten when we got to our own quarters and assembling round the mess table would join in the chorus: "It will never do to give it up so, Mr. Brown; it will never do to give it up so."[1]

The lieutenants were always our friends; and I cannot cite a better proof of the way these midshipmen performed their duties than by stating the fact that not one of them was ever punished during the cruise.

We sailed from Norfolk in March, 1846, and passing through the Turk's island passage and along the south side of Cuba, arrived at Vera Cruz early in April.

We found the squadron under Commodore Conner anchored under Sacrificios island, a much better anchorage than under Green island, and the usual anchorage for men-of-war visiting Vera Cruz. Sacrificios island lies E. S. E. 3¼ miles from San Pedro Bastion, Vera Cruz; and is about 4 miles from the castle of San Juan de Ulloa, which is 1600 yards N. N. E. from the same bastion. The island lies three-fourths of a mile from the main land, and the anchorage is between the island and the main; pretty close to the former for protection during the norther season.

The Spaniards under Grijalva landed on this island in 1518, and Bernal Diaz says of it: "Our people found on this last mentioned island two buildings of lime and stone, well constructed, each with steps, and an altar placed before certain hideous figures, the representations of the gods of these Indians. They found here also the bodies of five unfortunate persons who had been sacrificed on the preceding night, their hearts cut out, their limbs separated from the bodies and the walls and altars stained with their blood. This island was named *Isla de Los Sacrificios*. Opposite to it on the

---

[1]Apparently these are lyrics to a seamen's chantey, which is not, however, included in Stephen B. Luce's *Sailor Songs* (1902).

continent we landed, and constructing huts, remained some time in expectation of trading with the natives for gold."[2]

This landing place of Grijalva's followers was precisely the spot where General Scott landed his army in 1847.

In reference to the name of the castle of *San Juan de Ulloa*, Bernal Diaz says: "Our interpreter who showed some marks of intelligence being questioned as to the cause of these victims being put to death in that manner, made answer as well as he could, that it was done by the Indians of *Culva* or *Culchua*, meaning the Mexicans; but he pronounced this word *Ulua*, a name which ever after distinguished the place. It was called St. John partly because this was the day of St. John, and partly in compliment to our chief, Juan de Grijalva."[3]

The squadron at this time, as well as I recollect, consisted of the frigates *Cumberland* (flag ship), *Potomac* and *Raritan*; the steam frigate *Mississippi*; the sloop-of-war *Falmouth, John Adams*, and *St. Marys*; the steam sloop *Princeton*; and the brigs *Lawrence, Porpoise* and *Somers*. It was largely reinforced from time to time as I shall mention.

About the first of May we were unexpectedly signalled to get underweigh, and most of the vessels named stood to the northward in company. As the men were kept constantly exercising with small-arms in obedience to signal from the flag ship, we knew "something was in the wind," though war had not been declared. We anchored off Brazos Santiago, in Texas, about seven miles north of the Rio Grande river on the 6th, and the next day landed some 1200 men, sailors and marines, under Captains Gregory and Aulick, to reinforce the garrison at Point Isabel. We arrived in the nick of time. Previous to our arrival General Taylor with his army had advanced to the Rio Grande, established a post and completed

---

[2]Bernal Diaz del Castillo (1492–?1581) wrote *The True History of the Conquest of Mexico* in 1568. Parker probably used the translation by Maurice Keatinge published in London in 1803. The quotation cited here appears on page 28 of volume I.

[3]Ibid., p. 29.

a fort opposite to Matamoras. He then returned to Point Isabel, leaving the 7th Infantry to garrison this fort, which was afterwards called Fort Brown, in honor of Major Brown, of the 7th, who so heroically held it against all the attacks of the Mexicans from the 3d to the 9th of May, and who lost his life in the defence.

General Taylor having made his arrangements for the defence of Point Isabel (his base of supplies) again left to meet the Mexican army, which was now between Fort Brown and Point Isabel, and threatening the latter point. So that, as I have said, we arrived just in time.

Point Isabel was fortified, and we of the *Potomac* were assigned to some heavy guns at one of the angles. All the men were armed with muskets, but had not been much drilled in their use. Indeed, at that day it seemed impossible to get a regular "blue-jacket" to perform a soldier's duty. The prejudice against the small-arm drill was so strong among the men that during the whole war they made but little progress in learning even the company drill. They were always ready—*too ready*—to *load and fire*; but their awkwardness rendered them about as dangerous to friends as foes.

As soon as we got on shore at Point Isabel we expected we might have to march to join the army, so the lieutenants went immediately to work drilling their companies; and I thought the army officers who looked on would die of laughter at the sight. One lieutenant would persist in giving the order *double up*, when he wished to form two ranks; and we were all performing the most remarkable evolutions, none of which were laid down in Scott's Tactics.

The officers of the present day are so well instructed in infantry tactics at the Naval Academy, and the sailors are so well drilled, that they would find it hard to realize how very green we were at that day. However, we were all full of zeal and pluck, and were always able to hold our own in all our fights afloat or ashore. Each ship had a company of well-drilled and disciplined marines, and in our shore operations they formed a battalion, and this battalion formed the *nucleus* on which we rallied.

General Taylor met the Mexicans on the 8th of May, 1846, and fought the battle of Palo Alto. He stood on the defensive in this battle, and it was fought principally with artillery. He made good use of a siege train he fortunately had with him. I think it consisted of 18-pounders. The Mexicans made but one attempt to come to close quarters—towards the close of the day a body of lancers rode up as if about to charge, but were soon thrown into confusion by the 5th Infantry.

We at Point Isabel could hear the guns all day, and we knew by sound that our army, if not retreating, was not advancing. As may well be imagined we were in a great state of excitement, and the sailors were dying to go to the assistance of the army. About 12 o'clock that night a negro camp-follower came in and informed Major Jock Monroe, who was the senior army officer at the post, that General Taylor was defeated with great slaughter, and that he himself had barely escaped with his life. Captain Gregory of the navy was immediately called and begged to join the General with his men; and both he and Captain Aulick were keen to go; but Commodore Conner had to be consulted, and an express was sent off to him on board his ship. The commodore positively refused to send the men out; he said that unaccustomed as they were to the use of small-arms, and with no knowledge of formations, one regiment of cavalry could cut them to pieces, and that he would not risk crippling his squadron at the very beginning of the war; with many other good reasons no doubt, but here, in my opinion, he made his first mistake in this war:

> He either fears his fate too much,
>   Or his deserts are small,
> That dares not put it to the touch
>   To gain or lose it all!

If we had sent out a thousand men they would have reached General Taylor at daylight on the morning of the 9th of May when more than one officer thought help needed. It was afterwards said that General Taylor called a council of war on the night of the 8th, and after calling upon his officers for an opinion, which was to the effect *that the army should fall back on Point Isabel*, he broke it up with the remark: "Well, gentlemen, we will *advance* to-morrow morning at daylight." This was characteristic of the General; but even he, I think, would not have been sorry to see a thousand American bluejackets on the morning of the 9th.

It must be recollected that the Mexican army, under General Arista, consisted of six thousand men, while General Taylor had barely two thousand.

On the 9th of May General Taylor advanced upon the Mexicans at Resaca de la Palma and utterly defeated them. This battle was gained by an advance of our whole line, and as it was somewhat in the nature of a *scrimmage* the sailors would have given a good account of themselves, and it would have been said that the navy had saved the army. It was better for the army as it was; but the navy lost a glorious opportunity. We were all much disgusted at not being permitted to march out; but as no more stragglers came in, but on the contrary dispatches were received to the effect that the army had held its own on the 8th, we were relieved of our uneasiness as to its safety.

On the 9th we found the sound of the guns becoming more and more indistinct and towards nightfall our hopes were confirmed by the news of a glorious victory.

I knew Commodore Conner well; I was his aid for some time. He had served with distinction in the war of 1812, and was in the *Hornet* when she captured the *Penguin*; where he was badly wounded. He was an educated man and a brave officer; but during the war he always seemed to be too much afraid of risking his men; he lacked moral courage, and would not take the responsibility his position imposed upon him. Consequently he failed.

After General Taylor had defeated the Mexicans at Resaca de la Palma and relieved Fort Brown he returned to Point Isabel and had an interview with Commodore Conner. The newspapers in describing this interview pictured the commodore as appearing in a gorgeous full dress: cocked hat, epaulettes, &c., while the general was represented as being in an old coat and straw hat and very shabby. As well as I recollect the commodore wore a jacket on that occasion. I know he generally wore one, for he had very little of the "fuss and feathers" in his dress, though always scrupulously neat. But some persons have the idea that heroes must necessarily be dirty and cannot be disabused of it. Just as I have observed that passengers on board ship judge of a captain's qualifications by his size. Only those who are fat, with full round stomachs, are considered "fine old seamen!" Why if I were a ship owner I would not have a captain in my employ who weighed less than two hundred and fifty pounds and a large stomach should be a *sine qua non* if the vessel carried passengers.

But to return to my story. Although we knew on the 9th that General Taylor had gained a victory that day we were still on the *qui vive*, for it was thought that the Mexican cavalry might get round to the rear of our army and make an attack on Point Isabel; and considering that it was the base of General Taylor's supplies and the Mexicans must have known it was feebly garrisoned, it did seem reasonable. That night there came up a hard storm, with rain in torrents. In the midst of it the report was circulated that the picket guard had been driven in; and all was alarm and confusion. We of the *Potomac* manned our heavy guns, and I, being Captain Aulick's aid, was sent to a distant part of the post to call him. In performing this duty I had to pass through the encampment of the *John Adams'* crew, and just at this time the men commenced to discharge their muskets to see—as they explained—"if they would go off!" The balls whistled around me like hail, and how I escaped being hit is more than I can tell. I always regarded it as my narrowest escape during the war. However I got to the captain's quarters all right, and returned with him to our battery, which we reached about daylight. I shall never forget the appearance of things there. It seems it was the lowest part of the encampment, and the water had drained into the enclosure until it was knee-high. In the darkness our fellows had lost their clothing, hats and arms—everything that would float did so—and when we arrived all hands presented a pitiable, not to say comical, sight.

Now it is usual in a man-of-war to receive the captain with a certain amount of ceremony, and upon this occasion the "officer of the guard," Midshipman Murdaugh, did the best he could under the circumstances. Seeing the captain coming he managed to get on a pair of white trowsers and throw an old cloak over his shoulders, but he had no hat. One of the passed midshipmen had a straw one, but declined to loan it, (bless his stingy soul) saying it made no difference, seeing the general condition of affairs in the camp. "But it is just for the sake of *appearance*," said Murdaugh earnestly, and putting it on he received the captain in due form.

This became a by-word with us in the steerage, and Murdaugh never heard the last of it. If a midshipman had to keep an extra watch, go in a boat, or do anything disagreeable, he would remark that he only did it "for the sake of appearance." The incident was even commemorated in a song, one of the verses of which ran as follows:

> And then when we landed at Point Isabel,
>   To Taylor's assistance to go,
> Buck Murdaugh appeared in a battered straw hat,
>   And an old ragged cloak, and 'twas borrowed at that,—
> "For the sake of appearance," you know!

When General Taylor returned to Point Isabel after his victories, he was received with great enthusiasm, especially by the sailors, who were generally drunk. They had gotten the run of the sutlers' stores by this time, and knew where to get whiskey; but even without sutlers' stores they would have known where to have found it. I heard a lieutenant say that he once sent a watch of sailors ashore for recreation on an uninhabited island in the middle of the Pacific ocean, and they all came back drunk! I don't know anything about *that*, but I know that our men were drunk, and when General Taylor arrived the sailors almost carried him in their arms and could hardly be kept out of his tent. The General was very tolerant of them; and here as well as at Vera Cruz afterwards, when we were thrown much with the regular army officers, I noticed that they made a pet of Jack, and allowed him all kinds of liberties. They looked upon him as a sea-dog who should not be held responsible for anything he did on shore.

The wounded in the two battles soon commenced to come in,

and upon visiting the hospital it struck me as odd to see our soldiers and the Mexican soldiers lying alongside each other so sociably. Poor Major [Samuel] Ringgold of the Flying Artillery was brought in desperately wounded, and soon after died. We all attended his funeral. He introduced the drill of the flying artillery in the army, and commanded the first battery organized.

When General Taylor came in his escort was commanded by Captain Charles May who charged the Mexican artillery at Resaca de la Palma, and captured General La Vega who commanded it. He was the hero of the hour; six feet in height, and with his hair hanging over his shoulders, he was the picture of a dashing dragoon.

Just as May was about to charge the Mexican batteries, Lieutenant Randolph Ridgeley, commanding Ringgold's battery of artillery, and beyond a doubt the most distinguished officer at the battle of Resaca de la Palma, called out: "Hold on, Charley, until I draw their fire;" which he did, and May then charged. For his services May received two brevets; and Ridgeley but one, which he declined to accept. It was not May's fault, but there was much feeling on the subject among those who knew what Randolph Ridgeley's services really were at both Palo Alto and Resaca. When May returned home there was a dinner given him at New Orleans, and upon his rising to respond to a toast, a voice from the lower end of the table called out: "Hold on, Charley, till I draw their fire!"

In the interview between General Taylor and Commodore Conner it was agreed that there should be a combined attack upon a place called Burrita [or Barita] on the Rio Grande. Colonel Wilson, with the First Infantry, was to march by land and we were to send a boat expedition up the river. We accordingly weighed and anchored off the mouth of the Rio Grande; but there being rather a heavy swell on the bar the commodore would not risk the boats. We waited two days, and on the third the expedition started under Captain Aulick. When he got to Burrita he found the First Infantry in quiet possession of it—so here was another disappointment to the navy and another opportunity lost.

CHAPTER VI

War declared—blockade of the coast—rivers and towns on the
Gulf of Mexico—blockade of Vera Cruz—Green Island—the
pirates of the *Falmouth*—Passed Midshipman Hynson—burning
a vessel under the castle of San Juan de Ulloa—Midshipman
Rogers—loss of the brig *Somers*—unlucky vessels—affair at the
Rio Antigua—the gunboat *Reefer*—first attempt on Alvarado—
the British frigate *Endymion*

The war with Mexico was caused by the annexation of the
independent State of Texas (which was once a part of Mexico,
and had separated by means of a revolution) to the American
Union. The advance of the American army to the Rio Grande
brought about the first clash of arms. It now became the duty of
our squadron to blockade all the ports on the Gulf until such time
as we were prepared to take possession of them. These ports were
Matamoras on the Rio Grande; *Tampico* on the Tampico river;
Tuspan on the Tuspan river; *Vera Cruz* on the Gulf; *Alvarado* on the
Alvarado river; *Coatzacoalcos* on the Coatzacoalcos river, and *Ta-*

basco on the Tabasco river. This latter town is also called *San Juan de Bautista*. All these rivers—save the Rio Grande—are insignificant streams, and all have very bad bars at their mouths. Vera Cruz is the only one of the places named that has anything like a harbor. The others, are for vessels of any size, simply open roadsteads.

There are some ports in Yucatan, such as Laguna and Campeachy, but I think our vessels only visited them for the purpose of buying cattle during the war. To the best of my knowledge the State of Yucatan, though belonging to Mexico, took no part in the war. It *may* have been in a state of revolution at the time, but I do not know.[1]

Matamoras was immediately occupied without opposition by the army under General Taylor, and Commodore Conner proceeded to distribute the vessels of his squadron to blockade the other places. The larger vessels were generally assigned to the blockade of Vera Cruz, and of this number was our ship.

The squadron was largely increased, and among the vessels that joined it at one time or another were the sloops-of-war *Germantown, Albany, Saratoga* and *Decatur*; the steamers *Spitfire, Vixen, Alleghany, Scorpion* and *Scourge*; the brig *Truxtun*; gunboats *Reefer, Bonita* and *Petrel*, and (just before the bombardment of Vera Cruz) the *Ohio* 74, and bomb vessels *Vesuvius, Hecla* and *Stromboli*. There were more small steamers and gunboats, but I cannot recall them.

Upon our arrival off Vera Cruz we anchored under Green island where we had spent so many weary hours the summer before. Our anchorage was about 3¾ miles from the castle of San Juan; out of gun-shot in those days, but not by any means so in these days of rifled 100-pounder guns. The larger vessels remained generally at anchor, but the smaller ones were kept underweigh on the lookout for vessels approaching the harbor. Occasionally a vessel would arrive from Europe and anchor under Green island. I do not know what we would have done for mess-stores had it not been for these vessels. I think ninety days grace was allowed vessels from foreign ports to give them time to hear of the blockade of the coast; after

[1]It was.

that time they were made prizes if caught attempting to go in or out of port. Most of the vessels arriving were from German ports, with assorted cargoes, and their captains would break bulk and sell to our messes such stores as we were in want of. We always kept a prize master in them, and the midshipmen were glad to be detailed for this service as it insured plenty to eat and drink. Our mess was a poor one—we were always hard up for something to eat and for money to purchase it. I don't know how it was; we had the best set of fellows in the world in the steerage, lived in perfect harmony, but no one would act as caterer—we were divided up into little squads and lived from hand to mouth.

I recall a piratical trick played on us here by the midshipmen of the *Falmouth*. We had a gander belonging to the mess, brought from Norfolk, but he was in bad condition and not fit to kill—so one day while it was blowing half a gale of wind we thought we would send him ashore on the island for his health—we tied a label on his neck marked: "*Potomac*'s steerage mess," and set him adrift. He was bravely drifting towards the shore and we were congratulating ourselves upon the success of our manœuvre, when as he passed the *Falmouth* the midshipmen espied him and sent a boat to pick him up. We thought it was blowing too hard to lower a boat; but that was the last we ever saw of our gander—they literally "cooked our goose for us."

Officers from all the ships assembled every afternoon on Green island for exercise and bathing—there, too, we used to exchange ideas.

One of the finest fellows in the service I often met on Green island. I allude to Passed Midshipman [John R.] Hynson, of Maryland. He was drowned in the brig *Somers* when she capsized and sunk off Vera Cruz in the fall of this year. At the time of her sinking Hynson had both of his arms bandaged and in a sling, and was almost helpless. It was said that when the brig sunk he managed to get hold of a spar with another man, and finding it would not support two he deliberately let go his hold. It was like him. The way he happened to have his arms in a sling was this: While the *Somers* was maintaining the blockade of Vera Cruz a vessel managed to slip in—I think she was a Spanish schooner. The

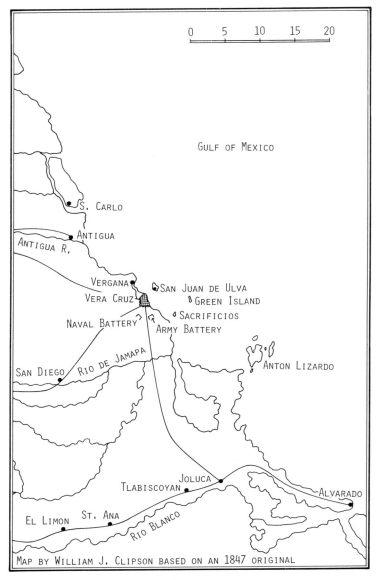

Veracruz, Mexico, and vicinity.

Mexicans moored her to the walls of the castle of San Juan for safety; but the officers of the *Somers* resolved to cut her out or burn her. Hynson was the leading spirit in the affair, though Lieutenant James Parker, of Pennsylvania, was the senior officer. They took a boat one afternoon and pulled in to visit the officers of an English man-of-war lying under Sacrificios island. It was quite usual to do this. After nightfall they left the British ship and pulled directly for the schooner, which they boarded and carried. This, be it observed, was directly under the guns of the castle and the muskets of its garrison. The crew was secured, and finding the wind would not serve to take the vessel out it was resolved to burn her. Her captain made some resistance, and the sentinel on the walls called out to know what was the matter. Parker, who spoke Spanish remarkably well, replied that his men were drunk and he was putting them in irons. The party then set fire to the vessel and got safely away with their prisoners. It was in setting fire to the schooner that Hynson got so badly burned.[2]

A short time after this Passed Midshipman [R. Clay] Rogers of the *Somers*, accompanied by Assistant Surgeon Wright, landed in the night on the beach to the southward of Vera Cruz, their object being to blow up a magazine outside the city-wall. A Mexican patrol coming up Mr. Rogers was made prisoner, but Dr. Wright escaped to the boat and got back to the brig. The Mexican authorities threatened to hang Rogers as a spy; but he wore his uniform at the time of his capture and they could not do so without violating the rules of war. Rogers was held a prisoner until the capture of Puebla by Scott's army in 1847; he then joined the Army and went into the city of Mexico with the captors.[3] He

---

[2]Unknown to the heroic midshipmen, the Spanish schooner that they burned, the *Criolla*, had entered the port with Conner's connivance as an American spy vessel.

[3]So concerned was Conner with Rogers's safety that he sent Lieutenant Raphael Semmes along with Taylor's army on its advance to Mexico City in order to seek Rogers's release. See Semmes's *Service Afloat and Ashore during the Mexican War* (1851).

resigned after the war, studied law and removed to San Francisco, where I believe he still lives.

Although it did not happen until late in this year, I will mention here the particulars in relation to the loss of the *Somers*. She was lying at anchor under Green island when a vessel was observed close to the main land, evidently with the intention of running the blockade. Captain R. Semmes, who commanded the *Somers*, got her underweigh and stood out under topsails and foresail to intercept her. The brig was nearly out of provisions and water, and flying light; so that it made her what sailors call *crank*. A heavy squall from the northward struck her as she was about the middle of the channel, and she went over before her sheets could be let go. She carried down with her Passed Midshipmen Clemson and Hynson and nineteen men.[4] The survivors were saved by boats from the English and French men-of-war lying at Sacrificios island. It was said at the time that if the tanks of the *Somers* had been filled up with salt water she would not have capsized.

The brig was named for Captain Richard Somers, who lost his life off Tripoli in 1804. He was in command of the ketch *Intrepid*, a fire-vessel loaded with bombs and combustibles, and his object was to destroy the Tripolitan gunboats in the harbor and perhaps the batteries. He intended to set fire to the ketch and to escape with his men in a small boat. The *Intrepid* blew up shortly after she entered the harbor, and all hands were lost in her. There was not a man left to tell the tale. Some of Somers' shipmates believed he blew her up to avoid capture. *He* was unlucky, and the *brig* was unlucky; and whatever may be said about the superstitions of sailors there *does* appear to be "something in a name"—why, look at the name "America," so popular with ship owners; I know myself of the loss of steamers *Central America, North America, South America*, and *two* named "America." I was not at all surprised at reading of the loss of the English sloop-of-war *Phœnix* the other day. If any man has a doubt in reference to unlucky names let him

---

[4]Actually 32 men were lost when the *Somers* went down.

take up a list of shipwrecks in the British navy and count up the "Phœnixes," "Pandoras," "Martins" and "Magnets." I do not hesitate to say that if I were a marine-insurance man I would charge a premium on vessels named after unlucky ones. *Bismillah! on my head be it.*

After lying at Green island for some months it became necessary to fill up our water tanks, and the commodore decided to do this at the river Antigua, a small stream not many miles to the northward of Vera Cruz. I shall always remember this river as it is the place where I first heard a hostile shot. We got underweigh with a number of other vessels, and passing just out of gun-shot of the castle, anchored off the mouth of the river about sunset of the same day. Our launch with the water casks was to go up the river the next morning in charge of passed midshipman Moore and midshipman Hunter, and I got permission to go in her as a volunteer.

In the morning at daybreak we started off, and in company with the boats of the other ships proceeded up the river. The bar was rough, and in crossing it we shipped several seas which wet the muskets packed away in the stern sheets. The expedition was composed of the launches with the water casks, and a number of cutters with armed men and marines to protect them. It was commanded by Captain [Frederick] Engle of the *Princeton*, an enterprising and dashing officer.

We anchored in the river and filled up our water casks; and I recall now the extreme beauty of the scene; it was a very narrow river, the shores were covered with tropical verdure, and through the groves of palm trees we could catch glimpses of thatched huts—we could hear the birds singing in the trees on the banks, and all bore the appearance of peace and quiet. We had been so long cooped up on board ship that I know I, for one, was wishing I could get on shore. The banks of the river were high, and away off in the distance was seen a solitary mounted vedette, the pennon of his lance gaily fluttering in the light morning air—he did not change his position while we were in the river and his appearance made the scene still more picturesque. He was the one thing wanted to give *life* to the landscape.

The boats having filled up their water-casks, we returned to our ships to discharge and get our breakfasts. We then returned to the river for another load. Captain Engle did not go the second time, and Lieutenant [Charles S.] Boggs was the senior officer. We crossed the bar safely, shipped a few seas as before, and anchored in the river. This time it was thought necessary to take more precautions and two marines were landed from one of the cutters to act as sentinels. They commenced the ascent of a small hill where they could command a better view, and had just reached the top of it when a volley was fired by the Mexicans lying in ambush. Having nothing to do with the boat I was sitting on the rail watching these marines and wishing I was with them when the firing commenced.

To me the scene instantaneously changed to a *drama*, and I fancied myself in a theatre. I enjoyed it very much. I saw the marines retreat down the hill; I saw one of them turn round when half way down and discharge his musket; I saw his hat fly away with a bullet through it; and then I saw both marines run madly into the water and the "play" concluded. Not to put too fine a point upon it, it became now a regular *sauve qui peut*.[5] There being no understanding as to what we were to do the boats commenced to go down the river and did not stand upon the order of their going. I saw the light boats come flying down the river and pass the marines who were standing up to their necks in the water and begging to be taken in. It began to look as though they would be left to their fate—(which would have been to our everlasting disgrace), and I was imploring Mr. Moore to pull to them when the last boat sheered in and picked them up. In the meantime the men in our boat did not remain idle spectators of the scene—*not by any means!* They were trying to weigh the anchor and be off with the rest; but being unable to do so I'm afraid they cut the cable—(we kept *dark* about this though, and it was not known in the squadron; other-

---

[5]*Sauve qui peut* is a traditional French military term of disaster. Roughly translated it is: "Get out if you can," or "Every man for himself!"

wise like Mrs. Gradgrind, "we should never have heard the last of it."[6] As soon as we commenced to retreat the Mexicans, who had never ceased their fire, showed themselves on the banks and followed us down towards the mouth of the river. One of our men received a ball in his shoulder about this time which brought me to a better appreciation of the state of affairs and convinced me that it was not a "play;" so Hunter and I commenced with the muskets in the stern sheets to see if we could not bring down a Mexican. The muskets being wet would not explode and after trying five or six I got careless in holding them, and the seventh happening to go off I was knocked heels over head in the bottom of the boat. The Mexicans reported afterwards that they had killed an officer, and I think they must have seen me fall. Our boat being a very slow one we had the honor of bringing up the rear, and we were, I need not say without any effort on our part, the last under fire.

The *first* boat out was the *Cumberland*'s first cutter, as she was anchored nearest the mouth of the river; but for a long time after, the officer who commanded her had a good deal to bear—nothing could be said about boating or racing that some devil of a reefer did not slyly say: "Well, I'll tell you what, the *Cumberland*'s first cutter is a fast boat."

Now it seems that this whole performance was witnessed from the ships, and the midshipmen by going aloft into the tops could see us all very well. As the current was running out the river, the boats appeared to leave the scene of action with remarkable speed—much to the disgust of our brave boys, who did not comprehend the state of affairs—so when we got back to the ship they were prepared for us.

To tell the truth I felt something of a hero. I had been in a battle and I had fired off a musket, (I really believe it was the first I had ever fired, and I was not a little proud of it), so when I went down to the steerage it was with a proud and lofty air. I was received with shouts of derision; remarks were made of boats rowing twenty

[6]A character in Charles Dickens's *Hard Times* (1854).

miles an hour, etc., etc., until I was glad to edge in a word and say meekly, that "I was only a volunteer."

The upshot of this expedition was that in the afternoon the *Princeton* anchored nearer the shore and shelled the woods; a force was landed which drove the Mexicans back, and the boats finished filling up their casks. They may have made one or two trips afterwards, but I do not think we got *all* the water we wanted for the squadron. The fact is the enemy had us at so great a disadvantage that they *should* have killed or wounded half of us when they first fired. Sailors in boats cannot row and fire at the same time; and even the marines fire at a great disadvantage. It seems the force attacking us had been sent from Vera Cruz, and the Mexicans claimed a great victory. The Vera Cruz papers were full of it, and stated that we had lost many men; but I think we had but one man wounded.[7]

It was while we were lying off the Antigua river that the first of the gunboats arrived. It was the *Reefer*, Lieutenant Commanding [Isaac] Sterrett. She was a very small schooner, mounting one gun. I went alongside her once in our barge, which was nearly as long, and not knowing any better stepped over her port quarter. The first lieutenant immediately informed me in no very gentle tone that "there was a *gangway* to that vessel!" Oh! there was a good deal of style kept up in these schooners, if they were little; they were gotten underweigh with the longest of speaking-trumpets and the hoarsest of voices; and I once saw one of them crossing the stern of the line of-battle-ship *Ohio*, and carefully throwing the lead. They drew about six feet of water! These gunboats did good service in Mexico, and took part in all the engagements. In port they looked very cosy and comfortable—at least in good weather—but at sea they were mostly under water; still I do not remember that one of them was lost during the war.

[7]After this skirmish, Conner abandoned attempts to bring water from the Antigua River and contracted with a Texas businessman to supply the army with water.

The first important expedition undertaken by us was for the capture of Alvarado, a town near the mouth of the Alvarado river, which is thirty-three miles S. E. of Vera Cruz. We went there with the squadron and anchored off the mouth of the river, outside the bar, which has only eight or ten feet of water on it. We were within long range of the batteries; at least I suppose we were within range, as we went to quarters and cast loose the guns. The gunboats anchored much closer in. We saw the Mexicans manning their batteries, and there were a number of small armed vessels lying in the river; among them a fine brig, which *should* have been cut out that night and added to our squadron.[8] We did not open fire from the ships, but during the afternoon and night the gunboats were engaged with the enemy, both with their heavy guns and small arms. A boat expedition was organized to go in the next day, and there was not much sleeping in the wardroom and steerage that night. The lieutenants selected for the boat-work were writing letters home, and probably making their wills. The midshipmen were sharpening their swords, loading their pistols, eating hard tack and salt junk, and boasting of what they intended to do the next day. There was no drinking in our steerage, but there was noise enough to scare all the Mexicans in Alvarado if they could have heard it. Those appointed to go in the boats were the operators and loud talkers, while we unfortunates who were to remain on board confined ourselves to criticising the commodore and growling generally. The morning broke cloudy and gloomy, but there was nothing particularly threatening in the look of the weather. About 9 o'clock a general signal was thrown out by the flag-ship, and words cannot express our astonishment at reading: "Return to the anchorage off Vera Cruz."

It was said that the pilots predicted a "Norther," but I believe that Commodore Conner's strongest adherents were shaken in

[8]Mexican defenses of Alvarado included one brig, three gunboats, and a small fort.

their faith after this *fiasco*. We returned as ordered, and in beating up the coast that day we were in company with the British frigate *Endymion*. The *Endymion* was one of a squadron of four frigates that captured the U. S. frigate *President*, Commodore Stephen Decatur, in 1814. On that occasion the *Endymion* was badly crippled by the *President*, and would have been captured had she been alone. The late Commodore [George N.] Hollins was a midshipman on board the *President* at the time, and I remember his giving me a full account of the chase and capture in 1876. After a lapse of sixty-two years the commodore related all the circumstances with as much minuteness as though it had happened but a month before.

The *Endymion* had accompanied the squadron to Alvarado to see the fun; and she saw it! and as if this was not mortification enough for one day, she beat us sailing. Whether it was that our captain was laboring under a fit of disgust or not, he would not make any effort to prevent it. Our yards and sails were not properly trimmed and set, and no attempt was made to trim ship—for the *Potomac* sailed very well when by the head.

Midshipman Hodge of the *Cumberland* "took the rise" out of the Britishers, though, a few days afterwards. He was sent to the *Endymion* with a dispatch, and upon leaving one of her midshipmen accompanied him to the gangway, and could not resist the temptation to say: "This is the ship that took the *President*, you know!" "Ah!" said Hodge, casting his eye aloft, "I see you have put extensive repairs on her since that day." The best of it was that Hodge, being just "caught," did not know one rope from another.

As I have said, this feeble attempt upon Alvarado satisfied the officers that Connor was "not the man for Galway;" and I can attest that while he commanded the squadron anything like enterprise or adventure was discouraged. The affair of burning the schooner under the walls of the castle was disapproved; if a boat at night, out looking for vessels trying to run the blockade, took an opportunity to reconnoitre the castle and defences of the town, it was disapproved—everything of the kind, in short, was frowned upon. We should at one time or another have cut out every gunboat at

Alvarado and every other place. We had the officers and the men to do it, and all we wanted was the word. Our *fiasco* at Alvarado was highly ridiculed by American papers and was a sore spot in our memories.[9]

[9]Conner made a second attempt on Alvarado on October 15. The city's defenses had been considerably reinforced, and once again the commodore called off the attack before it was well under way. See page 80.

CHAPTER VII

Capture of Tampico—slipping off Tampico in a "norther"—
the U. S. ship *Hornet*—vessels of the U. S. Navy lost between
1841–61—Pensacola—yellow fever—second attempt on Alvarado—Admiral Joshua Sands—attack on Tobasco—death of
Lieutenant Charles Morris—Captain French Forrest—incidents
of the blockade of Vera Cruz—Anton Lizardo—narrow escape
of the *Cumberland*—loss of the U. S. brig *Truxtun*—a man
hanged at the yard-arm of the U. S. ship *St. Marys*—visit Pensacola and return to Vera Cruz

Shortly after this attempt on Alvarado the squadron sailed to
attack Tampico, a town of about 7,000 inhabitants, on the
Tampico river 210 miles north of Vera Cruz, and next to that city
the largest and most important place on the coast. It was said that
the wife of the American consul, who remained in the city, had
long been in communication with Commodore Connor, and finally wrote him that the city would yield, without resistance, to
the appearance of force. This must have been so; for we went there,

and sending in the light steamers and gunboats, the town surrendered to us without a fight. I did not accompany the detail from our ship up to the city, and do not recall any incidents of interest in relation to the expedition.

The bar off the mouth of the Tampico river is considered the most dangerous on the coast, and many lives have been lost on it. Sharks are numerous in the vicinity, as though they knew of the dangers of the place and the probabilities of prey. We anchored off the bar in the *Potomac*, and remained for some time after the place fell. Tampico was immediately occupied by the Army, and the Army *may* have co-operated with us in its capture; but I cannot say positively. I only know that there were troops there immediately after its capture, if not before.[1]

It was the "Norther" season while we were there, and as vessels never attempt to ride these heavy gales out at anchor in the open roadstead, we had our topsails reefed before furling, and a slip-rope and buoy on the chain. These "Northers" spring up suddenly and blow with great violence along this coast from Galveston, Texas, to Alvarado; below Alvarado they do not, I think, blow *home*, as sailors call it.

One very beautiful evening we were all on deck watching the sunset and listening to the music of our band, when we saw a small steamer with troops (sick men I presume) coming out over the bar. She was a river-boat, and not intended for the ocean; but the exigencies of the times pressed into service many such "rattletraps" for the transportation of troops and stores. I did not wonder at hearing soldiers say they did not like "going to sea" when I saw the kind of vessels the quartermasters chartered to transport them from place to place during this war. Delightful as the sea is, especially off Cape Horn, in winter, a hard gale, with the hatches battened down and the water knee-deep in the steerage; or on the

[1] A column of troops under Major General Robert Patterson had been ordered to attack Tampico in September 1846. It was in response to this threat and not Conner's appearance that Santa Anna ordered the city abandoned in October 1846.

coast of Africa in a dead calm, thermometer at ninety degrees, and hatchways covered during a hard rain,—still, packed like herrings in an unseaworthy craft resembling what sailors call the ship *"Doodledeaddidee*, (I am not sure about the spelling of this tall word) *with three decks and no bottom,"* is quite another thing. But "this," as Mr. Toots says, "is a digression."[2]

The steamer crossed the bar safely and stood to the northward, bound to New Orleans. I do not know why, but we all watched this little vessel until she disappeared in the gloom of the night. I had no watch that night, and not feeling sleepy—which was an abnormal state for a reefer to be in—I passed the first watch with Hunter (familiarly known as "Nag.") About eleven o'clock a light breeze sprang up from the northward and Hunter was directed to inform the captain, who immediately came on deck and ordered all hands called. It seemed to me that the wind increased to a gale like magic. As we had close-reefed the topsails we had only to sheet them home and slip the chain to be underweigh.

The *John Adams* and the British brig *Daring* were in company, and it was a grand sight to see them rearing and pitching in the heavy sea that was soon raised. I do not remember ever to have known it to blow harder than it did on this occasion. As soon as we got well clear of the land we furled the fore and mizen topsails and hove to under a close-reefed main topsail and fore storm staysail, with the ship's head off shore. We lost sight of our consorts and did not see them again until we returned to our anchorage off Tampico.

It was under precisely similar circumstances that the U. S. sloop-of-war *Hornet*, Captain Norris, slipped from her anchorage here in September, 1829, and she has never been heard of since— foundered with all hands on board! She had previously touched at Havana, and while firing a signal gun her first lieutenant, the late Commodore Young, was so much injured by the recoil of a gun as to require the amputation of both of his legs. He was sent home

---

[2]Another reference to characters in Charles Dickens's *Dombey and Sons* (1848).

from Havana and lived for more than forty years after the loss of his ship.

During my twenty years' service in the U. S. Navy the following vessels were lost at sea, and never afterwards heard of: Schooner *Grampus*, Lieutenant Commanding Albert Downes, on our coast, in 1841; brig *Porpoise*, Lieutenant Commanding Bridge, off the island of Formosa, in 1853 or 4;[3] sloop-of-war *Albany*, Commander Gerry, in the West Indies, in 1855; and the sloop-of-war *Levant*, Commander William Hunt, near the Sandwich Islands, about 1860. Nothing has ever been heard of any of these vessels.

Upon our return to Tampico we heard that the little steamer I have mentioned put back as soon as she encountered the gale, and in attempting to cross the bar was lost with all hands on board. No wonder we watched her with so much interest the evening she sailed:

'Tis the sunset of life gives me mystical lore,
And coming events cast their shadows before,

sings Campbell.[4]

We had many of these "Northers" during the cruise, and I remember I rather liked them. Our hammocks were not piped up during their continuance, and we midshipmen had fine times below, sleeping as late as we pleased and skylarking. One of our amusements was to turn the mess-table bottom up, get on it, and slide to and fro as the ship rolled. Much we cared for gales of wind in those days!

From Tampico the *Potomac* went to Pensacola for provisions and water, and we arrived there in July, 1846. The yellow fever prevailed in the town and navy yard at the time; but we had only two cases on board, of which I was one, as I have previously stated. We remained here only a few weeks and were busily engaged in

---

[3]The brigantine *Porpoise* was lost in 1854.
[4]Thomas Campbell (1777–1844) was a popular Scottish poet noted for his sentimental and heroic verses. He was apparently a particular favorite of Parker's and is quoted frequently hereafter.

provisioning the ship during that time. Midshipmen Monroe, Carmichael, Somerville, Powell and Murdaugh left us here to report at the Naval Academy, Annapolis, for examination; so McLane, Pembroke Jones, Nag Hunter and I were left to "battle the watch" alone. Upon our return to the squadron at Vera Cruz we heard of the loss of the brig *Somers*, an account of which I have already given. We heard, too, that in our absence a second attempt had been made upon Alvarado. On this occasion the commodore had a larger force than upon the first. The force was divided into two divisions, each consisting of small steamers having in tow gunboats and cutters; and the intention was to make a dash across the bar and storm the place with the men in the boats.

Commodore Conner was on board the steamer *Vixen*, Captain Joshua Sands; his division had crossed the bar, and was nearly under fire when he saw that the second division, under Captain French Forrest, had grounded. "Well, Sands, what is to be done now?" said the commodore. "Go ahead and fight like h-ll," answered Sands. Unfortunately the commodore did not take his advice, but turned back, when if he had gone a cable's length farther the Mexicans would have surrendered. So ended the second attempt on Alvarado, and the papers sent up a howl of derision over its failure.

Captain Joshua Sands commanded the steamer *Vixen* throughout the war. The *Vixen* was a sister ship to the *Spitfire*, Captain [Josiah] Tattnall, and was in all the engagements with her. Sands' name was not so frequently heard, perhaps, as Tattnall's, but he proved himself a gallant officer on all occasions. He is now an admiral on the retired list, and the oldest officer in the navy.

When he was a lieutenant returning from a long cruise in the Pacific in the *Franklin* 74, bearing the flag of Commodore Charles Stewart, while she was lying to in a gale of wind off Cape Horn, under a close-reefed main topsail, a man fell overboard. Sands was under "suspension from duty" at the time and not allowed to go on the quarter-deck, but as the lee-quarter boat was being lowered to save the man, he sprang into it through one of the main-deck ports. The boat was lowered and got away from the ship's side when they found there were in it but Sands, the sailing master E. Peck, and two men. Peck who had been a foremast hand was a fine practical seaman, and getting an oar out aft he managed to keep the boat's head to the sea until the ship picked them up, which singularly enough under the circumstances, she managed to do. I forget whether the man was saved or not. Upon the return of the party on board Commodore Stewart put Sands under *arrest* for "leaving the ship without permission!" This anecdote was told me by Admiral Sands himself only a few years ago; he said Peck saved his life.

A short time after the Alvarado affair an expedition was fitted out to make an attack on Tobasco, a town on the Tobasco river, seventy-five miles above its mouth.[5] Tobasco contained about 5,000 inhabitants, and the troops of the state were assembled there under the command of General [Nicolás] Bravo, a bold and enterprising officer. I believe General Bravo had sent several messages to Commodore Conner inviting him to make an attack on Tobasco, and we knew pretty well that there would be an obstinate defence on his part. Indeed the Tobascans prided themselves on their courage and they were anxious to emulate their brethren of Alvarado. There is no doubt but that the native Indian of this part of Mexico *is* physically brave.

The river Tobasco was first visited by the Spaniards, under Grijalva in 1518. Cortez stopped here in 1519, and had a desperate encounter with the inhabitants. Bernal Diaz says that after his fight they dressed the wounds of the men and horses with the *fat of Indians*! I think the town called at that time Tobasco is the present Frontera, for Bernal Diaz says: "Our troops proceeded to the shore and disembarked at the Point of Palmare, which was distant from the town of Tobasco about half a league."[6] Cortez changed its name to *Santa Maria de la Vittoria*.

---

[5]Conner's second Alvarado expedition was on 15 October 1846. Perry's squadron departed for San Juan de Bautista (or Tobasco, more often spelled Tabasco) on 16 October.

[6]Bernal Diaz del Castillo, *op.cit.*, p. 57.

Our expedition was commanded by Commodore M. C. Perry, who had lately joined as second in command and who had his flag on the good old steamship *Mississippi*, a ship that did more hard work in her time than any steamer in the Navy has done since— and she was built as far back as 1841.

Commodore Perry's command, consisting of small steamers, gunboats and cutters arrived off the Tobasco river one afternoon, and dashing across the bar captured the town of Frontera, near its mouth, almost before the Mexicans knew they were there. Two river boats plying between Frontera and Tobasco were lying at the wharf; one of them with steam up and the supper table spread. The town and vessels where taken possession of without opposition, and the supper was enjoyed by the captors. In one of these steamboats I recognised the old steamer *Champion*, a boat that once ran between Richmond and Norfolk. She was very fast, and under the command of Lieutenant Lockwood, was very useful to the squadron afterwards as a dispatch boat. The commodore went up the river to Tobasco with his little fleet and captured a large number of small vessels lying off the town. The authorities, however, would not capitulate, and at the prayer of the foreign consuls the commodore forbore to bombard the place. The soldiers had evacuated it, and the commodore spared the town from motives of humanity, though I do not think the Mexicans appreciated it. While our men were taking possession of the various prizes the Mexicans kept up a fire from the banks by which Lieutenant Charles Morris, a son of the distinguished Commodore Charles G. Morris, lost his life. He was standing up in his boat when a musket ball pierced his heart. He was a very fine officer, and his death was much deplored by us all.

Commodore Perry finding the Mexican military had fallen back a short distance only from the town determined now to land a force and fight the enemy wherever he could find him. The landing party of marines and sailors was under the command of Captain French Forrest, a man who literally did not know the meaning of the word fear. He had a programme written out and after getting on shore was very particular in seeing that every officer and man took his position in accordance with this programme. This it took some time to do, and as the party was under a dropping fire of musketry the men became very impatient to advance, but Forrest would have his own way: all of a sudden he called out impatiently: "Where is that base drummer, where is that base drummer?" then pausing a moment he said quietly: "Oh! I forgot, he broke his drum-head this morning and couldn't come."

Before Captain Forrest had everything arranged to his satisfaction the commodore concluded it would be better not to send the men out from the cover of the guns of his squadron. He thought the game was not worth the candle, and it assuredly was not. The landing party was recalled and the commodore proceeded down the river with his prizes. As the town of Tobasco was not occupied by us the inhabitants affected to consider this a victory for their side, and became correspondingly "cheeky;" but we took the conceit out of them a few months after as I shall relate. This expedition to Tobasco took place while the *Potomac* was temporarily absent from the squadron. We were all very sorry not to have had a hand in it and to have been on what was known as Forrest's program-*me*. When we got back to the squadron we resumed the blockade of Vera Cruz, sometimes remaining some days under sail, and then again anchoring under Green island. While the vessels were at anchor they sent their boats out at night to cruise in the channel between Green island and the main. The service was arduous and dangerous. While out on this duty the launch of the *Mississippi* in charge of Midshipmen Pillsbury and Bridge capsized one night and Midshipman Pillsbury and some men were drowned. The survivors clung to the boat all night and were picked up the next morning in a pitiable condition. Bridge was afterwards drowned in the U. S. brig *Porpoise* off the island of Formosa. He was in command of her at the time. The *Porpoise* separated from the sloop-of-war *Vincennes* in a typhoon and has never been heard of since. This was in 1853–54.[7]

---

[7] See note 3.

Our boats caught a brig one night attempting to run the blockade, and brought her to us at Green island. We found several military-looking men among her passengers, and Captain Aulick sent for them to come on board the *Potomac*. They had a long interview with him in the cabin and finally were allowed to return to the brig, and it was understood by us that the brig was to be permitted to return to Havana, which was the port she had sailed from. She got underweigh that afternoon with the sea breeze, stood to the northward a short distance, and then putting her helm up, she squared away for Vera Cruz under all sail, and got safely in under the castle. We sent boats to chase her, and pretended to fire on her; but it was evidently a "put-up job." There was some *shenanigan* about it, but our captain never referred to it again. No doubt he had secret instructions.[8]

It is well known that we permitted General Santa Anna to return to the country (from which he had been banished in 1845) during the war. He landed at Vera Cruz with his staff in an English mail steamer; our boarding officer permitted him to land by order of the commodore. This was a wonderful stroke of policy on the part of our Government. It was thought that Santa Anna would immediately bring about a peace with us. He commenced his operations in that way at Buena Vista, and followed them up at Cerro Gordo, Contreras and Chapultepec!

It was some time in the summer of 1846 that Commodore Conner determined to make the anchorage at Anton Lizardo the general rendezvous for his fleet, which now began to assume large proportions. Anton Lizardo is twelve miles S. E. of Vera Cruz. The harbor is an excellent one, and is formed by the coral islands lying off the point, and which make a lee from the "northers." There are passages between the islands to the northwest and southeast, and as well as I can recollect, the anchorage is perfectly safe in all winds. It is a pity Vera Cruz had not been located there.

---

[8] Possibly a replacement for the spy vessel *Criolla* burned by the overanxious Parker and Hyndson on 26 November. See note 2, chapter 6.

The frigates *Cumberland, Potomac* and *Raritan*, with some sloops-of-war and numerous small craft started in company for this place one day, leaving the *Mississippi* and some other vessels on the blockade off Vera Cruz. Our station was immediately astern of the flag-ship *Cumberland*, and it soon became evident to Captain Aulick that we were not steering for the proper passage between the coral islands. He hauled his wind somewhat which brought him on the port quarter of the flag-ship. The commodore was warned by his pilot and others that he was attempting the wrong passage, but he was obstinate and held on until he brought up on the reef hard and fast aground. It is a wonder his masts did not go over the bows, but they held. When it was seen that the *Cumberland* had struck an amusing scene occurred. It reminded me of a large boy getting into trouble and being deserted by his friends. The vessels scattered in every direction. Our captain hauled on a wind and stood away to the northward as though he intended making for Pensacola, and even the little gunboats, which only drew six feet, steered for the open sea. The effect upon the commodore was to make him furious. He immediately made general signal to "anchor near the flagship;" but it took a verbal order, communicated by the flag-lieutenant, to bring the *Potomac* down within hail of the flag-ship. As it was we found a sunken rock not very far astern of us.

Signal was at once made to the *Mississippi*, and about ten o'clock she came to the commodore's assistance. The night was employed in taking out the *Cumberland*'s stores to lighten her—fortunately the weather remained good. The first thing Captain Aulick did the next morning was to take a boat and sound round his ship. I accompanied him, and it being very rough and before breakfast, I was seasick for the first and only time in my life.

The *Mississippi* now got her stream cable fast to the *Cumberland*, and during the morning she got her afloat; and if the *Mississippi* had not been at hand, I do not think the *Cumberland* would have gotten off. That afternoon the squadron anchored at Anton Lizardo, which ever afterwards was our headquarters. The *Cumberland* was so much damaged that it was found necessary to send her home to be docked, and as the *Raritan* had been a long time in commission and the times of her men were out, it was decided to exchange the officers and crews of the two vessels. This was accordingly done, and the *Cumberland* sailed for Boston under Captain [Francis H.] Gregory, and the *Raritan*, Captain Forrest, became the flagship. Upon reflection I think that this occurred in the summer of 1846, not very long after the return of the vessels from Point Isabel, and I think the capture of Tampico must have been in the *fall* of that year, *after* the visit of the *Potomac* to Pensacola, and not before as I have stated. In fact the "northers" only blow in the fall and winter.[9]

We were lying at Anton Lizardo when we heard of the loss of the U. S. brig *Truxtun*, Captain Carpenter.[10] The news was brought by Lieutenant Bushrod Hunter. The *Truxtun* was blockading the port of Tuspan, some 120 miles northwest of Vera Cruz, and got ashore near enough to the land to be under the fire of some small guns which the Mexicans brought down to the shore. The captain sent a boat under Lieutenant Bushrod Hunter to report the disaster to the commodore, and soon after determined to surrender. This was, I believe, opposed by his officers and crew. It was said afterwards that the quartermaster on duty positively refused to obey the order to haul down the flag. Either before this was done or immediately after Lieutenant Otway Berryman left with a boat's crew and got safely to the ships blockading Vera Cruz. The remaining officers and men were made prisoners by the enemy and sent to Vera Cruz, and the brig taken possession of. As soon as we got the news Captain Engle with the *Princeton* was sent there and he made short work of it. He drove the Mexicans out of the brig and burned her; not, however, before they had gotten some of her armament and stores on shore. The guns of the *Truxtun* were mounted by the

---

[9]The grounding of the *Cumberland* occurred on 28 July 1846, before the first assault on Alvarado. The expedition to Tampico took place in November.

[10]The *Truxtun* was commanded by Edward W. Carpender (not Carpenter). The events described here took place in August 1846.

enemy in the forts built to protect Tuspan; but we recovered them eventually as I shall mention.

Early in the winter of 1847 the *Potomac* went to Pensacola again for provisions and water. During our absence from the fleet a man was hanged on board the *St. Mary's* for striking an officer—he stepped from his gun at evening quarters and knocked down the lieutenant commanding the division. He was tried by a court martial and sentenced to be hanged. The commodore thought the discipline of the squadron required that the sentence should be carried into effect, and he was right. When this man was hanged at the yard-arm of the *St. Mary's* the crews of all the other vessels were mustered on the decks of their respective ships to witness it. He acknowledged the justness of his sentence, and was, at his own request, attended in his last moments by the very lieutenant he had assaulted. As soon as we got back from Pensacola in the *Potomac* we took up the blockade of Vera Cruz again as usual.

CHAPTER VIII

The fortifications of Vera Cruz—what Admiral Farragut
thought of them—campaign of General Taylor—Lobos Island—arrival at Vera Cruz of General Scott's army—a reconnoissance—landing of the army of General Scott at Vera Cruz,
March 9th, 1847—remarks on—investment of the city—services of the navy—opening of the bombardment—a heavy
norther—incidents connected with—sailors on shore—affair at
Medellin

The city of Vera Cruz contained at this time probably ten
thousand inhabitants.[1] Like all the old Spanish towns it is a
walled city, and defended by numerous fortifications to resist an
attack either by land or sea. There was a strong fort on the northern
point of the city, and another on the southern point, with guns
principally pointed seaward, and a number more along the walls
for the land defence. About half a mile off the city lies the castle of

[1]The population of Vera Cruz in 1846 was approximately 15,000.

San Juan de Ulloa, a well constructed fortification, built on a coral island of soft coral stone. The island is surrounded by reefs on the north-eastern, eastern and southern sides, and cannot be approached nearer than three-fourths of a mile; but on the face next the city vessels can go close up to the walls of the castle. The castle mounted it was said about one hundred guns of all calibres. There were a few mortars throwing a ten-inch shell, but the guns were, I think, principally 18 pounders.[2] The water battery was considered very powerful—between it and the citadel or main fort was a wide and deep moat with a drawbridge. If the water battery was carried by assault the citadel commanded it. This is in accordance with my recollection of the castle as it looked to me after its surrender. The castle of San Juan de Ulloa was taken by a French squadron under Admiral Baudin, on the 27th of November, 1838, after a bombardment of five hours.

The late Admiral Farragut witnessed it, being present in command of the sloop-of-war *Erie*. He took notes of all that occurred, and visited the castle a few minutes after its surrender. He says in his journal: "I visited the castle to ascertain the cause of its early surrender, and a single glance satisfied me that it would have been impracticable for the Mexicans to stand to their guns. The very material which formerly insured their safety was now a means of destruction, for the castle is built of a sort of limestone resembling coral, into which a solid shot will penetrate a short distance and remain buried, having little or no effect; but with shell it was another matter, they would explode and rend the stone in immense masses killing and wounding the men at the guns, in many instances shattering the walls from summit to foundation. I am satisfied that in a few hours more it would have been a mass of rubbish." "The Cavaliero Alto was very much shattered, and a few more shells would have reached the magazine. The guns were rendered useless, with scarce an exception, by the destruction of

---

[2]San Juan de Ulloa (or Ulúa) mounted 135 guns of all calibers, but only 36 of them were shell guns.

the carriages." The admiral does not state the exact force of the French; I think it consisted of three frigates, some corvettes, bomb vessels and steamers; but any French naval history will tell.[3] The officers of our squadron were very desirous of taking the castle before the arrival of General Scott's army, and some presented plans for doing so. The commodore *must* have had a correct plan of it, and he must also have known of the disposition of the French squadron in 1838. He, however, thought it had been greatly strengthened since that time, but subsequent events proved this untrue.

Captain John Wilkinson in his book, *Narrative of a Blockade Runner*, speaking of Admiral Farragut, says that during the Mexican war: "he [Farragut] had proposed to Commodore Perry, then commanding the gulf squadron, and urged upon him the enterprise of capturing the strong fort of San Juan de Ulloa at Vera Cruz *by boarding*."[4] The gallant captain's memory does not serve him in regard to this. Farragut was not in the gulf during the Mexican war until *after* the capture of the castle and town of Vera Cruz. He sailed in the *Saratoga* from Norfolk in February for Vera Cruz, and he says in his journal: "But we were just too late; the castle had surrendered to our forces under General Scott (March 26, 1847), and the flag was proudly floating over its walls." But it is well known that admiral, then commander, Farragut *was* of the opinion that the castle could be taken by the force under Commodore Conner, and it would have been a most fortunate thing for the navy if Farragut and not Conner had been in command at that time. There is no doubt in my mind but that we should have had it some months before we did, and the city of Vera Cruz fell with San Juan de Ulloa: for the latter commanded it.

[3]In what became known as the "pastry war" a French squadron of three frigates and some smaller vessels attacked Vera Cruz on 21 November 1838 in retaliation for damages to the shop of a French baker by a mob of Mexican citizens.

[4]John Wilkinson, *Narrative of a Blockade Runner* (1877), page 64.

General Taylor occupied Matamoras May 18, 1846, and on the 24th of September following captured Monterey after a desperate fight of three days. He then advanced in the direction of Saltillo. It was now decided by the authorities in Washington to abandon the advance on the city of Mexico by that line, but to capture Vera Cruz, make it the base of operations, and march on the capital *via* Jalapa and Puebla. The plan of this campaign was intrusted to General Winfield Scott, and all the *regulars* were taken from General Taylor save several batteries of light artillery and a squadron of dragoons. This caused much criticism and excited much feeling among General Taylor's friends; but the *volunteers* left with him had been drilled and disciplined by General Wool and gave a good account of themselves at the battle of Buena Vista—fought February 22, 1847. There General Taylor with 5000 men successfully resisted all the attempts of General Santa Anna with his army of 20,000 men to force his position, and the latter ingloriously retreated. This was the last battle fought by General Taylor's army. The transports containing the troops of General Scott's army were assembled at Lobos island, 150 miles north of Vera Cruz. Several of the vessels of the squadron were ordered there, and the senior captain took charge of affairs afloat. On the 24th of February, 1847, General Scott issued his final orders to his fleet at Lobos island, and we in the squadron now commenced to keep a bright lookout for the transports. About the end of the month the *Potomac* was lying under Green island in a moderate "norther," when shortly after noon the man at the mast-head reported a sail to the northward, and soon after we saw the long-expected fleet coming down before the wind. What number of vessels were there I do not know, but there were more than we could count—the little brig *Porpoise*, under her very efficient commander, Lieutenant William E. Hunt, gallantly led the way. The first thing that excited our astonishment was the great amount of sail carried by the transports, and the next the skilful manner in which their captains threaded their way between the reefs! But as one of them remarked to me afterwards, "any one could see the channel in a gale of wind;" meaning that the breakers on the reefs would show the deep water.

No words can express our excitement as ship after ship, crowded with enthusiastic soldiers, successively came in; some anchoring near us, and others continuing on for the anchorage at Anton Lizardo. We had been so long on board our ships, and for some months so inactive, that we were longing for something to do. I cannot answer for others, but the scene of that day—and I recollect it was Sunday—is so vivid, and the events so firmly fixed in my memory, that I can almost *see* the ship *Diadem* as she *grazed* our spanker-boom in her desire to pass near enough to speak us, and I can to this day whistle the "waltz" played by an infantry band on board a transport anchored near us that night, though I have never heard it since. It was indeed "a sight to dream of and not to tell." That night I went in charge of a boat to convey our marine officer, Lieutenant [Addison] Garland, to the transport containing the Fourth U. S. Infantry, which regiment was commanded by his uncle, Lieut. Colonel [John] Garland, and I shall never forget my welcome when it was known that I was a brother of the Parker who had died while belonging to the regiment in 1842. Many of the officers of this regiment were afterward killed—among them the gallant and genial Major [William M.] Graham.

After the landing at Vera Cruz I passed many hours at their encampment near the beach and I remember meeting a Lieutenant Grant—the present General Grant—both there and on board the *Potomac*; though I suppose he has long since forgotten all about it.

A few days after General Scott's arrival, Commodore Conner took him with a large number of the principal officers to make a reconnoissance of the fortifications of Vera Cruz, and to select a place for the disembarkation of the troops. The reconnoissance was made in a small steamer, and a bold one it was—the steamer went so close to the Castle and the northern land batteries that we expected to see her blown out of water. Why the Mexicans did not open fire was inexplicable to us; but I suppose it may have been their *siesta* time.

General Joseph E. Johnston, then Captain Johnston of the Topographical Engineers, was on board at the time and he has told me since how very rash he thought Commodore Conner on this occasion.

The reconnoissance decided General Scott to land the army on the main land abreast of Sacrificios Island. I do not see myself how there could have been two opinions as to its being the proper place; but perhaps the visit to the north side of the city was a *blind*. At all events all the transports were now assembled at Anton Lizardo and the final preparations made for landing the troops. Early on the morning of the 9th of March, 1847, the frigates and sloops of the fleet having taken on board as many troops as they could carry, and the steamers towing the transports with the others, we all got underweigh for Sacrificios Island, nine miles distant. It was a beautiful day and we had a fair wind, with a smooth sea. On board the *Potomac* we had two Pennsylvania regiments, under General [Gideon J.] Pillow, and among the privates I recognized to my great astonishment, a Mr. McDougall, who had been a midshipman with me in the *Columbus*. He had failed to pass his examination and had enlisted. Poor Mac, I never heard of him after this. The vessels anchored under Sacrificios Island about one o'clock, and we prepared to disembark the army, which consisted of about twelve thousand men, in three divisions, commanded by Generals [William J.] Worth, [Robert] Patterson and [David E.] Twiggs respectively.

The Government had previously sent out a large number of surf-boats for this service—these boats were built at or near Philadelphia, and were admirably adapted to the purpose. They were sharp at both ends, with flat floors and drew very little water. They carried one hundred soldiers with their arms and accoutrements, and were manned by one naval officer and eight or ten sailors. In landing in the surf our practice was to let go a kedge which we carried at the stern just before entering the breakers. Whatever may be said of Commodore Conner's management of affairs up to this time the arrangements for this service were simply perfect. The division of General Worth formed the advance and was the first landed. The men were put in the boats and the boats

The landing at Veracruz, March 9, 1847. Courtesy Beverley R. Robinson Collection, U.S. Naval Academy Museum.

were then towed astern of the several men-of-war at anchor. The mosquito fleet under Captain Tattnall ran close in to the beach and kept up a constant shelling; but not a Mexican was to be seen. I had in my boat a company of artillery commanded by Captain and Brevet Major [John L.] Gardner and Lieutenant [John P.] McCowan. Everything being in readiness a signal gun was fired from the flag ship, and we all cast off and pulled in line for the shore; the first boat to touch the beach was one containing a company of the Sixth Infantry, and Lieutenant Edward Fitzgerald sprang out and planted the regimental colors on the shores of Mexico. In less than two minutes after four thousand American soldiers were on the beach, and the landing was a fact accomplished. The boats returned to the ships and took on board and landed the division of volunteers under General Patterson; and finally the division of General Twiggs. By midnight General Scott and his entire army were in a position to commence the investment and siege of Vera Cruz.

Here I must pause awhile to say something in reference to the landing of troops upon a hostile shore. If the enemy will dispute the landing *boldly* it cannot be successfully accomplished. In the landing at Vera Cruz if the Mexicans had concealed themselves behind the sand hills until our boats were nearly in the surf, and had then come down and opened fire, it is my belief that half of the men would have been killed or wounded before reaching the beach. The gunboats could not have fired without endangering their friends, and the men in the boats crowded as they were would have been helpless. If there are no hills a moderately deep trench is all that is necessary for the shore party to shelter itself from the fire of gunboats. The idea is to keep under cover until the landing force gets about fifty yards from the shore and then let them have it with small arms and light artillery. Those of us who served on the James river in the civil war know how very few lives were lost by the shelling of gunboats. If the Russians had followed these tactics the allies would not have made good their landing in the Crimea, nor would the Federal troops have done so at Roanoke island had the Confederates adopted this plan.

Having landed the troops the work of landing material was now commenced. We who were engaged in it were called daily at 4 in the morning, and we worked until 9 or 10 at night. Each midshipman had charge of four surf boats, and we got our meals when and how we could. One of the officers of the flag ship had the general supervision of this work, and we went to the different transports as he directed. The officers and men worked very zealously in this business, and at the end of a week it was marvelous to see the amount of material put on the beach: guns, ammunition, tents, lumber, provisions, clothing, horses, mules, sutlers' stores, &c., &c. The landing place commenced to assume the appearance of a small town, and still the work went on. Transports sailed as soon as discharged and others were constantly arriving. The weather fortunately was good and the sea smooth.

The quartermaster of the Army and the other heads of departments seemed to have everything well arranged beforehand, and were always able to tell us which of the vessels they wished next to be discharged. There were no mishaps, no accidents, no men drowned; but everything went on with the utmost regularity and good order. It was a most creditable performance in every way, and the Navy had every reason to be proud of it. Without our assistance General Scott would never have advanced from Vera Cruz.

The Army after landing on the 9th quickly surrounded the city, and it was besieged in due form. General Scott gave the authorities a chance to send the women and children out before opening his fire, but his offer was declined; later in the siege they wanted to do so, but the general would not then consent; so they remained in the city during the whole of the bombardment. The castle of San Juan and the other forts kept up a constant fire upon the besiegers from this time till the close of the siege. Some mortars were mounted by our army, and I think they commenced firing about the 20th.[5] The army siege train was for some reason late in arriving.

We heard of General Taylor's success at Buena Vista a few days

---

[5]After the defenders refused Scott's demand for the surrender of the city, the Americans opened fire at 4:15 on 22 March.

after landing, and General Scott issued the news in a general order. Salutes were fired as a matter of course.

Before the regular bombardment of the city commenced the Army had two officers killed, Captain Vinton of the Artillery and Captain Albertis of the Infantry. Both were highly esteemed by their comrades.

We had at this time the heaviest "norther" I ever experienced. A large number of merchant ships dragged ashore in consequence of their being so badly provided with ground tackle; and the number of surf boats that broke adrift and went sailing down the coast was simply enormous. During the height of the gale a ship called the *Diadem* broke from her anchors and drifted across our hawse and it looked as if she would carry us on shore with her; but our captain promptly sent his men on board and cut away her masts. We then gave her the end of our stream cable which we secured to our mainmast, and veering her astern we held her safely through the remainder of the gale. The captain of the transport had the "cheek" to claim damages for the loss of his masts, but Captain Aulick did not admit the claim. Our men, however, rigged her up with jury masts afterwards and she went to sea.

No communication could be held with the shore while this gale lasted, but as soon as it subsided the Navy got most of the grounded vessels afloat, and one of the small steamers went down the coast and picked up many of the surf boats.

Happening to be on shore when this gale sprung up I was unable to get off to the ship, and many others were in the same category: among them my messmates, Midshipmen McLane and Jones. I suppose there were two or three hundred officers and sailors ashore. We of the *Potomac* hauled our boats up on the beach, and told the crews they must "shift for themselves," which they said very confidently they could do, and we then held a council as to what we should do for something to eat and a place to sleep. We knew nothing about sutlers' stores, and if we had were not provided with money. About 8 o'clock in the evening as we were disconsolately walking the beach we were accosted by a Lieutenant Ward of the Third Infantry, who said he had just heard that some naval officers were on shore unprovided with quarters, and he had come to look

for them. So we went with him to his tent where we found Captain
Dawson of the artillery. They had charge of some recruits and were
messing together temporarily. Dawson received us very hospitably, and we had some beefsteak for supper which we were glad to
get; though in consequence of the "norther" blowing it had more
sand in it than was agreeable. After supper a field bed was made in
the tent, and we all sat or lay about very comfortably and sociably.
We were treated to a small allowance of *pelos cochos*—two Greek
words signifying *neck oil*—the midshipmen of my time said—and
about 11 o'clock Ward informed us that he knew where some hand
grenades could be gotten, and he proposed that we should creep up
under the walls of Vera Cruz and throw them over into the city; he
said it would cause a *stampede*, as I have no doubt it would. My
messmates gladly caught at the idea; it seemed that a march of
three miles to reach the city, with a strong probability of being
captured by the enemy, if we were not previously shot by our own
sentinels, struck them as "just the thing." Captain Dawson, after
attempting to dissuade us from the attempt, positively refused to
accompany us and I must confess I had "my doubts." However I
could never let my messmates go without me; so we buckled on our
swords, and after several unsuccessful attempts to get through the
tent door which was tied, and our swords *would* act as "toggles,"
we emerged upon the plain. I can see Captain Dawson now rolling
on the tent floor with uncontrollable laughter. To obtain the hand
grenades we had fortunately to cross the encampment of the Fourth
Infantry; I say *fortunately*, for the night being very dark we kept
stumbling over the confounded tent pegs, and not being very
steady on our feet (probably in consequence of the furious
"norther" blowing) we could not hold a straight course; so that
Ward, after each of us had fallen down about twenty times,
proposed that we should give it up for that night and return to the
tent. He said that perhaps the next night would be better as we
could make an earlier start! To this we gladly acceded, and upon
getting back Jones insisted that we should take off our shoes before
creeping into the tent. This we did, and the next morning they
were gone, of course. Dawson said he had never heard before of

putting shoes out to be blacked in an encampment. We were much disgusted, but our men loaned us theirs to wear until we returned to the ship. We left our kind friends in the morning and wandered about all day; but when night came (although we declared that three were too great a tax on a mess of two) yet we had to go back as we knew of no other place to sleep, and we did this for three nights in succession and always received the same hearty welcome. We made no more attacks on Vera Cruz, however. Poor Ward was killed in the valley of Mexico, but Dawson still lives, a general on the retired list. Our men somehow managed to take good care of themselves—we used to go sometimes to their mess and get our dinners; they seemed all to be provided with muskets, though they brought none on shore with them, and they always had fresh beef for dinner. We thought it best to ask no questions. In the midst of this gale a report came that a vessel with a company of dragoons under Captain [Seth] Thornton had dragged ashore at Anton Lizardo, and it was proposed to send all the sailors down there to assist in getting the horses on shore. The Fourth Infantry was to march on our flank to protect us against an attack, as the sailors were *supposed* to be unarmed. We assembled on the beach about 10 o'clock at night, and I found, to my surprise, that most of my men were *mounted*, either on horses or donkeys. Finding that I intended making the march on foot my coxswain said that would never do, and going back from the beach towards the general encampment he soon returned with a horse. I mounted and said nothing. We did not go down, however, after all our preparations; though I have forgotten why we gave the expedition up. I saw Captain Thornton the next day on his way to report at headquarters—my *beau ideal* of a dragoon. He was captured by the Mexicans while on a scout before the battle of Palo Alto with his entire command, and had not long been exchanged when he joined General Scott. He was killed by the first gun fired by the enemy in the valley of Mexico.

The sailors having nothing to do wandered about, and a band of them went to Medellin (a small village some ten miles down the coast, and named for Cortez' birth place) and committed some outrages. General Scott was justly indignant and the offenders would have been severely dealt with if they had been caught. These stragglers met their punishment in some instances—every now and then we would find the dead body of a sailor terribly mutilated by the enemy. Most of the sailors though contented themselves with quietly getting drunk and riding about the camp. The army officers, as I have said before, took no notice of their pranks. One day an old "salt" rode by General Scott's quarters on a donkey, and some officers standing by observing that he was, as they thought, seated too far back, called out to him to shift his seat more amidships. "Gentlemen," said Jack, drawing rein: "This is the first craft I ever commanded, and it's d—d hard if I cannot ride on the quarter deck."

The second dragoons were sent down to Medellin about this time and had a fight with the Mexicans. One of the midshipmen of the squadron, Thomas Young by name, was sent with a dispatch to the commanding officer just before the battle. He was mounted on an old cavalry charger, and not being a very good horseman was unable to manage him. When the charge was sounded the horse started off, and Midshipman Young had the honor of leading the way across the bridge just below Medellin. He was highly complimented by the colonel of the regiment for his gallantry, and still lives to congratulate himself upon his narrow escape.

CHAPTER IX

Opening of the bombardment of Vera Cruz—Captain Tattnall
and the spitfire—Commodore M. C. Perry assumes command
of the squadron—Commodore Conner's mistake—the navy
lands six heavy guns—the Mosquito Fleet—the navy battery—
it opens fire on Vera Cruz—incidents—Passed Midshipman
Fauntleroy—surrender of Vera Cruz and the castle of San Juan
de Ulloa—our army takes possession—battle of Cerro Gordo—
a visit to the castle and city—our marines

As well as I recollect the regular bombardment of Vera Cruz by
the Army commenced March 22d, 1847.[1] On that day
General Scott formally summoned the town, and notified the
authorities of the consequences of a non-surrender.

I have omitted to say that the day after the landing, March 10th,
we were awakened by the sound of heavy firing, and going on deck
found that it was caused by Captain Tattnall in the *Spitfire*. He had

---

[1]At 4:15. See note 5, chapter 8.

gone in under Point Hornos and opened a fire upon the town and castle, *without orders*. He was quickly recalled by the commodore, and as he left his exposed position was loudly cheered by the Army. He lost no men by this affair, which was much regretted by the gallant captain—he could not rid himself of the old English idea that there *must* be a large list of killed and wounded to certify to a brave action. The "butcher's bill" at Algiers in 1816, in Lord Exmouth's squadron, must have satisfied the English nation in this particular.[2]

On the 21st of March, shortly after the hoisting of the colors we were electrified by the signal from the flagship: "Commodore Perry commands the squadron." I think Commodore Perry had gone north after the Tobasco affair, and had but lately returned in the *Mississippi*. Commodore Conner had been in bad health for some time, and willingly turned over the squadron to Commodore Perry; but the youngest reefer in the squadron felt that he had made a mistake in yielding the command when he did. He should have waited until Vera Cruz fell, at least.

The effect of this change was soon seen, and Commodore Perry's first order was to land six heavy guns (three 64-pounder shell guns and three long 32-pounders), and place them in battery to assist General Scott's siege guns. This was the most efficient co-operation we could give the army.

It is generally thought that Vera Cruz and the castle of San Juan were bombarded by the fleet. I have seen this stated in more than one "history," and recollect going to see a panorama in Boston shortly after the war which represented the fleet bombarding the castle while the troops were being landed on the *north* side of Vera Cruz.

The castle was thought to be too strong to risk the vessels of the

[2]British Admiral Edward Pellew, Baron Exmouth, commanded a naval attack on Algiers on 26 August 1816. After a nine hour bombardment, the Algerine dey apologized for his treaty violations and agreed to abide by the treaty requirements. For this victory Exmouth was made a viscount. Losses on both sides were very large.

fleet against it—there were no iron-clads then—but I believe that if it had not surrendered when it did, we were to have tried the effect of an escalade.

On the 22d of March the Mosquito fleet consisting of the steamers *Spitfire* and *Vixen*, and gunboats *Reefer, Bonita, Petrel* and two others, under Captain Tattnall, took up a position under Point Hornos, and opened on the town; and the next morning the *Spitfire* and *Vixen* each having two gunboats in tow stood closer in and opened on the town and castle both, and received their fire in return.[3] The vessels received no damage and there were no men killed. This diversion was ordered by Commodore Perry, and was the only bombardment of the castle by our vessels.

The *Spitfire* went the next day to the northward of the city to open communication with the left wing of the besieging army, which rested on the beach there.

Of the six guns landed from the vessels two were taken from the *Potomac* with their crews. Lieutenant A. S. Baldwin and three midshipmen went in command of them. Captain Aulick who was appointed to command the naval battery on the first day of its firing, ordered that all the passed midshipmen and midshipmen should draw lots to determine who should go with the guns, and it fell to McLane, Jones and myself. The lieutenants also drew lots for the service; of course every one wanted to go. The guns were landed on the 22d, and the one I was assigned to was placed in the *bottom* of a surf-boat instead of being put on skids across the gunwale, so when we got ashore we found great difficulty in getting it out; we finally accomplished it through the bottom of the boat! It was then hauled up on the beach by hundreds of soldiers and we waited for the "trucks," of which there were but two, to take it to the naval battery some three miles distant, and to reach which we had to plough through sand knee-deep, and cross many hills. There was

---

[3] On the 23rd, the combative Tattnall failed to acknowledge or obey Perry's recall signal and did not withdraw until the commodore sent an officer in an open boat with peremptory orders.

no particular road. Four of the guns were sent off the first day and night, but we remained on the beach with ours. The next day, 23d, Midshipman Jones was sent with the gun-carriages, ammunition and implements, and towards sunset one "truck" came back and Lieutenant Baldwin and Midshipman McLane started with one gun, leaving me to take up the other and last. I tried to keep my men together, but had much trouble with them; missing some of them I went to a sutler's store near by and found them round a cask of ale which they had tapped. I capsized the barrel as the best way to solve the difficulty. Towards midnight another "truck" arrived with two or three hundred "regulars" and their officers, and a number of mules. The sailors slung the gun, the mules were hitched, the soldiers manned the drag-ropes and off we went. I walked with the officers in advance. The batteries kept up a constant fire upon our lines and the bombs occasionally went over our heads, or burst near us. No one was hurt, however, and we kept steadily on. The bombs could be followed with the eye by the burning fuse and presented a grand sight.

The "truck" we were using was nearly worn out, and we broke down several times; but we managed to patch it up until we got very near General Patterson's headquarters, where the "regulars" were to be relieved by a detachment of volunteers, and here the "truck" broke down entirely. We found, after many attempts to sling the gun for one more effort, that we must make up our minds to wait for the other "truck," which had taken up Baldwin's gun, and must be on its return. One of my best men was a negro: a tall, powerful fellow who performed wonders in getting the gun slung, and helping along generally; he was the life of the party until we got to the battery; but he succumbed at the first gun from the enemy and was of no further use. After breaking down the last time the senior army officer said to me that if I made no objection he would take his men back to their camp as they had had much hard work, and could do nothing by remaining. Of course I made no objection, so I was left with about twenty half drunken sailors who threw themselves on the ground and were soon asleep. I took a seat upon the gun, and confess to feeling lonesome, and to make matters worse a snake ran over my legs, and that was more than I could stand—bomb shells were nothing to it. I knew General Patterson had been informed of my condition, and I made up my mind that if the other "truck" did not come, or if it broke down, I would make my way to the battery with my men. However, towards daybreak I heard the welcome creaking of wheels, and soon after the "truck" appeared with a large detachment of soldiers—my men sprung up refreshed and ready for anything; we slung the gun and were soon underweigh. We forded a small stream near General Patterson's quarters, and here Captain Aulick came out and directed me to come back from the battery as soon as I had gotten my gun mounted, and let him know "how affairs were going on." As I had been up for two nights I was not in the best of humors—indeed, for the first time in my midshipman's career I was insubordinate: so I told the captain that as soon as my gun was mounted we would open fire, and that I would not leave the battery after that! He eyed me keenly for a moment, and a pretty picture I must have presented after my two days experience in the sand and dirt, and then told me to take his clerk up with me and send the message back by him, and this I did.

Now the naval battery (as it came to be called) was placed by the engineer officers only about seven hundred yards from the walls of Vera Cruz. It was carefully *masked* and all the guns had been taken to it by night; so the Mexicans up to this time had no suspicion of its existence; but my gun being delayed, as I have said, it was broad daylight when we crossed a railroad which ran a short distance from the principal gate. I believe there were never any cars on it. We rushed the gun across the track as rapidly as possible, but the Mexicans, if they did not make out the gun, saw enough to excite their suspicion; and probably sent their engineer officers out to make a more careful examination of the surrounding hills. At all events we got safely to the battery, mounted the gun, and that completed the number. I went to the brow of the hill and looking through the brushwood which served to *mask* the battery saw the city of Vera Cruz stretched at our feet; and just over the city and within easy range the Castle of San Juan de Ulloa with its hundred guns. It was a beautiful scene, and in the early tropical morning everything looked so tranquil and sleepy that it was hard to realize that in a few minutes the silence would be broken by what Napoleon III. called a "fire of hell;" or what our volunteers more forcibly called a "hell of a fire!"

Some distance in the rear of the battery, lying in trenches, was a brigade of volunteers ready to support us in case the enemy attempted to storm our position. The first gun on the right of the battery was the *Raritan*'s 32 pounder, Lieutenant Harry Ingersoll; the next the *Potomac*'s 32 pounder, Lieutenant A. S. Baldwin; then there was a heavy "traverse," built of sand bags of six or more feet in thickness to prevent a raking fire; then came the *Mississippi*'s 64 pounder shell gun, Lieutenant Sidney Smith Lee; next the *St. Mary*'s 64 pounder shell gun, Lieutenant C. H. Kennedy; then another "traverse," and finally the *Albany*'s 64 pounder shell gun, Lieutenant Oliver H. Perry; and next on the extreme left, the *Potomac*'s 32 pounder, Commander Alexander Slidell Mackenzie.

Captain Mackenzie was Commodore Perry's fleet captain, and we did not know that he was in the battery. Midshipman Jones and I were of the same date and we had some conversation as to which of us would command the *Potomac*'s second gun; so when we saw Captain Mackenzie take charge of it we growled a good deal; but there was no help for it, so Jones stayed with the captain, and McLane and I with Baldwin. Captain John H. Aulick of the *Potomac*, being the senior captain in the fleet, was appointed to command the battery on the first day, March 24, 1847, and after that Captains [Isaac] Mayo, [Silas] Stringham, [French] Forrest and [Samuel] Breese were to command one day each in succession.

The guns were mounted on platforms, on their own carriages. The recoil was checked with sand-bags, and they were run out with the side-tackles and handspikes. Our gun was fired with a match, as we had the lock blown off early in the fight.

I should mention that the battery was constructed entirely of sand-bags. I do not know whether this was the first time that sand-bags were so used, but they answered their purpose so admirably this day that I wonder that any engineer who witnessed

The naval battery at Veracruz. Courtesy Beverley R. Robinson Collection, U.S. Naval Academy Museum.

the fight should ever have thought of any other fortifications than "earthworks." I am very sorry I cannot give the name of the officer who planned this work.[4] It resisted a very heavy fire for two days, and was not injured to any extent. What damage was done was repaired at night and I suppose we could have held it for an indefinite time.

We were sponging the last gun mounted, and getting the sand out of it, when the battery opposite us opened with a fire so well aimed that it was evident we were discovered. Orders were immediately given to unmask the battery, and it was soon done. The Mexicans had a cross-fire on us from seven forts and now opened on us from them all; and the castle threw 10-inch bombshells over the city in our midst. For the first five minutes the air seemed to be full of missiles, and it did really look as if it was "no place for the bugler." But our men soon settled down to their work and let them know what American sailors could do with navy guns.

We heard afterwards that when the Mexican engineers picked up some 64-pounder shells which had not exploded and 32-pounder solid shot they said the place must fall.

We fired with great accuracy and after a few hours the enemy's fire commenced to slacken, though it was still heavy. A few minutes after we opened I heard a peculiar "thud," and turning round I saw that a man's head had been taken off by a round-shot at the next gun. I saw Ingersoll wipe the man's brains off his own face with a white handkerchief, and coolly go on with his firing. This was the first man I ever saw killed by a solid shot.

Lieutenant Baldwin happening to say about this time that his gun was not entirely unmasked so that he could see Midshipman McLane and a man named Cavanagh sprang through the embrasure and cleared away the brushwood. For this gallant act they were very properly mentioned by Captain Aulick in his official report.

[4]The designer was none other than Captain Robert E. Lee, who was serving on Scott's staff.

Our fire was first directed against the batteries, or forts, and afterwards at the walls of the city. Lieutenant Baldwin fired with great coolness and deliberation and soon succeeded in cutting away the flagstaff of the battery opposite us—called by our men the "red" battery [Fort Santa Barbara], and the most spiteful devil of them all. At this all hands mounted the parapet and gave three cheers. We cut away the walls to the right and left of the forts as cheese is sliced with a knife and soon made a practicable breach, if it had been intended to assault. These breaches were filled up that night with sand-bags and were stronger than ever. This I noticed upon a visit to the town a few days after it had surrendered.

Several amusing scenes came under my observation during the day. Just in the rear of the guns a trench had been dug for the powder-boys to jump into for shelter. They would run from the magazine, a little farther back, and wait in the trench until the cartridge was wanted. A large shell happening to fall just back of the trench the order was given to lie down. A powder-boy threw himself upon the ground very near the shell, and I saw him eye it anxiously. He then commenced rolling himself towards the trench, and there being a gentle inclination the disturbance of the loose earth caused the shell *to roll after him*!

Dickens says that Miss La Crevy, the little portrait painter in *Nicholas Nickleby*, upon hearing of the death of Smike screwed her face, in the effort to prevent crying, into such remarkable contortions that "if she could have transferred it to canvas she would have made her everlasting fortune:" and so it was with that boy's expression if I could but paint it. Finally he rolled into the trench and the shell followed—fortunately not on top of him. No jack-in-a-box ever sprang up with more sprightliness than did that powder monkey! After all the shell did not explode.

Upon another occasion a shell fell in the battery and at the order "down!" a number of us fell on the ground together, with Passed Midshipman Charles M. Fauntleroy underneath. He had a self-cocking revolver in his hand and in the excitement involuntarily fired off two barrels; one of the bullets wounded me slightly in the left knee; and although it only broke the skin, it pained me for some weeks after. Where the bullets went, and why some one was not killed (unless it was because they were midshipmen) is more than I can tell.

Fauntleroy was stationed at the next gun to me: at the end of the day's fight hearing Captain Aulick express a desire to send a dispatch to the beach he volunteered to take it. As the Mexicans were playing upon us with all their guns at this time, we being out of ammunition and unable to reply, it was no joke to go from under the protection of our parapet. He got safely through, however, and he *should* have been specially mentioned for it; but he was not. He served with much distinction in the civil war on the southern side, sometimes in the navy and at others in the army. At one time he was the inspector general of General Jos. E. Johnston's army. A better officer or more chivalric man never trod a quarter deck; and a truer messmate never took his bean soup out of a cigar-box (with a sliding cover to prevent the other reefers from grabbing) as he told me he once did himself. By the way he was the fellow that bought the one-eyed game cock in San Domingo. As we got out of ammunition the embrasures were filled up with sand bags, and the men were directed to lie close in under the parapet and traverses. We were the last gun to expend our ammunition, and Lieutenant Baldwin being wounded, I had the honor of being left in command of it. At the very last fire we double shotted it, which was a rash thing to do as the gun was very much heated and there was danger of its bursting. Indeed Captain Aulick said the gun certainly would burst and ordered me to draw one of the shot; but we had no means to do it; so sending the men out of the way after aiming it, McLane stood on one side of the breech with a match and I on the other, and we fired it. I suppose our idea in doing this was that if the gun *did* burst we would not live to be reprimanded by "old Aulick." After filling up all the embrasures we had nothing to do but sit under the parapet and await the arrival of our "relief" under Captain Mayo. The Mexicans having returned to their guns, most of which we had previously silenced, sent a storm of shot and shell over our heads and it was rather fun to watch the new fellows coming up, though they probably "did not see it." Our loss this day was four killed; and one officer and five men wounded. I never heard what the loss of the enemy was from our fire.[5]

Upon Captain Mayo assuming the command we were ordered to make the best of our way to the beach, and the *Potomac*'s men left in charge of Midshipmen Jones and McLane. I went down in a wagon to take care of Mr. Baldwin who was wounded. We had four wild mules hitched to an army wagon, and as the road was frequently blocked by other wagons, and one of our mules had his tail shaved off by a cannon shot, it was with much difficulty and danger that we got through. However by 8 P. M. we were all safely on board the old *Potomac*, eating our supper of hard tack and salt junk, and telling the other fellows "all about it." On the next day, 25th, the navy battery continued its good work under the gallant Captain Isaac N. Mayo. The fire from it confirmed the Mexicans in the belief that the town must fall, and on the evening of that day they sent out a flag of truce preparatory to surrendering. Our loss in the battery was Midshipman T. Shubrick of the *Mississippi* and several men killed and a few wounded.

On the 27th commissioners were appointed to arrange the terms of the capitulation, and Captain Aulick represented the navy on the occasion. The fall of Vera Cruz did not necessarily involve that of the castle, for the latter commanded the city. For this reason preparations were being made in the fleet to carry the castle by an escalade in case it held out. For some reason it did not do so, and its commander gave up when the city did. Some said that General Scott would have assaulted the city on the night of the 25th had the flag of truce not come out that afternoon; but I know nothing as to the truth of this report. General Scott probably kept his own counsel.[6] The enemy surrendered five thousand prisoners, and five

[5]Mexican authorities estimated casualties of 600 soldiers and 400 civilians. These figures were almost certainly exaggerated by the Mexicans in order to justify their capitulation. Actual losses were probably less than a fourth of this total.

[6]In fact Scott did plan an attack on Vera Cruz and his preparations were well advanced when negotiations opened on 26 March.

hundred pieces of artillery of all calibres.[7] Taking everything into consideration they made a brave defence. The loss of life among the soldiers was not great; but I am sorry to say that many women and children were killed. This was not General Scott's fault, as he gave the authorities a chance to send them away which they declined to avail themselves of. When our advance guard entered the town on the 27th to take possession they saw just as they passed through the gate the naked corpse of a woman lying in the middle of the street, placed there for effect, of course. During the bombardment the citizens took refuge in the churches, which was unfortunate for them as the steeples and towers made them conspicuous objects by which to "lay" the mortars. On the 27th our army marched in, as I have said, and many of the naval officers were allowed to go on shore to witness the ceremonies. I went in a boat to the mole to be ready to transport our captain to the castle. It seemed to me strange to pull in under the guns of the castle without being fired at. We had been watching it *at a distance* for so many long months that I could not divest myself of a feeling of awe as we approached it. The mole was occupied by the *lazzaroni* who were civil enough while we waited there. After some hours the "advance" arrived, and I took General Patterson and Captain Aulick to the castle of San Juan. I had a good opportunity to examine it, both then and afterwards. I have recorded my opinion as to its strength. It is only that of a young midshipman. When I first visited it, it was certainly the filthiest place I had ever been in; and as for the *smells* the city of Cologne itself could not surpass them.

General Scott's plans for the capture of Vera Cruz and prosecution of the campaign were admirable. As the troops detailed for the garrison of the castle and town marched in to take possession the division of "regulars" under General Twiggs took up the line of march for the city of Mexico. Only twenty-two days after the fall of Vera Cruz Scott defeated the Mexicans at Cerro Gordo, where Santa Anna was strongly posted with an army of twelve thousand

[7]The numbers here are actually 3,000 and 300.

men. Captain Joseph E. Johnston of the topographical engineers (the present General Johnston) was badly wounded the day before this battle while reconnoitring, and Midshipman McLane of our ship who was his brother-in-law went up to look out for him; so when he returned he told us much about this fight. The marines of the fleet were on shore with the army during the entire siege and behaved with great gallantry, as indeed they did in all the naval operations of the war. A few days after our occupation of the city I went on shore and visited the forts, &c.—they were badly battered. In the churches the organs, pictures and images were generally knocked to pieces, and men were hard at work glueing on the arms and legs of the saints. I thought it characteristic of these people to be at this when there were so many suffering people outside to be attended to. I saw many sad sights that day in the way of wounded non-combatants, and was glad to get back to the ship again.

The *Potomac* now went up and anchored near the castle. We sent a number of the captured guns home. I spent many an hour in carrying them to the transports—they were generally very long eighteen pounders, cast of brass or bronze—the metal was very valuable and the original cost of the armament of the castle and city must have been enormous. Some of the guns were very old, and no doubt had a history. All had names and mottoes inscribed on them; one was called "the terror of the North Americans." Many of these guns are now at the naval academy in Annapolis—to me they recall days of hard work, whatever may be the thoughts of others in viewing them.

CHAPTER X

Expedition to Alvarado—"Alvarado" Hunter and the steamer *Scourge*—a coincidence—an allegory—capture of Tuspan—Jack Beard's disappointment—grand expedition to Tobasco—attack on the gunboats by the enemy in ambush—landing at the Devil's Bend—the march—incidents—the steamers raise the *chevaux de frise* and take the fort—capture of the town of Tobasco—Captain Bigelow appointed governor—an unfortunate affair—sail for home in the frigate *Raritan*—yellow fever—arrival at Norfolk

A fter the capture of Vera Cruz, in which the Navy had played so conspicuous a part, Commodore Perry determined to take Alvarado, which place it will be remembered had successfully resisted two attempts made on it by the vessels under Commodore Conner. Alvarado, situated near the mouth of the river of the same name, is a small town, thirty-three miles S. E. of Vera Cruz. At this time it was blockaded by the *Scourge*, Lieutenant Commanding Charles G. Hunter. The *Scourge* was a very small steamer, carrying one gun, and a crew of perhaps forty men. She had but lately joined the squadron.

The Commodore made great preparations for this attack, and to make assurance doubly sure a brigade under General Quitman was to march along the beach and co-operate with the vessels.

We accordingly sailed in the *Potomac*, and as the signal was made to the ships to make the best of their way, we, being out of trim and consequently a dull sailer, did not arrive off Alvarado until towards the last. As we approached the bar we saw that something was wrong as the vessels were all underweigh instead of being at anchor. Very soon the *Albany* hailed us and said that Alvarado was taken. "By whom?" asked our captain." "By Lieutenant Hunter, in the *Scourge*," was the reply. And so it was. Hunter, the day before had stood in pretty close and observing indications of *flinching* on the part of the enemy he dashed boldly in and captured the place almost without firing a gun. Not satisfied with this he threw a garrison, *consisting of a midshipman and two men*, on shore and proceeded in his steamer up the river to a place called Tlacatalpan which he also captured.

When General Quitman arrived with his brigade and the place was gravely delivered over to him by Passed Midshipman William G. Temple (the present Commodore Temple), he was greatly amused and laughed heartily over the affair. But it was far otherwise with Commodore Perry; he was furious and as soon as he could get hold of Hunter (which was not so easy to do as he continued his way up the river, and we could hear him firing right and left), he placed him under arrest, and preferred charges against him. This was a mistake—he should have complimented him in a general order, and let the thing pass. Lieutenant Hunter was shortly after tried by a court-martial and sentenced to be reprimanded by the Commodore; the reprimand to be read on the quarter-deck of every vessel in the squadron. This was done, and the reprimand was very bitter in tone and unnecessarily severe.

The reprimand said in effect: "Who told you to *capture* Alvarado? You were sent to *watch* Alvarado, and not to take it. You have taken Alvarado with but a single gun, and not a marine to back you!" and it wound up by saying that the squadron would soon make an attack on Tobasco, in which he should not join; but that he should be dismissed the squadron. This action on the part of the Commodore was not favorably regarded by the officers of the squadron; and as to the people at home they made a hero of Hunter. Dinners were given him, swords presented, etc., and he was known as "Alvarado" Hunter to his dying day.[1]

Poor Hunter, his fate was a sad one after all. Soon after his arrival at home his friends got him the command of the schooner *Taney*, and in her he made a sort of roving cruise in the Mediterranean. He was not allowed a purser, and being extremely careless with his accounts found himself heavily involved upon his return to the United States. His friends came to his assistance and succeeded in getting him another command. He went to the Brazil station in command of the brig *Bainbridge*. I think this was in 1854 or '55. After being on the station for a year or so, he got into some difficulty with the commodore and deliberately *ran away from the squadron* in his brig, and brought her home to New York. Relying upon his popularity he issued an "address" to the people as soon as he arrived. As well as I remember he found fault with his commodore for not sending the *Bainbridge* to the Falkland islands to adjust some matters in dispute and for which business the commodore no doubt considered him too rash. The "address'" fell to the ground. It would not do—the offence was of too serious a nature to be overlooked, and he was immediately dismissed the service by the President. Not very long after, he died in a New York hospital. In many respects he was one of the best naval officers of his day.

Looking over Bernal Diaz' *Conquest of Mexico* not long ago I came across an incident related by him which strikes me as a rather remarkable coincidence: he says, in speaking of the voyage of Juan de Grijalva in 1518, and in which Pedro de Alvarado (afterwards a captain under Cortez) had a command: "Alvarado discovered and entered the river called by the natives *Papalohuna*, but by us

---

[1]Perry's anger was due to the fact that the point of the expedition to Alvarado had been to obtain much-needed transport animals, and Hunter's premature seizure of the town gave the Mexicans an opportunity to remove or destroy their military stores and drive the livestock out of reach before the squadron arrived.

afterwards the river of Alvarado; where the natives of a place named *Tlatocalpa* presented him with some fish. *Our chief was much displeased with the conduct of this officer,* for whose return we were obliged to wait for the space of three days, and gave orders that in the future no ship should ever separate from the squadron."[2]

Upon my return to the United States after the war, while traveling between Baltimore and Philadelphia, I bought a New York paper which contained an article which seems not to have been generally read; at least I have never mentioned it to a man who had read it. It was headed: *An Allegory*, and was so apropos that I am tempted to repeat it:

"Once upon a time the inhabitants of a certain village were much annoyed by the depredations of a wolf. Two expeditions had been organized and sent out to kill this wolf, but failed to find him. One day, however, a man came in and reported that he had seen the wolf *go into a cave,* and he thought that if they went out soon enough they would catch him. The Selectmen of the village immediately called up a countryman and directed him to go out *and watch the mouth of the cave* to see that the wolf did not escape; and he, throwing a hoe over his shoulder, and whistling up his dog, started out to do so. The Selectmen now organized a grand expedition with music and banners, and marched out to the cave. Upon their arrival there the countryman met them with the information that the wolf was dead; he said that while he was watching the mouth of the cave the wolf got his head in a hole and could not draw it out again; seeing which *he went in and chopped his head off with his hoe.* The Selectmen were highly indignant at this information, and the chief man stepped forward and reprimanded the countryman in these words: "Who told you to *kill* that wolf? You were sent to *watch* that wolf and *not* to kill him. You have killed that wolf with a single hoe, and only a dog to back you! But I'll tell you what it is; we are going on a *coon hunt* to-night, and

[2]Bernal de Diaz, *op.cit.,* p. 38. The emphasis is Parker's.

d—n you, you shan't go." I never knew who of Hunter's friends wrote this article, but it struck me as clever.

Commodore Perry next turned his attention to the capture of Tuspan. The *Potomac* sent a detachment of fifty men on this expedition, under a lieutenant. Midshipman Hunter went from our mess. The bar at Tuspan is a dangerous one and the small steamers had their masts hoisted out to lighten them. Commodore Perry hoisted his flag on the *Spitfire* and led the way up the river with boats of the squadron in tow. The first fort on the river below the town, called the *Pana*, was silenced by the guns of the *Spitfire* and then stormed by the sailors; two other forts were taken in the same way and the town was occupied.

The Mexicans made a spirited defence. Captain Tatnall, Commander [William C.] Whittle and Lieutenant James Parker were wounded, with some men. We lost but one man killed. The guns taken from the brig *Truxtun* were found in one of the forts, and restored to the fleet.

Upon Hunter's return from this expedition he had many amusing yarns to spin. We had a man named John Beard, captain of the maintop, who was an original in his way. Hunter told us that in the attack on the town of Tuspan Beard pushed ahead after the retreating enemy and succeeded in capturing a soldier; taking his musket from him, and tying his hands behind his back with his neckerchief, he proceeded to take him to headquarters. On his way he invited those of his shipmates whom he met to turn back as he intended to show his prisoner to the commodore, and then take him out and shoot him. This interesting spectacle he thought they would not like to miss. Upon the commodore's ordering the prisoner to be put in the guard-house, Jack preferred his modest request to take him out and deal with him in accordance with his deserts. To his surprise the commodore pitched into him most savagely, and came near giving him a dozen with the "cat-o'-nine-tails" there and then.

"Well," said Beard, "if I had supposed he was to be put in the guard-house I would have shot him when I had the chance." He always considered himself badly treated in this affair.

There remained but one place of importance on the coast in the hands of the enemy and to that we now turned our attention. It was Tobasco, which I have already described; and as it was well garrisoned and commanded by a brave officer, General [Nicolás] Bravo, we expected a serious resistance.[3] Great care was taken in organizing the attacking force. It consisted of the light vessels and cutters. I can recall, of the vessels which went up the river, the steamers *Scorpion* and *Spitfire*; the bomb vessel *Vesuvius*; the brig *Washington* and detachments from the *Raritan, Potomac, Mississippi, Germantown* and *Decatur*. Doubtless there were other vessels represented.[4] The force was divided into two grand divisions; and we had a thousand sailors and marines, and ten pieces of light artillery ready to land. The guns were the Army six-pounders and were drawn by hand. I was detached from the *Potomac* and ordered to the frigate *Raritan*, then lying off the mouth of the Tobasco river, and went down in the flag-ship *Mississippi* to join her.

A detachment of fifty men from the *Potomac*, under Lieutenant [Henry S.] Stellwagen and Midshipman A[ugustus] McLaughlin, took passage in the *Mississippi* as part of the attacking force. Commodore Perry kindly offered me a place on his staff; but finding an old shipmate, Lieutenant L. Maynard, in command of a company of pioneers I preferred joining him.

Arriving off the river in June, 1847, the *Scorpion* bearing the flag of Commodore Perry with the first division in tow crossed the bar and commenced the ascent of the river, followed by the second division, commanded by Captain Forrest, in tow of the *Spitfire*.

I was in a small whale-boat with Midshipman King and the company of pioneers. Our boat towed astern of the brig *Washington* and she was in tow of the *Scorpion*, Captain [Abraham] Bigelow.

The city of Tobasco, called also *San Juan de Bautista* and *Villa*

---

[3]In fact, General Bravo had been replaced by Colonel Domingo Echagaray in April.

[4]In addition to the vessels named by Parker, the steamers *Scourge* and *Vixen* and the brig *Stromboli* participated in the attack.

The Tabasco expedition at Seven Palms, June 16, 1847. Courtesy Beverley R. Robinson Collection, U.S. Naval Academy Museum.

Hermosa, is seventy-five miles from the mouth of the river. We anchored off the town of Frontera the first day [June 13] and made our final dispositions. The next morning at dawn we started again. About three o'clock in the afternoon as we were going along in fancied security we were fired on by the Mexicans lying in ambush on a high hill. We had no one hurt, the shots going over us, and we returned the fire without stopping. We continued on up the river and about sunset anchored at a place called the "Devil's Bend," seven miles below the town of Tobasco. Here the river was known to be obstructed by a *chevaux de frise*; and it was the intention of the commodore to land the men here if it was found impossible to raise the obstruction. As soon as the vessels anchored we youngsters assembled on board the *Scorpion* and commenced discussing the attack made on us in the afternoon. Passed Midshipman [William] Nelson (known as Bully Nelson) was expatiating in a loud voice, after his manner; the subject of his remarks was that he did not believe that we *had* been fired into at all—that it was all gammon, etc. Now the commodore did not intend to have any part of our work depreciated, so Mr. Nelson was promptly suspended and sent below. This was my first introduction to this officer, who was a brave man if he *was* a bully. He became a major-general in the U. S. Army, distinguished himself at Shiloh, and was finally killed by one of his own brigadier-generals for some affront, real or fancied.[5]

The vessels and boats all lay huddled together at the Devil's Bend, and just about dark a Mexican came to the bank of the river and deliberately shot a man on board the *Vesuvius*. A bold fellow whoever he was, and although we opened with great guns, field artillery, and small arms I do not believe he was hit!

The next morning at daylight Lieutenants [James] Alden and

[5]Major General William Nelson was shot to death by a fellow Union general, ironically named Jefferson Davis, over a personal matter in a Louisville hotel lobby in September 1862. After a temporary suspension, General Davis was restored to his command and remained in the army after the war.

[William] May were sent up the river in their boats to sound over the obstructions. They had hardly commenced operations when the enemy opened a fire upon them from the banks by which Lieutenant May and some men were wounded. It being impossible to continue the work under this fire the boats returned, and the commodore determined to land the men and march to the city. This was done, and in a short time we had a thousand men and ten field pieces on shore. It was hard work scrambling up the bank, which was steep, and how the guns were hauled up I never knew; but it was done, and a pretty sight it was as seen from the vessels. Of this force two hundred were marines under Captain [Alvin] Edson, and a fine body of men they were. They order of march was that the pioneers should constitute the advance guard, then the marines, and next the companies of sailors, with the field pieces in the centre. As soon as the pioneers landed, we pushed ahead to look for the road, and having found it the order was given to the command to march. After marching a few miles we came upon the Mexicans who opened fire upon us from an intrenchment. A halt was called by the commodore, and the field pieces were ordered to the front; they commenced firing as they got up. The marines deployed on our right, and we were all in line eagerly waiting for the word to charge. Now I was "flying light" upon this occasion; instead of being loaded down with arms and ammunition as most of the officers were I had but my dress sword, which I carried in my hand, and a small double barreled rifle pistol in my breast pocket. My haversack I threw away, and being clothed in simple jacket and trousers, with not even a vest, I was ready for a "fight or a foot-race." Commodore Perry was well in front with a sailor holding his broad pennant immediately behind him, presumably as a good mark for the enemy. After a few rounds from Blunt's and Frank Murray's guns the order was given to charge, and away we went, pioneers with their axes, marines, artillerymen and sailors in a mass. For my own part I had no definite idea as to what I expected to do; but I determined at all events to get to the front, and I did so. We went over the intrenchments, from which the enemy fled as soon as they saw us coming. I was by this time in the lead, and was one of the very few who caught sight of a Mexican at this place. I had one in sight and did my best to capture him. Lieutenant Maynard, long as his legs were, could not keep up with me, and I could hear him shouting in an exhausted voice, "catch him Parker." After running my man a half mile or so, we came to a hamlet; he ran through a hut, or open shed, and I after him; and when I got to the other side he had disappeared and was not to be found. It was a narrow escape—for *me* I mean, not the Mexican, for as I weighed about one hundred pounds only I suppose if I *had* caught him he would have coolly cut my throat and continued his flight. As our men came up we resumed the search, but without success; and it has always been a mystery to me where in the mischief he *did* go. Maynard could testify that he was not like Sarey Gamp's Mrs. Harris![6]

The march was resumed and soon the men commenced to suffer from the heat, and want of water. The artillerymen, especially, were breaking down. Most of the guns had been thoughtlessly landed without the limbers, and it was almost impossible to draw them with the trails dragging on the ground; so two men had to stand by to lift them. All the ammunition, too, was in boxes, slung to handspikes, and carried across the men's shoulders. It was heartbreaking and backbreaking work, and many men succumbed. It took all the men we had to keep the guns up in position. Sailors cannot march, however ready they may be to attempt it.

We struck the river about this time and the men rushed in to drink without much regard to order, and just then to our great surprise the steamers passed by and gave us a broadside. Fortunately no one was hurt, and we hastened to show our flags.

The way the steamers happened to be there was this: a certain Captain [George W.] Taylor had invented a method of raising sunken obstructions, and had been sent out with his apparatus. He

---

[6]Sarah Gamp was a character in Charles Dickens's *Martin Chuzzlewit*, who continually referred to a mythical friend, Mrs. Harris.

was with us at this time. His method consisted simply in this: India rubber bags were attached to the obstructions by divers; the bags were then inflated with air by means of tubes from above; and their buoyancy would cause them to rise and bring up the obstructions. In this way the *chevaux de frise* had been raised at the Devil's Bend; and Captain Bigelow immediately started up the river with the vessels under his command.

As we advanced with our tired men the pioneers would frequently be called back from the front to assist in getting the guns across the rough corduroy roads and bridges we had previously constructed; and this gave us an extra amount of walking; but our men stood it very well and we were in the advance when we came in sight of the fort, situated on the left bank of the river, a few miles below Tobasco. We knew the fort contained some heavy guns.

Midshipman King was sent back to notify the commodore and we continued to advance. We were in single file, I remember, and I proposed to Maynard that we should form "line abreast," giving as a reason that a raking shot would bowl us all down like nine-pins. Maynard adopted the suggestion. When we got near enough to distinguish the flag, which was flying from a tall flag-staff, "what words can express our disgust and surprise" when we saw that it was the American flag!! We had had our toilsome march for nothing. The steamers had arrived before us, and after a short action had captured the fort—the garrison retreating from it. I have always thought that this was a fortunate thing for the land party, as we would have lost many men in taking it by assault with our limited knowledge of military tactics. We would have had to advance a mile across a plain in the face of a fire from a number of heavy guns, and I do not suppose it would have entered our heads to try a flank movement. Upon our arrival at the fort the commodore ordered a halt to allow the line, which now extended for some miles, to close up. We found a well here, and were glad to get a glass of cool water. After some fifty of us had drank, Commodore Perry came up and directed that no one should drink from the well as it was probably poisoned. We who had already done so now suffered excruciating pains for a short time; but there was nothing the matter with the water, and we soon forgot all about it.

When the line was closed up we took up the line of march for the city. There was a wide, paved road to it from the fort, and as we marched along in company front, with a fine band of music at the head of the column and flags flying, we no doubt presented a gallant appearance. Most of the inhabitants had fled, I think, and the only persons left to admire us were a few foreigners. We entered the city about sunset, and were assigned quarters by our acting quartermaster. The few people remaining in the town were not at all disturbed by us. There was some drinking by our men the first night, but it was soon put a stop to. The first thing I saw the next morning was the provost guard marching off a lot of sailors to the guard house. Most of the men were dressed in women's clothes and presented a ridiculous appearance. Captain Bigelow was appointed governor of the town, and a garrison of several hundred men detailed; the rest of the men were sent back to their vessels; the pioneers among the number.

The afternoon we left Tobasco on our return, the boats assembled alongside the *Vesuvius* at the Devil's Bend. I suppose there were six or seven hundred men collected there, and one of them happening to discharge his musket a *fusilade* commenced which the officers found it impossible to stop, and finally we had to take refuge in the cabin of the vessel to avoid being shot. The men kept it up until they got out of ammunition. That night one of the steamers towed us down the river and the next morning we joined our respective ships. The garrison at Tobasco was not left in quiet possession by the Mexicans. They kept it in a constant state of alarm. Captain Bigelow marched out on one occasion and fought a battle with them and defeated them. The *Potomac*'s men behaved very well in this combat.

An unfortunate affair occurred during the summer. The Mexicans were in the habit of stealing up on our outposts at night and opening an annoying fire. Passed Midshipman Bradford of the *Spitfire*, to stop it, took a number of his men out one evening after sunset and concealed them in the *chaparral*:—the idea being to surprise the enemy,—but unfortunately the officer in command of the field piece at the outpost, Midshipman A. McLaughlin, was not notified of this manœuvre; so when Bradford opened on the Mexicans about 10 o'clock that night McLaughlin opened on Bradford and killed and wounded a number of his men. Fortunately Bradford made himself known before the field piece was fired a second time. The capture of Tobasco was the last of the naval operations of the war, and all the ports were now in our possession.

The yellow fever broke out during the summer along the entire coast; it was particularly virulent at Vera Cruz and Anton Lizardo and the navy lost many valuable officers and men. General Scott took possession of the city of Mexico on the 14th of September, 1847, which practically ended the war. The treaty of peace was signed at Guadalupe Hidalgo on the 2d of February, 1848. By this war the United States came into possession of New Mexico and California.

Upon my arrival at the mouth of the river Tobasco I went on board the frigate *Raritan*, Captain Forrest, for a passage home. My old ship, the *Potomac* sailed also for home at the same time from Vera Cruz. We sailed for Norfolk about the 1st of July and the yellow fever broke out the day after. The first case was that of Midshipman Robert B. Storer, a most promising young officer, and he died almost before I realized that he was sick. The surgeon at first concealed the fact that "yellow jack" had made its appearance, but we very soon had from 150 to 200 officers and men down with it. It became evident that the worst cases were those whose duties kept them much *below decks*, such as the purser's clerk, the captain of the hold, &c., and the captain very wisely ordered us all to remain on the spar and main decks, and not to go below under any circumstances. The ward-room officers messed on the spar deck and the midshipmen on the main deck. All etiquette was laid aside, drills were suspended, and everything done to make all hands as comfortable as possible. Of four doctors but one remained on duty; most fortunately he escaped entirely. Captains [William J.] McCluney and [Samuel H.] Walker (passengers in the cabin) were down; all the ward-room officers but the four lieutenants, and all the midshipmen were sick. I have mentioned in a former chapter the fact that it was my second attack. The ship became a floating hospital, and to make matters worse we were frequently becalmed, and when we *did* have a wind what distance we made to the *eastward* we would lose by the strong current setting to the *westward* through the Yucatan channel. Captain Forrest's conduct in this trying time was admirable; he frequently visited the sick, and at all hours of the day his cheerful voice could be heard singing in his cabin. No doubt he did it to encourage us. As for myself I *determined to get home* and that alone saved my life. Those who gave themselves up to despair soon died. I cannot attempt to describe the appearance of the ship, nor the many weary days we passed— "many a day to night give way, and many a morn succeeded"—but at last we got to Havana where we put in for medicines—we were out of nearly everything. The authorities at Havana treated us in the handsomest manner. We were put in quarantine, of course, but supplies of every kind were sent us—among other things *ice*!

I have always been fond of music—in fact I may say I have an ear for music—in my youth I had heard the wonderful Clara Novello, and since then I have listened to the melodious tones of the divine Patti; but no music ever equalled in my ears the *rattling* of the *ice* on a large platter which the hospital steward carried round to the sick that morning, and for which I lay in my hammock awaiting my turn![7]

We remained in Havana but twenty-four hours, and as soon as we got outside the harbor we hove to, and buried Captain Alvin Edson of the Marines and two of his guard with him. We lost on the passage Captain Edson, Midshipman Storer, the purser's clerk, the purser's steward and a good many men—the exact number I do not know. We arrived at Norfolk the latter part of July, and the *Potomac*, with my old messmates, arrived the very same day. There

[7]Clara Novello and the divine Patti (Aldelina Juana Maria Patti) were popular soprano vocalists of the nineteenth century.

was no fever on board the *Potomac*; so, as they said, if I had not left her I would not have had the yellow fever a second time—but then again I would not have been on the famous Tobasco expedition.

Captain Forrest ran the *Raritan* up to the town and anchored off the naval hospital; the sick were immediately landed, the remainder of the officers and crew granted leave of absence and discharged, and the ship was taken down and anchored off Craney Island. The fever did not spread, and I never heard that a case occurred in Norfolk or Portsmouth this summer. But if men had been put to work on the *Raritan* breaking out her holds, etc., it might have been different; for that the steamer *Ben Franklin* carried the yellow fever to those cities in 1855 is "as true as taxes," as Mr. Barkis says.[8]

As soon as I obtained my leave of absence I started for Boston. I had had my head shaved, was as yellow as gold, and weighed about ninety pounds, and to crown all my tailor made my clothes too small. Smike himself did not present a more ridiculous appearance.[9]

Upon my arrival at Boston I got into an hotel coach which had many other passengers in it; the driver said he would drive them to their several destinations in Boston and then take me to the Charlestown Navy Yard, which my father commanded. One young man would not get out at the Lowell depot, but said he would wait. The driver told him that if he went to Charlestown he would miss his train: still he persisted that he would wait; and I saw that he had made up his mind to see the last of me. I could not understand his behavior at the time, but I knew afterwards. He thought I was being taken to the penitentiary, which is located in Charlestown!

During the summer I remained "on leave" and my physician tried to "build me up," for in the autumn I was to go to Annapolis to prepare for that grand climacteric of a Middy's life, his examination for the grade of Passed Midshipman.

---

[8]A reference to a character in Charles Dickens's *David Copperfield* (1850).
[9]A reference to a character in Charles Dickens's *Nicholas Nickleby* (1839).

CHAPTER XI

Ordered to Annapolis—the Naval School of 1847—Captain
George P. Upshur—duels—the battle ground of Bladensburg—Professor William Chauvenet—swapping yarns—
Pat Murphy and the coon skins—Captain X's dilemma—
Commodore Chauncey—a precise message—a sailor's testimony—Van Ness Philip's visit to Troy—Thompsonian treatment—Mad Jack Percival—pass my examination—a bad
quarter of an hour on board the *bay state*—a friend in need—
hard work at the Boston Navy Yard

I reported for duty at the Naval School, Annapolis, in September, 1847. The school had been established here in 1845 by the
Hon. George Bancroft, then Secretary of the Navy. Previous to
that time the school was held at the Naval Asylum, Philadelphia.
The first class to graduate at Annapolis was that of the midshipmen
of the date of 1840—the class graduated in July, 1846. The class
of 1841 was very large, and when the time came for it to report at
Annapolis we were in the midst of the Mexican war, so the
Secretary of the Navy decided to divide it into two parts—all those

appointed between January and July, 1841, joined the school in the fall of 1846 and graduated in 1847; and the other part, to which I belonged, went there in the fall of 1847 and passed in 1848. The class was the largest ever appointed in the navy, numbering 245 I believe, and owing to various causes there remained some forty who went to the school in 1848 and passed in 1849. It was not until the three divisions had passed that the "numbers" were assigned. At the time I joined the school it presented a far different appearance from what it does at the present time. The place had been known as Fort Severn and was transferred to the navy by the War Department March 15, 1845. The fort was build in 1808 and mounted a few 24 pounders *en barbette*, at which we were drilled. Near the water's edge six 32 pounder guns were mounted on a platform built to represent a section of a ship's deck, and we were also exercised at these guns. The walls enclosed but nine acres in all and the professors and midshipmen used the buildings left by the army. There was not a new building on the grounds. The large barrack-rooms were used as recitation rooms and quarters. Two small gun-houses were turned into quarters also. We called them "Brandywine Cottage," and the "Abbey;" the long barracks were called "Apollo Row" and "Rowdy Hall." The curriculum embraced gunnery, infantry tactics, steam, mathematics, navigation and nautical astronomy, natural philosophy, chemistry, English grammar and French— seamanship the midshipmen were supposed to be prepared in and there were no vessels attached to the school. Commander George P. Upshur was the superintendent; having just relieved Commander Franklin Buchanan, to whom is due the honor of having organized the school. Professor William Chauvenet taught mathematics, nautical astronomy and navigation; Professor H. H. Lockwood, gunnery, steam, infantry tactics and natural philosophy; Professor Arsène N. Girault, French; Dr. John A. Lockwood, chemistry; and Chaplain George Jones, English grammar. Captain Upshur was assisted in his executive duties by Lieutenant Sidney Smith Lee. The instruction in mathematics, nautical astronomy and navigation was very good, and that in natural philosophy,

French, gunnery and steam was fair. The chemistry, English grammar and infantry tactics we paid but little attention to; the two last were taught only on Saturday and we made quite a farce of the recitations.[1]

In the spring of 1848 Mr. Copeland, a distinguished engineer of New York, gave us some interesting lectures on steam; and about the same time Lieutenant [John A.] Dahlgren (afterwards a rear admiral) drilled us a few times at the guns, and gave us some practical instruction in filling shells, driving fuses, etc. There were about one hundred men in the class, and as we had all been to sea for six years I fear we gave our good superintendent much trouble.

There have been stricter disciplinarians than Captain Upshur at the naval school, but never a more honorable, high-toned gentleman than he; and I doubt if any young man was ever thrown in his company without being the better for it—for my own part I have never ceased to remember his gentle manner, his high honor, his pure character and unexceptionable life. If *example* counts for anything we had it before us in him, and if we did not profit by it it was our own loss. As a rule we studied hard—the class was so large that many were struggling for the first honor—for to be the "number one" of the 41's was almost equal to a patent of nobility in our estimation.

The Hon. John Y. Mason was the secretary of the navy at this time. In many points he resembled Captain Upshur—they were both Virginians. As might be expected of so large a number of young men assembled together we gave the citizens of the quiet old town something to talk of: the nocturnal revels of the "Owls" and the "Crickets;" the "Corn Hill Riot," etc., rather surprised these staid old gentlemen; but take it all in all there was not much disturbance created.

Two duels were fought during the session. The first one was fought *inside the walls of the school;* the parties left the supper-table

---

[1] For personal sketches of each of these men, see Jack Sweetman, *The U.S. Naval Academy: An Illustrated History* (1979), chapters 2–3.

in advance of their classmates, and going behind the ten-pin alley in a few minutes one of the principals had a ball in his hip, and the "affair" was over. When he was carried to his room Doctor Lockwood was sent for and it was intended to pass it off as the result of an accident. The doctor silently probed the wound, and then suddenly said: *"What distance?"* *"Ten paces"* replied two or three Middies without pausing to think. A short time after this another duel was fought at Bladensburg and one of the party was wounded in the hip as before.[2] The secretary of the navy was very indignant at these affairs; the *impudence* of the parties in the first case in selecting the *grounds* of the school for fighting was what he said he "could not get over." All the parties engaged—seconds as well as principals—were dismissed the service by President Polk. About three years after they were re-instated by President Taylor. Only two of the principals chose to return to the navy; they were the ones who had been wounded, and are at present commodores in the navy.[3] The seconds are all dead. If these duels had both been fought at Bladensburg I think the Department would have over-looked them. I know Captain Upshur would have "winked" at them; for though no duelist he did when a passed midshipman resign to fight his first lieutenant; but the commodore would not accept his resignation. Bladensburg has been a duelling ground since the "Bladensburg races," as the battle fought in 1814 is facetiously called. A Washington poet celebrated this battle in the following lines:

[2]Bladensburg, outside Washington, was a traditional dueling ground. Captain Samuel Barron mortally wounded Stephen Decatur in a famous duel there in 1821.

[3]In the duel on academy grounds on 4 May 1848, Byrd A. Stevenson wounded Walter W. Queen. Both young men received reprimands. Stevenson subsequently failed to graduate for unrelated reasons; Queen eventually became a rear admiral. The duel at Blandensburg was between Francis C. Dallas and John Gale and was fought on 7 June of the same year. Both men were dismissed from the academy.

THE BATTLE GROUND

And here two thousand fought, three hundred fell,
And fifteen thousand fled; of these remain
The *three* where Barney laid them,—*they* sleep well.
Of the *fifteen*, part live to run again,
And part have died of fever on the brain,
Potions and pills—fell agents—but the worst,
As Sewell in his pamphlet proves is thirst.

And General Winder, I believe, is dead,
And General (———) retired to learned ease,
Posting a ledger. He has exchanged the bed
Of fame for one of feathers, and the fees
Of war for those of trade: and, where the trees
Shook at his voice, all's still, as ere began
The fight; for, when it did, they cheered, and—ran.

All, save old Handspike and his crew—they stood
Drawn up, one coolly buttoning his breeches,
Another his cheek helping to a quid
Of purser's pigtail. No long windy speeches—
For valor, like a bishop, seldom preaches—
They stood like men prepared to do their duty,
And fell as they had done it—red and smutty.

Peace to them! men I still have found
Though sadly looked on by us land-bred people,
High-souled, warm-hearted—true, it must be owned,
They've no great predilection for a steeple,
And too much for a bottle. But the ground
Strongest in tares is so in wheat; the sod
May flower as here, whose very earth is blood.

But to return to the naval school. To Professor William
Chauvenet is due more credit for its establishment than to any
other man. Appointed a professor in the navy in 1841 he went to
sea in the *Mississippi*, and here very soon discovered the defects in
the method of instructing the midshipmen as pursued at that day.
He was soon after sent to the Naval Asylum in Philadelphia to take

charge of the school there, and from that time he applied himself to the task of establishing a school more fitted to the wants of the navy. He saw from the beginning that such an institution must be a growth and not a creation. He remained in the navy until 1859 when he resigned to accept a professorship in Washington University, St. Louis. In 1862 he was chosen chancellor of the university. Up to the time of his resignation he was the life of the naval school. He was, next to Professor Peirce of Harvard, the best mathematician in the country, and as an instructor he stood second to none. He left the navy because his salary was too small for him to support and educate his family. A miserable economy on the part of the Government permitted him to leave without an effort to retain him. Professor Chauvenet died in 1870; but he lived long enough to see the naval school attain the growth he always predicted for it, and to achieve which he gave eighteen years of his life.

It was our custom to meet on Saturday nights and hold what Van Ness Philip called "reformed banquets." Coming from different stations we were in the habit on these occasions of "swapping yarns;" and although I never wrote them in my journal, as Brown did, yet many remain in my memory, and some few I will relate.

A mid who had served on board the *Pennsylvania*, lying off the Norfolk navy yard, said that one morning at sunrise an old darky who had come down through the Dismal Swamp canal in a canoe came close to the ship, and seeing a man standing in the gangway, inquired: "Is Master Pat Murphy on board dar?" "Yes," was the reply, "what do you want with him?" "Missis sent him a peck of sweets and a couple of coon skins," said the old man. Another story was of Captain Arthur X. It seems that his friends got him the command of a brig upon condition that he would take no liquor to sea with him in his cabin—he being somewhat addicted to it. After being at sea a week or two the captain felt an inordinate desire for a drink. In that day the ration of grog was served to the men on the upper deck in small vessels. At 12 o'clock the grog tub was brought up, and the captain, after passing it several times, walked up to the purser's steward and said: "What's this complaint I hear of the ship's whiskey?" "Give me a tot;" he drank it with gusto, and remarked: "It's as good whiskey as ever I drank; let me hear no more complaints." It is needless to say there had been none.

Old Commodore Chauncey commanded the New York navy yard at the time when there was "no law for post captains." One Sunday in the chapel of the yard the chaplain read a notice which he said was by order of the bishop of the diocese: "By *whose* order did you say?" inquired the commodore, standing up: "By order of the bishop of the diocese," mildly replied the chaplain. "Well, the notice will not be obeyed," said old Chauncey: "I'll let you know that *I am the bishop of this diocese.*"

One of our classmates was very precise and it was told of him that being directed by the lieutenant of the watch to report to the captain that "there was a sail in sight," he did so in these terms: "Captain P. the officer of the deck desires me to inform you that there is visible on the extreme verge of the sensible horizon a small speck, which he conceives to be a sail."

Discussing sailors one day the opinion was expressed that a man-of-war's man would not tell the truth if his interests or desires lay the other way: and no amount of "swearing" would make him do it; in illustration of which a story was told concerning one Passed Midshipman C. He had been on shore from his ship in some port of the Mediterranean and upon his return to his boat, lying at the mole, was intoxicated. Here he happened to fall in with an English chaplain who was waiting for a boat to take him to his ship, and after some words C. knocked him overboard. A shore boat picked the unfortunate man up and took him to his vessel. C. was too drunk to know what he was about. The fact coming to the ears of the commodore he promptly brought C. to a court-martial, and, as the chaplain generously declined to appear as a witness, the judge advocate had to rely upon the boat's crew to make out his case. The first witness testified "that Mr. C. was down on the mole when he saw the chaplain approaching *in an intoxicated condition. The chaplain walked up to Mr. C., and in making a pass at him,* he fell overboard." This was the coxswain's testimony and the remainder of the boat's crew swore to the same effect. Of course C.

was acquitted, and equally of course he made the *amende honorable* to the chaplain.

This C. was a very humorous fellow, though he would "crook his elbow." Being at the old Bowery theatre one night—in that happy condition when "another glass of claret would spoil him"— he went in front of the curtain and gave out the following announcement: "Gentlemen and ladies, tomorrow night will be performed the drama entitled, 'The babes and the woods;' Babes, Mr. Brown; Woods, Mr. C.; to be followed by the roaring farce called 'Moses and the bulrushes:' Moses, Mr. C.; Bulrushes by the troop."

Mr. C.'s sailors may or may not have given testimony attributed to them; but I have often noticed their great objection to appearing before a court as a witness. They seem to have some extraordinary superstition in regard to their "committing themselves" as they call it. Old Junius B———— as a witness in a case of assault and battery once testified that he "saw the accused give the accuser several kicks, or," he cautiously added, "words to that effect."

Midshipman Van Ness Philip used to tell a very good story on himself: He once carried his niece to Troy and entered her at Mrs. Willard's famous school. He was invited to attend a party at Mrs. Willard's the same evening and remained in town to accept it. Philip enjoyed a joke more than most men, and during the day he came across a *conundrum* which amused him much. It was: "What is the difference between Tom Thumb and Queen Elizabeth?" The answer was: "He is a wonder and she was a Tudor." He said that when he attended the party that night this abominable conundrum kept running in his thoughts and he was dying to ask it; but he did not know a soul in the room save Mrs. Willard. After awhile, however he seized an opportunity and propounded it to her. It seems the old lady was somewhat deaf, and after Philip had asked it she said: "What did you say, sir?" Philip repeated the conundrum in rather a loud voice, and as this drew the attention of all in the room he said he began to get pretty red in the face. "Ah!" said Mrs. W., "what is the difference between Queen Elizabeth—and *whom* did you say, sir?" "*Tom Thumb*," roared Philip in a stentorian voice and much to the astonishment of the company assembled. Of course Mrs. W. gave it up, and Philip had to repeat the answer several times in a loud voice and was then doubtful whether the old lady "took." He said he left the party as soon after as possible and determined never to ask a conundrum unless sure of his listener.

One of our fellows told a yarn concerning the "practice" of a merchant captain who treated his crew by the Thompsonian method, in which all the medicines were marked from number one to ten. On one occasion a man complained of being unwell and the captain judged he required the medicine marked number six; but on looking in the medicine chest he found that he was out of number six, so he gave the man *two threes*.

Many of our stories were of the captains we had sailed with, and old Captain Percival, or mad Jack, as the sailors called him, came in for his share. Captain Jack *was* eccentric, but he always took a fatherly interest in his midshipmen. He wrote once to the father of one of them that his son had entered a profession "where he would either go down to his grave wept, honored and sung, or unwept, unhonored and unsung." A few days after, he got angry with the young man and at once sat down and wrote to his father: "Dear Sir—Your son is going down to his grave unwept, unhonored and unsung."

Captain Jack being upon a board for the examination of midshipmen announced the passing of one of them to his father (who was a commodore in the Navy) in the following delicate way:

"Dear X—Your son has passed. Do you recollect our taking the *Columbus* out of dock? *She just grazed.*—Yours truly,
PERCIVAL."

But this is a digression. "When to the sessions of sweet silent thought I summon up remembrance of things past," I get off the regular track as it were.

The Board of Examiners, consisting of Commodores Morgan, Wyman, Mayo, Dulany and Gwinn assembled in Annapolis in June, 1848, and in July I passed my examination and became a passed midshipman, *eligible* to promotion to all grades above it and entitled to wear a star on my collar to back the anchor already worn there. I could bring in a great many elegant quotations here in relation to stars, but I'll "pass." Upon passing my examination I received orders to the Boston navy yard and upon getting as far as New York on my way there found myself short of funds. There was nothing remarkable in this, because I generally got home in that condition. Upon going to Brooklyn and applying to a friend for a loan, he informed me that *he* was going to Boston that afternoon and would meet me on the boat, pay all my expenses, &c. I gave myself no further trouble and at 5 o'clock went down to the *Bay State*, Captain Brown, of the Fall river line. Having some small change I bought the evening papers and a magazine or two and ensconced myself comfortably on the hurricane deck which was crowded with ladies and gentlemen on their way to Newport—it being the height of the season there. As the boat shoved off I happened to look up and words cannot express my dismay when I saw my friend standing on the wharf carpet bag in hand, *left*! My first feeling was that of anger that he should have *allowed* himself to be left under the circumstances, and I felt a diabolical desire for a rifle that I might put a bullet in his block of a head; but that soon gave way to despair and I felt in a moment that the ladies *all knew I had no money*! What to do was the question; the fare was five dollars, and I had but one.

Now the *Bay State* had been repaired in the dock of the Boston navy yard a short time before this and my father having extended some civilities to Captain Brown, he (the captain) had since been especially polite and hospitable to him and his family. I had heard of this, and though I had no personal acquaintance with the captain, I resolved to make myself known to him and explain my peculiar (or pecuniary) condition; so I went to the purser's office and asked to see the captain. "He is in the pilot house," said the purser; "won't I do?" (I'm *sure* the rascal suspected my impecunious state). "No," I answered, "I wish to see Captain Brown," and I went to the pilot house.

One of the waiters pointed out the captain. He was a stout man, with a white beaver on the side of his head, and as he stood talking with a number of gentlemen to save my life I could not introduce myself and break the subject to him; so I walked aft. The confounded negro rang his bell and requested the passengers to "call at the purser's office and settle" oftener than I had ever known him to do before. Not feeling able to remain on the hurricane deck where I felt that all hands knew I was short of funds I went down on the main deck. I had no sooner gotten there than I saw the mate belaboring a shabby-genteel man, and upon my interfering and inquiring as to the cause of such harsh treatment the mate said: "Well, sir, this man has no money"—(just my case thought I)—"and he knows we cannot put him on shore until we get to Newport: We have many such stowaways," he continued. Well! to make a long story short, while I was deliberating whether to make another attempt to see Captain Brown, or jump overboard, I was accosted by a young man who seemed to know me well; he said he had been on board the *Ohio* with me in 1842. He informed me that he had just returned from a cruise in the *Albany*, where he had served as captain's clerk, and had just been paid off. These words sounded well, and as soon as he got through *his* story, I told *mine*. I will never forget the joy with which he pulled out a handful of bank-notes and thrust them upon me. He wanted me to take a hundred dollars, but I only took twenty which I put in my pocket and became "a man again."

I saw this gentleman the following day in Boston at the old United States hotel and returned the loan. I have never been able to recall his name, nor have I any recollection of his being with me on board the *Ohio*. I have never met him since. I have always believed that he was in some humble position on board the *Ohio* and that I had done him a service of some peculiar kind; for he could not have been kinder if he had been my own brother; and, as I have said, it seemed to be a real *joy* to him to be able to assist me. Even Macaulay's "schoolboy" can see the moral of this story.

I remained attached to the navy yard in Boston about two months and cannot say I rendered any material service to the Government in that time. In fact there seemed to be no scope for a young man of my transcendent ability. I was a *passed* midshipman, and *consequently* a "gnostic;" moreover I was a 41, and we 41's did not hold ourselves cheap, I assure you. It rather surprised me to see everything going on all right without my assistance, but so it was. I was zealous enough, but for the life of me I never could find anything to do. One day the executive officer, Lieutenant Timothy Hunt, tired I suppose of seeing me "standing about" told me to see what Lieutenant Handy was doing, and to help him. I called upon Lieutenant H. and asked him what he was doing; he replied: "nothing;" "well," said I, "I've come to help you." This was all the duty I remember to have done at the yard.

CHAPTER XII

Ordered to the sloop-of-war *Yorktown*—sail from Boston—
arrival at Porto Praya—first cruise on the coast of Africa—the
Gambia River—Monrovia—battle between the Liberians and
natives—President Roberts—a cruise to windward—Cadiz,
Funchal, Teneriffe, Palmas—Porto Praya again—an old city—
riding out a gale on a lee shore—rescue of the American brig
Copperthwaite

In September of this year [1848] I was ordered to the frigate
Constitution, fitting out at the Boston navy yard for the
Mediterranean; but the ship was largely stocked with passed and
other midshipmen and not wishing to pass another cruise on the
forecastle or quarter deck carrying messages and calling the "relief," I applied to have my orders changed to the *Yorktown*, a
sloop-of-war fitting out for the coast of Africa. The Secretary of the
Navy granted my request and remarked that he expected I was the
only officer who had preferred a sloop-of-war on the coast of Africa
to a fine frigate in the Mediterranean; but I was looking forward to
promotion and a "watch," and I got it.

The *Yorktown* was a third-class sloop-of-war of 560 tons, and carried a battery of sixteen 32-pounders of 27 cwt. She was a staunch little craft and a good sea-boat. We went into commission in October, Captain John Marston. The other officers were: Lieutenants, Rootes, Spottswood, Frailey and Fleming; Sailing Master, Caldwell; Purser, Semple; Surgeon, Fox; Passed Assistant Surgeon, Potter; Passed Midshipmen, Coleman, Seawell, Selden and Parker; Midshipmen, Bruce, J. Parker, Fyffe and Means; Boatswain, Young; Gunner, Oliver; Sailmaker, Frankland, and Carpenter, Mager. Our junior lieutenant left us as soon as we got on the station, and the passed midshipmen were promoted to fill vacancies; otherwise there were absolutely no changes in our officers, which in a two years' cruise is rather remarkable, especially on what is called a sickly station. We had a very fine crew and numbered in all 150 souls. Commodore Benjamin Cooper took passage with us; he was appointed to succeed Commodore [William C.] Bolton in the command of the African squadron and intended to hoist his flag on board the *Portsmouth*, a very fine first-class sloop.

I do not propose to give a detailed account of the cruise. A two years' stay on the African coast does not, as a general thing, present much variety of incident. The object of keeping vessels on the coast was to capture slavers and protect our own lawful traders. The English and American Governments kept squadrons of a certain number of guns in accordance with a special agreement or treaty— (since abrogated).[1] The English took many slavers but our vessels, being bound by our interpretation of the "right of search" took very few indeed. The explorations of Livingstone, Burton, Stanley and others have added very much to our knowledge of Africa in the last thirty years; and the introduction of steam-packets along the

---

[1] Article VIII of the Webster-Ashburton Treaty of 1842 required both the United States and Britain to maintain "a sufficient and adequate squadron of naval forces," defined as no fewer than 80 guns, off the coast of Africa to suppress the slave trade.

coast has no doubt made the aspect of it very different from what I remember it in 1848–9–50.

We sailed from Boston November 22, 1848, and had a very rough passage across the Atlantic. I had been in heavy gales in the Gulf of Lyons, *pamperos* off Monte Video, and "northers" in the Gulf of Mexico and thought I knew what bad weather was; but this experience in the Atlantic on the "fortieth parallel" exceeded anything I had before dreamed of. When we were not scudding we were lying to; and had not the little ship been, as I have said, a very good sea-boat she must have foundered. I have seen her hove to with only a tarpaulin in the mizen rigging and not a rag of sail on her forward rising to the seas and not *shipping* one. She had a way as Joe Seawell said of making two "butts" at a sea, and then going around it. For many days we in the steerage did not pretend to wear shoes and stockings—everything was wet for the steerage was ankle-deep in water. However, we arrived safely at Madeira and found the *Jamestown*, Commodore Bolton, in port. Remaining but a few days we sailed for the Cape de Verde islands, looked in at Porto Grande, and early in January, 1849, anchored at Porto Praya. Here we found the *Portsmouth*, and Commodore Cooper transferred his flag to her. Lieutenant Fleming accompanied him as "Flag"; Caldwell was made junior lieutenant, and I succeeded him as sailing master. After filling up our provisions and water we sailed to make the usual four months' cruise on the coast. While crossing the Atlantic we found that our rudder-post was decayed, and as Porto Praya did not offer the facilities required we went first to Bathurst on the Gambia river to repair it. The Gambia is a pretty sheet of water and the appearance of Bathurst is picturesque in the extreme. It was from Pisanea on this river that Mungo Park set out on his last expedition to discover the mouth of the Niger river, in 1805. We found here several companies of one of the English West India regiments. These regiments have white officers, and the privates are recruited from the captured slaves. All the English posts on the coast were garrisoned by these troops. The officers of the regiment at Bathurst were individually very polite and hospitable; but I observed here, what I afterwards noticed at the other posts, that the officers did not agree well together and were split up into several small messes. I had expected to see them a "band of brothers"—exiles in a sickly clime as they were—but it was otherwise. Thinking of this curious state of affairs I came to the conclusion that it must be the effect of the climate; their livers get out of order and they become irritable and quarrelsome.

We put an iron band on the rudder-head which we thought would answer temporarily and then sailed for Monrovia. This town is situated on Cape Mesurado which is elevated about 80 feet above the ocean. The small river Mesurado enters the sea on its northern side. Monrovia was named in honor of President Monroe, one of the earliest friends of the American Colonization Society, and is the capital of Liberia. The first settlement was made in Liberia in 1822; it remained under the protection of the Colonization Society until 1847 when it became a free and independent republic, and Mr. [Joseph Jenkins] Roberts, formerly a slave in Petersburg, Virginia, was elected President. The republic was modeled after the government of the United States. At the time of our first visit the town of Monrovia was much excited at the probability of a war with a tribe on the southern coast. It appears that some Spaniards (slave dealers) held possession of a strip of coast which the Liberians claimed to have purchased some years before and refused to give it up. They had a factory in the neighborhood of Sinou, and a large quantity of stores, such as rum, cotton-cloths, muskets, powder, &c., &c. on hand for the purchase of slaves. It must be understood that the tribes on the coast are not opposed to the slave trade, for the reason that the "slavers" make it a rule never to carry them off—the coast tribes make war upon those in the interior and all the slaves they capture they sell to the "factors," who put them in *barracoons* until an opportunity occurs to ship them. The Spaniards, therefore, felt perfectly safe in arming the tribe at Sinou and defying the Liberians.

Great preparations were going on at Monrovia, reinforcements were arriving from the different settlements, and Queen Anne muskets, second-hand uniforms, swords, epaulettes, cocked hats and top boots were at a premium. President Roberts, a mulatto, (about three fourths white I should judge), was a man of character and some education. As he was on board the *Yorktown* a month or more I had an opportunity of observing him. He was very quiet in his deportment and modest withal. We were of course full of curiosity as to the object of the grand expedition and Roberts being close-mouthed we used to "pump" one Colonel Hicks who kept the hotel in Monrovia where we were in the habit of dining when on shore. Hicks was a regular old time darkey and very talkative. Upon one or two occasions where the Liberians had come in collision with the natives Hicks had incontinently fled—he was a born coward, and it was well understood. Hicks, however, did not know much about matters although he was on the President's staff. As he himself acknowledged, upon his propounding a few questions to the President, he had replied: "Colonel Hicks mind your own business." "Oh!" said Hicks in relating this: "That Roberts is a smart nigger!" It was well for him that Roberts did not hear him!

When all was ready the army under Brigadier General Lewis, (also a mulatto, and a former slave in Virginia) was put on board some small schooners, and these were taken in tow by a French steam gunboat which co-operated with the Liberians. We sailed in company with President Roberts on board and soon anchored off Sinou. The force was landed the next morning and although we had orders to take no part yet at the request of Roberts our captain consented to let four unarmed boats pull in with them, for effect. I went in charge of one and had a good view of the battle.

When Colonel Hicks landed, which was towards the last, he was a sight to see, in his cocked-hat, epaulettes and top boots. Our purser, an old acquaintance, chaffed him unmercifully because he did not go to the front; but Hicks did not advance; he "saw from the beach when the morning was shining" all he wanted to see.

The opposing parties with their old fashioned arms kept up a heavy fire *at long range* the whole of the first day. The natives lay hidden in the woods or bushes and the Liberians would not leave the sea-side. The second day the French captain thinking he might be kept there a lifetime decided to take a hand in it himself; so twenty sailors were landed under a lieutenant, the woods were

shelled by the steamer, and with the Frenchmen in advance the
Liberians advanced into the country. Having given them a "start"
the Frenchmen returned and left the army to pursue its victorious
career; the enemy retreating up the country to the factory where
the Spaniards had established their head quarters, and which was
General Lewis' objective. After the Frenchmen left, the advance
was led by a company of Congo negroes who had been captured in a
slaver and were now apprenticed in Monrovia. They were the
bravest men in the army. The Liberians were absent four or five
days and at night we could track them by the burning villages.
They reached the factory and burned it and returned to the beach
with the Spaniards as prisoners. There was great rejoicing in all the
land when the victorious army got back to Monrovia. We had
orders to take President Roberts on board again, which we did,
and visited Cape Palmas, Grand Bassa, Tradetown, Cape Mount
and other places. The president lived in the cabin and conducted
himself with much propriety.

We fell in with an English man-of-war at Cape Mount and as
soon as her captain saw the Liberian standard at our masthead he
came on board in full uniform to call upon President Roberts. In
fact, at all the places visited he received the same honors as would
have been extended to a crowned head. We carried Mr. Roberts
back to Monrovia, and in June returned to Porto Praya. Here we
replenished our stores of provisions and water and sailed for Cadiz
in Spain. This was off our station; but our rudder-post was in such
bad condition that it became necessary to replace it, and this could
not be done at any port on the coast. It may readily be believed that
we were glad to have so pleasant a break in our cruise. We touched
at Madeira on our way for a few days. We found the *Portsmouth* in
port and Commodore Cooper whose health had long been failing
went home in her. In a few months she rejoined the squadron
bearing the flag of Commodore F. S. Gregory.

We were in Cadiz some weeks while a new rudder-post was
made for us at the dock-yard. We then sailed and spent the
summer in visiting Madeira, Teneriffe and Palmas; and in October
returned to Porto Praya. The cruise to windward was a most

delightful one, and was of much service to us all. The merchants of Funchal, Madeira, are famed for their hospitality and the people of Palmas, Grand Canary, we found equally kind. I shall have more to say of these islands in my next chapter.

Porto Praya is on the island of St. Jago, one of the Cape de Verdes. It is a small town, inhabited by a few Portuguese, half breeds, and negroes; the latter constitute the bulk of the population. It is situated on a high bluff overlooking the bay and is not particularly unhealthy or warm.

The harbor is a good enough one during the continuance of the "trades," which blow about ten months in the year. In the months of August and September heavy gales sometimes blow from the southwest, and as the harbor is open in that direction vessels which happen to be in the port must slip their cables and go to sea.

It was to Porto Praya that Commodore Charles Stewart brought his two prizes, the *Cyane* and *Levant*, which he had captured in the frigate *Constitution* eighteen days before: February 20th, 1815. While lying there an English squadron of superior force made its appearance and the commodore fearing it would not observe the neutrality of the port stood out to sea with his ships, and endeavored to make his escape. The *Constitution* and the *Cyane* got safely to New York, but the *Levant* was recaptured.

On the north side of the island are the ruins of an old Portuguese city. It was abandoned in consequence of having no harbor; but from the appearance of the ruins it must have been rather an imposing place. I saw there the stone walls of the churches and other public buildings. Upon the occasion of my visit I went to a monastery, some portions of which are inhabitable; indeed we found several black monks in possession. There was a library there and some of the books were in a good state of preservation. These books must have been very old and rare and would be worth their weight in gold in London. Being fond of old books I have since regretted not purchasing some of them which I could readily have done.

The Cape de Verdes were discovered in 1449, and I expect this city was founded not many years after. It was called Santiago, and it was here that the *Vittoria*, one of Magellan's squadron, touched, July 10th, 1522, upon her return to Spain after having accomplished the first circumnavigation of the globe. The old city presented a mournful appearance; but we found a few negroes there. Dr. Potter being with me all the sick were brought out for him to prescribe for as soon as it became known. It is indeed sad to fall in with people in these out-of-the-way places and witness their sufferings for the want of medical and especially surgical assistance. The fever they can manage themselves, but any accident to body or limb must go uncared for. The only people more to be pitied in this respect are the American merchant sailors.

The Government established a depot at Porto Praya some time in 1842 I believe, and it was the general rendezvous of the squadron. The island furnishes very fair mess stores—fruits in great abundance, and the oranges the best I have ever seen anywhere. The inhabitants raise turkeys in great numbers, and at all the places on the coast we found them in abundance. This rather surprised me, for I do not remember seeing them in any numbers in the tropics anywhere else.

We were caught here on this visit by a southwest gale which came near driving us ashore. The wind sprang up at night and increased so rapidly that our captain did not think it prudent to attempt to get underweigh and he decided to ride it out. All hands were called about two A. M., the topmasts were housed and the lower yards sent down. We were riding by the starboard bower anchor, and immediately let go the port bower and sheet anchors; we veered chain on all until the starboard bower had 120 fathoms out. I had never before seen a vessel ride out a gale on a lee shore; and as the sea rose and came rolling in it seemed impossible that anything could hold the ship. The port chains did not get an even strain with the starboard bower, and as the ship rose to a sea she would straighten the latter out as stiff as an iron bar and the strain would squeeze the stay-bolts out of it. But it held. We were in the habit of overhauling our chains once a quarter and knew that everything was in good order. The stern of the ship was not very far from the rocks at the base of a steep cliff, and if the ship had gone ashore not many of the hundred and fifty men on board would have reached the shore alive. We were up all night and well into the next day making all snug. The starboard sheet was hemp and it took some time to bend it, which we did. At noon just as the order was given to pipe to dinner an American brig—called the *Copperthwaite*, from Philadelphia on a trading voyage—dragged ashore and hoisted her colors union down. It was my special duty, as Master to attend to this kind of work so I volunteered to go to her assistance. The captain hesitated some time about lowering a boat—indeed there was such a fearful sea running that most of the lieutenants thought that a boat could not reach the shore—but he finally consented to let me make the attempt. The boatswain was ordered to call down the main hatch for volunteers and the whole ship's company promptly responded. Passed Midshipman Selden volunteered to go with me and we picked out thirteen men, most of whom were petty officers. The boat was lowered with Selden, two men and myself in her, and towed astern by a hawser; the other men jumped overboard with lines and we pulled them in the boat as best we could. Watching a favorable opportunity we let go the hawser, pulled short round, and made for the stranded brig. I cannot attempt to describe the trip; but we could only see the top of our ship's masts when we went down in the hollow of the waves, and from the ship they did not see *us* at all.

There was an American whaler between us and the shore and her boats were much better adapted to the work than ours but her crew looked upon it as our "pigeon," and contented themselves with giving us three cheers as we went flying by. The brig was lying broadside to the beach, the sea was making a clean breach over her and the men were lashed in the rigging. I pulled in under her lee to turn round, and having done so, pulled directly for her main rigging in which I saw her captain waiting. As we got near I ran forward to be the first on board and as the boat touched the brig's side I made a spring and caught the captain's hand, at the same time the receding wave carried the boat back towards the shore. I hung on for a moment, but our hands being wet and perhaps a little greasy, my hold slipped and overboard I went. The anxiety of my men to save me came near drowning me; for as soon as my head appeared one fellow stuck a boat-hook in the back of my neck which pushed me under again, and I could not get a chance to catch my breath. When I *did* catch it I ordered them in terms more forcible than polite to let me alone, and being a tolerable swimmer I was soon on board the brig and my men after me. As is the custom in such cases I took command of the brig and gave some necessary orders as to sending down the upper yards and masts, and to execute which my men sprang aloft like cats. The captain relieved of all responsibility seemed another man, and his first words were: "Well gents, what will you take to drink?"

At sunset the gale had somewhat moderated; but fearing the brig might go to pieces during the night, and knowing that no assistance could be expected from the shore, we decided to leave her and watch her from the beach. As I had previously sent the boat ashore under the lee of the brig, where she had been hauled up by the natives, we all jumped overboard and swam ashore in a body. The gale still moderating we went off to the brig again shortly after midnight and got an anchor out to windward. About daylight the land breeze made, we set sail, and by 8 A.M. she was afloat. The brig was really not much injured; she leaked a little, but not more than the pumps could clear very handily; the men however were tampered with by the Portuguese merchants in Porto Praya and went before the American Consul and protested against going to sea in her. The Consul ordered a survey, and we sent a gang of men, discharged her cargo, and hove her down. Our carpenters stopped the leak, and we put her all *a taunto* again; the men still refused to go in her and she was sold. She was worth about six thousand dollars and brought fifteen hundred. A few days after, she sailed for the coast under a Portuguese captain with a full cargo of rice! Not the first American vessel sacrificed in this way in a foreign port by a long shot. I felt very much for the poor captain, and after all the men did not make very much by their motion as most of them died of fever. In spite of the exposure and hard work our men did not suffer at all. We did not have a single case of fever. For my services on this occasion I, some months afterwards, received a letter from the Hon. Secretary of State; all I remember about it is that it was tied with a blue ribbon.

CHAPTER XIII

Kroumen—the brig *Porpoise*—a boatswain's mate's poetry—a
narrow escape from drowning—Accra—Elmina—Cape Coast
Castle—grave of L. E. L.—slavers—a Yankee trick—the slave
trade—the *Bridgton*—Whydah—Dahomey—Prince's Island—
African fever—second cruise to windward—Madeira—Canary
Islands—wreck of the *Yorktown* on the island of Mayo—return
home—how to find the moon's age

Upon our first visit to Monrovia we had provided ourselves
with twenty *Kroumen* to do the boat work of the ship. These
men belong to a tribe on the coast near Tradetown; but there are
always a number of them to be found at a little village of their own
near Monrovia. They are sober and obedient, and the best boatmen
in the world. They are regularly enlisted and borne on the ship's
books and as their proper names cannot be pronounced—much less
spelled—the purser names them to suit himself. These names are
printed inside their Sunday hats and if the hat is lost the man loses
his identity. On Sundays they were mustered with the rest of
the crew, and it was hard to resist a smile at hearing called out

such names as: Jack Fryingpan, Giraffe, Upside Down, Bottle of Beer, &c.

When I went on shore to take observations with the artificial horizon (a small trough filled with quicksilver) the boat's crew of *Kroumen* would sit on their haunches near by and gravely watch the operation. As they saw me do this always before sailing from a port they not unnaturally gathered the impression that as I looked in the quicksilver with the sextant *I was looking for the way to the next port!* I encouraged them in this belief to keep them quiet. At Porto Praya, especially, they were always very anxious to know what vessels were anchored off Monrovia, and as I generally knew what vessels *should* be there I could give a correct answer.

We sailed from Porto Praya on our second cruise down the coast in November, 1849. Upon our arrival at Monrovia we found the brig *Porpoise* at anchor (as I had previously predicted). The second lieutenant of the brig, Israel Waite, was one of the most humorous men I have ever known. Alas poor Yorick! he lost his commission a few years after this time and went to Nicaragua with Walker's filibusters where he was either killed or died of fever. The captain of the *Porpoise* was a nervous man and had a habit of calling everything a "chap;" he would say: "What do you think of that chap," meaning perhaps a rising squall. Waite in turning over the deck to his relief would frequently say: "It looks a little *chappy* on the lee bow." The *Porpoise* had a fine set of fellows in her wardroom and we were very intimate with them. She had, too, that *rara avis*, a poetical *boatswain's mate!* Here is one of his parodies which I happen to recall:

1

I knew by the smoke that so gracefully curled
Around the fore hatch that dinner was nigh;
And I said if there's anything good in this world
'Tis made in our mess and they call it sea-pie.

2

'Tis 12 and the boatswain is ordered to pipe,
His mates they stand ready to answer and bawl;
The grog-tub is out and the line stretched along,
Each hand is awaiting the sound of the "call."

3

By the side of yon grog-tub how sweet 'tis to stand
And listen to catch the dear sound of your name:
But oh! how much sweeter when the tot's in your hand
You drink and are off some sea-pie to claim.

4

And thus in a snug man-of-war did I say,
With a cook to attend me and make me sea-pie;
With my half pint of whiskey to drink every day,
How sweet could I live, and how calm could I die!

The mess on board the *Porpoise* kept a book called the "goss" book; I do not know the etymology of the word "goss;" but that was its name. All such effusions as the above were entered in it, which is why I remember it. My memory preserves, fortunately for the reader, but one more.

TO ANNAPOLIS

For many months we happy were
In drinking juleps, eating crabs,
Without a thought, without a care,
We smoked away—*not* penny grabs!
But oh! the day at length arrived
To pony up the good and just
Round sum of three seventy-five
But very few put down the dust.

But: *Satis superque, de reste, bastantemente!*[1] All this is digression and a long one too. Let me pull myself together and resume.

While at Monrovia upon this visit I made a pretty narrow escape from drowning. When we went on shore we never attempted to land in our own boats—the custom was to lie outside the breakers and wait for a canoe to come out and take us in. One morning I started with two of our lieutenants to go on shore to hold a survey on some naval stores, and when we got near the beach the senior officer said it was too rough to land. My friend, Dr. Thomas M.

---

[1] A Latin/Neapolitan Italian expression of exasperation.

Potter, (now a medical director on the retired list) was in the boat and as we wanted to go on liberty we waited for a canoe and very imprudently both got in her—I in the bow and he in the stern. When we entered the breakers the first one went completely over and swamped us. I knew the *Krouman* was all right, but as soon as I got my head above water I turned to look for Potter; seeing him *diving for his umbrella* I concluded he could take care of himself, so I struck out for the shore which I was the first to reach. Fortunately there were a number of *Kroumen* on the beach watching us and they joined hands and hauled us up as soon as we struck the beach: otherwise we would inevitably have been carried back by the undertow and drowned. I remember that when I struck the beach the sand seemed to me to be receding at the rate of 40 miles a minute; "or words to that effect."

In January, 1850, we sailed from Monrovia for a cruise down the coast. We first stopped at Cape Palmas, which struck me as the prettiest of all the settlements in Liberia, and I believe it is the most healthy. From there we went down along the gold coast into the Gulf of Guinea, stopping at Accra, Elmina, and Cape Coast Castle. Elmina and Cape Coast Castle are fortified places; the former is held by the Dutch and the latter by the English. All these places were originally held by the Portuguese who made the first discoveries on this coast; they discovered Madeira in 1419; Cape Bojador in 1439; Cape Verde in 1446; the Cape de Verde islands in 1449; Sierra Leone in 1450; Congo was visited in 1484; and finally Bartolomeo Diaz reached the Cape of Good Hope—called by him the Cape of Storms—in 1486. They were the great navigators of the world at this time.

Cape Coast Castle presents a very imposing appearance from the sea. It is built of brick or stone, and mounts some large guns, principally for the land defence. It has resisted several attacks by the Ashantees.[2] It was here that the poetess, Miss Landon

---

[2]The British fort of Elmina, though undermanned, resisted the attack of an Ashanti army of some 12,000 during the Second Ashanti War (1873–74).

(L. E. L.), died. She married Governor McLean, and died soon after her arrival at the Castle under somewhat mysterious circumstances.[3] I had a commission from a lady to gather something from her grave—a flower or even a tuft of grass—but I found only a slab to mark where she had been buried in the parade ground, and no green thing within a mile of it.

At Elmina and Cape Coast Castle we were most hospitably entertained by the officers. Poor fellows, they were much cut off from the world and a strange face was a real pleasure to them. These places along the coast, called factories, were originally established for the trade in slaves. At Accra we fell in with H. B. M. brig *Contest*, Captain Spencer, who told us of a certain American brig *Bridgton* being on the coast and strongly suspected of being a slaver. I had always had a desire to catch a slaver with the slaves on board, for I wanted to see if what I had heard of them was true; but I knew the trouble it gave if one were only taken on suspicion. The difficulty with these vessels was that the slavers took out the same cargo as the regular traders, viz.: rum, tobacco, cottoncloths, fire arms, &c., &c. Under a cargo of this kind the slavers had lumber for the slave deck, water casks, &c. When they arrived at the place where the slaves were ready to be shipped they would discharge cargo, fill up their water, take the negroes on board with inconceivable rapidity, and put to sea.

A neat trick was played upon the English brigs *Contest* and *Kingfisher* by the captain of one of these vessels. He was in port with them, and at first was suspected; but as he flew the American flag the Englishmen were chary of searching him. After some time, as he continued to sell his goods as a regular trader, their suspicions were allayed and he became quite sociable with the two English captains. He had just arrived on the coast, had plenty of good

---

[3]Letitia Elizabeth Landon (1802–1838) was a popular romantic poet and novelist better known by her initials as L.E.L. In June 1838 she married George Maclean who was then governor of the Gold Coast, but she died only a few months later of an accidental overdose of prussic acid.

liquors and cigars, and was very hospitable. The captains frequently dined with him and no doubt found it pleasant to be relieved of the restrictions of a man-of-war. One evening the conversation turned on the sailing qualities of their respective vessels and the American said he would like to give them a trial. The next morning he got underweigh with the land breeze and in passing the English brigs hailed their commanders and challenged them to a race. They both got underweigh, followed him out, and in the afternoon when the usual sea breeze set in they had a trial of speed "on a wind." At sunset the English vessels parted company as they were obliged to return to their stations. The American bid them an affectionate adieu. When the brigs got back they found he had taken on board a full cargo of slaves the preceding night, and as he had 24 hours start it was useless to pursue.

When slaves are actually on board a vessel it is hard to say whether their condition is ameliorated by being recaptured or not. If they are recaptured they cannot be restored to their homes; for they are taken from the interior, and if landed, the coast tribes make them prisoners again: so some other disposition must be made of them. If captured by an English man-of-war they are sent to Sierra Leone, or enlisted in the West India regiments; if an American man-of-war captures them they are landed at Monrovia and apprenticed to the Liberians for a term of years; and if they are not slaves their condition is so near it that I was unable to perceive the difference.

On our way down to Whydah we fell in with the brig *Bridgton*. I boarded her and brought her captain back with me, with his "papers." He was a Portuguese and had not an American in his crew. He was evidently much frightened, but after some conversation with our captain he convinced him that his "papers" were all right: as indeed they seemed to be. The brig was cleared from Bahia and her "papers" were countersigned by the American consul. When the captain found we intended to let him go he became as saucy as a Pasquotank man in the herring season. We furnished him with an anchor and cable, for which he gave us an order on his owners in Philadelphia. The *Bridgton* accompanied us to Whydah, and here we found the launch of the *Kingfisher*, commanded by a Lieutenant Hamilton.

The English used to keep their boats stretched along the coast, at intervals of ten miles, and in this way one vessel watched a long strip of coast. The brig *Perry*, commanded by Commander [Andrew H.] Foote (afterwards a distinguished admiral) was the only vessel of our squadron that adopted this plan and she was rewarded by the capture of several slavers. One was a large ship with six or eight hundred slaves on board. The *Perry* was under English colors when she saw her, and the ship hoisting American colors, Captain Foote took possession of her. Hamilton of the *Kingfisher* had been after the *Bridgton* for some time. He was very glad to spend his nights with us while at Whydah; but I observed he kept a bright lookout for the *Kingfisher*, and was always off bright and early. He was a capital fellow and we were glad to have him. He told us that the captain of the *Bridgton* was very "cheeky" since our arrival and would point to our flag and tell him he could not "touch him now." Hamilton always told him he was only waiting for him to get his slaves on board to capture him. We heard afterwards that the *Bridgton* got off with a full cargo of slaves a few days after our departure, in spite of Hamilton.

Whydah is the principal seaport of the kingdom of Dahomey, of which we have heard so much of late years. An Englishman who had been in the country for some time gave me an interesting account of the king and his people. Speaking of their snake temples—for they worship snakes—he said that an English cooper, not long in the country, was one day coopering a cask, and seeing a large snake near by he chopped its head off. It was with much difficulty that the foreigners saved his life; he was sent out of the country and a large fine paid. He told me that when the king desired to send a message to a deceased friend or relative he would send for a slave, give him the message and have his head cut off; he said he had never seen a slave exhibit any fear, and I have been told the same of the Chinese when about to suffer death.

From Whydah we went to Prince's island to water ship. This is a beautiful spot, nearly on the equator; the land is very high and as vessels anchor near the shore the hills seem to be nearly overhead. We enjoyed our visit here very much, principally on account of the fresh-water bathing. Many streams run into the sea from the mountains near the village, and in a hard rain it is wonderful to see the rapidity with which the water rises. In company with half-a-dozen officers I walked across the island to visit an old city which had been abandoned. I found there the ruins of stone churches, monasteries, etc., similar to the old city on St. Jago island. It had evidently been a place of importance. These old cities all have romantic histories if one could only get at them. The Portuguese seemed in those days to build cities first, and look for a harbor afterwards. St. Paul de Loanda, in about nine degrees south latitude, was the largest and most important of all their cities on the west coast. It still belongs to Portugal, but is of little consequence now; though the recent operations on the Congo river may resuscitate it.

Our ship was perfectly healthy the whole time we were on this station. We were never allowed to remain out of the ship after sunset, and the ship never entered the rivers. In 1844 the *Preble* lost many of her crew while lying in a river on the coast, since which time it is forbidden by the Department to do so. I think the health of the station compares favorably with the West Indies or coast of Brazil. We had but one case of real African fever and the patient recovered.

Leaving Prince's island we sailed for Porto Praya, touching at many ports on our way up the coast. We sailed from Porto Praya for a cruise to windward in June, in company with the *Portsmouth*. We beat up through the islands (Cape de Verdes) and I was much surprised at the strength of the trades. As we got to the northward of Mayo the wind freshened to double reefs, and at noon we were actually hove to under a close-reefed main topsail and fore storm staysail. At 4 P. M. the same day we had the royals set. We arrived at Funchal on the 1st of July and for the month we remained there did nothing but enjoy ourselves. It was our third visit and we had many acquaintances. We commenced the round by having all of our friends on board to a *déjeuner à la fourchette* on the 4th of July,

and after that there was a succession of picnics, dinner parties, etc.
Mr. Howard March, our consul, kept open house and his partner,
Mr. Beyman, did the honors.

About the 1st of August we left Madeira for the Canary islands
and spent another month between Teneriffe and Palmas. These
islands belong to Spain. They were known to the ancients under
the name of the *Fortunate Islands*. One can readily understand why
they were known as they can be *seen* from the coast of Africa. The
peak of Teneriffe, 12,000 feet high, is visible in clear weather at a
distance of 150 miles. The Spaniards discovered these islands
about 1330. They were inhabited at that time by a race called
Guanches, probably Arabs from the adjacent coast. All trace of
these people is now lost, which is much to be regretted. The
Spaniards extirpated them during the 16th century. From
Gomera, the most westerly island, Columbus sailed to discover the
new world.

We sailed from Palmas about August 30th, 1850, on what was
to prove the last cruise of the *Yorktown*. We had fresh trades and
fine weather and steered to make *Bonavista* the northernmost of the
Cape de Verde islands. We expected to meet our relief, the
sloop-of-war *Dale*, at Porto Praya whence we would sail for home.
It may be imagined that we were all in fine spirits. Our cruise was
up; we had lost but one or two men by sickness; there had been no
courts-martial, and nothing had occurred to break the harmony
existing on board. The second day out I remember that when I
marked the chart in the wardroom I called attention to the fact that
we were abreast the point where Captain Riley was wrecked in the
brig *Commerce* in the early part of the century, and he and his crew
made prisoners by the Arabs.

We made the island of *Bonavista* as expected, and on the 4th of
September ran along the eastern side of the island of *Sal* with a
strong trade wind blowing. At sunset that day we hauled round
the south point of that island and shaped a course to pass to the
northward of the island of *Mayo*. There was some discussion as to
this, for the usual course was to go to the southward of *Mayo;* but
no danger was anticipated as there was plenty of room and to spare

between *Mayo* and the island to the northward of it. The ship was
under top gallant sails and the lee clew of the mainsail, and
running 9 knots, with the wind on the starboard quarter. At 1
A.M. we hauled up the mainsail. I had the morning watch and at 4
A.M. relieved Lieutenant Caldwell, who, after passing the orders,
expatiated upon the good breakfast he expected to wake up to in
Porto Praya, where we expected to arrive by 8 A.M.

The island of *Mayo* was in sight on our port beam, and the island
of *St. Jago* ahead; the weather was clear with flying trade clouds.
The captain who had been up all night came out of his cabin and
asked me how far I thought we were from Mayo. The peaks visible
to us were some distance inland, and it was difficult to judge. Our
lookouts were cautioned to be on the *qui vive*, and I had scarcely
issued the order when the forecastle lookout called out: "breakers
ahead." It was just before 5 o'clock, and the day was beginning to
dawn. I immediately slapped the helm hard down and manned the
lee main braces, intending to brace up aft, brace abox the head
yards, and wear short round on her heel; but she had hardly come
up a point when she struck, and fetched up all standing. It was a
miracle that the masts did not go over the bows. We now braced
up fore and aft, and attempted to force her over. Upon sounding
the well it was found that there was already much water in her, and
we manned the pumps and commenced pumping. By this time all
hands were on deck, and the first lieutenant, Mr. Rootes, had just
relieved me when the carpenter came up, and in a low, calm voice
said: "It is of no use to pump; *the ship's bottom is knocked out!*" And so
it was; she had struck on sunken, sharp-pointed rocks, and as she
rose and fell with the sea which was pretty heavy the bottom was
crushed in, and the water tanks, &c., in the hold were rammed up
against the berth deck beams. Finding that it was useless to
attempt to save the ship we now turned our attention to the saving
of life and material. The boats were hoisted out and lowered and
towed a-stern with marines in them to prevent any one getting in
without orders, and the upper masts and yards were sent down on
deck. The ship had now settled down on the rocks with the water
about knee-deep on the berth deck.

When day broke we found we were on the north end of Mayo island about a mile from the shore. Outside of us, at a distance of a mile, was a reef on which the sea was breaking heavily; had we struck on that reef not a man would have been saved. The purser's safe with the ship's money and books were taken up into the cabin, and the men were ordered to bring their bags up on the spar deck. While we were engaged in this the ship suddenly fell over on her starboard beam ends, and there was a rush for the boats, which were soon filled with marines, landsmen and idlers. The officers and our best men, however, stuck to the ship and clambered up the sides to the weather rail. The masts were cut away, and although some men were aloft at the time they were rescued unhurt. As soon as I got on the weather side I turned to take a view of the scene, and the first man I noticed was Caldwell sitting on the weather main brace bumpkin with a loaf of bread under his arm, and a very tall plume sticking up in his old straw *sombrero*. It seems that as the ship capsized he had grabbed at the captain's flower-pots and seized the plume which he stuck in his hat. The ship now lay completely over on her starboard side, with the water over her hatchways. Lieutenant Frailey who was below when the ship went over made a narrow escape; he found all the ladders carried away and could not get on deck; as the water came pouring in it swept him aft, and with a receding swell he was carried to the hatchway, where the boatswain caught sight of him, and with the assistance of the gunner hauled him up on deck in an exhausted condition. The ship had no air-ports and the lower deck was lighted by dead lights let into the spar deck. As the ship capsized, the pressure of the air forced out all those on the port side. Two of the wardroom servants (Portuguese) who were caught below took refuge in the master's room, and thrust their hands through these openings with loud cries for assistance. The boatswain, Mr. Young, and the gunner, Mr. Oliver, who were conspicuous for their activity and courage on this occasion, cut the hole larger with axes and soon got them on deck. They certainly came up through a *very small hole*, and were so dreadfully frightened that they forgot all the English they had previously learned, nor did they recover it while I was with them. The boats being loaded to the water's edge were sent ashore to land their men, and we hung on to the wreck to await their return. Our best men stuck by the officers and were perfectly unconcerned; the only fear I had was that she might slip off the rocks and go down in deep water. In the course of an hour the boats returned, and the ship was formally abandoned *without the loss of a man*. Mr. Rootes was the last man to leave the wreck.

As soon as we got on shore we picked out good boats' crews and returned to the ship where we commenced getting sails and spars for tents and sent them on shore. All the provisions we could get at were also landed. The water was spoiled five minutes after the ship struck, and it was well for us that we found it on the island. As it was we suffered much for the want of it the first day. By sunset we had sent ashore many necessary articles and we all landed. I shall never forget the headache I had when I got on shore, nor the magical effects of a cup of tea which a sailor brought me in a tin pot. We slept that night on the beach in the tents we had erected. The next morning we went again to the wreck, and the *Kroumen* who were demoralized the first day now proved very efficient. The ship's money which consisted of doubloons and silver dollars in bags had been put on the transom in the cabin, and was now lying to leeward of it under water with *débris* of all kinds. The *Kroumen* recovered a good deal of it by diving. I noticed that when they became exhausted they would say they would make one more dive and stop. At the last dive they would come up with both hands full of money and *their mouths also*! We winked at this proceeding, remembering the old adage that you should never "look a gift horse in the mouth."

Had it not been for these water-dogs we would not have recovered a cent. As the ship broke up, different articles floated on shore; among them many quarter casks of good Madeira wine. These we had to stave to prevent the men from getting at it. We remained here several days and then removed to the southern end of the island, where there was a town inhabited by negroes. Some of us went by land and the rest in the boats. Upon our arrival the officers and men were distributed among the houses, and Lieutenant Spottswood was sent in the launch to Porto Praya to notify the Consul of our condition. He soon returned with a schooner loaded with provisions from the naval store-house. There were a few Portuguese in the village; a *commandante*, of course, and about twenty black soldiers. The American Consul was a Portuguese negro who had received some education in Lisbon. We found him a very sensible and hospitable man. Mayo exports salt only. Ships go to the town I am writing of for it. There is no harbor, and the salt is taken off with much difficulty; it is collected in pans. We remained on the island 33 days anxiously looking for the arrival of the *Dale*. Our amusements were salt-water bathing, riding donkey races and shooting. We found large numbers of quail and guinea fowls on the island; the latter the most difficult bird to shoot I have ever met with. Our men remained healthy and we lost but one man by sickness. The huts we lived in were comfortable enough in dry weather; but in rainy weather the roofs leaked badly. Calling upon one of the midshipmen one morning I found him in bed reading Shakespeare; he was smoking a pipe and had a glass of aguadiente convenient; and to make himself still more comfortable had an umbrella hoisted to protect himself from the rain which was falling heavily, and from which the roof of his shanty did not protect him. On the 8th of October the *Dale* arrived, and the next day we went in her to Porto Praya where we found the *Portsmouth*, Commodore [Francis H.] Gregory, and the *John Adams*, Captain [Levin M.] Powell. To this latter ship we were now transferred and sailed in her for home. We ran the trades down to the island of St. Thomas where we stopped to water. We remained but a few days and then sailed for Norfolk where we arrived in December, 1850. Captain Marston was tried by a court martial for the loss of his ship and honorably acquitted.

Before closing this chapter I am reminded to give a "rule for finding the moon's age," given me by Captain Marston—not that it is *new*, for I have seen it in almanacs many times since then, but because I have never known any one, save myself, to make a proper practical use of it. I am reminded of it here, because I wanted to know if there was a moon on the night the *Yorktown* was wrecked and have applied the rule to find out. Of course all almanacs give the moon's age; but then one cannot always have an almanac at hand.

The rule is used by the Church in determining festivals, feast days, etc. It is as follows: "To the epact, add the day of the month, and to this sum add the number of the month from March (*inclusive*). This sum if less than 30 will be the moon's age; should the sum exceed 30, subtract 30 and the remainder will be the moon's age." The moon's age calculated in this way *may* be one day in error.

The epact can be found in the Book of Common Prayer of the Episcopal Church. Knowing it for one year it is easily calculated, as it increases by 11 from one year to the next, and 30 is dropped when the sum exceeds 30. It should be observed that the epact is reckoned from March to March. I will give an example of the application of this rule:

Required the moon's age on the 5th day of September, 1850.
Epact for 1850 17
Number of months from March to September (inclusive) . . . 7
Day of the month 5
                                                                                            ‾‾
Moon's age 29

So there was no moon on that night.

CHAPTER XIV

A morning call—ordered to the surveying brig *Washington*—
survey of Nantucket Shoals—Block Island and No Man's
Land—pilot Daggett—the pilot of the *Bibb*—anecdotes—
ordered to the *Princeton*—a night with the "spirit-rappers"—
am detached from the *Princeton* and ordered to the *Cyane*

Upon the conclusion of the court-martial on Captain Marston,
before which I appeared as a witness, I was granted the usual
three months' "leave." While at home on this "leave" I was
frequently requested by my mother and sister, who were not
visiting at the time, to call on their friend Miss Zanes, who was
living at one of the largest private boarding-houses in the city. I
never returned from a walk that I was not asked if I had called upon
Miss Zanes, until it became at last a household word. Being very
bashful I did not like the idea of calling alone and introducing
myself, but finally I screwed my courage up to the sticking place.

Calling at the house I inquired if Miss Zanes was in, and being answered in the affirmative, I sent up my card and entered the parlor. I had not been long seated when the door opened and a lady appeared. I met her, introduced myself as Passed Midshipman Parker of the navy, and shook hands with her. I thought she seemed embarrassed, but she advanced to the fire and sat down. I drew up a chair and commenced the conversation with an allusion to certain atmospherical changes, etc., but I made but little headway. Miss Zanes is quiet and timid, I thought, I must endeavor to bring her out. While revolving in my mind the best manner of accomplishing this the door opened and another lady appeared; she had her hat on. It flashed across me in a moment! I had made a mistake. *This* was Miss Zanes; she had been out walking, and had just come in and heard of my being in the parlor. I advanced to the door, bowed, introduced myself as Passed Midshipman Parker of the navy, and shook her warmly by the hand; at the same time congratulating myself upon my self-possession and perception. She went to the fire, took a seat, and entered into conversation with the first lady. I also took a chair and occasionally tried to get a word in edgeways, (so to speak); but in a little while they both rose and went to the window and sat down in the alcove. Well, I thought, this is a most extraordinary proceeding on the part of Miss Zanes! But I could not remain alone at the fire-place, so I picked up a chair and followed them. The mischief of it was that I was not certain now *which was Miss Zanes*! I became somewhat confused and rather red in the face. I did the best I could under these novel circumstances and put in a remark now and then to which they did not deign to reply. While meditating a retreat, and not exactly sure as to which one *to shake hands with* in making *mes adieux* the door opened, and a third lady appeared upon the scene!

By George, said I to myself, I have been all wrong, *this* must be Miss Zanes! I advanced to meet her, introduced myself as before, and fortunately for my brain it *was* Miss Zanes: the real Simon pure. I begged her to explain to the other ladies that I was *not* an escaped lunatic with a mania for introducing myself to people;

shook her *very* warmly by the hand and evaporated through the front door. If Miss Zanes had not made her appearance when she did I would have introduced myself to all the boarders in the Butler house (as it was just before the dinner hour) and would probably have ended by being sent to an asylum. I have not had the pleasure of meeting Miss Zanes from that day to this.

At the expiration of my "leave" I was ordered to the surveying brig *Washington*, lieutenant commanding S. Swartwout.[1] The party was in charge of lieutenant commanding Charles H. McBlair, and consisted of the steamer *Bibb*, the brig *Washington* and a small schooner which we chartered for the season. We spent the summer of 1851 in surveying the Nantucket Shoals, and what with gales of wind and fogs we did not get a great many working days. I had the command of the "tender," and when we did have fair weather would have to sit upon deck from about 4 A. M. till 8 in the evening taking an angle every five minutes. I found it uninteresting as well as hard work and was not sorry when the season was over.

Happening to ride out a gale on the shoals I comprehended how so many small fishing vessels are lost on the banks; for if one holds on too long she will swamp before a man can get forward to slip the chain; indeed it is impossible to do so.

We did some independent work in the *Washington* afterwards off Block island and No-man's-land. Block island and Nantucket were primitive places in those days, but are now popular summer resorts. Our pilot, Mr. Daggett, had been the pilot of the frigate *Congress* in the war of 1812, and related many interesting incidents concerning it. He said they were once nine months at sea without going into port. The present Commodore Ingraham who was a midshipman in the ship has since corroborated many of Daggett's

---

[1] The *Washington* (the sixth U.S. warship to bear that name) was a six-gun brig built as a revenue cutter. She was transferred to the navy in 1838 and returned to the revenue service ten years later.

statements.[2] The pilot of the *Bibb* was quite another character; brought up on Nantucket island, going to sea in the summer and working at his trade in the winter, he was one of the most original men I have ever met. He had a fund of anecdotes, and most of them were out of the usual run of sea-yarns; one was of a man who was taken very ill from having eaten twelve lobsters. The doctor not relieving him of his pain, he went off and commenced praying as follows: "Oh Lord, you know I am not like those Methodist fellows who are always praying for help and doing nothing for them-selves—but if you will relieve me of six of these lobsters I'll try and grapple with the other half-dozen myself."

We laid the *Washington* up in New York in October, and then went to Washington for the winter, where we were employed in office work.

In the spring of 1852 preparations were being made for Com-modore Perry's Japan expedition. I was ordered to the *Princeton*, a new screw sloop just completed at the Boston Yard and designated as one of the vessels of the squadron.

I had a very curious experience with the "spirit rappers" the night I arrived in Boston. It was in the midst of the excitement caused by the revelations of the Fox girls, and there were more or less believers in every town in New England.[3] I met at the Tremont House my friends Passed Midshipmen Hare and Selden, the first a "true believer," the latter a sceptic in the rapping business, and they proposed that we should visit a "medium" that night. Before starting it was decided that Hare should be the questioner and that he should summon up the spirit of a Passed Midshipman Sim-

---

[2]Commodore Duncan Ingraham (1802–1891) was born in Charleston, S.C., of a family of naval officers. His father had fought with John Paul Jones on the *Bonhomme Richard*. Like Parker, Ingraham subsequently chose to resign his commission to serve in the Confederate States Navy.

[3]Margaret Fox (1833–1893) was a popular medium who conjured up "spir-its" by tapping under the table with her toes. She was exposed as a fraud in the 1880s at about the time Parker wrote, but nevertheless continued to act as a medium until her death.

mons, who had been drowned off the coast of Brazil a year before. Simmons was a friend of mine, but an enemy of Hare. We got to the house of a Mr. Leroy Sunderland[4] about midnight and were ushered into a back parlor where we found the "medium" seated. She was a pale, delicate-looking young woman, of nervous temperament and a frightened air. She had the appearance of a person addicted to the use of narcotics. She was very lady-like in her dress and manner, and for a few minutes we sat around the table, which was an ordinary mahogany centre-table, engaged in conversation. After awhile the spirit of Simmons made its arrival known by a series of *raps* under the table, and we proceeded to business. I should mention that we were each provided with a pencil and a card with the alphabet printed on it. All communications were made by means of this alphabet, the questioner putting his pencil on each letter in succession, and the spirit designating the correct one by a *rap*, until the word was spelled out. Suffice it to say that all Hare's questions were answered with the most remarkable accuracy, though we knew the "medium" could have no suspicion of who we were. Finally the spirit said to Hare: "I do not like you and will not answer any more questions." I must say I was staggered at this reply and I suspect showed it. The "medium" then said to the spirit: "Is there any person in the room you *will* answer?" The reply was indicated by the table moving sharply up against my breast! The "medium" directed me to ask a question and I confess that the whole proceeding had astonished me so much that I could scarcely keep my hand from trembling. However, I asked a question, and it being by this time very late I thought it well to break up the séance; so I put my foot under the table and tilted it. The "medium" instantly rose and said there would be no more communications, that some one had tilted the table. I "acknowledged the corn" (no pun-ish-ment), and we all engaged in conversation

[4]La Roy (not Leroy) Sunderland (1804–1885) was a Methodist minister who became a rabid abolitionist and organized the first antislavery society in the Methodist Church.

again. The "medium" now turned her attention especially to me; she said I *could* become a first-class medium; that she knew I was sceptical then, but that if I would only have faith I would become a far better medium than she; that my *appearance* indicated it; (by the way, considering the appearance of the young lady, and that of Mr. Leroy Sunderland himself, this was not so much of a compliment as one might suppose), and gave many other good reasons for her belief. So earnest was she in this that after we had left the room she called me back and said the "spirits" would do almost anything to make me a "true believer," and that if I wished it they would *rap* on the head of my bed that night! I assured her that I would come again to see the "spirits" and that I did not wish them to *rap* on the head of my bed; I was most impressive on this point. I felt nervous enough without that.

We returned to the hotel and I went to bed. I was awakened by hearing a spirit talking to me. I opened my eyes and saw a dim outline of *something* clothed in white robes. Although I could not exactly *hear* the words I knew that the spirit said: "We are anxious to convert you; get up and you will see something wonderful;" I rose in bed and saw directly in front of me a *cross of fire!* I lay down again completely dazed, and convinced that this was a revelation. Just then I heard the "boots" in the passage, and this gave me courage. I rose again and at first saw the cross of fire as before— gazing steadily at it I rose and walked towards it. The inside shutters of my room were *in two parts*, and the first gleam of the rising sun shining on them had made the burning cross. It was not until I had actually touched the shutter that the illusion was dispelled, and if I had not risen the second time I suppose I should have become a spiritualist. I went many times after this to see them, and I observed that while my friend Hare's questions were always answered correctly, mine never were. I thought that perhaps the "mediums" were expert physiognomists—they watched the face of the questioner as he rested his pencil on the letter, and remembered that "the wish is father to the thought."

I reported for the *Princeton* as ordered. She was a long, narrow vessel with a great shear, and not at all adapted to the naval service.

We were towed to Baltimore by the *Mississippi* to take in the machinery, which had been contracted for. Commander Sidney Smith Lee was ordered to command her, and my dear friend and mentor, Frank Murray, was one of the lieutenants. I should have been charmed to sail with them, but finding there was no chance of the ship getting to sea became impatient and exchanged into the sloop-of-war *Cyane*, Captain George N. Hollins, at Norfolk, bound to the West Indies.[5] I may say here that the *Princeton* never *did* get to sea; she was a miserable failure in every respect, and was finally sent to Philadelphia to end her days as a receiving ship.

[5]The *Cyane*, an 18-gun sloop launched in 1837, was 132′3″ in length, 34′3″ across the beam, and displaced 792 tons. She was decommissioned and sold in 1887.

CHAPTER XV

Join the *Cyane*—bad navigation—Havana—the Lopez expedition—Key West—the Dry Tortugas—Pensacola—Commodore
J. T. Newton—Greytown—the Nicaragua route—a trip up
the San Juan del Norte—Castillo—join a flying squadron at
Portsmouth, N. H.—Eastport—St. Johns—the Bay of
Fundy—Captain Geo. N. Hollins—a sunken rock—an old
time Dutch commander—the Gulf of St. Lawrence—detached
from the *Cyane*—the *Cyane* bombards Greytown—the Isthmus
of Darien—Strain's expedition—Captain Prevost's experience—
the Darien and Mosquito Indians

I reported on board the *Cyane* in July, 1852, and did not much
fancy going into the steerage again after having been sailing
master of a ship for two years; but my rank did not entitle me to be
detailed as such from the navy department, so I had to take my
chance of an acting appointment as I had done in going to the coast
of Africa. We went from Norfolk to New York for a draft of men to
complete our crew, and in the Fall sailed for Havana. Our master
was not by any means an expert in the art of navigating a ship, and

in attempting to go through the Hole in the Wall came very near
plumping us on Abaco Island;[1] however we got to Havana without
further mishap and after remaining there a few days sailed for
Pensacola. Here we found orders to return to Havana. On this trip
our master got entirely out of his reckoning; we made the land on
the fourth day out, and at sunset hove to off what *he* said was
Havana. We thought it very strange that the *light* could not be
seen; but there is always much delicacy observed in such cases in
the navy, and no one had a word to say. That night I had the mid
watch, and at 12 o'clock relieved the master who told me the
orders were *to keep the beach in sight*. The ship was under topsails,
foresail and jib and was sailing along the land with a light breeze,
instead of being hove to with her head off shore as she should have
been. Not liking the look of things I made the master write the
orders on the log slate.

About 1 o'clock the lookout in the lee gangway reported a boat
in sight, and stepping to leeward I saw a fishing boat at anchor.
Knowing we must be pretty close to the land I wore ship close
around the boat, and stood off shore. At 3 A. M. I tacked ship and
stood in shore again for the purpose of putting the ship as near the
position in which I took charge of her as possible. At 4 when the
watch was called we were nearly as close to the land as at 12, and
when my relief (who was a slow coach) came up we just had the
beach in sight as directed. I told my relief that he had better tack
ship at once, stand off shore for an hour, and by that time it would
be light enough for him to see. He said he would do so. I went
below and waited anxiously to hear the order "ready about," which
at last came. As the ship went round I commenced to undress, but
just as she came head to wind *she struck* and was soon hard and fast
aground. All hands were soon on deck and the stream anchor was
carried out astern. The ship did not make any water, and by 8
o'clock we had her afloat again without having had to start the

[1]The Hole in the Wall was the narrow passage between Grand Bahama Island
and Little Abaco Island.

water or throw anything overboard; but it was a narrow escape. We found upon inquiring of some fishermen who came off that we were near Bahia Honda, 45 miles west of Havana!

Captain Hollins was a very cool, prompt seaman, and handled his ship well on this occasion. I was much struck with his manner upon reaching the deck. He did not ask any unnecessary questions; he recognized the fact that the vessel was on shore and must be gotten off, and he proceeded to take steps to accomplish it. Indeed he never *did* call the master to account either for being so much out in his reckoning, or for not heaving the ship to with her head off shore as he had ordered him to do. I thought myself he should not have overlooked this latter point.

Upon our arrival at Havana our third lieutenant was invalidated which promoted me to master, and a few days afterwards the *Fulton* came in with Vice President [William R.] King on board, short of officers. Our former master was sent to her, and I became an acting lieutenant, and Passed Midshipman Van Zandt was made master.

Our stay at Havana was not marked by any incidents of importance. The relations between the United States and Spain were rather strained in consequence of the expedition of Lopez in 1850.[2] In April of that year Lopez landed at Cardenas with about six hundred men, and after an obstinate engagement succeeded in taking the town. He was afterwards forced to fly, and with some others escaped to the United States. The Cubans treated the prisoners with unnecessary cruelty, not to say barbarity; and the feeling against Americans was very bitter at this time.

It will be remembered that Lopez made another attempt in the summer of 1857 with 480 men. On the 11th of August he landed on the northern coast of Cuba, where he left Colonel Crittenden and 100 men, and started to the interior expecting to be joined by

[2]Narciso López (1798–1851) was a Venezuelan soldier and filibuster. He led an abortive Cuban revolutionary movement in 1843 and another expedition backed by American southerners in 1850, when he succeeded in capturing the city of Cárdenas. Subsequently, as Parker notes, López was captured, convicted, and publicly garroted by the Spanish.

the people. He was disappointed. His army was attacked and dispersed. Crittenden and his party were captured and shot. Lopez and six of his companions were also captured, and afterwards executed at Havana by the *garrote*. The recent attempts of the Cubans to attain their independence, and the shooting of Captain Fry and others need not be repeated here. These expeditions cannot be justified by any international laws or customs.

We gave a ball during our stay, but it was principally attended by Americans and English, and we saw but little of Cuban society in any of our subsequent visits. We managed to enjoy ourselves riding about the neighborhood in volantes, visiting the Tacon theatre and the café Dominica, the most charming café I have ever seen in any country.

From Havana we went to Key West where we spent two weeks very pleasantly. The citizens we found very kind and hospitable and several balls were given us. The *Cyane* had now been several years in commission and was overrun by rats. The men were so much annoyed by them that they could find no comfort in their hammocks. Reinforcements joined them at every port in spite of all our precautions, and it had come to such a point that we had to take steps to get rid of them; so Captain Hollins decided to go to the Tortugas islands and "smoke" the ship. The Tortugas were surveyed in 1829 by the late Commodore Tattnall and the following year the Government commenced extensive fortifications on them. At the time of our visit the fort was not garrisoned, an ordnance sergeant being in charge.

We ran the ship alongside the coral reef and made her fast as though alongside a wharf. The air ports and hatches being carefully caulked in, charcoal fires were lit along the berth deck and in the holds, on platforms of sand. The carbonic acid gas formed, being heavier than the air, sinks and the rats are driven up from below. Tubs of water were placed along the deck, and as the gas makes the rats thirsty they are found around these tubs. The officers and the crew bivouacked on the island for two days and nights. We then returned to the ship and removed the hatches. I am afraid to tell how many dead rats we took from the berth deck and store rooms; but we were not troubled with them again during the cruise, nor did any seem to have died in the hold of the ship.

From the Tortugas we went to Pensacola where we found the frigate *Columbia*, bearing the flag of Commodore John T. Newton.[3] Commodore Newton, though brave and intrepid, met with almost as much ill fortune at sea as Admiral Byron who was nicknamed by his sailors "Foul-weather Jack." He was a lieutenant on board the *Hornet* when she took the *Penguin* in 1815, and a sword presented to him for his gallantry on this occasion bore the inscription, *"Fortune favors the brave."* It did not apply in his case, however. He was unfortunate enough to once lose an officer and boat's crew off Havana; he commanded the old steamer *Fulton* which blew up at the New York Navy Yard by the explosion of her magazine; in 1852 he was ordered to command the steamer *Missouri*, a sister ship to the *Mississippi*; in her he went to Washington—the ship got ashore in the Potomac, and a lieutenant and some men were drowned in carrying out an anchor in the launch; finally the *Missouri* was burned at Gibraltar. The commodore was a remarkably handsome man, of tall, elegant figure and graceful carriage. He was extremely courteous to his officers.

At this time (March, 1853,) the Nicaragua route between New York and San Francisco was doing a good business; the trip between the two places was sometimes made in nineteen days, which was shorter than *via* Panama. The steamer from New York went to Greytown (San Juan di Nicaragua) and there the passengers were put on board light-draft, stern-wheel steamboats, which went up the San Juan river to Lake Nicaragua. Here, at a village called Fort San Carlos, they were transferred to commodious side-wheel steamboats in which they crossed the lake to Virgin Bay, and from Virgin Bay they crossed in a conveyance of some kind to San Juan del Sur, a distance of ten miles, and went on board the ocean steamer for San Francisco.

---

[3]The *Columbia* was a 44-gun frigate launched in 1836. She was burned by Federal forces during the evacuation of Norfolk in April 1861.

Greytown on the Mosquito coast claimed to be under the protection of England, though this was a matter of dispute. The whole Mosquito coast had been under the protection of the British for many years; but in 1850 the jealousy of the United States having long existed on this subject, the two governments covenanted "not to occupy, or fortify, or colonize, or assume or exercise any dominion over any part of Central America." The matter was finally settled in 1857 by Nicaragua taking possession of it.

The town at the time of our visit in the spring of 1853 was inhabited by a lawless set of desperadoes, of all nations, who had organized some kind of a city government. The mayor was said to have been an escaped convict from Sing Sing, and I believe it was so, for the others were evidently tarred with the same brush. They resembled the old buccaneers in everything save courage.

These people made a living by preying upon the passengers passing to and from California, of whom large numbers were detained at Greytown a day or two at a time on their passage: more by design than by accident. Nearly every house in town was a hotel. The harbor here is formed by an island at the mouth of the river lying opposite Greytown; on this island the steamship company had its store-houses, and as long as the passengers were detained occasionally and sent ashore in the town to pass a night or two everything went smoothly; but finally the company decided to build a hotel on the island to keep the passengers on *their* side of the river during the transit and to prohibit their landing at Greytown at all; to do all the "skinning" itself in fact. This was more than the Greytowners could stand and they declared war to the knife. Getting wind of this state of affairs the *Cyane* went there to keep the peace. We arrived the very night the island was to be stormed and sacked, and landed a force to protect it. The Greytown gentlemen decided to postpone the attack until our departure. We kept our men on the island for a few days and the captain then issued a proclamation which he had posted in Greytown forbidding the inhabitants going there without first obtaining permission from the *Cyane*. He was soundly abused by them for this, but bore it philosophically, especially as the proclamation was obeyed. We remained here seventy mortal days, the dreariest time I ever passed in any foreign port, and that is saying a good deal. Our only excitement was caused by the arrival of the steamers from New York and New Orleans which made fortnightly trips and brought us our mails, and the arrival of the steamers from Lake Nicaragua with the San Francisco passengers.

I noticed a difference in the deportment of the outgoing and incoming passengers; those going out were full of fun and frolic, while those returning were more quiet, I suppose because they had either lost all hope or had made small fortunes which they carried about their persons and were careful not to exhibit. In company with some of our officers I made a trip up the river as far as Castillo in one of the company's boats. Castillo, so called from an old Spanish fort built here to command the river, is about 15 miles from the lake. It was once taken by the English under Lord Nelson (then a post captain) and he lost a large number of men by fever.[4] It is situated on a high hill overlooking a bend in the river and presents a most romantic appearance—all *ruins* do. In traveling in these countries one is surprised to see so many solidly built fortifications. The old saying is: "The Spanish build forts, the French take them, and the English hold them." We remained in Castillo a week and then went down the river in a crowded boat with the California passengers which we had not bargained for— there was no distinction made between cabin and steerage passengers, and as the latter made a practice of *shooting across the deck* at alligators on the banks, promenading was unhealthy—so we had to sit huddled together for three days. The man next me had the small-pox.

To add to our discomfort on board the *Cyane* we would occasionally find *snakes*; they would come floating down the river on

[4]In February of 1780 Nelson, then a 20-year-old captain in his first command, was ordered to escort 500 British soldiers to the isthmus. Characteristically he exceeded those orders by landing personally with the troops and participating in the siege.

drift wood, &c., and run up our cables. This was a thing I never could become used to, though they were said to be harmless. Our amusements consisted in fishing, and shooting alligators, or I should say of shooting *at* alligators—for I never saw one killed. We caught one in our seine once, and wild work he made of it. The men towed him off to the ship, and we hoisted him on board with the yard-tackle. The seine was about ruined; *but we got the alligator*! I here first eat the *Iguana*, cooked by a Mosquito Indian, and found it very palatable.

At last the time came when we were getting out of provisions, so we sailed for Pensacola. Here we found orders to sail for Portsmouth, N. H., there to join a flying squadron under Commodore W. B. Shubrick. We met the squadron at Portsmouth, having touched at Norfolk on our way up. The object of this flying squadron, which consisted of four vessels, was to protect the fisheries.

The vessels now separated, each to visit different ports. We went first to Eastport, Maine, and thence to St. Johns, N. B. The tide rises and falls from twenty to twenty-five feet at these places and it is necessary to bear this in mind in selecting an anchorage. St. Johns, as seen from a vessel, presents at high water quite a different appearance from what it does at low water. We sailed from this place with a southwesterly wind, and proceeded to beat out of the Bay of Fundy. The night following was one of the most disagreeable I have ever passed at sea. I was navigating the ship again, and we were trying to make the light on Seal island. It was blowing and raining: thick as mud; the tide running four or five miles an hour, and no soundings to be had. Take it all in all it was a most trying night. The Seal islands are marked by the wrecks of many vessels, and no wonder—the frequent fogs alone are enough to account for it, to say nothing of the tides and the absence of soundings. We made the light at 4 A. M. and shortly after, I shaped a course for Cape Sable and turned in. I had a good joke on the captain a little later in the day. We were running along the land, about seven miles off, and steering due south. While I was breakfasting, the captain (who was a very bold navigator but much

given to "chaffing") looked down the hatchway and inquired why I
kept so far from the land, and "what I was afraid of?" I replied that
I would explain, and going to his cabin I pointed out to him on the
chart a rock marked with twelve feet water on it, about four miles
off the land and directly in our track. It was marked "doubtful,"
and was not on all the charts, but as I said, the sea was so smooth it
would not break on it and there would be nothing to indicate it;
that it *might* be there, and I thought it better to "guard against all
precautions," to use a slang of his own. The captain laughed at it,
said there was no rock there, and compared me to old Bainbridge
who "went forty miles out of his way to avoid a fly-speck," etc.,
etc., and directed me to haul the ship in to within three or four
miles of the land. This I did, and soon forgot all about the matter.
At meridian I observed the latitude and reported the result to the
captain as usual, and then went to my room to compute the
longitude. I had hardly reached it when the orderly came down and
said the captain wanted me immediately. I hurried up to the cabin
and found Captain Hollins plotting our position, from the latitude
and estimated distance from the land, and it put us *right on top of
the rock!*

He had consulted some other charts which had the rock marked
down, and I found him somewhat disturbed. We were under
starboard studding-sails and royals, and not knowing what better
to do—for he knew we would strike the rock before seeing it if it
were really there he took in all sail and hove the ship to. This
extraordinary proceeding on a fine, clear day, with a fair wind, no
doubt caused "Jack" much surprise: but we gave no explanation,
and "Jack" is not much given to asking one. About 2 o'clock we
filled away and made all sail without seeing any signs of the rock;
whether it exists or not I do not know, but it was a long time before
the captain said "rocks" or "fly-specks" to me again.

Captain Hollins was one of the most agreeable men I have ever
sailed with; a prime seaman, he did not bother himself about
trifles; but in a time of danger all under his command looked up to
him and depended upon him. As an example of his readiness I may
mention one incident, although it occurred after I had left the

ship. The *Cyane* was running along the coast of New Jersey, in thick weather, and getting too close in struck on one of the dangerous shoals off Little Egg harbor. Captain H. sprang up on deck, clewed up everything, and let go the anchor. The weather clearing up just at this time several boats were seen making for the ship (which was then afloat and riding to her anchor) in great haste. As the first boat got alongside a man sprung up the ship's side and called out in an excited manner: "I'll wreck this ship; I claim her," etc., etc. Captain H. in a quiet manner asked him what he meant. "Why, I thought you were on shore and wanted assistance," said the man. "Oh no," said Hollins-—"I've only come in to take a look at the harbor." After some conversation of the same kind the man agreed to pilot the *Cyane* out through the shoals for the sum of ten dollars!

The captain used to relate a conversation he once had with a Dutch captain who took part in the bombardment of Algiers under Lord Exmouth in 1816. Three Dutch frigates which happened to be lying at Gibraltar when the English squadron arrived asked for and obtained permission to join it in the proposed expedition and they rendered good service. The Dutchman was complaining to Captain Hollins that the English papers did not give them proper credit for their action, &c., &c. "But," said Captain H., "the *Dutch* papers mentioned it, did they not?" "Oh yes!" was the reply, "de *Dutch* papers mentioned it, but who de debble ever reads de *Dutch* papers?"

It used to be said when I was a midshipman that one of our vessels once killed a man on board a Dutch frigate while firing a salute—the gunner had neglected to draw the shot from one of the guns. The American captain was much mortified and distressed at the occurrence and sent a lieutenant on board to express his regrets. The lieutenant found the Dutch captain coolly smoking his pipe and made the proper explanations, &c. "Oh!" said the captain: "There are plenty more Dutchmen in Holland!"

We rounded Cape Sable, and passing by Halifax went through the Straits of Canso into the Gulf of St. Lawrence. We saw here some of the grandest scenery I have ever beheld; Cape Breton island

on one side and Nova Scotia on the other. I really had no expectation of it as I had never seen it mentioned. It only proves, what is
often said, that Americans need not leave their own continent for
magnificent scenery. I should like to describe the appearance of
these straits as we entered them in the *Cyane* in September, 1853. I
have the *idea*, but cannot find words to express it. I am, in point of
fact, somewhat in the condition of Mr. Toots' tailor "who had a
pair of pantaloons in his mind, but *couldn't* cut them out."[5] Not the
first author who has found himself in the same predicament.

Our orders were to "sight" the Magdalen islands, and then sail
around Cape Breton island on our way home. We had a fair wind
and shaped a course directly for these islands which we expected to
see about 11 P. M. I had read in the sailing directions that the
"light" was very carelessly kept and sometimes not lighted at all,
and as the night was very dark I could not help feeling uneasy and I
several times remarked to the captain that perhaps he had better
heave to until daylight. But he was anxious to get home and did
not wish to lose any time; he told me that all he wanted was to
"make the light," and he would then bear away for Cape North. I
went forward and told the boatswain, whom I found on the
forecastle this, and remarked that all we wanted was to make the
light which we should do at 11 o'clock. The boatswain said he
would keep a lookout himself, and that *he had no doubt but that we
would make the light very soon!* Singular to say just as the bell struck
for 11 the lookout forward reported a light *right ahead!* "Hard
aport" said the captain, and directing me to set the course he went
below and turned in, and I shortly after followed his example. We
returned to Portsmouth where we found the commodore and
reported the particulars of our cruise. We then went to Philadelphia where I was detached and ordered to the Naval Academy,
Annapolis, as an Assistant Professor of Mathematics.

The *Cyane* returned to Greytown in 1854 and bombarded it. I
have really forgotten on what grounds Captain Hollins did this;
but it was a nest of pirates, and the pity is he did not destroy the

---

[5]A reference to a character in Charles Dickens's *Dombey and Son* (1848).

inhabitants and spare the houses. We often hear by the way of a man-of-war knocking towns down, blowing them to pieces, &c.; but it is easier said than done, and this I have always held to. Greytown was built entirely of wood, yet it stood a fire of shot and shell for four or five hours, and then a landing party had to be sent to *set it on fire!*[6]

In the years 1853–4 great interest was felt in the explorations of the Isthmus of Darien, the object being to find a suitable place for a canal between the two oceans. Not that the idea of a canal was a new one by any means, for the Emperor Charles V sent a peremptory order to his governors on the isthmus to "cut a canal," and this was not many years after the discovery of the Pacific ocean or South sea as it was then called. It had long been thought that the Darien Indians knew of a short route across the isthmus if they could be gotten to reveal it. But these Indians were known to be jealous of strangers and very warlike in their disposition. They remain unconquered to the present day. Dampier who knew them well, having crossed the isthmus from the Gulf of San Miguel in 1681, says in speaking of a tribe living on the Atrato river: "They are very dreadful to the Spaniards and will not have any commerce with them nor with any white people. They use tubes about eight feet long out of which they blow poisoned darts."[7]

Several travelers about this time (1853) professed to have crossed the isthmus in a few days time, and to have met with no very high elevations. These stories are now known to be false. In reading the accounts of Davis, Ringrose, Wafer, Dampier and others—all buccaneers, and who were frequently crossing in the latter part of the 17th century—I observe that the journey occupied from twelve to twenty days. The Indians did not know of a shorter route then or they would have shown it, because they were friendly to the buccaneers who they knew were crossing to the

[6]The *Cyane* bombarded and virtually destroyed Greytown on 13 July 1854 in retaliation for the temporary detention of the American minister to Nicaragua.

[7]William Dampier (1652–1715) was the author of *A New Voyage Round the World* published in London in 1697. The quotation, somewhat paraphrased by Parker, appears on page 41.

South sea to make war upon the Spaniards whom they held in deadly enmity. Lieutenant Isaac G. Strain of the navy got permission to organize a party and attempt to cross. The *Cyane* took him and his companions to Caledonia Bay in January, 1854. Captain Hollins called a council of the Indians in his cabin and finally they consented to allow the party to cross and to furnish guides. We all know the fate of this expedition. They started with 12 officers and 13 men on the 20th of January with ten days provisions—their guides left them the second day after starting and they wandered helplessly in the woods until the men commenced to fall down and die of hunger. They were searching for the Savanna river to lead them into the Gulf of San Miguel and they struck the Chuquinaque which leads there by a much longer route. February 13th, Strain seeing that he would lose his entire party if help was not obtained took two of his strongest men and pushed on ahead leaving the others to follow under Passed Midshipman W. T. Truxtun (the present Commodore Truxtun). Strain succeeded in getting to the Gulf of San Miguel on the 9th of March, and there fortunately found the English man-of-war *Virago*. A boat expedition was immediately fitted out and sent up the river with the necessary supplies. It found the party, March 23d, on the banks, in a half starved condition. It arrived just in time. Had it not been for the indomitable courage and perseverance of Truxtun and Jack Maury (an assistant engineer in the navy) the whole party would have died of starvation. Messrs. Polanco and Castilla, the Columbian commissioners, and six men perished. The survivors were taken to Panama, and finally returned to the United States in the *Cyane*, sailing from Panama April 25th.[8]

---

[8]Lieutenant Isaac Strain participated in two expeditions to the Isthmus of Darien. The first, in 1843–44, collapsed in part because of Strain's own inexperience. The second, ten years later, was an international consortium in which Strain led the American contingent. His party wandered through the wilderness for three months and was given up for dead before reappearing tattered and emaciated. This march was the subject of a three-part series of articles by J. T. Headley that appeared in *Harper's Magazine* in 1855. *See* Vincent Ponko, *Ships, Seas, and Scientists* (1974), pp. 160–76.

The mistake made by Strain was in taking *sailors* for a land exploration; he might as well have taken a party of children. These men, with arms in their hands, were starving in a country abounding in game! Had he taken a few western hunters the fate of the expedition would have been different. The history (so called) of this expedition was written by Headley, and published in *Harper's Magazine*. It is much to be regretted that Commodore Truxtun, almost the only survivor, cannot be prevailed upon to write out a full account of it.

In 1858 I met in the Pacific a Lieutenant Moore of the British Navy who gave me an interesting account of *his* experience on the Isthmus. He set out with Captain Prevost and a number of men to cross from the Pacific to the Atlantic side. They went up to the head of the Gulf of San Miguel (I think) in boats and there, hiding a portion of their provisions, they left four men to guard the boats, and started for the interior. They met with such difficulties that they made but slow progress, and finally had to return. When they got back to the boats they found the four men lying dead, shot by the Indians with poisoned arrows. The rest of the party got back safely to their ship. These Indians told Captain Prevost afterward they would not have killed these men had they known they were English. They thought they were Spaniards, for whom they have an undying hatred. It is curious to note how this feeling has been handed down among them by tradition. They still remember that the English crossed the Isthmus in the early days to fight the Spaniards, who at the time held their ancestors in the most cruel servitude wherever they could lay hands upon them.

The same friendship for the English exists at this day among the Mosquito Indians, the foundation of which was laid by these same buccaneers. Dampier says of them: "They are tall, well made, raw-boned, lusty, strong and nimble of foot, long visaged, lank black hair, look stern, hard favored, and of a dark copper-color complexion. They are but a small nation, and not one hundred men of them in number, inhabiting on the main near Cape Gratias à Dios. They are very ingenious at throwing the lance, fishgig, and harpoon. They have extraordinary good eyes, and will descry a sail at sea farther, and see anything better than we. Their chief employment in their own country is to strike fish and turtle. For this they are esteemed and coveted by all privateers; for one or two of them in a ship will maintain a hundred men; and it is very rare to find privateers destitute of one or more of them when the commander or most of the men are English. But they do not love the French, and the Spanish they hate mortally.''[9]

[9]Dampier, pp. 7–9.

CHAPTER XVI

Report for duty at the Naval Academy—ordered to the *Merri-mac*—auxiliary steam power—sail from Boston—arrival at Rio—the *Ganges* 74—double Cape Horn and arrive at Talca-huana—brilliant performance at Valparaiso—Chincha Islands—the Chinese coolie and the Peruvian cholo—first inhabitants of North America—Callao—Lima—the Spanish American repub-lics and population—Payta—the buccaneers—Alexander Sel-kirk—Juan Fernandez—Dampier—circumnavigators—Magel-lan—Drake—the early Spanish voyagers

I reported for duty at the Naval Academy in October, 1853, and remained there until June, 1857. For the first two years I was an instructor in mathematics, and afterwards, in navigation and astronomy. In the summer of 1855 I made a cruise in the practice ship *Preble*[1] with the midshipmen, as instructor in navigation and

[1]The *Preble* was a 16-gun sloop built in 1839 and subsequently burned at Pensacola in April 1863. She was 117′7″ in length and 33′10″ across the beam with a displacement of 566 tons.

watch officer; we visited Eastport, Portland, Cape Cod and Boston. I found the Academy much improved since my examination; the curriculum more expansive; the grounds greatly enlarged; and many new buildings erected. In September, 1855, I received my commission of lieutenant; having served just fourteen years for it. In the fall of 1857 I was ordered to the screw frigate *Merrimac*, fitting out at Boston for the Pacific. She bore the flag of Commodore J. C. Long, and was commanded by Commander [Robert B.] Hitchcock. The *Merrimac* was one of a class of steam frigates just built. She was over 3,000 tons, and carried a battery of 9 inch Dahlgren guns on her main deck; and on the spar deck two 11 inch Dahlgren guns as bow and stern chasers, and sixty-four pounder shell guns. She and her sister ships were much the largest frigates of their time. She was a fine-looking ship, and her main deck with its powerful battery was a picture for a sailor to behold; but I cannot say much for either her sailing or steaming qualities. She was very long (for those days) and correspondingly sluggish in her movements. She *could* "tack," however, and in that had the advantage of some of the men-of-war of the present day; but I believe that with a smart breeze an old time line-of-battle ship would have worked round her in spite of her "auxiliary" steam power. Before I joined her she had made a six months trial cruise and her officers gave fabulous accounts of her speed under sail. I never discovered it myself though I was in her over two years. I recollect we made the passage from Panama to Callao in company with the *Decatur*, and she beat us in all the weather we experienced on the trip, yet she was the ship that Joe Watkins said, one morning got under the shade of a large tree while sailing along the coast of Africa, *and did not get out of it though she had a fair wind all day!*[2]

I cannot tell how the truth may be;
I say the tale as 'twas said to me.

[2]The *Decatur*, a sister ship of the *Preble* (see footnote 1), was launched in 1839 and sold after the war in 1865.

As for her speed under steam, 7 knots was the maximum when we left Boston; at the end of the cruise 5 knots was all she could keep up for 24 hours. The fact is the "auxiliary" steam power was an absurdity; the ships would neither steam nor sail. It has always seemed to me that men-of-war should be provided with engines and boilers calculated to give them very great speed; they need not use steam in cruising unless in a case of emergency, and the exercise of a ship under sail would be of inconceivable benefit to the younger officers. While the "naval officer" is really a soldier, that is a *military* man, and must not be confounded with the merchant captain who simply follows a mercantile pursuit, yet it must be borne in mind that it is just as essential that he should know how to manage a ship as it is that a dragoon should know how to ride; therefore too much attention cannot be paid to this important point in the education of the young officers of the navy.

The *Merrimac* had a full complement of officers and men and we mustered about six hundred souls. On the 17th of October we sailed from Boston on what was to prove a dull uninteresting cruise. We had on board the Hon. R. Kidder Meade who had just been appointed Minister to Brazil. We had fine weather on our way out, and arrived at Rio Janeiro in December. Here we found the English 74, *Ganges*, Admiral Baynes, on her way to the Pacific. We frequently fell in with her afterwards and knew her officers well. Burgoyne, who was lost with most of his crew in the iron clad ship *Captain* in 1870 was her commander. He was a bright, pleasant fellow, and I remember was very popular with his messmates though he had been promoted (for his services in the Crimea) over most of their heads.

We sailed from Rio towards the latter part of December for the Pacific ocean. We had intended going through the Straits of Magellan, but for some reason the idea was abandoned when we got near the entrance; so passing through the Straits of Le Maire we rounded the much dreaded Cape Horn without encountering any bad weather, and arrived safely at Talcahuana, Chili, early in February, 1858. We remained here a couple of weeks to refit and paint ship. It is the seaport of the more important town of

Concepcion, situated a few miles inland, and is a large and safe harbor. We gave our men liberty here—a watch at a time. They got into a row with the native police, or *vigilantes*, and many came off with cracked skulls.

We sailed from Talcahuana for Valparaiso, where news had been received of our being on the coast, and where our arrival was anxiously looked for. They had heard of the splendid new steam frigate *Merrimac*, and expected to see us dash into the port at the rate of twenty miles an hour; consequently when we were signalled every man, woman and child made haste to arrive at a point where they could view this magnificent spectacle. They feared the ship would arrive before they could reach the points selected. It is to be hoped they carried their dinners with them. We "slowed down" to about four knots an hour as soon as we made the land, and towards sunset *crept in*, and after making a "Judy Fitzsimmons" of ourselves, anchored so far out that if it had been at all hazy our arrival would not have been known in town.

This was our usual method of taking up an anchorage: but I have seen the *Ganges*, a ship of reasonable length and beam, run a half-mile inside of us under all sail and make a "flying moor," somewhat after the manner of the "ancients."

From Valparaiso we sailed for the Chincha islands. These islands lie a few miles off Pisco on the Peruvian coast, about 120 miles southeast of Callao. The custom house is at Pisco and all vessels going to the islands for guano enter and clear there.

The use of guano was known to the ancient Peruvians. [Friedrich H. A.] Humboldt was one of the first by whom it was brought into notice in Europe, and its importation into England commenced about 1839. At the time of our visit there were forty or fifty American vessels here—all large, fine ships and all of which we boarded.

Nothing can be more dismal than the appearance of these islands, and nothing more horrible than living on them. Not a green thing to be seen—nothing but guano; the men live in it; they smell it, breathe it, and I suppose taste it in their food. The laborers were Chinese coolies, in charge of a few Peruvian soldiers.

I was told that they would become so desperate that gangs of them would commit suicide together by joining hands and leaping from the cliffs into the sea. I could well believe it after a brief visit to the islands; and when a Chinaman once makes up his mind to take his life nothing will stop him. It is well known that when the Panama railroad was being built the Chinese would drown themselves *in two feet of water* by sticking their heads in the mud and keeping them there until life was extinct.

The coolies in Chili and Peru are (or at least were at this time) little better than slaves. They are brought over from China, where they are bought or kidnapped, and bound for a term of years. Very few live to return to their own country. I have been on board the Spanish vessels engaged in the coolie trade, and with their armed officers, iron gratings over the hatchways, etc., they are *fac-similes* of the African slavers.

By the way, I frequently heard while on the coast that the first Chinese taken to Peru could communicate with the native Indian or *Cholo*. I do not know if this be true, but I heard it from several sources. That a point of so much importance should not excite much attention will not surprise those who know the very little interest these South Americans attach to anything relative to the former history of their country. Now I have very little doubt that North America was peopled by tribes coming from Asia by the way of Behring's Straits. They could have crossed in their canoes without trouble, and the climate probably modified the type of the North American Indian. More than one traveler has noticed the similarity of the Indians on different sides of the Straits; their customs, some of which are very peculiar, are the same. There is absolutely no reason for looking any further than this for the actual peopling of the continent.

But the Aztecs of Mexico, and the Children of the Sun in Peru, who were they? Chinese or Japanese in all probability. Chinese and Japanese junks have been wrecked and cast away on the coast of Oregon, we know; they are brought over by the *Kuro Siwo*, or Japan current, and a vessel could be drifted down the coast towards Mexico by the coast current. Supposing such to have been the case would it not be just like a Chinaman, with his intelligence and cunning, to take advantage of an ignorant tribe and announce himself as a superior being? This is my theory in regard to the matter: and it need not interfere with the theory that Yucatan was a Phœnician colony, as its monuments, etc., would seem to indicate. The equatorial current would carry a vessel there fast enough from the Canary Islands, which were known to the ancients certainly as far back as 140 B. C. Columbus found the mast or rudder of an European vessel at one of the West India islands!

When the *Merrimac* got to Callao, we found a revolution in progress. The Peruvians had two fine screw frigates, the *Apurimac* and the *Amazonia*, and the party holding these commanded the coast. At this time Montero commanded the *Apurimac* and we heard much of him. The rumor was that he would attack Callao, so we were on the look-out for him. One fine morning I was surprised to see the frigate steaming quietly into port. Montero landed and went to Lima. There was no excitement—*Cosa de España*, I suppose. He gave up the ship, and no doubt got his reward. I expect it is the same Montero who now claims to be the President of Peru. He was considered an enterprising officer, and would have been a good one in a navy under proper discipline.[3]

Lima, the City of the Kings, has been often described. I believe the name is a corruption of the Peruvian word *Rimac*, a river. It was founded by Pizarro, in 1535, who gave it the name of *Ciudad de los Reyes*. It has frequently suffered from earthquakes; in that of 1746 not more than twenty houses out of three thousand were left standing, and of twenty-three ships in the harbor of Callao nineteen were sunk. The town of Callao was utterly destroyed by a tidal wave during this earthquake; of four thousand inhabitants but two hundred escaped. The town was rebuilt farther back from the old

---

[3]Lizardo Montero was vice president of Peru (1880–81) in the García Calderón administration. He was one of many caudillos who claimed power during this volatile era.

site. Vessels now anchor where the first city stood. Lima is 700 feet above the sea and is to be seen from Callao, from which it is distant six or eight miles. A railroad connects the two cities. The city of Lima is beautifully laid out, and small streams of water, conducted from the river Rimac, contribute to its cleanliness. It has many fine public buildings, and on the plaza are situated the magnificent cathedral, the government house (once the vice-regal palace, where Pizarro was assassinated), and the hall of independence. The convent of the Franciscans, the mint, the palace of the inquisition, and the cabildo are all worthy of notice. Under the cathedral I saw the skeleton of Pizarro, at least the priest said it was Pizarro; and Mr. Clay, our minister, who had been a long time in the country said he saw no reason to doubt it. The bones of the hands and feet had been carried off by visitors, and I am afraid that one of our party imitated this abominable example. There is much of interest to be seen in Lima, and I spent many hours in endeavoring to identify the places mentioned by Prescott and other writers, such as the stream the conspirators had to cross on their way to assassinate Pizarro, his palace, etc.

A friend told me he one day met a well-dressed man on the plaza and inquired of him if he could tell him where the palace of Pizarro formerly stood. "What Pizarro?" said the gentleman. "Why, the *great* Pizarro, the grand conqueror," replied my friend. "I do not know him," said the man, and, bowing politely, he walked off. In my visits to different parts of Central and South America and Mexico I have observed much ignorance exhibited by the inhabitants of the early history of their country. They not only do not know, but they seem to take no interest in learning anything about it. One can readily account for this. It is caused by the frequent revolutions. The schools are broken up; and the people, children included, are kept in a constant state of excitement. Why, what must be the condition of affairs in Peru at the present time?[4]

<hr>

[4]At the time Parker wrote, Peru was engaged in fighting the War of the Pacific and a Chilean army was advancing on Lima.

The Chilians are better informed than most of these people. They are much better men; not on account of the climate, as some suppose, but because they have not intermarried to so great an extent with the negro and Indian. It is this which causes the degeneration of the white man. We hear a great deal of the regeneration of Mexico. It is all humbug; it is an absurdity if applied to the present inhabitants, because *it isn't in them!* What *is* a Mexican? Is he a Spaniard, or an Indian, or does the fact of a man's being born in Mexico, be he white, red or black, make him a Mexican? The best man in Mexico is the man of pure Spanish descent (very hard to find); the next best man is the pure Indian, and the next the pure negro. The mixed race is the worst and unfortunately by far the most numerous; and this applies to every country on the continent south of the United States. The only regeneration of Mexico will be by throwing open the doors and introducing some millions of pure-blooded white men.

None of the Spanish American Republics, save perhaps Chili, are in as prosperous a condition as they were under the old Spanish rule. They want a strong government to keep them in order. Brazil is kept quiet by it; and Brazil has the most detestable population of all these countries.

We sailed from Callao in March and first stopped at Payta, some 480 miles up the coast. Payta is the site of an old Peruvian village, and I think Pizarro landed here in 1526 on his way to Cuzco. It is the seaport of the town of Piura, which lies in the midst of a fertile country; but Payta not only has no vegetation, but there is absolutely no fresh water within ten miles of it. All the water is brought from a river at that distance; and the road to it is strewed with the bones of dead donkeys: Sam Weller, to the contrary, notwithstanding.[5] The dogs here have a hard time of it; they are forced to go to the river to drink, and by the time they get back home are so thirsty they have immediately to start back again; so

---

[5]Sam Weller was "boots," the servant to Mr. Pickwick in Charles Dickens's *Pickwick Papers* (1837).

that their lives are spent in travelling. I believe the English Steam Navigation Company have works here now and distil water for the inhabitants as well as for their steamers. Payta has a fine harbor and a good climate. It was taken and burned by Lord Anson in 1742, and before his time was several times sacked by the buccaneers.

Speaking of the buccaneers, I know of no more interesting reading than is to be found in the pages of Dampier, Ringrose, Wafer, Woods Rogers and others giving an account of their exploits on the western coast of North and South America in the latter part of the seventeenth century and the beginning of the next. Alexander Selkirk was a buccaneer who sailed with Captain Stradling in the Cinque Ports in 1703. Quarrelling with his captain he requested to be put on shore at the island of Juan Fernandez, which lies about 375 miles due west of Valparaiso. He was landed in 1705 and remained solitary and alone until 1709, when he was taken off by Woods Rogers. He must have been a good hater; for it is said that when Captain Rogers sent a boat for him the first question he asked was whether Stradling was on board, for if he was he would remain on the island. Selkirk's adventure gave De Foe the idea of his romance of Robinson Crusoe, published in 1719, and Juan Fernandez is generally known as Crusoe's island; but in point of fact De Foe places his hero on one of the Windward or Carib islands; for his ship sailed from Brazil for the coast of Africa and was blown off her course by contrary winds. *N'importe*.

Dampier tells of a Mosquito Indian who passed three years alone on the island twenty years before Selkirk's time. He says: "March 22, 1684, we came in sight of Juan Fernandez and presently got out our canoe and went ashore to seek for a Mosquito Indian, whom we left here when chased hence by three Spanish ships in 1681, a little before we went to Arica. This Indian lived here alone above three years and although he was several times sought after by the Spaniards, who knew he was left on the island, yet they could never find him."[6] After describing the manner in which this Indian

[6]Dampier, *op.cit.*, p. 84.

contrived to live he says: "He saw our ship and came to the sea side to congratulate our safe arrival. And when we landed, a Mosquito Indian named Robin first leaped on shore and running to his brother Mosquitoman threw himself flat on his face at his feet, who helping him up and embracing him fell flat with his face on the ground at Robin's feet, and was by him taken up also. We stood with pleasure to behold the surprise, tenderness and solemnity of this interview which was exceedingly affectionate on both sides."[7]

Juan Fernandez was discovered in 1567, and is named for its discoverer. It is at present a penal settlement belonging to Chili. It has no harbor. Dana in his *Two Years Before the Mast* gives a good description of it.[8] Of all the buccaneers this man Dampier was the most remarkable. He wrote a full account of his voyages, and his book not only abounds in nautical information, but is full of philosophical remarks. Nothing seemed to escape him, and his chapters on winds and currents may be read to advantage at the present day. He was born in Somersetshire, England, in 1652; served in the Dutch war in 1673; was an overseer of a plantation in Jamaica; and in 1675 was a logwood cutter in Campeachy. He gives an excellent description of the country and his trade. We then hear of him in Virginia, from whence he sailed to the coast of Africa, and thence to the South sea—from the South sea he went overland to the Caribbean sea, and home to England. He sailed again for the South sea, and gives a most interesting account of his operations on the west coast from Chiloe island, Chili, to Acapulco in Mexico. He then crossed the Pacific ocean to Nicobar and New Holland where he made valuable discoveries, and after remaining some time in the East Indies he returned to England, having been absent on his last voyage more than eight years.

The first circumnavigator of the globe was Magalhaens or Magellan as he is generally called, a Portuguese in the service of

[7]Ibid., p. 86.

[8]The description of Juan Fernandez appears in chapter seven of Richard Henry Dana's *Two Years Before the Mast* (1840).

Spain. He sailed in 1519 and discovered the straits which bear his name. He sailed with a squadron of five ships, but only one succeeded in making the voyage. An account of the voyage was written by the Chevalier Pigafetta, an Italian, who accompanied Magellan as a volunteer.[9] It is in this voyage that the first mention is made of the log line. Pigafetta gives an amusing account of the origin of the name Patagonia. He says that the natives with whom they communicated had their feet bound up in hides which made them so awkward in their movements that the sailors called them *patagones* (clumsy-footed)—hence Patagonia. The island of *Tierra del Fuego* was named from the large number of fires observed on the land.

The straits of Magellan were used by all the first circumnavigators, for Cape Horn was not discovered by Le Maire until 1616, nearly a hundred years after Magellan. The Spaniards had a fort here, called Fort Famine, because the garrison perished for want. Magellan proceeded across the Pacific (which he so named from its smoothness) until he arrived at the Philippine islands. He remained there some time and taking sides with the natives in their wars was killed. His ship finally reached Spain under one of the subordinate officers by the way of the Cape of Good Hope, having been absent just three years and twenty-nine days. They had been long given up, and when they stated that they had "sailed round the world" were not believed. Upon examining the log-book it was found they were a day behind in their "reckoning," and this was to the scientific the best proof of their assertion, for as they sailed to the westward and had not corrected the "reckoning" by dropping a day at the 180th meridian (as is now the custom) they naturally were a day behind the time in Spain, or as sailors say had lost a day.

---

[9]Antonio Pigafetta, *Magellan's Voyage, A Narrative Account of the First Circumnavigation*. This story is not included in the most recent scholarly translation by R. A. Skelton (Yale University Press, 1969) who suggests that the name derives from *patacones* (in Spanish) or *patas de cao* (in Portuguese) meaning "dogs with large paws."

The first Englishman to sail round the world was Sir Francis Drake, in 1577–80, and to read the English accounts of him one would suppose he was really the first circumnavigator. The fact is the Spaniards sent many vessels to the Pacific ocean between Magellan's time and Drake's. One has only to read Navarrete's *Collection of Spanish Voyages* to be assured of this; and by the way, interesting as the books of Irving and Prescott are, they do not in my opinion compare with Navarrete's accounts of the early Spanish voyages to the South Sea and East Indies.[10]

Some time after Magellan sailed the Spanish government commenced to send out vessels to look for him; and even Cortez, who had just completed the conquest of Mexico, actually built vessels at Tehuantepec and sent them to the East Indies on the same errand.

The Portuguese it will be remembered were prosecuting their discoveries by the way of the Cape of Good Hope, which had been doubled by Vasco de Gama in 1497. Vasco de Gama went to Goa on the west coast of Hindostan; and as I have mentioned that Columbus found the rudder of a European ship in the West Indies, I will also mention that the natives of Goa told Vasco de Gama they had been visited by three ships similar to his before his arrival. Where did they come from and what became of them?

As the navigators of those days did not correct their "reckoning" at the 180th meridian, instances are known of islands in the East Indies where the people on the western end are a day ahead in their computation of those on the eastern end: the western end being discovered by the Portuguese sailing east, and the eastern end by the Spaniards sailing west.

---

[10]Martín Fernández de Navarrete (1765–1844) was the author of the *Colección de los Viajes y Descubrimientos que hicieron por Mar los Españoles desde fines del Siglo XV* (1825–1837). Washington Irving (1783–1859) used Navarrete's account to write two books: *History of the Life and Voyages of Christopher Columbus* (1828) and *The Voyages and Discoveries of the Companions of Columbus* (1831). William Hickling Prescott (1756–1859) wrote, among other works, the *History of the Reign of Ferdinand and Isabella* (1837).

I confess that in reading of the performances of the Spaniards in those early days I am filled with surprise. Cortez completed the conquest of Mexico in 1520, and a few years after we find him fitting out vessels to look for Magellan. The rapidity with which Cortez, Pizarro and their companions spread over the countries conquered by them is marvellous to read of. Alvarado, having conquered Guatemala, thinks nothing of going to Peru to join Pizarro. A few years after, we hear of his building ships and sailing for Navidad, in Mexico, to assist in suppressing an insurrection in Guadalajara. This is a long voyage for sailing ships at the present time.[11]

He was killed near Colima by his horse rolling over a precipice. As for traveling across the country for hundreds of miles these men thought nothing of it. There were no roads, and any one who has seen an Indian cutting his way with his *machete* wonders how an armed man could ever pass. Acosta says that soon after the conquest of Peru the Spaniards were constantly crossing the isthmus of Darien, and penetrating the country towards Bogota. He says that men in armor and on horseback crossed the mountains by paths which a naked Indian of the present day can hardly travel on foot.[12]

Whatever the old Boatswain may have said of iron men, the old Spaniards were iron if ever men were. But after all it was the search for *gold* that made them iron.

As Hood sings:[13]

Gold! gold! gold! gold!
Bright and yellow, hard and cold;
Molten, graven, hammered and rolled;
Heavy to get, and light to hold;
Hoarded, bartered, bought, and sold,

[11]Pedro de Alvarado was an early Spanish explorer and governor of Guatemala in 1534.

[12]José de Acosta (1539?–1600) was a Jesuit missionary and author who wrote *The Natural and Moral History of the Indies* (1590, English translation 1604).

[13]Thomas Hood (1799–1845) was an English poet and popular satirist.

Stolen, borrowed, squandered, doled:
Spurned by the young, but hugged by the old
To the very verge of the church-yard mould;
Price of many a crime untold:
Gold! gold! gold! gold!
Good or bad a thousand fold!
    How widely its agencies vary—

CHAPTER XVII

Cook's voyages and discoveries—Anson's voyage around the world—the mutiny of the *Bounty*—Panama—Indian names and their signification—Tumbez—Callao again—Lieutenant Denny, R.N.—the Sandwich Islands—Realejo—Nicaragua—Chinandegua—a voyage in a bungo—Panama again—Commodore J. B. Montgomery—Valparaiso—the *Levant*—the *Lancaster*—sail for home—Rio Janeiro—John Brown's raid—the frigate *Congress*—arrival at Norfolk

The first English circumnavigator was Drake; and he was followed by Cavendish, Cowley, Clipperton, Anson, Byron, Wallace, Carteret and Cook. The last was the most celebrated, and made three voyages. He made many important geographical discoveries; but of all his discoveries the most important was his establishing the fact that it was possible for a ship to make a long voyage without losing half her crew by the scurvy; such had been the case up to his time. He was killed by the natives of Owhyhee, Sandwich Islands, in 1779.[1]

But of all these early voyages, commend me to the history of Lord Anson's voyage, as related by the Chaplain of the *Centurion*. It is simply a romance from beginning to end. Anson left England September 18th, 1740, with eight vessels—the *Centurion*, *Severn*, *Gloucester*, *Wager*, *Pearl*, *Tryal*, and two store-ships,—the object of the expedition being to attack the Spanish vessels in the South Sea.

The vessels separated off Cape Horn, where they experienced frightful weather. Here the *Severn* and *Pearl* put back to England, and the *Wager* was wrecked on the coast of Patagonia, north of the Straits of Magellan. Byron, afterwards a commodore and a circum-navigator, was a midshipman on board, and wrote an account of the shipwreck and subsequent sufferings of the crew. His book, called *Byron's Narrative*, is a poem in itself.[2] The survivors were conducted by the Indians to Chili, and got back to England in 1745. The shipwreck and sufferings of Byron and his companions are commemorated by Campbell in his "Pleasures of Hope:"

And such thy strength-inspiring aid that bore
The hardy Byron to his native shore.
In horrid climes, whence Chiloe's tempests sweep
Tumultuous murmurs o'er the troubled deep,
'Twas his to mourn misfortune's rudest shock,
Scourged by the winds and cradled on the rock,
To wake each joyless morn, and search again
The famished haunts of solitary men,
Whose race, unyielding as their native storm,

---

[1]James Cook (1728–79) was an English naval officer and explorer who discovered Hawaii, or as Parker spells it Owhyhee, on his last voyage in 1779.
[2]During the War of Jenkins's Ear, English Admiral Baron George Anson (1697–1762) led a squadron of six ships around Cape Horn late in the season of 1740. The *Wager* was wrecked on the coast of Chile, and two others turned back. By 1742 Anson had only one vessel left, but with that vessel he crossed the Pacific and captured the Spanish treasure galleon in 1743 (see p. 206). Parker's reference is to John Byron *The Narrative of the Hon. John Byron* (1769).

Knows not a trace of Nature but the form;
Yet, at thy call, the hardy tar pursued,
Pale, but intrepid,—sad, but unsubdued,
Pierced the deep woods, and, hailing from afar
The moon's pale planet and the northern star;[3]
Paused at each dreary cry, unheard before,
Hyenas in the wild, and mermaids on the shore,
Till, led by thee o'er many a cliff sublime,
He found a warmer world, a milder clime,
A home to rest, a shelter to defend,
Peace and repose, a Briton and a friend![4]

The *Centurion* was three months trying to double Cape Horn, and finally succeeded in doing so, and made her way to Juan Fernandez with the loss of half her crew. The remainder were in so enfeebled a condition that it was with the utmost difficulty the vessel could be brought to an anchor. Though many had died from the effects of the unheard-of weather, yet the most fell by that fearful scourge of the early navigators, scurvy.

The commodore and most of his men were landed and buried up to their necks in the earth, this being the treatment for scurvy at that time. Indeed, I have known officers in my time who had experienced this treatment.

Bad as was the condition of the *Centurion* that of the *Gloucester* was worse, and when she made her appearance off Juan Fernandez men had to be sent to her to bring her in. The *Tryal* and one store-ship arrived in like condition. Having refitted his ships, Anson with his two frigates cruised along the coast of Peru. The *Tryal* was burned, and the store-ship sent back to England. He burned Payta, and then stood to the northward to Acapulco, in Mexico, with the intention to intercept the royal galleon, sailing between that port and the Philippine Islands.

---

[3]"Hailing from afar the northern star" in this southern latitude must be taken *cum grano salis*: it is a poetical license. [Author's note]
[4]See *The Poetical Works of Thomas Campbell*, W. A. Hill, ed. (1863), pp. 1–48.

The trade between Spain and the Philippines was at that time carried on by the way of Vera Cruz and Acapulco; the goods being shipped to Vera Cruz, and then sent overland to Acapulco. The Royal galleon sailed yearly, leaving Acapulco in April and arriving at Manilla in June, and leaving Manilla so as to arrive at Acapulco about Christmas—"never more than eight or ten days before or after," as old Dampier observes. The old Spanish books give very quaint descriptions of the galleons and their voyages, and their cargoes being immensely valuable great care was taken in selecting their commanders. The sailing directions for making the voyage to and fro were minutely drawn up and required to be strictly adhered to. In going to Manilla they had only to get into the "trades" and run them down to the Ladrone islands (where they stopped a few days to refresh), and thence to Manilla; but in returning it was far different, as it was necessary to stand to the northward to about the fortieth parallel in order to get the westerly winds. They then stood to the eastward until they made the coast of California which they ran down to Cape St. Lucas. Here they communicated with the shore to learn if any enemy were on the coast and so to Acapulco.

Dampier says that before reaching Acapulco they stopped off *Sallagua* to land the passengers for the city of Mexico; this I take to be what is now known as Navidad bay. This was before the days of chronometers which have only been in general use since the beginning of the present century; and the longitude was found by lunar observations. It was often two or more degrees in error; so that the instructions to the returning galleons required them to be very careful to notice the color of the water, appearance of the sea-weed, and even a particular kind of fish in approaching the coast of California. Cuts of these vessels show that they carried large jars of water suspended from their rigging to lengthen their supply. The route from Manilla to Acapulco was first followed by Urdaneta in 1654, and was called for many years after "Urdaneta's Passage."

Anson arrived off Acapulco and saw the galleon in the harbor; but she was moored close to the shore, and the entrance being defended by a strong fort (another of those grand works of the early Spaniards which I have often visited) did not think it prudent to attack her. From the chaplain's narrative it is easy to locate, as I have myself done, the exact spot where the galleon was moored. After blockading the port for some time he went up the coast to Point Tejupan to water ship; he then returned to Acapulco and finding the galleon would not come out he at last bore away with his two ships for China. To show the fearful ravages made by the scurvy among his men he was actually forced to burn the frigate *Gloucester* on the passage to get men enough to handle the *Centurion*!

The *Centurion* stopped at Tinian, one of the Ladrone islands, and here again landed most of her officers and men for treatment against the scurvy. Whilst here it was discovered that an attendant of one of the officers was a female. She *may* have been the heroine of the old sailor-song of Billee-i-Taylor which says:

Then she took a sword and pistols,
Took a pistol in each hand;
And she fell to shooting on Billee-i-Taylor
As he was walking along the strand.

Which the captain when he heard it,
Very much approv'd what she had done,
And straightway made her First Lieutenant
Of the gallant Thunder Bomb.

If Captain Luce has omitted this elegant production in his *Naval Songs* it is *à su disposicion.*[5]

The *Centurion* being left with but few men on board was blown to sea in a gale of wind. The party on shore waited anxiously for her return and she not making her appearance they commenced building a schooner, on which the commodore worked with his own

---

[5]"The Ballad of Billy Taylor" is included in Stephen B. Luce's *Naval Songs* (1902). It is a story of a woman who disguised herself as a man in order to be with her sailor lover. She subsequently discovered him to be unfaithful and shot him.

hands, to carry them to China. Fortunately the ship got back and they all embarked for Macao, where the ship arrived in 1743. The English flag was then hardly known in the East, and the authorities at Canton refused to furnish the ship with provisions, of which they stood in great need. When the Mandarins visited the ship, Anson to make a show had the marines drawn up on the quarter-deck; and so many of the guard had died that he supplied the deficiency by dressing some of his sailors in marines' uniform, much to their disgust no doubt. Upon the Mandarins refusing to furnish provisions, Anson told them he regretted their decision as his men *must* have meat; and if they could not obtain it in any other way they would seize the Chinese in their boats, and eat them! This brought them to terms and the supplies were forthcoming. It must be remembered that at this time the Portuguese had the trade with China, as the Dutch had with Japan.

After remaining a month Anson announced his intention to sail for England, *via* Batavia, and he actually took the mails on board. He sailed accordingly, and after getting out of sight of land he called up his crew and announced his intention to cruise off the Philippine islands and try to intercept the galleon from Acapulco. The men responded with three hearty cheers and the *Centurion* proceeded to cruise off Espiritu Santo in the hope of encountering her. To show how sanguine all hands were as to the result of an engagement it is recorded that the commodore having asked his steward why he did not have a certain turkey, or something of the sort, for dinner, he replied that he was keeping it to entertain the captain of the galleon when he dined with the commodore. The galleon at last made her appearance, and although superior to the *Centurion*, was captured, and with her the largest sum of prize money ever taken in a single bottom.

The *Centurion* having sold her prize (worth two million dollars) in Macao, sailed for England, where she arrived June 15, 1744, after an absence of three years and nine months. Prize money to the amount of five million dollars was divided among her crew. The freaks of her discharged sailors, the reckless scattering of money, etc., were long remembered in England, and have been preserved in the songs of Dibdin and others.

What romance exceeds in interest the story of the Mutiny of the Bounty? Lady Belcher has written a full and interesting account of it; but I believe I can add a few particulars not to be found in her book.[6] The brig *Bounty*, Lieutenant Commanding Bligh, sailed from England in December, 1787, for the Society Islands, the object of the voyage being to take a number of bread-fruit trees to the West India Islands. [This was afterwards done.] The vessel met with unusually rough weather off Cape Horn, and Captain Bligh finally determined to proceed by the way of the Cape of Good Hope, which he did, and arrived safely at Otaheite. Here he took on board the trees and sailed for the West Indies in April, 1789. Three weeks after sailing the crew mutinied under the officer next in command to Bligh—one Christian, a mate. Captain Bligh and eighteen men were put in an open boat, with a scant allowance of food and water, and set adrift. He made a most remarkable voyage. The *most* remarkable *boat* voyage probably ever made. He sailed from the Friendly Islands to the island of Timor, a distance of nearly 4000 miles, and arrived without the loss of a man. It was only by the utmost firmness in keeping his men on a proper allowance of food and water, and refusing to land on unknown and probably unfriendly islands that he accomplished this. From Timor he got back to England with his party. In the meantime the mutineers under Christian, twenty-five in number, returned in the *Bounty* to Otaheite, and here most of the men determined to remain, among them a young midshipman named Heywood. Christian, Midshipman Young and eight men took on board a number of Otaheitan men and women (four men and eleven women) and sailed away to the eastward. For some years nothing was heard of them.

---

[6]Lady Diana Belcher, *The Mutineers of the Bounty and their Descendents in Pitcairn and Norfolk Islands* (1870).

As soon as Captain Bligh reported the facts to the ministry the frigate *Pandora*, Captain Edwards, was sent to look for the mutineers. She proceeded to Otaheite and there took on board Mr. Heywood and thirteen others; but all search for the *Bounty* proved ineffectual. The mutineers were treated with unnecessary severity on board the *Pandora*, (their place of confinement was afterward called the "Pandora's Box,") and to add to their sufferings the vessel was wrecked and some of them were drowned. The others finally arrived in England and were brought to trial in 1792. Captain Bligh who was a tyrant and one of the last men who should have been put in authority over others, (he was afterwards made Governor of Australia, and for his tyranny was deposed by an insurrection in 1808), was also one of the most vindictive of men. He did his utmost to have every man, old or young, hanged. Midshipman Heywood was a mere lad—he knew nothing of the projected mutiny; but when in the morning he was offered the choice to remain on board or go in the boat he elected to remain: *no doubt because he did not fully comprehend the situation*. His youth and ignorance of the plans of Christian and his associates would account for this. He was, however, condemned to be hanged with the rest, and Captain Bligh tried to have it carried into effect. Fortunately he had influential friends, and his case being properly presented to the throne he was pardoned with two of the men—the others were hanged. Heywood lived to become a captain in the navy, and devoted his whole life to expiating what he considered his crime; but what others considered an error of judgment. He was at sea twenty-five years out of twenty-seven years in the service, and I was told by an officer who knew him that never was a man so passionately loved by his officers and crew. One of the men pardoned with him never left him afterward; he went with him on all his cruises as his coxswain, and at the end of the cruise lived at the captain's home. Captain Heywood died universally beloved and esteemed, which is more than can be said of Captain Bligh.

Nothing more was heard of the *Bounty* until 1808 when Captain Folger of Boston touched at Pitcairn's island in the Pacific expecting to find it uninhabited. As he approached it he was much surprised at seeing a canoe coming off with two men in it, and still more surprised at hearing one of the men exclaim as he got alongside the ship, in good English, "throw us a rope." When he came on board the captain asked him his name, and he replied: "Thursday October Christian."

Captain Folger found upon the island one of the mutineers who called himself John Adams, but who is supposed to have been Alexander Smith, who gave an account of the colony. He was the only survivor of the *Bounty*'s crew. Christian had destroyed the vessel soon after their arrival. A few years afterwards the English were all killed by the Otaheitans except three who concealed themselves. The Otaheitan men quarreled among themselves and were all killed or died of their wounds. Two of the Englishmen died soon after, and Adams or Smith with several women and children remained the only inhabitants of the island. Adams described Christian's remorse to have been extreme. The whole story is most agreeably told by Lady Belcher, who is a grand-daughter of the late Captain Heywood.

In 1814 the island was visited by the British frigates *Briton* and *Tagus*. The visitors thus described the inhabitants at that time: "This interesting new colony consists of forty-six persons, mostly grown up young people, besides a number of infants. Their native modesty, assisted by a proper sense of religion and morality, instilled into their youthful minds of John Adams, has hitherto preserved these interesting people perfectly chaste."[7]

An English officer who had visited Pitcairn's island told me that when the British frigates arrived there in 1814, old Adams thought they had come for him, and that he would be taken to England and hanged. When the captain of the frigate landed, Adams stood on one side with his hat off, as is the custom of English sailors in the presence of an officer, and his long, white hair flowing over his shoulders. The government, however, if it

[7]The account of the visit by the *Briton* and the *Tagus* is on pp. 169–88 of Belcher, *op.cit.*

did not pardon him, never took any notice of his crime. He died in 1830. The officer told me that Adams kept a journal which he had read—after telling of the killing of the Otaheitans, and there being but three white men left—it went on to say: "It was observed of Jack B. that his conduct was strange, and we feared he might kill us in our sleep; it was therefore decided to put him to death, which we accordingly did *with an axe!*" The Pitcairn islanders were removed to Norfolk Island in 1856. A few years after, some of them returned to Pitcairn's Island, where they still are.

But avast! Should I go on with these reminiscences I will exhaust the patience of my reader. The truth is, that being very fond of this kind of reading I had, during my four years' stay at the naval academy, taken advantage of an excellent library to read up the early voyages of the Spanish, English, and French in these seas; and now, being on the spot, I was in the habit of recalling these incidents during many a weary night's watch.

We left the *Merrimac* in Payta. From Payta we went to Panama, and here, being within eight days' sail of New York, we felt almost like returning home after our long voyage around Cape Horn. Old Panama was founded soon after the discovery of the Pacific. It was built principally of cedar. About 1673 it was sacked and burned by the buccaneers under Morgan. The present city is situated about four miles west of the old town. It is a walled city, and was in its day strongly fortified. The bay of Panama, in spite of what the "sailing directions" usually say, affords good anchorage. Vessels cannot lie very near the shore, 'tis true, and southerly gales sometimes blow. I have known it *well* for twenty-five years, and have never in that time heard of a ship dragging on shore.

Should Lesseps succeed with his canal (and I think he will), he will find no difficulty as to making a harbor at Panama.[8] The anchorage under Perico Island is now a perfectly safe one; and a

---

[8]Six years after the publication of Parker's book, on 4 February 1889, de Lesseps's *Compagnie Universelle du Canal Interoceanique* went bankrupt. See David McCullough, *The Path Between the Seas: The Creation of the Panama Canal* (1977).

moderate sum spent in building breakwaters will make a basin large enough to hold all the vessels that will ever want to use it.

The name *Panama*, it is said, means in the Indian language "a place abounding in fish;" (it *should* be filth). I confess I have no great faith as to the rendering of these Indian names into English. When Cordova, in 1517, landed on an unknown coast he asked the name of the country, and was answered by the natives: "*Tectetan;*" meaning "I do not understand you;" and this the Spaniards corrupted into *Yucatan!* And on the same voyage Bernal Diaz says the natives came off to the ship in their canoes, and tried to induce them to land, saying: "Con Escotoch," meaning "Come to our town:" and from this we get Cape *Catoche!* It has long been a wonder to me how Mungo Park managed to translate the touching song of the negro woman in Africa: considering that he did not understand the language! *Verb umsap.*

From Panama the *Merrimac* went to the south coast again, touching at Tumbez, on the Guayaquil river, and Payta, on the way. At Callao I met my friends Moore and Denny of the English steamer *Vixen.* Moore had accompanied Captain Prevost in his attempt to cross the isthmus. Denny had served in the *Baltic* under Admiral Napier during the Crimean war, and used to relate many interesting particulars of it. He was telling me one day of their raising a torpedo (or *"infernal machine"* as we called them *then*) and taking it aboard Vice Admiral Seymour's ship. The admiral who was walking the deck with a cane professed to "know all about it;" so he attempted to explain how it was made, and in so doing gave it a rap. It exploded; killed some men, and the admiral lost an eye. "What a dreadful thing!" said I; "Oh no! not at all," said Denny: "He gets a pension; he is laying back in Greenwich hospital— two-six a day!" "but," he continued in the same breath, "There was a poor beggar of a marine officer had his shin knocked off; *he* didn't get anything." I *could* have said to Denny "a pension covers a multitude of shins;" but I regret to say I did not. It was one of those vexatious *arrière-pensées.* [9]

[9] Afterthoughts.

This was the same Denny who told me of the fight at Simonoseki, where he was wounded.[10] He was not promoted as he thought he should have been and this was his "grievance;" "for," he would say in a melancholy tone, "perhaps I shall never have another chance to get hit!"

In September, 1858, we sailed from Callao for the Sandwich islands, and arrived at Honolulu in October. Here our commodore went on shore for the first time since leaving Boston. In inspecting the ship there he fell down a hatchway and injured his leg. During the entire cruise he passed his days seated in a chair with his leg propped up. The Sandwich islands were named by Cook for Lord Sandwich. The English claim that Cook discovered this group, but the Spaniards knew them a century before his time. The islanders *were* an amiable race, and though they have been accused of being cannibals it is not probable. The early voyagers were very fond of scoring men down as man-eaters; in some cases—notably the Indians of Alaska—because it was the custom to keep the bones of their ancestors in their huts. There are few pure-blooded islanders to be seen now, and the decrease in the population since Cook's time is simply frightful—in another century there will be none left to tell the tale. The natural result of the intermixture of races. The little *Dolphin*, Captain Percival, was the first American man-of-war to visit these islands, I have been told.[11]

We had expected to remain some time at Honolulu; but the unsatisfactory relations existing between the United States and Nicaragua called us there. One cannot wonder that the expeditions of the filibusters under Walker had caused bad feeling in Nicaragua.[12] Indeed Nicaragua and Costa Rica appealed to the

[10]See footnote 7, chapter 3.

[11]The *Dolphin* visited Hawaii in 1825 while searching for mutineers from the whaling ship *Globe*.

[12]William Walker (1824–1860) was the most famous of American filibusters. After invading Mexico with an armed band in 1853, he was forced to return to the United States and stand trial (he was acquitted). His most successful such venture was to Nicaragua where he succeeded in establishing a government in 1855. His regime was recognized by the United States in 1856,

great European powers for protection in May of this year. We arrived at Realejo in December. We anchored off what is now called Corinto, Realejo being in fact situated on a small creek seven miles distant. It shows the terror caused by the buccaneers on this coast—most of the towns were located away from the shore. The squadron assembled here in January, 1859; and we had a visit from the President of Nicaragua and his cabinet. We were here about three months. The harbor is an excellent one and the climate tolerably good. We took advantage of our long stay to land our battalion of small-arm men frequently, and have what the marine officer in Cooper's "Pilot" so often longed for: "a good steady drill." The *Merrimac*'s crew were the smartest men at their guns, great and small, I have ever seen. The ship passed an excellent ordnance inspection upon her return home, and I doubt if her "time" in transporting, dismounting, and general handling of guns has ever been equalled.

The town of Realejo is small, and is now an insignificant place, though one can see the ruins of an old stone cathedral and other public buildings. We used to go to the town of Chinandegua occasionally for a few days' stay. I met there an American doctor, from Tennesseee, who kept a hotel or boarding-house; he had married a native and had a large family. Asking him how he happened to find himself in the place, he told me his history. In 1849 he started for California to dig gold. Upon reaching Panama he found it crowded with "gold searchers," and no vessels in port to carry them on their way. He and a number of others bought a *bungo* (a large canoe), and in it actually started for San Francisco, a distance of more than three thousand miles. The party chose for leader one Chris. Lilly, a pugilist, who had just before killed a man named McCoy in the prize ring. They coasted along the shore, landing frequently for provisions and water. Upon landing at

---

but he ran afoul of Cornelius Vanderbilt, who sponsored a coalition of Central American states against him and drove him from the country in 1857. See his account of these adventures: *The War in Nicaragua* (1860).

Realejo the doctor left; he said he had enough, and I suppose he is in Chinandegua now. Inquiring about this *bungo* subsequently, I was told that she got past Cape St. Lucas, and was wrecked. The party, still under Lilly, made their way to San Francisco on foot. This voyage of over two thousand miles in a *bungo* almost, if not quite, equals Captain Bligh's.

About March, 1859, we went to Panama, and here Commodore Long was relieved by Commodore John B. Montgomery—a most estimable man and gallant officer. He served with distinction on the lakes in the war of 1812. In the summer the *Merrimac* went to Valparaiso to await the arrival of her relief—the new ship *Lancaster*. We found here the *Levant*, Commander Wm. E. Hunt. She was afterwards lost at sea, as I have before mentioned. She had a fine set of officers, and not a vacancy in her complement when lost.

In October the *Lancaster* arrived, and we sailed for home. Our captain made great preparations for rounding Cape Horn; he considered the ship "top heavy," and everything was sent below that could be stowed there, even the oars of the boats! At my earnest solicitation the oars were kept in *one* boat, in case of a man falling overboard! We had a good passage to Rio de Janeiro, and no bad weather off the Cape. In fact we did not experience a gale of wind during the entire cruise. We heard in Rio of John Brown's raid against Harper's Ferry. It created great excitement and some warm discussion, but not an officer on board justified it.

We found in Rio the frigate *Congress*. The *Merrimac* was to meet this vessel in Hampton Roads not many months after, under far different circumstances.[13] We arrived at Norfolk in December, 1859, after a monotonous cruise of 26 months. I wrote *Naval Light Artillery* during this cruise, which was adopted by the Navy Department, and has ever since been the text-book at the Naval Academy. I also translated the French *Tactique Navale*, which was also used at the Academy.

[13]The *Merrimac*, partially burned by the evacuating Federals, was raised, armored, and rechristened the *Virginia* by the Confederates. In her first sortie on 8 March 1862 she attacked the *Cumberland* and the *Congress*, sinking the first and forcing the other to surrender. See chapter 23.

CHAPTER XVIII

Ordered to the Naval Academy—secession of the Cotton
States—occupation of Annapolis by troops under General Butler—secession of Virginia—resign my commission in the
U. S. Navy and enter the Confederate Navy—Governor Hicks
and the state of Maryland—secession of the border states—the
northern democrats—Harper's Ferry—General Harney—the
appearance of Richmond at the beginning of the war—the
"*pawnee* war"—arrival of troops—a naval howitzer battery—
evacuation of Norfolk—Captain A. B. Fairfax—the *Patrick
Henry*—Lieutenant Powell—our first iron-clad—the battle of
Manassas—affair at Acquia Creek

In the summer of 1860 I was ordered to the Naval Academy for
the second time, and in September reported for duty as an
instructor of seamanship and naval tactics, and entered upon my
duties. Captain George S. Blake was at this time Superintendent of
the Academy, and Lieutenant C. R. P. Rodgers the Commandant
of Midshipmen.

Instructors in the strictly professional branches at the Academy at the present time, with text-books, models and apparatus at their command, can scarcely understand how extremely arduous we found our duties in 1860. There were no books on seamanship or naval tactics exactly adapted to the wants of the Midshipmen, so that the instructor had to do a good deal of compiling and translating. I wrote the *Seamanship* used by the senior class, and translated Chopart's *Naval Tactics* for them also; and as the class had to copy the manuscript it gave them much additional labor.

My book on Naval Light Artillery being adopted as a text-book, I was put in charge of that branch in addition to my other duties, and found I had my hands full.

The secession of South Carolina in December, quickly followed by that of Mississippi, Alabama, Florida, Georgia, Louisiana and Texas, convinced all reflecting minds that a civil war was impending; indeed I had long been of that opinion myself. I was satisfied in 1857 that the subjects in dispute between the Northern and Southern states would finally be decided by an appeal to arms. I have my opinion as to the *cause* of the war—and a pretty decided one it is—but it is not my intention in this book, which is simply a memoir of what I saw myself of the war, to obtrude it. At some future time I may bring up some points which have not yet been considered—contenting myself with saying that the men who suffered most by the war (the Southern army and navy officers *inasmuch as they lost a profession*) had less to do with bringing it about than any other class of citizens.

It may well be imagined that the constant state of excitement in which we were kept was not conducive to hard study; yet so good was the discipline that everything went on as usual, and the midshipmen were kept closely to their duties. As the states seceded, the students appointed from them generally resigned with the consent of their parents; but their departures were very quietly taken, and the friendships they had contracted at the school remained unimpaired. Affairs remained in this state until the bombardment of Fort Sumter, April 11–13; but after that, as war was now certain, the scholastic duties were discontinued and the place assumed more the appearance of a garrison.

I resigned my commission on the 19th of April, 1861, upon hearing of the secession of Virginia. On the afternoon of that day a collision occurred in Baltimore between a Massachusetts regiment and a mob, and the railroads in the vicinity of the city were torn up to interrupt travel. Troops were sent to Annapolis on their way to Washington which was supposed to be threatened by the Confederates. The first troops to arrive were the New York 7th regiment, a Rhode Island regiment and battery, and a Massachusetts regiment all under the command of General B. F. Butler.

The authorities of the Academy were under the impression that an attack upon the school and the frigate *Constitution* was projected by the secessionists in the neighborhood; but I think there never was any serious foundation for their fears. While waiting to hear of the acceptance of my resignation I remained on duty, and was one night placed in a most unpleasant position. An alarm was given that the secessionists were coming up the river to attack us; the long roll was beaten, and all hands were sent to their stations. I was in charge of the howitzer battery, and like many of the midshipmen manning it who had resigned and were waiting to hear from Washington, had either to refuse to do duty or fire on our friends.

The alarm was a false one; I do not hesitate to say, however, that had we been attacked I should have stood by my guns and performed my duty by the school. I was still an officer of the navy; and, moreover, Maryland had not seceded, and if it had, war had not been declared.

It was now determined to remove the school to Newport, R. I., and preparations were made accordingly. About the 23d of the month (April) I received private information from a friend in Baltimore that a steamboat would be at the wharf that night at 9 o'clock to take Governor Hicks to Baltimore, and was advised to seize the opportunity to leave. I did so, and many of my brother officers were at the boat to see me off. As we approached Baltimore the boat sheered in to a wharf near Fell's Point, landed the Governor and his friends, and then went on to her usual wharf. This was done to prevent the secessionists from getting hold of the governor. Not very long before, they had done so in Baltimore, and he had on that occasion made a very good secession speech. The object of Governor Hicks was to get to Frederick where he had called the Legislature to assemble, and where those members professing southern sympathies were arrested and cast into prison a short time after. Thus was the State of Maryland seized by the throat by the United States government before the beginning of hostilities.

The State of Virginia seceded on the 17th of April, and was soon followed by Arkansas, North Carolina and Tennessee. This action was precipitated by President Lincoln's call for 75,000 troops on the 15th of April. I confess I could never see the philosophy of it. The Union men of these States by their persistently voting against secession, in convention and otherwise, induced President Lincoln and his advisers to believe that they would not consent to it under any circumstances, and they strengthened his hands to that extent. In a measure they *invited* him to issue his call for 75,000 men! After, as I say, voting against secession and thus preventing their States from making preparations for war they suddenly turned round and voted *for* it when the U. S. government had taken the action their attitude had seemed to approve![1] This inconsistency was rivalled by the action of the northern Democrats. They had generally supported the attitude of the seceding States, and were patting them on the back with the advice "to go in and win;" but as soon as the "flag was fired on" (to use the expression of the day) they jumped over the fence. Why? The South had only done what the northern Democrats had encouraged it to do! Did they not see that everything was tending to an appeal to arms, and that they were inciting the South to it? or did they suppose that "war" meant throwing oyster shells at each other? I think I could give a pretty good reason for *their* action if this were the place for it! I suspect

[1]Virginia's convention had voted against secession 88-45 on 4 April in the belief that some compromise might yet solve the crisis. Lincoln's apparent determination to coerce the South, however, provoked a reconsideration, and on 17 April the convention voted 88-55 to join the Confederacy.

that at the meeting of the northern governors the manner in which the war was to be precipitated was all arranged. Not the only thing of the kind concocted by "the party," both before and *after the war*, if I am not mistaken.

Whatever our wise statesmen may say, I thought then, as I think now, that after the action of the six extreme Southern States and the formation by them of a Southern Confederacy, the Border States—if they held the ground that a State could not be lawfully coerced,—and if, also, they were opposed to the abolition of slavery—*had no choice* but to join their sister States; and true statesmanship should have shown them this, and their action should have been united and prompt. It *might* have averted the civil war.

To return to my narrative. Upon my arrival in Baltimore I found it would not be prudent to attempt to reach Norfolk by the Bay Line, and I decided to go to Richmond via Harper's Ferry, which was then occupied by the confederates. As we approached the bridge at the Ferry the cars were stopped and several confederate officers walked through the cars and gravely inspected the passengers. I am sure I do not know what for, nor did they probably. In fact the whole proceedings at this time—in Virginia at least—seemed so like a comedy that were it not for the fearful tragedy which followed one would be tempted to indulge in a hearty laugh over them. I stopped at Harper's Ferry and took the cars for Winchester; they were crowded with colonels and majors, but few privates were to be seen. I learned to my surprise that they were either going off on leave or were "bearers of dispatches." The carrying of dispatches—no matter of how little importance—seemed to attach a certain dignity to the carrier. Accustomed as I had been all my life to order and discipline I was somewhat depressed at the absence of it, as well as by the total ignorance of military affairs everywhere observed while on my way to Richmond. How little could I foresee that these men were to fight and gain battles which were to be immortalized in history! I found in the cars next day General [William S.] Harney of the army, who had been made prisoner at Harper's Ferry, while on his way to

Washington. There was of course no reason in this, as war had not been proclaimed, and he was promptly released upon his arrival in Richmond. We stopped a night at Manassas Junction and here, as in every other town through which we passed, we saw the people drilling—in companies, however. At this time the State had not one organized regiment. Where we had companies, the North had regiments.

Upon my arrival in Richmond I reported to Governor [John] Letcher, and was immediately commissioned a lieutenant in the Virginia State Navy; and I may as well say here that as soon as the State was regularly entered into the Confederacy I was commissioned a Lieutenant in the Confederate Navy. Richmond at this time was in a state difficult to describe. The hotels were thronged, troops were coming in, messengers were riding to and fro, and everybody *was in motion*. I particularly noticed this fact: even at the hotels the seats were not occupied; no one could sit still. I suppose the great excitement accounted for this. The dispatches coming in hourly, the reports spread from mouth to mouth, the *news* contained in the daily papers even, were enough to drive a *reasonable* man crazy. We heard the most wonderful rumors; nothing was too absurd or ridiculous for belief, and men's time seemed to be taken up in spreading stories that would have put Gulliver to shame and made Munchausen hide his diminished head. The emanations from the brain of a maniac were logical in comparison!

Only the Sunday before my arrival there had been what was afterwards called the "Pawnee War." The steamer *Pawnee* was reported to be coming up the river, and all Richmond went to arms. What they thought the *Pawnee* with her few guns and men could do with the city of Richmond, or what *they* expected to do by arming themselves with shot-guns, horse-pistols and broadswords and going down to Rockett's wharf to meet her, I could never discover. No doubt they only regretted that they could not arm themselves, in addition, with a few *culverines*, *falconets* and *sakers* (whatever they may be)! Hector's arming at the siege of Troy was nothing in comparison. But the *Pawnee* did not come up the river and the good citizens returned to their homes to lay aside their arms and anxiously await new "reports."

The companies coming in from the country were dressed in the most extraordinary uniforms the eye ever rested on; but they were full of fight. As they arrived they were sent to a camp near the city to be drilled. It is useless to say they stood in need of it. "What," said a drill-master to a captain who was speaking of his ignorance of the company drill, "What, then, do you propose to do with your men in time of battle?" "Just turn them loose," was his reply, and this appeared to be the general idea as to how the impending war was to be fought. Men insisted upon carrying a bowie-knife and revolver in addition to a musket, in the belief that a battle was a *scrimmage*; but they soon knew better, and after the first campaign our generals could say with Moliére's mock doctor, *nous avons changé tout cela.*[2]

I was ordered to organize a battery of howitzers, to be manned by sailors to serve with the army, and as I had to have the guns cast at the Tredegar works, the carriages made, etc., I was kept in Richmond some months, and had an opportunity of seeing all that was going on.

Soon after Virginia seceded the Southern troops commenced coming in, and were sent to the front as they arrived. I recollect that when the first regiment arrived from South Carolina the men announced that they "had come to fight the battles of old Virginia;" and the city papers inculcated about the same idea. One would have supposed that South Carolina was not at war with the United States and had had nothing to do with bringing it about! Nothing was said about "old Virginia" bearing the brunt of it, as she was about to do! There was no use in trying to combat the nonsensical ideas that were put in circulation; the fact is that about this time one half of the people were crazy and the other half *non compos mentis*, both north and south.

The evacuation of Norfolk by the Federals was a most fortunate

---

[2]We changed all that.

thing for the Confederates. Why the Federal authorities did this was always beyond my comprehension. They had the place, and with the force at their command could not have been driven out. No batteries could have been put up by the Confederates in the face of the broadsides of their ships, and it being only twelve miles from Fortress Monroe (Old Point Comfort) it could have been reinforced to any extent. But they did give it up, and had hardly done so when they commenced making preparations to retake it.[3] The navy-yard contained a large number of heavy cannon, and these guns were used not only to fortify Norfolk and the batteries on the York, Potomac, James, and Rappahannock rivers; but were sent to North and South Carolina, Georgia, Florida, Alabama, Mississippi and Louisiana. They were to be found at Roanoke Island, Wilmington, Charleston, Mobile, New Orleans, Vicksburg, and many other places.

Soon after our occupation of the Yard Commander Archibald B. Fairfax was put in charge of the ordnance department, and he immediately turned his attention to the banding and rifling of the 32-pounders of 57 and 63 cwt. I do not know who invented the machine for rifling the guns (the *banding* was taken from the Parrott gun probably), but the work was done under the supervision of Captain Fairfax, and was, in my opinion, the most important improvement made in our ordnance during the war. I well remember that when the first gun was finished he mounted it on the small steamer *Harmony* and experimented with it on a frigate lying off Newport's News: taking a position outside the range of her guns, he succeeded in hitting her several times. Large numbers of these banded and rifled guns were prepared for the ships and batteries. I never heard of any of them bursting, though I saw them fired many times; the charge was eight pounds, and the projectile weighed about 70 pounds. After the battles of Roanoke island and Elizabeth City, Admiral Louis Goldsborough, U. S. N., in his report to the Secretary of the Navy, says: "His (the confederate's)

[3]Parker's analysis is accepted by most historians. The Federal commander, Commodore C. S. McCauley, simply lost his nerve.

favorite gun is the 32-pounder of 57 and 63 cwt., beautifully fortified at the breech-end by a long and massive wrought-iron cylindrical ring, and so rifled in the bore as to admit of the use of round shot and grape as well as shells by the simple interposition of a junk wad between the charge of powder and the shot or stand of grape. His ordnance arrangements throughout exhibit great skill and ingenuity." Our vessels in these battles were fitted out by Captain Fairfax. I am glad to render him this tribute as he never received the credit due him.

Whilst I was organizing my battery the steamer *Patrick Henry* was fitting out at Richmond for a cruise on the coast; she had been called the *Yorktown*, and belonged to the Old Dominion line running between New York and Richmond.[4] She was not at all fitted for a man-of-war, but we had to take what we could get, and by taking off her upper cabins, strengthening her decks, etc., made her answer pretty well. She carried a bow and stern pivot, and ten guns in broadside, 32 and 64-pounders. Lieutenant William Llewellyn Powell was her executive officer. He was, from the very beginning of the war, impressed with the necessity of having iron-clad vessels. I had many conversations with him on this subject. He was certainly the first man I met in the Confederate navy who saw that all navies must eventually come to it. He communicated his views to the Secretary of the Navy and got permission to try iron on the *Patrick Henry*. She was our first iron clad!

Powell put one-inch iron on her hull abreast the boilers—it extended a foot or so below the water line, and ran a few feet forward and abaft her engines and boilers. One inch was not much protection, but it was all she would bear. On the spar deck he put iron shields, in the form of a V, forward and abaft her engines.

[4]The *Patrick Henry* (formerly the passenger and mail steamer *Yorktown*) was a side-wheel steamer of 1,400 tons. She was seized by the state of Virginia at the outset of hostilities and armed with 10 guns and a crew of 150. Parker would later command this vessel as part of his duties as superintendent of the Confederate Naval Academy.

These shields were of heavy timber and covered with one or two inches of iron. In fighting head or stern on, they afforded good protection against a raking shot, and it must be remembered that as the *Patrick Henry* was a side-wheel boat with a walking-beam engine this protection was very important to her. It must not be understood by the non-professional reader that the use of iron to protect ships was original with either the Federals or Confederates. The French had iron-clad gunboats or batteries in the Crimean war, 1854; and at the beginning of our civil war they had the powerful iron-clad frigate *Gloire*, and the English had the *Warrior*. For the matter of that, Haydn in his dictionary of dates, says: "The *Santa Anna*, the property of the knights of St. John, of about 1700 tons, *sheathed with lead*, was built at Nice about 1530. It was literally a floating fortress, and aided Charles V in taking Tunis in 1535. It contained a crew of 300 men and 50 pieces of artillery."[5]

Lieutenant Powell seeing no chance of distinction in the navy resigned to enter the army. He was made a brigadier general and ordered to command Fort Morgan at Mobile. Here he put everything in a good state of defence; but he died of fever before the place was attacked by the fleet under Farragut. He was one of the purest of men and a most reliable and accomplished officer.

July 21, 1861, the battle of Bull Run or Manassas was fought. We in Richmond knew very little of it until the next day; but when the news *did* come we had the most marvelous accounts of it. The regiments *decimated* were innumerable, and the meaning of this word was as little understood then as it is now. The men-of-war (?) on the James river at this time were the *Patrick Henry*, *Jamestown* and *Teaser*. The *Jamestown* was a sister ship to the *Patrick Henry*, but not so strong. She mounted two 32 pounder rifled guns. She was christened the *Thomas Jefferson* by the Confederate government; but she was always known by her old name of *Jamestown*. The *Teaser* was a tug boat mounting one gun. It was found impossible to ship crews for these vessels; there was a great scarcity of sailors at the South, and the landsmen naturally pre-

[5]Haydn's *Dictionary of Dates* was a popular reference encyclopedia of the time.

ferred the army. About the time I had my guns ready and the men enlisted, they were taken for the *Patrick Henry*, and Commodore Samuel Barron who had been put in command of the squadron destined to operate in the waters of North Carolina offered me the command of the gunboat *Beaufort*.[6] I gladly accepted the offer as I had given up all hope of getting my howitzers into action with the army after the battle of Manassas. I saw soon after I commenced drilling the men, that guns drawn by hand cannot operate with troops to advantage unless very near their base of supplies. It was wise in the Secretary to send my men back to their legitimate sphere, and I cheerfully consented to it. They were a fine set of fellows, and Captain Tucker stationed them together at the bow gun of the *Patrick Henry* where they never failed to give a good account of themselves afterwards.

The first hostile shot I saw fired in the war was at Acquia Creek, where I went in June or July simply to see what was going on. Upon arriving there I found several small steamers bombarding our Fort at Cockpit Point. Captain William F. Lynch commanded the battery, and General Ruggles the department. He had quite a force assembled to resist an invasion; but I thought any one might have seen that the enemy had no idea of landing troops—indeed there were no transports in sight. The bombardment was, I suspect, only for the purpose of drawing our fire, that they might see the strength of the battery. It was carried on at long range and there was nobody hurt. Upon my return to Richmond the next day I met at a "turnout" a train conveying the 1st Arkansas regiment to the seat of war. The men were greatly excited and eager for the

[6]Because of his father's service in the American Revolution, Samuel Barron (1809–1888) was admitted to the U.S. Navy at the remarkable age of two—his commission as a midshipman was dated 1 January 1812. He made captain in 1855, but resigned in 1861 to accept a commission as captain in the Confederate Navy. He was captured after the surrender of Fort Hatteras, exchanged a year later, and spent the rest of the war in Europe attempting to gain increased foreign aid for the Confederacy. The *Beaufort* was a converted canal boat that had operated on the Albemarle Canal. Armed with one rifled 32-pounder (banded) and one 24-pound carronade, she carried a complement of thirty-five.

fray. I gave them the news as the trains stopped side by side. When their train moved off every man who could get his arm out at a window did so, and the flourishing of bowie-knives made it look like a steel-clad!

The result of the battle of Manassas which filled our people with joy and gladness was, I confess, a disappointment to me, and though it may seem a strange thing to say I lost hope of our final success at the time of our first great victory. I do not care to enter into my reasons for this impression; but that such was the case a few of my most intimate friends know. I trust I did not exhibit this feeling in my after career, but the results of our after victories only tended to confirm it. *Ay de mi, Alhama!*

CHAPTER XIX

The North Carolina state navy—I join the reinforcement for Hatteras—capture of Cape Hatteras—Commodore Samuel Barron—Lieutenant Wm. H. Murdaugh—Roanoke Island—Oregon Inlet—I assume command of the *Beaufort*—Fort Macon—Colonel Bridges and his command—a pleasant day—reading under difficulties—public school education—the *Beaufort*'s crew—my cabin boy—the Neuse River—Teach, the pirate—a pilot's yarn—visit to Jacksonville—a false alarm—Washington, N. C.,—a cruise on a canal—arrival at Norfolk

T he Governor of North Carolina had, before the state regularly joined the Confederacy, been going it on his own hook, as it were.[1] He fitted out privateers, sent out blockade-runners, etc., and got in so many stores, that it was observed at the beginning of

---

[1] Henry T. Clark (1808–1874) became governor of North Carolina on 7 July 1861 with the death of John W. Ellis. It was Clark who organized North Carolina into military districts and supervised the raising of state troops in the first year of the war.

the war that the North Carolina troops were the best armed, and best clothed men that passed through Richmond. The steamer *Winslow*, a small side-wheel boat, under Captain Thomas M. Crossan, formerly of the Navy, was very active in cruising outside of Cape Hatteras as a privateer, and captured some valuable prizes. The men found in them were generally foreigners and many of them entered our service, as I have reason to know. When the State became one of the Confederate States, her vessels were all turned over to the navy and became men-of-war, and not privateers. The vessels thus turned over were: the *Winslow*, Commander Arthur Sinclair; the *Ellis*, Commander W. B. Muse; the *Raleigh*, lieutenant commanding Alexander; and the *Beaufort*. The *Winslow* and *Ellis* were at Hatteras; the *Raleigh* at Oregon Inlet, and the *Beaufort* at Newbern.

Commodore Barron being in Norfolk, I went there early in August to report. He directed me to remain and fit out a launch for service in Albemarle and Pamlico Sounds, and when ready to take her to Cape Hatteras and leave her. The three entrances into Pamlico Sound,—Oregon, Hatteras and Ocracoke inlets,—were guarded by fortifications and garrisoned by North Carolina troops. Hatteras, being the principal entrance, was especially well fortified. I had the launch well fitted out with sails and a howitzer and when ready to start, began to consider how I was to get to Hatteras, as I had no men. About the 24th of August we heard that a squadron under Flag Officer [Silas] Stringham, with troops under General Butler, had appeared off the place; and the 3d Georgia regiment, which up to this time had been stationed at Norfolk, was ordered to reinforce the garrison there. Captain Thomas Hunter of the navy was put in command of the expedition. The 3d Georgia was a remarkably fine regiment, commanded by Colonel Wright, and was afterwards highly distinguished. Up to this time it had never been in action, and the men were very eager for one.

Captain Hunter offered to tow me down, and I gladly accepted his offer. We had one small steamer for the officers, and the men were towed in canal boats. We left Norfolk about the 27th of

August, and went through the Chesapeake and Albemarle canal. We stopped at several places along the canal, and at landings on the Croatan river, but got no news. I think it was on the afternoon of the 30th that, as we were making the best of our way down Albemarle Sound, we met a schooner under full sail for Edenton. Upon hailing her, we were told that Hatteras had fallen the day before, and all but a few of the garrison were prisoners. There were a few officers on board who had escaped in small boats. I never knew much about this affair; but it seems that after the ships had bombarded the two forts for a day or two, a force was landed. Our men abandoned the upper fort, and retreated to the lower one, seeing which the enemy took possession of it. Commodore Barron who arrived at this time landed with his Flag Lieutenant William Sharpe, and Lieutenant W. H. Murdaugh, and was earnestly solicited by Colonel Martin, who commanded the fort, to assume the supreme command. This he unwisely did, in his great desire to render all the aid and assistance in his power. The Federals in the upper fort now opened a fire with their rifles in addition to the fire from the ships, and on the 29th the place surrendered. The steamers *Winslow* and *Ellis* got away, the former to Newbern and the latter to Washington on the Pamlico river, after taking off the garrison at Ocracoke inlet.[2]

Lieutenant Murdaugh was badly wounded while serving a gun by the explosion of a shell; but was gotten off to the *Winslow* and escaped being made prisoner. The officer who gave us the information spoke of his gallantry in the highest terms as well as of that of Commodore Barron. Murdaugh who resembled Somers, inasmuch as he "had no more dodge in him than the mainmast," suffered for some months from his wound; but he did gallant service to the end of the war. He as well as Powell were midshipmen with me in the old *Potomac*. Our papers were loud in their remarks about the

[2]The Union capture of Hatteras Inlet on 29 August 1861 was the first successful combined operation of the war. Commodore Silas Stringham's fleet of four steamers, a revenue cutter, and a tug opened a bombardment on 28 August and two army transports landed a force under Major General Benjamin Butler. Both Confederate forts surrendered unconditionally the next day.

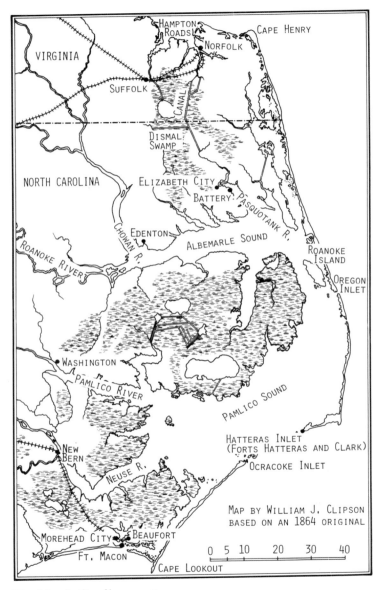

The North Carolina coast.

Hatteras affair (of course) and Commodore Barron's action was the subject of much unkind and unjust criticism. The fact is the gallant commodore in his desire (as I have said) to do all he could for the cause, acted as nine out of ten men of spirit would have done under the circumstances. I have spoken of it as unwise for the reason that his command was afloat; and it was a thankless task to have the command ashore forced upon him at the eleventh hour. The commodore had the satisfaction of knowing that Colonel Martin and his men highly appreciated his services and the department approved his action. If the attack on Hatteras had been made a few months later in the war, when our men had learned how little damage the fire of ships does to earthworks, the fort would not have fallen—witness the defence of Fort McAllister March, 1863.[3]

Upon our receiving the news of the fall of Hatteras we landed the Georgians on Roanoke island and proceeded in the small steamer to Oregon Inlet, which was still held by its garrison. Upon our arrival, a council was held and it was resolved to evacuate the place and remove the guns, &c. to Roanoke Island; this was done, and Alexander in the *Raleigh* rendered great assistance in it. There was really a strong and very well constructed fortification at Oregon Inlet, and some objection was made to evacuating it— among others the engineer who constructed it was very loth to abandon it—but after the fall of Hatteras it became of absolutely no importance. The principal entrance to the sound being open what earthly reason could there be for holding the other two? I do not think the Federals occupied the forts at either Oregon or Ocracoke Inlets during the war—they had no occasion to! I returned to Roanoke Island with Captain Hunter and was sent by him to Norfolk with dispatches to Commodore Forrest. The launch, I left in charge of Boatswain [Charles H.] Hasker— afterward Lieutenant Hasker, an energetic, valuable officer—to be

[3]Fort McAllister, south of Savannah, held out against Union naval attacks and fell to General W. T. Sherman's army after its march across Georgia in 1864. Parker's assessment that Hatteras Inlet was as defensible as Fort McAllister is questionable.

used in landing stores for the troops on the island. Upon my reporting to the commodore he insisted upon my going immediately by rail to Newbern and taking charge of the *Beaufort*, which I proceeded to do. Upon my arrival there I found the *Beaufort* at the wharf with a few officers on board, but no crew. She had been commanded by Captain Duval while in the State service, and he and his officers and men had left. The *Beaufort* was a small iron propeller, built for service on the canal. She was 94 feet long and 17 feet broad; her iron was one-fourth of an inch in thickness. Her deck had been strengthened and shored up, and forward she carried a long 32 pounder which was soon afterwards exchanged for a banded and rifled 57 cwt. 32 pounder. Her magazine was just forward of the boiler, and both magazine and boiler were above the water line and exposed to shot. She carried 35 officers and men.

From Hatteras the Federals could advance on Norfolk by the way of Albemarle Sound, attack Newbern on the Neuse, or Washington on the Pamlico river. The entrance to Albemarle Sound was defended by batteries on Roanoke Island, then being hastily constructed. Newbern was defended by a small fort on the river, a few miles below, and Washington in the same manner. The enemy made a great mistake in not taking possession of the sounds immediately after capturing Hatteras; there was nothing to prevent it but two small gunboats carrying one gun each. Two of the small steamers under Flag Officer Stringham should have swept the sounds, and a force should have occupied Roanoke island.[4] This at least could have been done had the Federals seized their opportunity; but, as is so often the case in war, they failed to make use of it. A striking instance of this occurred when General Butler landed at Bermuda Hundred, on the James river, in the summer of 1864: he advanced cautiously in the direction of Howletts. Had he advanced promptly and boldly he could have taken Drury's Bluff (Fort Darling), and even Richmond itself. But, as the soldier said: "our hind sights are better than our fore sights!"

[4]Federal forces did not occupy Roanoke Island until 7 February 1862. See chapter 20.

While I was getting the *Beaufort* ready, Commodore W. F. Lynch, who was appointed to succeed Commodore Barron (then a prisoner) in the command, arrived at Newbern; and, as great anxiety was felt concerning Fort Macon which it was thought would soon be attacked, General Gatlin, who commanded the department, and the Governor of the State met him for consultation. I had gone to my room and was about retiring when a rap at the door announced Lieutenant Pat M. who said the Commodore desired to see me immediately. "What does he want?" said I. "Well," said M., "he wants you to go into Fort Macon as chief ordnance officer." "Why does he send *me*," growled I, "when he knows I'm fitting out my vessel, and there are plenty of other officers about, doing nothing?" "Well," said M., "we talked it over, and decided *you* were the man for the place." Now be it known that after Commodore Barron's experience at Cape Hatteras we of the Navy had no particular desire to follow his example; but there was no appeal: so when I presented myself before the council and was told by Commodore Lynch that he had offered my services to General Gatlin, I thanked him for the honor and said how extremely happy I should be to render any service, etc., etc. It was arranged that I should go down in a special train next morning at daylight, and I made my preparations; growling to myself all the time like a quarter gunner, and then turned in for a few hours' sleep.

Upon reaching the depot the next morning, I found Commodore Lynch and all the naval officers there, with the crew of the *Winslow*, the only vessel in port. I learned to my great satisfaction that the Commodore had determined to go into the fort with his entire force; information having been received during the night that it would probably be attacked that day. This pleased me very much; for though I strongly objected to "going it alone," being inclined rather "to pass," I had no objection to being "ordered up" with the entire party.

Most of the naval officers present, objected to going though, of course, not in the commodore's hearing; it was not that they would not gladly have gone in their ships (had they had any), but the impression made by the harsh reflections upon Commodore Barron was too strong to be removed. Just as the cars were about to start, Pat M.—made his appearance—his face as red as fire, a carbine over his shoulder, and a jug of *pelos cochos* in his hand—and said he had been ordered to remain in Newbern to take charge of the few men left behind. He growled about it so much that one of officers (upon what we all considered good grounds) offered to take his place and let him go. "No," says M.—, "I'll obey orders." "Well give us your jug" said the officer, and off we went.

Upon our arrival at Fort Macon we were received with great joy by Colonel Bridges, the officer in command. The colonel had distinguished himself at the battle of Bethel as a captain, had been promoted, and placed in command of Fort Macon. As he said himself he knew nothing about heavy artillery or the defence of fortified places. "I only know," said he, "that that flag must not come down" and no one who knew this gallant man could doubt that it would only be lowered after a desperate defence, if at all. The colonel received me as the ordnance officer most cordially. "Now," he remarked, "my mind is at rest;" and I am sure that as soon as he felt that his men had been properly instructed and that his ammunition was all right, he would have welcomed the presence of an attacking force.

We found in Fort Macon Mr. [Edmund] Ruffin, who had fired the first gun at Fort Sumter. He was an old man, an Englishman by birth, and I thought, was very much out of place.

The first thing I did upon assuming my duties was to send a few crews to their guns and direct them to fire at a target which had been already placed. I had previously made up my mind not to openly correct any small mistakes, fearing to discourage the garrison on the eve of an engagement; but I was glad to see that the men did their work very well, and made some fair shots. I expressed myself to the colonel as very well pleased, but my pleasure was nothing compared to that exhibited by the other naval officers. Their delight, surprise and admiration were loudly expressed; they said that the sailors were not wanted, that they could not do as well as the soldiers, and in fact, that they might as well return to

Newbern. So by the afternoon train the whole "kit and boodle" of them (so to speak) left, and I was alone in my glory.

Fort Macon was garrisoned by six companies of North Carolina troops, recruited in the neighborhood; and a more orderly, obedient, well-behaved set of men I did not fall in with during the war. Lieutenant Colonel Sloan was the second in command, and Lieutenant Coleman was the ordnance officer. I only wish I could recall the names of more of the officers, the adjutant's especially, for their hospitality to me was unbounded. The spirit of the colonel was reflected by the men. All hands were full of enterprise and pluck; and I had been with them but a few days when I felt ready to go into an engagement with them with pleasure. Fort Macon at that time would not have fallen without a brave defence. The fort is on a strip of sand lying about two miles off the main land, and is reached from Beaufort and Morehead City by boat. On the beach below the fort was encamped a regiment commanded by Colonel Zebulon Vance, afterwards Governor of the State, and at present U. S. Senator. I recall a very pleasant day sailing over to his camp from Morehead City, in company with Commodore Lynch, of the Dead Sea Expedition, Colonel Vance, and Mr. Burgwyn, of North Carolina, all brilliant conversationalists. Mr. Burgwyn's son was the Lieutenant-Colonel of Vance's regiment—he was killed at Gettysburg, while in command of it.

I could never account for the feeling of confinement I used to experience in the fort. It is true I had never lived in casemates before; but I had passed years in small vessels, in apartments ten feet square. Yet when the gates were closed at night I always had a "shut up" feeling—I could not seem to breathe freely—and as soon as they were thrown open in the morning I was the first man out, and many were the long walks I took with Colonel Bridges on the beach.

On one occasion I had to pass some days alone at the tavern in Morehead City. I do not recollect now why I was there, but I not only had no companions, but no books. Not a book was to be had on the premises. One afternoon after walking wearily about the village looking in vain for reading matter I went to my room, and my eye happening to rest on my trunk I observed that it was lined with newspapers; it was what is known as a "shoe trunk." I took out the clothing, held the trunk up in a good light, and read everything I could get at without twisting my head off! This was not the only time during the war when, if I did not regret knowing how to read, I did regret being fond of it. I have always held the opinion that it is of more importance to a man who has to make a living by making boots, (for example), to know how to make a good one than to know how to read and write; and it would be well if our wiseacres in their howl for more public-school education would pause to reflect whether the country is not feeling the want of skilled labor, and our streets are not being filled with idle young men—whether, in fact, the public schools are not teaching the working classes everything but how to make an honest living! It is not all of education to know how to read and write. I have seen many a man-of-war's man who could do neither, and yet be quick of apprehension, prompt to execute, truthful, brave and self-denying; and as far superior to the city hoodlum or country bumpkin in all the qualities that go to make a *man*, as it is possible for one man to excel another.

During the dreary time I was watching the movements of the enemy at Hatteras in the *Beaufort* whilst I was bored to death for the want of something to read—there being little else to do after the morning exercise—my pilot, who had passed his life on these waters, managed to pass his time very pleasantly, every bird that flew overhead, or fish that swam alongside gave him some occupation or food for thought. He was a philosopher, inasmuch as he had learned to live in the present. It is a mistake to say that education (understood in its ordinary sense) cannot injure a man. It depends upon his manner of living, and in many cases it renders his life unhappy, and to that extent injures him. "Oh," said the keeper of a lock on the canal when I remarked upon the loneliness of the place: "I don't know, sometimes we have as many as five or six boats passing in a day!" So after all every man looks upon life from a different standpoint and all happiness is comparative.

But all this philosophizing has nothing to do with Fort Macon! During my two weeks' stay the U. S. steamer *Susquehanna* arrived to blockade the port.[5] She anchored out of gunshot of the fort, though near enough to the beach to have shelled Vance's regiment if Captain [James L.] Lardner had felt so inclined. Beaufort which is 25 miles from Newbern has an excellent harbor, and I wonder that more blockade runners did not use it the first year of the war. The *Nashville*, Captain [Robert B.] Pegram, was the only one I knew to go there. The fort was taken and the town occupied by the Federals in April, 1862.

Upon the arrival of an army officer to relieve me I left the fort and returned to Newbern to resume the fitting out of the *Beaufort*. I made up a crew principally of men who had been in the prizes captured by the *Winslow*. I had but one American in the crew—a green hand who shipped as a coal heaver. My officers at this time were midshipmen Charles K. Mallory and Virginius Newton, pilot James Hopkins, engineer Hanks, and captain's clerk Richard Byrd.

The crew was composed of Englishmen (two of whom were splendid specimens of man-of-war's-men), Danes and Swedes. I never sailed with a better one, and I never knew them to fail in their duty; indeed I used to wonder at their eagerness to go into battle considering the fact that they knew nothing at all about the cause of the war; but a sailor is a sailor all the world over. I found it difficult to ship a cook and steward, and finally took as cabin-boy a youth of 14 years of age who told me he had been "raised in the neighborhood." I did not doubt it, for as captain Simon Suggs says: "You could see the marks on his legs where he had stood in the swamp while gathering berries the previous summer." I remember his appearance well. The first day he came into the cabin

[5]The *Susquehanna* was a side-wheel steamer of 2,450 tons displacement, laid down in 1847 and launched in 1850. She had been M. C. Perry's flagship when he entered Tokyo Harbor in 1853. Captain James Lardner (1802–1881) was a career naval officer who later commanded both the East and West Blockading Squadrons. He retired in 1864 and was made a rear admiral on the retired list in 1869.

to announce dinner he stuck his head suddenly into my very small state room and, as I was sitting in my bunk, this brought his face within six inches of mine; this seemed so to startle him that he could only open his eyes and mouth: "Well!" said I, "what do you want?" "The vittels is up," he gasped and evaporated. That night he deserted, and I saw him no more. My appearance, whatever it was, was too much for him.

During the month of October, 1861, we remained in the *Beaufort* at the mouth of the Neuse river on the lookout for any movement from Hatteras. No enemy appeared, but as I had occasion frequently to go up and down the river I ran some risk from the fort below Newbern. I could never get them to understand my signals. When I passed them at night they would give me a shot first and then send off a boat to make inquiries! However it did me no harm and it gave them practice. I used to hold long conversations with a pilot I met at the mouth of the Neuse river. He had passed his life on the sound, and was a real old-fashioned fellow, a believer in signs and tokens. He told me of his many attempts to find the money buried by Teach the pirate.[6] Teach frequented Pamlico Sound and used to lie at an island in it from which he could watch Hatteras and Ocracoke Inlets. I visited this island and every square foot of earth on it had had a spade in it in the search for Teach's money. Everybody hereabouts believed that Teach had buried a large amount of money *somewhere* on the shore of the sound. This pilot told me he had sometimes seen lights on the shore, which lights indicated the spot where the money was buried. The great point was to get to the place before the light was extinguished. He said he had several times jumped into a boat and pulled for one, but unfortunately the light always disappeared before he could reach the shore.

Such was the tale that was told to me
By that shattered and battered son of the sea.

[6]Edward Teach (d. 1718), better known as Blackbeard, was an English pirate in the Caribbean from the end of the War of Spanish Succession (1713) until his death.

I went in the *Beaufort* one afternoon to a place called Jacksonville, situated on a creek emptying into Pamlico Sound. I had some doubt about leaving the mouth of the Neuse, but something of importance took me to Jacksonville. I arrived there at sunset and made fast to the wharf. The inhabitants knew nothing of the *Beaufort* and thought it was a gunboat from Hatteras; so every man, woman and child took to the woods. There was not a soul left in the town when I arrived. My pilot went on shore and by throwing out friendly signals at last brought them down, and very soon the vessel was crowded with people. About 10 o'clock that night a report came that the enemy had landed at the mouth of the Neuse river; it was brought by two young men who said they were there and had barely time to jump on their horses and escape. Here was a "category" as Captain Truck says. The creek was so narrow and intricate that my pilot said he could not take the steamer down before daylight, and by that time the enemy would be well on the way to Newbern. After some delay I persuaded a man to ride back to the river for further information. I do not think I ever suffered more in my life than while awaiting his return. Towards morning my scout returned. It was a false alarm—there was no enemy there. It seems that near the mouth of the river there lived a widow with two pretty daughters who were the belles of the neighborhood. The two Jacksonville young men were paying them a visit when some soldiers on leave from Newbern arrived. The soldiers saw one of the young ladies outside the house, and learning of the presence of the two young men determined to get rid of them; so they put up a joke which the ladies entered into with spirit. They charged up to the house hurraing at the top of their lungs, the ladies cried "Yankees," and our two heroes "vamosed the ranche." The next morning I made the best of my way back to my station, and about the end of October went to Newbern for coal.

Shortly after, Commodore Lynch arrived in the *Seabird* accompanied by the *Raleigh*, *Fanny*, and *Forrest*. The *Fanny* which had been captured near Oregon Inlet by the *Seabird* and *Raleigh* was commanded by Lieutenant Tayloe, and the *Forrest* by Lieutenant Hoole. Each carried a 32 pounder rifled gun. I was sent in the

Beaufort to Washington to relieve the *Ellis*, Captain Muse. We went up the Pamlico river by night, passed the fort without being seen, and went through the "obstructions" (of which we knew nothing) without difficulty. This "obstruction" consisted of piles driven in the channel, and like all such amounted to "a row of pins." The good people of Washington were much surprised at seeing us quietly at anchor the next morning, and it taught them a lesson.

It being the opinion of the authorities in Richmond that the enemy would soon make an attempt on Roanoke island Commodore Lynch determined to assemble his squadron there.

The *Beaufort* was ordered to Norfolk to have the gun replaced by a rifled 32-pounder. We went through the Chesapeake and Albemarle canal, which was my first experience in that kind of navigation. I believe we kept the mast-head lookout as usual. We had fine weather and a smooth sea in the canal, doubled the locks without difficulty, and arrived at the Norfolk Navy Yard about the middle of December.

CHAPTER XX

A visit to Newbern—change of officers—join the squadron at Roanoke Island—Wise's brigade—the defences of Roanoke Island—Commodore Lynch's squadron—the Burnside expedition—Flag-Officer Goldsborough's fleet—an evening with Commodore Lynch—battle of Roanoke Island—incidents—retreat of the squadron to Elizabeth City

On the 24th of December I was sent by Commodore Lynch by rail to Newbern to appraise a small steamer bought by him for the Navy. I found Newbern in an excited state, fearing an attack from Hatteras, and the scene of constant alarms. Only the night of my arrival I was sent for by the colonel in command to whom I had offered my services, and informed that they had signalled from one of the posts below that the enemy was coming up the river. While we were waiting further news a captain came in and requested to be relieved from the command of a battery on the river. He said he knew nothing about guns, and if the enemy was coming up he wished to be relieved. He proposed that I should take his place. This did not look well, but I suppose it was an isolated case. Newbern made a good defence when the time came for it.[1]

Upon my return to Norfolk I found the *Beaufort* nearly ready. Mr. Hopkins, my pilot, left me here and I secured another. Mr. Bain relieved Mr. Byrd as my clerk, and Lieutenant [John H.] Johnson joined as executive officer. Johnson, who was from Fredericksburg, was a classmate of mine. He had been engaged in a duel, as second, while at the Naval Academy and was dismissed, as I have before mentioned.[2] He went in 1848 to California, and though afterwards reinstated in the Navy declined to return. He told me he was living on his *ranche* in California when he heard of the secession of Virginia, and that he turned the key in his door and left for home. He left me after the battle of Elizabeth City and was ordered to New Orleans. After the fall of that city he went to Wilmington where he was drowned while going to the assistance of a blockade runner. He was a very modest man, but a most determined and courageous one—every inch a gentleman he was as cool a man under fire as I ever saw.

About the middle of January I proceeded in the *Beaufort* to join the squadron at Roanoke Island. This island, which lies on Croatan Sound between Pamlico and Albemarle Sounds, was garrisoned by a regiment of North Carolina troops, in command of Colonel [Henry M.] Shaw. The district was commanded by General Henry A. Wise, and his brigade was ordered to assist in the defense of the island. His brigade, as far as I have been able to find out, was distributed between Elizabeth City and Nag's Head. Nag's Head, which is abreast of Roanoke Island, on the sea shore, about three miles across, was General Wise's head-quarters. Why General Wise when he was ordered to the command did not establish his headquarters on Roanoke Island, and order all his troops and artillery there, was what I have never been able to discover. Nag's

---

[1]Newbern (or New Bern or New Berne) fell to a combined attack by Commodore Stephen C. Rowan and General Ambrose P. Burnside on 14 March 1862.

[2]See pp. 131–32.

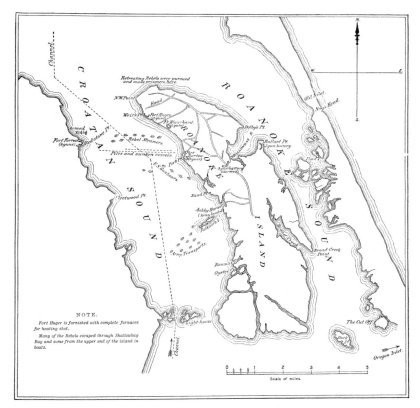

Roanoke Island, North Carolina, from *Official Records of the Union and Confederate Navies*, Series I, Vol. 6.

Head itself could have been rendered untenable by the fire of one Federal gunboat.

Three forts had been constructed on the island to protect the channel. The upper one was on Weir's Point and was named Fort Huger. It mounted twelve guns, principally 32-pounders of 33 cwt., and was commanded by Major John Taylor, formerly of the Navy. About 1¾ miles below, on Pork Point, was Fort Bartow; it mounted seven guns, five of which were 32-pounders of 33 cwt., and two were rifled 32-pounders. This fort, which was the only one subsequently engaged in the defense, was in charge of Lieutenant B. P. Loyall, of the Navy. Between these two points was a small battery. On the main land opposite the island, at Redstone Point, was a battery called Fort Forrest. The guns, which were 32-pounders, were mounted on the deck of a canal-boat which had been hauled up in the mud and placed so that the guns would command the channel. The channel itself was obstructed a little above Fort Huger by piling. It was hoped that these batteries, with the assistance of Commodore Lynch's squadron, would be able to prevent the enemy's ships from passing the island. The great mistake on our part was in not choosing the proper point at which to dispute the entrance to the Sound. The fortifications and vessels should have been at the "marshes," a few miles below, where the channel is very narrow. I do not know who was responsible for the selection of the points fortified as I was not at the island when ground was first broken.

The squadron under Commodore Lynch consisted of the *Seabird* (flagship), Captain McCarrick; *Curlew*, Captain Hunter; *Ellis*, Captain Cooke; *Appomattox*, Captain Sims; *Beaufort*, Captain Parker; *Raleigh*, Captain Alexander; *Fanny*, Captain Tayloe, and *Forrest*, Captain Hoole. Of these vessels the *Seabird* and *Curlew* were side-wheel river steamboats; the *Seabird* of wood and the *Curlew* of iron. The others were screw tug-boats, built for the canal, and were similar to the *Beaufort*. The *Appomattox* and perhaps the *Fanny* were wooden—the others of quarter-inch iron. Each mounted one 32-pounder rifled gun, except the *Seabird* which had a smooth-bore forward and a 30-pounder Parrott gun aft. In addition we had a fine large schooner called the *Black Warrior*, armed with two 32-pounders and commanded by Lieutenant Harris.

The expedition under General Burnside and Flag Officer Goldsborough was assembling at Hatteras Inlet, and although we did not know positively that it was not intended to attack Newbern yet the chances were in favor of Roanoke island. About the 1st of February the *Curlew* and *Raleigh* were sent to Hatteras, and upon their return reported the enemy nearly ready to move. The com-

The naval battle of Roanoke Island. Courtesy Naval History Division.

modore now held a council of war to determine whether the vessels should dispute the advance of the enemy's ships at the "marshes," or assist in the defence in conjunction with the forts. It was decided to adopt the latter plan, though some of the captains favored the first. The majority thought it better not to divide our forces at the eleventh hour.

It was at nine o'clock on the morning of February 6th, 1862, that the enemy's fleet made its appearance. It consisted according to the report of Flag Officer [Louis M.] Goldsborough, of the *Stars and Stripes, Louisiana, Hetzel, Underwriter, Delaware, Commodore Perry, Valley City, Commodore Barney, Hunchback, Southfield, Morse, Whitehead, Lockwood, Brincker, Seymour, Ceres, Putnam, Shawsheen* and *Granite*. These vessels were armed with 100-pounder rifled, 80-pounder rifled, 30-pounder rifled, 20-pounder rifled, 12-pounder rifled, and 9-inch, 8-inch and 6-inch smooth bore guns. Some of them carried four guns each. Their number of guns, exclusive of the *Commodore Perry*, and *Commodore Barney*, was forty-eight; if these two vessels carried three guns each, the total number of guns opposed to us was fifty-four. The enemy's fleet was accompanied by a large number of transports bearing the troops of General [Ambrose] Burnside; and it was evidently his plan to silence our batteries—particularly the one at Pork Point—and land the troops under the protection of the guns of the ships.

The weather at the time the enemy made his appearance was cold, gloomy and threatening, and about 10 a.m. we observed that he had anchored below the "marshes." We had gotten underweigh and formed line abreast, in the rear of the obstructions, and we remained underweigh all day, as the weather was too thick to see very far, and we did not know at what moment the ships might commence the attack. The galley fires were out, and we could have no cooking done, and as the weather was cold with a drizzling rain at intervals, we passed considerably more than one *mauvais quart d'heure!*

About 4 in the afternoon Captain Sims in the *Appomattox* was sent down to reconnoitre. He went very close to the enemy, but was not fired at. Flag Officer Goldsborough says in his allusion to it: "She met with no opposition from us simply because we were not unwilling that she should accomplish her wishes." I presume he wanted us to know what we were to expect the next day. Sims gave a very correct report of the number of men-of-war in the fleet; the number of transports was what "no fellow could find out;" there were too many to count. At sunset, as we saw no disposition on the part of the enemy to move, we anchored and all hands went to supper. We kept guard boats out during the night to avoid a surprise. After getting something to eat I went on board the *Seabird* to see Commodore Lynch. I found him in his dressing gown sitting quietly in his cabin reading *Ivanhoe.* He expressed great pleasure at seeing me and said he had thought of signalling me to come aboard, but knew I must be very tired and he did not wish to disturb me; and I must say for the commodore that I never served under a man who showed more consideration for the comfort of his officers and men. We talked for a long time of what the next day would probably bring forth, and our plans for defence, &c. We neither of us believed that we would be successful, not was there a naval officer in the squadron who thought we would. The force opposed to us both naval and military was too overwhelming. Ten thousand men to our two thousand on land, and nineteen vessels and 54 guns to our eight vessels with 9 guns on the water. After talking some time on the subject, we insensibly got upon literature. Lynch was a cultivated man and a most agreeable talker. He had made some reputation in the navy by his book upon the Dead Sea exploration.[3] We commenced on Scott's novels, naturally, as he held one of the volumes in his hand; incident after incident was recalled and laughed over, and I never spent a more delightful evening. We were recalled to our senses by the ship's bell striking 8 (midnight). I jumped up exclaiming that I did not know it was so late and that I had not intended keeping my gig's-crew up so long. The commodore's last words to me at the gangway were: "Ah! if we could only hope for success;" "but," said he: "come again when you can." For my own part I looked upon it as an *adieu* and not an *au revoir*; for I had made up my mind that it would be death or a prisoner before the next day's sun had set; but as I rowed back to my vessel I thought what strangely constituted and happily constituted beings we are after all. Here were two men looking forward to death in less than 24 hours—death, too, in defeat not victory—and yet able to lose themselves in works of fiction. Well may Scott be called the Wizard of the North! Unknown to ourselves it must be as Campbell writes: "Hope springs eternal in the human breast!"[4]

At daylight the next morning the *Appomattox* was dispatched to Edenton, and as she did not return till sunset and the *Warrior* did not take any part in the action, this reduced our force to seven vessels and eight guns. At 9 A. M. we observed the enemy to be underweigh and coming up, and we formed "line abreast" in the rear of the obstructions. At 11.30 the fight commenced at long

[3]Navy Lieutenant William F. Lynch led an American scientific and exploring expedition to the Jordan River and the Dead Sea in 1847–49. See W. F. Lynch, *Narrative of the United States Expedition to the River Jordan and the Dead Sea* (1852).

[4]Sir Walter Scott was known as the Wizard of the North. Campbell is, of course, Thomas Campbell, *op. cit.*

range. The enemy's fire was aimed at fort Bartow and our vessels, and we soon became warmly engaged. The commodore at first directed his vessels to fall back in the hope of drawing the enemy under the fire of forts Huger and Forrest; but as they did not attempt to advance, and evidently had no intention of passing the obstructions, we took up our first position and kept it during the day. At 2 P. M. the firing was hot and heavy, and continued so until sunset. Our gunners had had no practice with their rifled guns, and our firing was not what it should have been. It was entirely too rapid and not particularly accurate. Early in the fight the *Forrest* was disabled in her machinery, and her gallant young captain (Lieutenant Hoole) badly wounded in the head by a piece of shell. She got in under fort Forrest and anchored. Some time in the afternoon, in the hottest of the fire, reinforcements arrived from Wise's brigade, and were landed on the island. The Richmond Blues, Captain O. Jennings Wise, were, I think, part of this force.

Pork Point battery kept up a constant fire on the fleet, and the enemy could not silence it. The garrison stood to their guns like men, encouraged by the spirited example of their instructor, Lieut. B. P. Loyall. Forts Huger and Forrest did not fire, the enemy being out of range; but the small battery between Pork Point and Weir's Point fired an occasional gun during the day. Towards 4 o'clock in the afternoon a shot or shell struck the hurricane-deck of the *Curlew* in its descent, and went through her decks and bottom as though they had been made of paper. Her captain, finding she was sinking, started for the shore, and as he passed me, hailed; but I could not make out what he said, and he being a very excitable fellow (the North Carolinians called him Tornado Hunter) I said to Johnson that I thought there was nothing the matter with him. "Oh, yes there is," said J., "look at his guards." And sure enough he was fast going down. I put after him in the *Beaufort*, but he got her ashore in time. Hunter put his vessel ashore immediately in front of fort Forrest, completely masking its guns, and we could not fire her for fear of burning up the battery, which, as I have said, was built on an old canalboat. As it turned out, it did not much matter. To show what an excitable fellow Hunter was: he told me afterward that during the fight this day he found to his surprise that he had no trousers on. He said he could never understand it, as he had certainly put on a pair in the morning. I told him I had heard of a fellow being frightened out of his boots, but never out of his trousers. Poor Hunter; he served gallantly during the war, and was second in command at the battle of Sailors Creek, where he was made a prisoner. He dropped dead as he was taking an evening walk, a few years after.

We in the *Beaufort* did our best in maintaining our position, and I had reason to be proud of the way in which every officer and man performed his duty. Johnson as staunch as the mainmast, the two midshipmen full of zeal, and my clerk, Mr. Bain, standing by me on the hurricane deck coolly taking notes of the fight. The first shell that exploded over us scattered the pieces over our decks. Midshipman Mallory, a youth of 14, brought some of the pieces to me with much glee; he looked upon the whole proceeding as great fun. Poor boy! he met with a sad end at last. After serving with me in three engagements he was ordered to the gunboat *Chattahoochee* at Columbus, Ga., and lost his life by the explosion of her boiler. He was from Hampton and was an honor to his birth-place; had he lived and had the opportunity he would have become a great naval officer. My men worked their gun coolly and deliberately, and as the captain of it, Jack Robinson, was an English man-of-wars man, trained on the gunnery ship *Excellent*, I think we did some good firing. My gunner's mate, John Downard, was also from the same ship and knew his duties thoroughly. Both of these men had the Crimean medal. I must not forget to mention my engineer, Mr. Hanks, who was always ready with his engine.

About 4 P. M. I observed that the enemy's troops were landing to the southward of Pork Point [at Ashby Harbor] under the guns of a division of their fleet, and could not perceive that any successful resistance was being made to it. A little after sunset the firing ceased on both sides, and as we felt sure the enemy would not attempt to pass the obstructions by night as he had declined to attempt them by day we ran in and anchored under fort Forrest. We lit our galley fires, and as we had been fighting all day were glad enough to get something to eat. Upon the whole I was rather surprised to find myself alive, and congratulated myself upon having one night more before me. I directed my steward to serve out the cabin stores to the men and let them have a good supper— that was about what I thought of what would be the result of the next day's fight.

During the afternoon when the battle was at its height I ordered the engineer to send me all the men he could spare from the fire-room to work at the gun; one of the men sent up was my green coal-passer, who evidently did not like the appearance of things on deck. However he went to the side tackles of the gun as ordered; after awhile a shell bursting overhead I called to the men to lie down, and when it was over I ordered them to jump up and go at it again. All promptly obeyed but the coal-passer, who still lay flat on his stomach. "Get up," I called to him from the hurricane deck just above him: he turned his head like a turtle and fixed his eye on me, but otherwise did not move. "Get up," I said, "or I will kill you," at the same time drawing a pistol from my belt and cocking it. He hesitated a moment and then sprang to the gun, and behaved well during the rest of the engagement. As I went aft to my cabin after the battle, my steward being busy forward, I called to the engineer to send a man to make a fire in my stove. I had just seated myself before it when who should come in but my friend the coal-passer—he kneeled down in front of me and commenced blowing up a fire. Knowing that the man had not the slightest idea of the discipline of a man-of-war, and wishing to encourage him, I remarked, "Well, my man! I am glad you did your duty so well at the gun after I spoke to you." He blew awhile, and then looking back he said: "I tell you what, captain, I was mighty skeered;" "but," said he after another blow, "I saw you were going to kill me so I thought I *mout* as well take my chances with the enemy." After a few minutes more blowing, he said: "I warn't much skeered after that; it's all in getting *used to it*, Cap." Well, I thought, you have got at the philosophy of it, after all.

I do not remember our loss in the squadron in this day's

engagement; but Lieutenant Hoole was dangerously wounded, and lost an eye, and Midshipman Camm of the *Ellis* lost an arm.

Soon after we anchored signal was made by the flag ship for the captains to report on board. Upon my entering the cabin I was informed by Commodore Lynch that we must retreat from Roanoke Island. Much surprised and mortified, I asked why, and was told that the vessels generally were out of ammunition. A council was held as to whether the vessels should retreat to Norfolk through the Chesapeake and Albemarle Canal, or go to Elizabeth City on the Pasquotank river. We would have saved the vessels by going to the former place, but the commodore's orders were to do his utmost to defend the waters of North Carolina; so we decided to go to the latter, where it was understood a fort had been built to protect the town. Elizabeth City was the terminus of the Dismal Swamp Canal, and we hoped to get ammunition that way from Norfolk in time to act in conjunction with the fort. I was sent to Roanoke Island to communicate all this to Colonel Shaw, and confess did not relish my mission. It looked too much like leaving the army in the lurch; and yet to have remained without ammunition would have been mere folly. I took an officer on shore with me who had gotten on board the *Seabird* somehow—probably he had come in the *Appomattox* from Edenton—he had just been released from a northern prison, and here he was going to meet the same fate again, as we all knew—but he did what he considered his duty. I think he was a Major Dinwiddie,—a noble fellow, whatever his name.

I met Colonel Shaw at his quarters, and stated the facts in relation to the vessels, and then returned to the *Beaufort*. All lights were now extinguished, and the squadron got underweigh for Elizabeth City, the *Seabird* taking the *Forrest* in tow. It was one of the darkest nights I ever knew, and as none of the vessels showed a light it was difficult to avoid a collision. My pilot got confused early in the evening and I had to do the best I could alone; and, considering I had but a faint idea of where Elizabeth City was, I did remarkably well. We fell in with some vessels carrying reinforce-

ments to the island on our way—I think it was Green's battalion—
and the *Beaufort* had the credit of colliding with them. This was
not true, however,—for while I was speaking one of the schooners,
another of our gunboats carried away her head booms.

I anchored in the mouth of the Pasquotank river some time
during the night, and the next morning went to Elizabeth City,
where I found the remainder of the squadron. This was on Saturday, February 8th.[5]

---

[5]Shaw's command on Roanoke Island was overwhelmed the next morning by
the Federal Army under Burnside. Nearly 2,500 Confederates were taken
prisoner.

CHAPTER XXI

The defences of Elizabeth City—Henningsen's Artillery—
reconnoissance by Commodore Lynch—he is chased back to the
Pasquotank—I am placed in command of Fort Cobb—the battle of Elizabeth City—incidents—the destruction of the Confederate squadron—Commodore Lynch—retreat from Elizabeth
City—cross the Dismal Swamp—incidents along the route—
Henningsen's men—march to Suffolk—arrival at Norfolk—
find the *Beaufort* there—join General Wise at Great Bridge—
return to Norfolk and report to Commodore Buchanan—his
squadron

Elizabeth City is on the Pasquotank river, twelve miles from its
mouth. The river here is very narrow and on the right bank, at
Cobb's Point, some two or three miles below, was a battery of four
32-pounder smooth-bore guns. The fort, as it was called, was a
wretchedly constructed affair and not by any means a credit to the
engineer officer who built it. I afterwards met this officer. He
acknowledged that it was badly done; he said that when the

citizens of Elizabeth City applied to General Huger to have a battery put up to protect the town, he was sent to do it. He thought that "Elizabeth City was the last place the Federals would attack," and slighted his work. It shows how uncertain war is, and how important *discipline* is.

The magazine of this fort resembled an African ant-hill more than anything else, and had its door fronting the river, and was of course entirely exposed. The guns were good enough, but they were badly mounted—only one could be trained to fire across the river, the others looked down the channel. We found at Elizabeth City General Henningsen with one or more batteries of light artillery, and after our arrival the militia were called out, and some of them were sent into the fort. We learned that the Dismal Swamp canal was out of order, and vessels could not pass through. Commodore Lynch sent Captain Hunter by express to Norfolk for ammunition, and men to repair the canal.

We could hear firing in the direction of Roanoke island until about noon of this day; it then ceased and we knew the island had fallen. We felt sure Elizabeth City would be the next place attacked, and the commodore appointed me to concert a plan of defence with General Henningsen.

My idea was to land the guns of the vessels and mount them on shore, not together, but distributed on both sides of the river, and to place Henningsen's guns in pits or behind temporary embankments in the same way. By this method the enemy, after getting up with the fort, would have been brought under a very heavy cross fire, and his vessels being of light construction Henningsen's guns would have done them as much damage as our large cannon. The infantry were to seek the best cover they could find and act as sharpshooters along the bank of the river, which was not two hundred yards wide. But there not appearing to be time enough to make this disposition of our guns, it was decided that the schooner *Black Warrior* should be put over on the left bank of the river a little below the fort, and the remainder of the squadron which now consisted of the *Seabird, Ellis, Appomattox, Beaufort, Raleigh* and *Fanny*, should form line abreast across the channel, opposite the fort, and that Henningsen's artillery should be held in reserve. After making these dispositions Commodore Lynch started in the *Seabird* on the 9th for Roanoke island to reconnoitre, and took the *Raleigh* with him. During the afternoon of this day the *Beaufort* towed to the mouth of the canal a schooner loaded with quarter-master's stores; she eventually got to Norfolk with her very valuable cargo. About sunset Commodore Lynch returned in the *Seabird* having been chased by the enemy's vessels, which anchored at the mouth of the river about ten miles below the fort at 8 P. M. The *Raleigh* was either sent to Norfolk *via* the C. and A. canal, or she escaped in that direction while being chased.

The enemy's squadron consisted of fourteen vessels, mounting 33 guns; to oppose which we had six vessels, mounting 8 guns, and the guns of the fort. The *Curlew* had been left at Roanoke Island, where she was burned by her crew. The *Forrest* was hauled up on the ways at Elizabeth City, and the *Raleigh* was probably in Norfolk. Commodore Stephen C. Rowan was in command of the Federal vessels, and we knew him to be a dashing officer.

We anchored abreast the fort in our position, and spent most of the night in dividing the ammunition, so that each vessel should have an equal share. I passed the evening talking over matters with the commodore, and we both concluded that affairs looked blue. The canal being out of order, escape was impossible in that direction, and nothing remained but to fight it out. I went back to the *Beaufort* about two o'clock in the morning and sent for Johnson to give him directions for the next morning. After telling him to give the men breakfast before daylight and then to have everything ready for action, and to call me as soon as he saw the enemy getting underweigh, I went to my cabin and threw myself on my berth "all standing." I really believe I did not take off my sword and pistol; and I know I did not remove my cap. I never was so tired in my life. For more than a week I had not had my clothes off, had had but little sleep, and been in a constant state of excitement. I soon dropped off, and in less than a minute (as it seemed to me) Johnson called me to say the enemy was underweigh and coming up.

"Have the men had their breakfast?" said I. "Yes, sir," said

Johnson. "Is the gun cleared away and ready for action?" "Yes, sir," he replied, "the men are at their quarters, the fires are out, the magazine is opened, and we are all ready for battle." "Very well," I answered; and Johnson went forward. I fell back on my pillow and commenced to moralize: how delightful, thought I, 'twould be to be on shore in the woods where I can hear the birds welcoming the rising sun:

> The breezy call of incense-breathing morn,
> The swallow twittering from the straw-built shed,

and all that sort of thing; here are these confounded fellows coming up to break the peace when I so particularly wish to remain quiet; why will men fight, and before breakfast, too; why not lead a life of peace? why not————. "Look here, Captain," said Johnson, "the enemy is right on top of us!" I sprang up and bade adieu to my moralizing. Upon reaching the hurricane-deck I think I saw the relieved expression of my men. I had not thought of it before, but my non-appearance had given rise to some anxiety.

The enemy were coming up at full speed and our vessels were underweigh ready to abide the shock when a boat came off from the shore with the bearer of a dispatch for me; it read: "Captain Parker with the crew of the *Beaufort* will at once take charge of the fort—Lynch." "Where the devil," I asked, "are the men who were in the fort?" "All run away," said the messenger. And so it was; they had recollected that:

> Souvent celui qui demeure,
> Est cause de son meschef, &c.[1]

and had taken to their heels. The enemy's vessels were by this time nearly in range, and we were ready to open fire. I did not fancy this taking charge at the last moment, but there was no help for it, so I put the men in the boats with their arms and left the *Beaufort* with the pilot, engineer and two men on board. I directed the pilot to slip the chain and escape through the canal to Norfolk if possible,

---

[1]Roughly translated, this is: He who hesitates is lost.

otherwise to blow the steamer up rather than be captured. He "cut out," as Davy Crockett says, accordingly. While pulling ashore the officers and men were engaged in tearing some sheets into bandages to be used for the wounded men: a cheerful occupation under the circumstances! but it was one of the delights of serving in these gunboats that no surgeons were allowed. All the wounded had to be sent to the flag ship for treatment. Upon getting into the fort I hastily commenced stationing the men at the guns, and as quickly as possible opened fire upon the advancing enemy. Some of the officers and men of the *Forrest* made their way to us upon learning that the militia had fled. I must not forget to say that the engineer officer who had been sent from Richmond for service in the fort remained bravely at his post. He asked me to report this fact in case he was killed. He was a Prussian, and I think his name was Heinrich. He was not the engineer who built the fort. I found Commodore Lynch on shore; his boat had been cut in two by a shot and he could not get off to his ship, as he informed me, and he furthermore said I was to command the fort without reference to his being there; that if he saw an opportunity to get off to the *Seabird* he should embrace it.

The enemy's vessels came on at full speed under a heavy fire from our vessels and the fort. The fire from the latter was ineffectual. The officers and men were cool enough; but they had not had time to look about them. Everything was in bad working order, and it was difficult to train the guns. Just before we commenced to fire two of my men brought a man to me and said in the most indignant manner: "Captain here's a man who says he don't want to fight!" The idea of one of the *Beaufort's* not wanting to fight seemed to irritate them exceedingly. I looked and beheld my poor cook trembling before me. The men held him up by the collar, for his legs refused to do duty. He was a delicate-looking Spaniard and, poor fellow, could speak very little English. He had been captured in a prize and had shipped in the *Beaufort* for the want of something better to do. He knew nothing about the war and cared less. In the fight at Roanoke he had been stationed in the magazine, and as it was pitch dark there had fondly imagined himself in a safe place; but it was different here in the broad daylight. *"Que diable allait-il faire dans cette galère!"*[2] Falling on his knees before me, he could only say: "captain, me no wantee fight," which he kept repeating. Poor fellow, I thought, I don't wantee fight either—at least, not until after breakfast. "Put him in the magazine," said I, recalling his former station, and thought no more about him. But he was to be my *bête noir* that day, for in the heat of the battle two of Henningsen's horsemen brought him to me between them. He had fled from the magazine, and they had captured him. He was in an exceedingly limp condition; but I said, as before, "put him in the magazine," which was done. He got away again, however, and beat us all to Norfolk—and that's saying a good deal.

Commodore Rowan's steamers did not reply to our fire until quite close, and without slackening their speed they passed the fort and fell upon our vessels. They made short work of them! The *Seabird* was rammed and sunk by the *Commodore Perry*. The *Ellis* was captured after a desperate defence, in which her gallant commander, James Cook, was badly wounded. The schooner *Black Warrior* was set on fire and abandoned, her crew escaping through the marshes on their side of the river. The *Fanny* was run on shore near the fort and blown up by her commander, who with his crew escaped to the shore. Before the *Ellis* was captured some of her officers and men attempted to reach the shore—among them, Midshipman Wm. C. Jackson, a handsome youth of 17—he was to have joined my ship the next day. He was shot in the water while swimming on shore. I do not blame the enemy for this—it was unavoidable—but it was a melancholy affair. He was taken on board the U. S. steamer *Hetzel* and received every attention. He died at 10 P. M. the same day, and was buried on shore. Captain Sims, of the *Appomattox* kept up a sharp fire from his bow gun until it was accidentally spiked; and he then had to run for it. He had a howitzer aft which he kept in play; but upon arriving at the mouth

---

[2]A line from Molière's *Les Fourberies de Scapin*. Roughly translated it is: What the deuce was he doing there?

of the canal he found his vessel was about *two inches* too wide to enter; he therefore set her on fire, and she blew up. The *Beaufort* got through to Norfolk.

We in the fort saw this work of destruction going on without being able to prevent it. As soon as the vessels passed the fort we could not bring a gun to bear on them, and a shot from them would have taken us in reverse. A few rounds of grape would have killed and wounded all the men in the fort, for the distance was only a few hundred yards. Seeing this, I directed Johnson to spike the guns, to order every man to shoulder his musket, and then to take down the flag. All this was promptly and coolly done, and upon the fact being reported to me by Johnson, I pointed to some woods in our rear and told him to make the best of his way there with the command. All this time Commodore Lynch had stood quietly looking on, but without uttering a word. As his command had just been destroyed under his eyes, I knew pretty well what his feelings were. Turning to him I said: "Commodore, I have ordered the fort evacuated." "Why so, sir?" he demanded. I pointed out the condition of affairs I have just stated, and he acquiesced. Arm in arm we followed the retreating men. The enemy had by this time turned their attention from the ships to the fort and commenced firing shot and shell in our direction. We had to cross a ploughed field, and we made slow progress. I wished very much that the commodore was twenty years younger. I felt that instead of a slow walk, a sharp run would have been better exercise—more bracing, as it were. We had nearly reached the woods when I met my two men, Robinson and Downard, posting back in great haste. They took their hats off when they saw me and looked a little sheepish. "Were you not ordered into the woods?" I inquired. "Yes, sir," answered they. "Then where are you going?" I demanded. "Come back to look for you, sir," said Robinson. They had missed me in the woods, and fearing I had been killed or wounded were going back to carry me off! And here was my first lieutenant, Johnson, aiding and abetting them! As soon as we struck the road we procured a guide, and as we had to pass Elizabeth City which was now in possession of the enemy, we hurried up for fear of being taken prisoners. We had observed that some of the vessels carried troops—in fact there was a Rhode Island regiment present—and we expected they would land and intercept us. The officers and men of the *Fanny* and *Forrest*, and stragglers from the other vessels, reported to me and I found I was, next to the commodore, the senior officer on shore. I soon got the commodore off in a buggy, and I begged him to make the best of his way to Richmond. It was the most extraordinary-looking vehicle I ever laid my eyes on, and I felt sure it would cause a sensation in Richmond if the commodore's report did not.

I had been told by Commodore Lynch that if I evacuated the fort I was to fall back on Henningsen. I fell back as fast as I could, but did not see anything of his command. After we had gotten by Elizabeth City we felt pretty safe against capture, particularly as by twelve o'clock I had my entire command mounted or in country wagons, and I got them in something like military organization, with commissary, quartermaster, etc.

The scenes along the road were distressing, and yet sometimes so comical that one found himself laughing with the "tear in his eye." We passed at one place the smoking ruins of a house. The neighbors told me it had been occupied by a Union man who upon learning of the success of the Federals at Elizabeth City had refused even water to the retreating troops of Henningsen. Locking up his house he took up a position in the upper story, and finally ended by firing on the soldiers who were about the house and killed one of them. The soldiers burned the house with the man in it. Passing another place I saw a young girl in convulsions and screaming at the top of her lungs. Her parents were trying to pacify her in vain. I added my persuasions, I told her everything would be all right, the war would soon be over, etc. "Oh! what does it matter," said she, "if the war *is* soon over, if all the *men* are killed?" I "passed."

The kindness and hospitality of the people along the route was unbounded. Just before sunset my quarter-master, who had been riding in advance, reported that a gentleman living near by had offered to give us all supper and a night's lodging. I gladly accepted his offer. At this time I overtook General Henningsen and his staff—I never did catch up with his guns. The general was opposed to my remaining on that side of the river for the night, and said we would be captured. I told him the offer was too good to be declined, and added (for the recollection of his troopers bringing back my unfortunate cook to the fort, and their remarks, had left a sore spot): "General, I was told to fall back on you and have been doing so all day; now I intend to stop." I wish I could recall the name of the gentleman who entertained us. I had about 150 officers and men, and to supply us all was no light tax—to say nothing of the animals. The men were given a good supper and quarters in the barn, and the officers received in his house. There were many ladies there—refugees from Elizabeth City. They forgot their own troubles and insisted on waiting upon us at table. It was only one of the many instances of the noble and inspiriting conduct of the Southern women. *They* never gave up. In the darkest hour of the war they had an encouraging word. As for the sick and wounded, God knows what they would have done without their kind nurses. Scott has rendered woman a tribute; but the wars of the world have never produced the equal of the Southern woman.

We left our kind friends at 3 o'clock next morning, and I sent our quarter-master on ahead to order breakfast at a tavern where I knew we should arrive about 8 o'clock. I was told that it would take us two days to reach Suffolk as the road across the Dismal Swamp would not permit of rapid traveling; but I made up my mind I would be there that night if it were possible. The *Merrimac*, I knew, would be soon ready for her crew, and it was most important to get the men with me to Norfolk as quickly as possible. There were no sailors to spare at the South. We arrived at the tavern and breakfasted—the ladies there (refugees) attending to our wants at table, and everybody doing all in their power to assist us in getting on. The proprietor would take no pay, so we could only offer our thanks, and after giving three cheers we started. About 12 we came to a cross-road country store and were told that Commodore Lynch had passed and ordered dinner for the men; but as they had so lately breakfasted I would not stop. I rode in the rear of the command and kept the horses moving. About 3 in the afternoon I was hailed from a house and found there Commodore Lynch. The hospitable owner would not hear of our continuing on our way without stopping for some refreshment, so I consented to remain; and in a short time he and his wife and daughters, with their servants, were busily engaged preparing it. The commodore started off alone in his gig for Suffolk. We remained an hour and then left, and traveling at good speed arrived at Suffolk at 9 P. M. We had made nearly forty miles since leaving the fort the day before, which, under the circumstances, was not bad traveling. The first news I got was that the commodore had not arrived. He told me afterward he took the wrong road and did not get to Suffolk until the next day. We were most kindly received at Suffolk, and learning that a special train was about returning to Norfolk I put my command on board and sent the horses and wagons back to their owners. We got safely to Norfolk, and at midnight I awakened Commodore Forrest at the Navy Yard and reported the disastrous result of the battle of Elizabeth City. I learned to my great gratification that the *Beaufort* was safely alongside the wharf at the Yard. Upon Captain Hunter's arrival a force had been put to work on the canal, and the *Beaufort* had succeeded in getting through.

After the fall of Roanoke island General Wise had retreated from Nag's Head in the direction of Norfolk on the line of the Chesapeake and Albemarle canal, and I was sent up the canal in the *Beaufort* to co-operate with him. We went up about the 12th of February, and after making a reconnoissance as far as North river I returned to Great Bridge where I met the General and his men. We had very cold, disagreeable weather, and Wise's men as they arrived looked in bad condition. The General's son, Captain O. Jennings Wise, was killed at Roanoke island, and he himself seemed in poor health and worse spirits. In fact the result of the past week's fighting had dispirited us all, and the cold, sleeting weather did not tend to cheer us up. Wise had in his brigade all the Nicaragua *filibusters* I had ever heard of. I do not know how they happened to congregate in his brigade, but they did. The most noted of these men and the one who particularly interested me was Henningsen. He had been Walker's right hand man and military adviser in all his operations in Central America. He was a tall, gaunt man with sandy hair and florid complexion—of Scandinavian origin, he looked the picture of an ancient Viking. He wore a slouched hat and a monkey jacket and walked with a staff. Commencing life as an officer in the British army he had served in the Don Carlos war in Spain, and after serving in various armies of Europe and in Nicaragua had finally turned up in the confederacy. He was the most perfect Major Dalgetty I ever met, and he frequently came on board the *Beaufort* to see me. At this time he was a colonel in the Confederate army; but for some reason he was not employed after the operations I am describing.

As I have before said, Wise's brigade was scattered between Elizabeth City and Nag's Head at the time Roanoke island was attacked. Why it was not concentrated on the island I have never learned. A portion of it was in the battle and a battalion belonging to it was on its way there. One regiment was at Nag's Head and Henningsen with his artillery was at Elizabeth City. There may have been good reasons for this, want of transportation or something, but I have failed to discover them. I know now that if our force had been assembled at the "marshes" and proper fortifications put there we could have kept the Burnside expedition at bay. And even as it was, if there had been more men on the island and they had stood to their guns the troops of Burnside could not have landed. The vessels not only did not pass the island, but did not attempt to do so until the forts had been turned and captured by the army. Pork Point battery which stood the brunt of the bombardment on the 7th was hardly damaged. Captain Loyall has since told me that by the aid of some thirty negroes they had there on the night of the 7th, the fort was in as good condition on the morning of the 8th as it was the morning before. Only another instance of the impossibility of demolishing an earthwork by a distant and non-continuous bombardment.

I returned to Norfolk about the 20th of February for repairs. My executive officer was here detached and ordered to New Orleans, otherwise there was no change in my officers. I was now ordered to report to Flag Officer Franklin Buchanan who had been put in command of the vessels in the waters of Virginia. His command consisted of the *Merrimac* (iron clad), *Beaufort* and *Raleigh* at Norfolk, and the steamers *Patrick Henry*, *Jamestown* and *Teaser* on the James river. There were several vessels building in Richmond and five or six new gunboats in Norfolk. Two of the latter, the *Hampton* and the *Nansemond*, were nearly ready. I shall speak of these vessels in another place. They were none of them engaged in the operations in Hampton Roads which were so soon to follow.

CHAPTER XXII

The evacuation of Norfolk by the Federals—ordnance left at the Navy Yard—vessels burned—the *Merrimac*—is converted into an iron-clad—her designer—her construction and appearance—her armament—her engines and speed—her draft

As I have said before, the evacuation of Norfolk by the Federals on the night of April 20th, 1861, was one of the most extraordinary proceedings of the war. They were in possession of the navy yard with its large amount of ordnance stores; they had several vessels in commission, and were within 12 miles of reinforcements from Fortress Monroe. By keeping the *Pawnee* running between Old Point and Norfolk they could have prevented any attempt to obstruct the channel, and the corvette *Cumberland* with her broadside sprung upon the town would have kept the citizens quiet. The spirit of madness or folly prevailed, and I know of no better exhibition of it than the fact that while they were trying to get out, our people were actually trying to obstruct the harbor so as to keep them in.

During the seven days' fights around Richmond, after the Federals were driven to Harrison's Landing on the James river, I was one day in the Spottswood hotel. Officers were constantly arriving with the latest news; and the most wonderful rumors were put in circulation. We heard that "Lee was about to bag McClellan's entire army;" "that they could not get away;" "that they wanted to get away," etc., etc. An old planter, who had been driven from his farm on the river, after listening to all this, impatiently exclaimed: "then why, in God's name, don't we let them go."

One would have thought the people of Norfolk would have looked upon the going of the United States vessels in the same light.

To say nothing of the other stores left at the Navy Yard and afterwards used by the Confederates, the following is a list of the guns as given in the report of Mr. Wm. H. Peters, who took an inventory by order of the Governor of Virginia:

      1 11-inch columbiad.
      2 10-inch guns.
     52 9-inch   "
      4 8-inch   90 cwt. guns.
     47 8-inch   63   "   "
     27 8-inch   55   "   "
      1 8-inch   57   "   "
      4 64-pounders, of 106 cwt.
    225 32-pounders, "   61   "
    173 32-pounders, "   57   "
     44 32-pounders, "   51   "
     28 32-pounders, "   46   "
    116 32-pounders, "   33   "
     44 32-pounders, "   27   "
    235 61-cwt. guns, old style.
     50 70-cwt.   "   "
     44 40-cwt. Shubrick guns.
     63 42-pounder carronades.
     35 32-pounder   "

Here we have 1195 guns of large calibre!

The vessels destroyed or partially destoyed were the *Pennsylvania*, three-decker; the *Delaware*, 74; the *Columbus*, 74; the frigates *Merrimac*, *Columbia* and *Raritan*; the sloops-of-war *Germantown* and *Plymouth*, and the brig *Dolphin*. The old frigate *United States* was left intact, and was used by the Confederates as a receiving ship most of the war. Of these vessels the steam frigate *Merrimac* was scuttled and sunk, and burned to her copper-line and down through to her berth-deck, which, with her spar and gun-decks, was also burned. She was raised, and the powder in her magazine (put up in air-tight copper tanks) was found to be in good condition; and it was afterwards used by her in her engagements.

Who first proposed to turn the *Merrimac* into an iron-clad I am not prepared to say. It was claimed by Commander John M. Brooke and by Naval Constructor John L. Porter. I have previously stated whom I believe to have been the first officer in the Confederate Navy who fully appreciated the use of iron in naval warfare and advised its adoption, Lieutenant Wm. L. Powell. In the case of the *Merrimac*, the originality consisted in the design and not the use of iron. Lieutenant Catesby ap R. Jones says that on the 21st of June, 1861, the Hon. S. R. Mallory, Confederate Secretary of the Navy, ordered that the *Merrimac* should be converted into an iron-clad on the plan proposed by Lieutenant John M. Brooke, C. S. Navy.

The ship was raised as I have said, and what had previously been her berth deck became now her main gun deck. She was 275 feet long as she then floated, and over the central portion of the hull a house or shield about 160 feet long was built. This shield was of oak and pine wood two feet thick; the sides and ends inclined, according to Lieutenant Jones, 36 degrees, and the roof which was flat and perhaps 20 feet wide was covered with iron gratings, leaving four hatchways. Upon this wooden shield were laid two courses of iron plates two inches thick—the first course horizontal and the second perpendicular, making four inches of iron armor on two feet of wood backing. The iron was put on while the vessel was in dock, and it was supposed that she would float with her ends barely submerged. So great was her buoyancy, however, that it required some 800 tons of pig iron (according to boatswain Hasker in his account of her) to bring her down to her proper depth. I know myself that a quantity of iron was put on, though I cannot say how much. Now as this iron was put on, the whole structure sunk, and when she was ready for battle her ends, which extended about 50 feet forward and abaft the shield, were submerged to the depth of several inches and could not be seen. I have reason to recollect this, for I had occasion to go close alongside her several times in the *Beaufort* on the 8th of March, and I was always fearful of getting on top of her extremities. I could not see where she commenced or ended!

The appearance of the *Merrimac* was that of the roof of a house. Saw off the top of a house at the eaves, (supposing it to be an ordinary gable-ended, shelving-sides roof), pass a plane parallel to the first through the roof some feet beneath the ridge, incline the gable ends, put it in the water and you have the *Merrimac* as she appeared. When she was not in action her people stood on top of this roof which was in fact her spar deck.

Lieutenant Catesby Jones says: "The prow was of cast iron, wedge shaped, and weighed 1500 pounds. It was about two feet under water, and projected two feet from the stem; it was not well fastened." I may mention that it was so badly fastened that the best judges said it would certainly break off when used. It will be seen hereafter that perhaps it was as well that it was not well fastened. Lieutenant Jones says: "The rudder and propeller were unprotected. The battery consisted of ten guns; four single banded Brooke rifles, and six 9 inch Dahlgren guns. Two of the rifles, bow and stern pivots, were 7-in. of 14,500 pounds; the other two were 6.4-in. 32-pounder calibre, of 9,000 pounds, one on each broadside. The 9-in. gun on each side nearest the furnaces was fitted for firing hot shot. A few 9-in. shot with extra windage were cast for hot shot. No other solid shot were on board during the fight. The engines were the same the vessel had whilst in the U. S. Navy. They were radically defective and had been condemned by the U. S. government. Some changes had been made, notwithstanding which the engineers reported that they were unreliable. They performed very well during the fight, but afterwards failed several times, once while under fire. Commodore Tattnall commanded the *Virginia* (*Merrimac*) forty-five days, of which time there were only thirteen days that she was not in dock or in the hands of the navy yard. Yet he succeeded in impressing the enemy that we were ready for active service."[1]

The chief engineer of the *Merrimac*, Mr. H. Ashton Ramsay, had been a shipmate with me in the last cruise of the *Merrimac* in the Pacific. He was then a passed assistant engineer. He knew the engines well, and I doubt if another man in the Confederate Navy could have gotten as much out of them as he did. He deserved all the credit Admiral Buchanan afterwards gave him. The draft of water of the *Merrimac* upon her first appearance in Hampton Roads was about 21½ feet. After she was docked on the 9th of March and more iron put on, she drew about one foot more. When she went down to the Roads on the 8th of March she steamed about seven knots an hour. Ramsay and I agreed that she steamed quite as well as when we made our cruise in her. After docking, her speed was reduced about one knot per hour. She carried a full complement of officers and 320 men—among the latter were not many regular man-of-war's men. She was christened the *Virginia* by the Confederate authorities and was officially known by that name; but I shall continue to call her by the name which has become historical.

[1]Captain Catesby ap R. Jones, "Services of the *Virginia* (*Merrimac*)," *Southern Historical Society Papers* (1883), pp. 65–75.

CHAPTER XXIII

The Federal ships in Hampton Roads—the *Merrimac* and her consorts leave Norfolk—the battle of Hampton Roads—the sinking of the *Cumberland*—arrival of the James River Squadron—the batteries at Newport's News—the frigates *Minnesota*, *Roanoke* and *St. Lawrence* come up from Old Point—they get aground—surrender of the *Congress*—fire from troops on shore—incidents of the battle—the Federal loss—the Confederate loss—the ram and iron-clad—Confederate gunboats—services of the wooden vessels in this battle

About the 6th of March, 1862, the *Merrimac* being ready to go out, the Norfolk papers published an article to the effect that she was a failure, and would not be able to accomplish anything. It was intended, of course, to deceive the enemy, who we knew regularly received our papers. The Federal squadron then in Hampton Roads, consisted of the following vessels, viz.: the *Congress* and *Cumberland*, lying off Newport's News; and the *Minnesota*, *Roanoke* and *St. Lawrence*, at anchor below Old Point. There were also at Old Point the store-ship *Brandywine*, the steamers *Mt. Vernon* and *Cambridge*, and a number of transports and tugs; these, however, took no part in the subsequent engagement. The *Congress* was a sailing frigate of 1867 tons, mounting 50 guns, principally 32-pounders, and a crew of 434 men; the *Cumberland* was a large corvette (a *razee*) of 1700 tons, mounting 22 nine-inch guns, and a crew of 376 men; the *Minnesota* was a steam frigate of 3200 tons, mounting 43 guns, of 9-inch and 11-inch calibre, and a crew of about 600 men. The *Roanoke* was similar to the *Minnesota*, and the *St. Lawrence* to the *Congress*.

Newport's News is 6½ miles from Old Point and 12 miles from Norfolk. It is on the left bank of the James river, and above Old Point. The enemy had a large number of guns mounted there to protect the mouth of the river, and it had a large garrison. At Seawell's Point, 3½ miles from Old Point, the Confederates had a powerful battery to protect the entrance to the Elizabeth river. It also, in a measure, commanded the approach to Newport's News; but the main ship channel is at a distance of 2 or 2½ miles from it. At Seawell's Point was mounted the only 11-inch gun we had in the Confederacy.

Everything being ready, it was determined by Commodore Buchanan to make the attack on the 8th of March. The night before, he sent for me and gave me my final orders. The last change made in our signal-books was that if the Commodore's flag was hoisted under number "one," it meant "sink before you surrender." Mr. Hopkins, who had formerly been my pilot, came on board the *Beaufort* as a volunteer, and Midshipman Ivy Foreman, of North Carolina, reported to me as volunteer aid. They both rendered excellent service the next day.

At 11 A.M., March 8, 1862, the signal was made to sail, and the *Beaufort* cast off from the wharf in company with the *Merrimac* and *Raleigh*, and stood down the harbor. The weather was fair, the wind light, and the tide half flood; the moon was nine days' old. Nearly every man, woman and child in the two cities of Norfolk and Portsmouth were at the same time on their way to Seawell's Point, Craney Island and other points, where they could see the great naval combat which they knew was at last to take place. Some went by land, others by water. All the batteries were manned; all work was suspended in public and private yards, and those who were forced to remain behind were offering up prayers for our success. A great stillness came over the land.

Flag Officer Forrest who commanded the station, accompanied by all the officers of the navy yard went down with us in the *Harmony* as far as Craney island, 4½ miles below Norfolk. Everything that would float, from the army tug-boat to the oysterman's skiff, was on its way down to the same point loaded to the water's edge with spectators. As we steamed down the harbor we were saluted by the waving of caps and handkerchiefs; but no voice broke the silence of the scene; all hearts were too full for utterance; an attempt at cheering would have ended in tears, for all realized the fact that here was to be tried the great experiment of the ram and iron-clad in naval warfare. There were many who thought that as soon as the *Merrimac* rammed a vessel she would sink with all hands enclosed in an iron-plated coffin. The least moved of all, were those who were about to do battle for the "Cause" they believed in. On board the *Merrimac* the officers and men were coolly employed in the multifarious duties that devolved upon them, while the men of the *Beaufort* and *Raleigh* were going into battle with the same careless *insouciance* they had exhibited in the battles of Roanoke island and Elizabeth City.

The James river squadron, consisting of the *Patrick Henry*, *Jamestown* and *Teaser*, under the command of Captain [John R.] Tucker, had been previously notified by Commodore Buchanan that the *Merrimac* would go out on the 8th, and Tucker was directed to come down the river as close to Newport's News as he deemed prudent, so as to be ready to dash by the batteries and join our division when the action commenced. The commodore could not have given the order to a better man—eager to engage the enemy, Tucker, the most chivalric and bravest of men, ably seconded by his gallant captains, Nicholas Barney, Webb, and Rochelle, was only too ready to fly the Confederate flag in Hampton Roads. At daylight that morning he was at anchor off

Smithfield Point—some ten miles above Newport's News—and in full view of the enemy, as afterwards reported by Lieutenant George Morris who, in the absence of her commander, fought the *Cumberland*. As we got down towards the mouth of the Elizabeth river, about 12.30 P. M., the *Beaufort* took a line from the port bow of the *Merrimac* to assist her in steering—being very near the bottom she steered very badly. Mr. Cunningham, one of her pilots, came on board at the same time by order of Commodore Buchanan. This gave the *Beaufort* three pilots; the *Merrimac* remained with three, and the *Raleigh* with one. We turned up the James river. The *Congress* and *Cumberland* were lying off Newport's News and were riding to the last of the flood tide. They had their "washed clothes" up at the time we saw them, I remember, which shows how entirely unexpected our appearance was—in fact the captain of the *Cumberland*, Commander William C. Radford, was at this time on board the frigate *Roanoke* below Old Point attending a court-martial. Lieutenant George Morris was left in command, and the ship could not have been better fought by any officer of the U. S. navy.

The *Cumberland* was lying at anchor just above Newport's News, and the *Congress* abreast the Point. As soon as our vessels turned up the James river the enemy saw that our attack would be made upon the frigates, lying off Newport's News, and the two ships there commenced getting ready to receive it.

At 1.30 P. M. we cast off the line from the *Merrimac*, and all three vessels steamed for the enemy, the *Beaufort* maintaining her position on the port bow of the *Merrimac*; and exactly at 2 P. M. we fired the first gun of the day, and at the same time hoisted the battle flag we had used at Roanoke island at the mast-head. This flag resembled the French flag—it was, I think, the colors reversed. It was devised by Commodore Lynch and was used by his squadron. I had not thought of referring the matter to Commodore Buchanan; but I determined to hoist it "for luck," and I will not deny that I had some superstition in connection with it. The men were all for hoisting it, and that decided me. I do not wonder that

Captain Marston of the *Roanoke* said in his report: "It was the impression of some of my officers that the rebels hoisted the French flag."[1]

The *Merrimac* now hoisted the signal, "close action," and from that time until the surrender of the *Congress* she made no signal, nor did she answer one. I mention this particularly as it caused me to consider that I must use my own judgment during the battle—only recollecting to obey the signal for close action—and I know that other officers commanding gunboats thought as I did.

The fire of the *Cumberland* on the *Merrimac* was so heavy while it lasted that it was impossible for a man to stand on her upper deck and live—so perhaps was the fire of the *Congress*. I only mention the fact stated; and I have no recollection of seeing a man on the deck of the *Merrimac* from the beginning of the fight until after the *Congress* surrendered. During the afternoon, in the heat of the action, the *Raleigh* came alongside me and her commander, Lieutenant Alexander, told me the carriage of his gun was disabled and he could not fire a shot. He said he could not get his signals answered by the *Merrimac*, and wanted to know what he should do. I directed him to return to Norfolk. This is in corroboration of what I have said above. Fortunately Alexander repaired the damage and did not have to leave the fight.

As we approached the enemy, firing and receiving their fire, the *Merrimac* passed the *Congress* and made for the *Cumberland*—which vessel was either just turning to the ebb tide, or had her broadside sprung across the channel. The *Beaufort* and *Raleigh* engaged the *Congress* and shore batteries, and the firing became fast and furious. I took up a position on the port quarter of the *Congress* and used the rifled gun with effect. The *Merrimac* rammed the *Cumberland*, striking her just forward of the starboard fore channel—firing and receiving a heavy fire in return—and stove her bow in so completely that she at once commenced to go down. As she took the

---

[1]Captain John Marston's report to Navy Secretary Gideon Welles is printed in *The Official Records of the Union and Confederate Navies in the War of the Rebellion* (Hereafter cited as *O.R.N.*), Series I, 7:8–9.

bottom she turned over on her beam-ends. She made a gallant defense, her crew fighting their guns to the last, and went down with her colors flying. This was at 2.40 P. M. precisely. Boats went off from Newport's News to save the drowning men. The *Merrimac* reversed her engines immediately upon ramming the *Cumberland*, and had some difficulty in extricating herself—indeed her bow sunk several feet. When free, she proceeded a short distance up the river to turn round, having done which she stood for the *Congress*.

As soon as the *Congress* observed the fate of her consort she slipped her cable, set her fore-topsail flying, and with the assistance of a tug, ran on shore below Newport's News. At this time I observed the James river squadron coming gallantly into action; they were under a very heavy fire while passing the Newport's News batteries, but got by without receiving much damage. All of our vessels now directed their fire upon the *Congress*. I took up a position on her starboard quarter and kept it until she surrendered. The fire on this unfortunate ship was perfectly terrific. She returned it with alacrity, principally from her stern guns, and was assisted by the batteries on shore.

We saw now the frigates *Minnesota*, *Roanoke* and *St. Lawrence* coming up from Old Point to the assistance of the *Congress*, towed by powerful tugs. They were under a heavy fire from the batteries on Seawell's Point as they passed, and received some damage. The *Minnesota* received a rifle-shot through her mainmast, "crippling it," according to her captain's report. Strange to say all three of these vessels ran aground; the *Minnesota* about one and a half miles below Newport's News, the *St. Lawrence* farther down, and the *Roanoke* below her again. The *Minnesota* was near enough to take part in the engagement and the *St. Lawrence* fired a few broadsides. The *Roanoke* and *St. Lawrence* were soon pulled off by the tugs and made the best of their way back to Old Point. They took no farther part in the battle. The *Minnesota* remained aground. The *Congress* made a gallant defence and did not surrender until one hour and twenty minutes after the sinking of the *Cumberland*. Her decks were running with blood, and she bore the brunt of the day. At 4 o'clock she hoisted a large white flag at her mainmast head, and as it went up, Midshipman Mallory in charge of our bow-gun, waved his cap and exclaimed: "I'll swear on the Bible that we fired the last gun!" So the *Beaufort* fired the first and last gun in this memorable battle. When I saw the white flag, I immediately lowered a boat, and sent Midshipman Mallory and Foreman with a boat's crew of three men to take possession of the prize and bring her commander on board the *Beaufort*. As the boat approached the *Congress* a marine at the gangway levelled his piece, and threatened to fire; but Mallory told him he was ordered to board the vessel, and was "bound to do it," and pulled alongside. He and his companions got on board, and Midshipman Foreman hauled down the colors and brought them to me.

The firing having ceased, the *Merrimac* signalled me to come within hail, which I did. Commodore Buchanan then ordered me to "go alongside the *Congress*, to take the officers and wounded men prisoners, to permit the others to escape to the shore, and then to burn the ship." I went alongside her in the *Beaufort*, at the port gangway, and sent an officer to direct her commander to come to me, at the same time sending my men aboard to help to get the wounded men to the *Beaufort*. I did not think it proper to leave my vessel myself as I had but two young and inexperienced midshipmen with me, and I saw an enemy's gunboat not very far off. In a few minutes Lieutenant Austin Pendergrast came down the side of the *Congress* accompanied by an officer whom I took to be the purser or surgeon of the ship. It proved to be Captain William Smith who had been in command until a few days before, when he had been relieved by Lieutenant Joseph B. Smith. Lieutenant Smith was killed in the action, which left Pendergrast in command. Captain Smith was acting as a volunteer; but this I learned afterwards. These two officers landed on the hurricane deck of the *Beaufort* where I was standing, and surrendered the ship. As they were without side-arms I thought it proper to request them to return to their ship and get them. This they did, though Pendergrast delivered to me a ship's cutlass instead of the regulation sword. I now told Pendergrast my orders and asked him to get his officers and wounded men on board as quickly as possible as I wanted to burn the ship. He said there were 60 wounded men on board the frigate and begged me not to burn the vessel. I told him my orders were peremptory. While we were engaged in this conversation the wounded men were being lowered into the *Beaufort*, and just then the *Raleigh* came alongside me. Lieutenant [James L.] Tayloe came on board and said Captain Alexander had sent him to me for orders. I directed him to take the *Raleigh* to the starboard side of the *Congress* and assist in getting off the wounded men. I had scarcely given him the order when a tremendous fire was opened on us from the shore by a regiment of soldiers—Medical Director Shippen says it was the 20th Indiana. The firing was from artillery as well as small arms. At the first discharge every man on the deck of the *Beaufort*—save Captain Smith and Lieutenant Pendergrast—was either killed or wounded. Four bullets passed through my clothing; one of which carried off my cap cover and eye glass, and another slightly wounded me in the left knee, precisely in the spot where my friend Fauntleroy had accidentally wounded me at the siege of Vera Cruz. Lieutenant Pendergrast now begged me to hoist the white flag, saying that all his wounded men would be killed. I called his attention to the fact that they were firing on the white flag which was flying at his mainmast head directly over our heads. I said I would not hoist it on the *Beaufort*; in fact I did not feel authorized to do so without consulting Commodore Buchanan. I said: "Tell your men to stop firing;" he replied: "They are a lot of volunteers and I have no control over them." This was evident. The lieutenant then requested permission to go on board the *Congress* with Captain Smith and assist in getting the wounded down. This I assented to; in the first place, I was glad to have their assistance; and secondly, I would not have been willing to confine them in my cabin at a time when the bullets were going through it like hail—humanity forbade it; I would not have put a dog there.

I now blew the steam-whistle, and my men came tumbling on board. The fire of the enemy still continuing from the shore, I cast off from the *Congress* and steamed ahead so that I could bring my bow gun to bear. I had no idea of being fired at any longer without returning it, and we had several deaths to avenge. We opened fire, but could make little impression with our single gun upon the large number of men firing from intrenchments on shore. The sides and masts of the *Beaufort* looked like the top of a pepper-box from the bullets, which went in one side and out at the other. Being much encumbered with the prisoners, five of whom were wounded, and having no medical officer on board, I ran alongside the steamer *Harmony* and delivered them to Flag Officer Forrest. They consisted of Master's Mate Peter Hargous and 25 men. We then steamed immediately back and joined the other vessels in the attack on the *Minnesota*, which vessel was still on shore. The air seemed to be full of shot and shell from this time till some time between 7 and 8 P. M., when we hauled off in obedience to signal, and anchored between Seawell's Point and Craney island. Dr. Herbert Nash kindly came off from the latter post and attended to the wants of the wounded on the *Beaufort*.

At midnight the *Congress* blew up. According to the report of Lieutenant Pendergrast she had been on fire from the beginning of the action; and Medical Director Shippen, who from his station would be likely to know, says: "We were on fire in the sick-bay, in the main-hold, and under the ward-room near the after-magazine. Some of these fires were extinguished, but the most dangerous one, that near the after-magazine, was never extinguished, and was the cause of the explosion, which, during the following night, blew the ship to pieces."

The results of this day's operations were the total destruction of the frigate *Congress* and corvette *Cumberland*, and the partial crippling of the frigate *Minnesota*. The loss in killed and drowned on board the *Cumberland*, as reported by her commander, was 121; and the surgeon reports 14 wounded, which makes 135 casualties. I find it difficult to ascertain from Lieutenant Pendergrast's report how many men the *Congress* lost in all. He gives the total number of killed and missing as 136; he then deducts 26 wounded, taken on shore, which leaves 110. If there were 60 wounded men when I went alongside, as he said (and this number was certainly not exaggerated), and if he sent 26 on shore, these, with the 5 I had, would account for 31; which leaves 29 unaccounted for, or still on board; and there is reason to fear that some wounded men were left on board to be consumed by the flames, who would have been taken off by the *Beaufort* and *Raleigh*, under the flag of truce, had they not been fired upon by the troops on shore. The fire of these troops killed their own wounded men as they were being lowered over the side, and rendered it impossible for us to continue the work. The *Raleigh* did not take a man on board from the *Congress*. The *Minnesota* lost 3 killed and 16 wounded, and there were some casualties reported among the other vessels. From what I can gather, I think the loss in the Federal fleet in killed, drowned, wounded and missing amounted to nearly 400 men.

On our side the *Merrimac* lost 21 in killed and wounded; the *Patrick Henry*, 14; the *Beaufort*, 8; the *Raleigh* had Lieutenant Tayloe and Midshipman Hutter killed, how many men I do not know; nor have I any information as to the number of killed and wounded in the *Teaser*. The *Jamestown* had no casualties. Our total loss, however, did not exceed 60. On the *Merrimac*, Commodore Buchanan and his flag lieutenant, Robert D. Minor, were wounded. Captain Webb, of the *Teaser*, and Alexander of the *Raleigh*, received slight wounds, but not enough to disable them. Lieutenant Tayloe and Midshipman Hutter fell at the first murderous discharge from the shore, while the *Raleigh* lay alongside me; in fact, I had just assisted Mr. Tayloe to step over to the hurricane deck of the *Raleigh*, after giving him his orders, when he was shot. They were both killed under the flag of truce. Their loss was deeply felt by their comrades. Young and full of promise, it did indeed seem hard that they should fall at the end of a battle in which they had rendered such gallant service. Commodore Buchanan and Lieutenant Minor were sent to the Naval Hospital at Norfolk on the morning of the 9th, and the command of the squadron devolved upon Captain John R. Tucker, of the *Patrick Henry*. He did not leave his own vessel, however, and Lieutenant Catesby ap R. Jones succeeded to the command of the *Merrimac*.

The result of this day's battle—which was to revolutionize the navies of the world, as showing the power of the ram and ironclad—has immortalized the name of the *Merrimac*; this all will concede. But in all descriptions of this battle the *Merrimac* has so completely overshadowed her consorts that if they are alluded to at all it is in a light way; and the gunboats are frequently denominated tugs. Indeed the people on both sides formed such extravagant notions concerning the *Merrimac* that they seemed to think that from that time forward a gun could do no damage unless mounted upon an iron-clad vessel. The Confederate accounts of the battle were full of the *Merrimac*, the fire from her guns, etc.,—and but little was said of the smaller vessels whose fire was equally effective. Justice to those who served in these vessels and especially to those who died upon their decks, requires that I should establish this fact. As Campbell sings:

> And yet, amidst this joy and uproar,
> Let us think of them that sleep,
> Full many a fathom deep,
> By thy cold and stormy steep, Elsinore,

premising that it is difficult to make anyone at the present day understand what absurd and ridiculous men-of-war our gunboats really were. The magazine and boiler being above the waterline, and the hull of one-fourth inch iron, or one inch planking, a man serving in one of them stood a chance of death in four forms: he could be killed by the enemy's shot, (this was the legitimate form); he could be drowned by his vessel being sunk, (this might also be called a legitimate form); he could be blown up by a shot exploding the magazine, or he could be scalded to death by a shot passing through the boiler—the last two methods I always considered unlawful, and (strange as it may appear) strongly objected to!

To prove the services of the wooden vessels in the battle of Hampton Roads I shall quote only the Federal accounts. The italics are mine. The Secretary of the Navy, Hon. Gideon Welles, in his report of 1862 says: "Having thus destroyed the *Cumberland*, the *Merrimac* turned again upon the *Congress*, which had in the meantime been engaged with the smaller rebel steamers [the *Beaufort* and *Raleigh*,] *and after a heavy loss*, in order to guard against such a fate as that which had befallen the *Cumberland*, had been run aground. The *Merrimac* now selected a raking position astern of the *Congress, while one of the smaller steamers poured in a constant fire on her starboard quarter. Two other steamers of the enemy also approached from James river firing upon the unfortunate frigate with precision and severe effect."* The *Minnesota*, which had also got aground in the shallow waters of the channel, became the special object of attack, and the *Merrimac* with the *Yorktown* and *Jamestown* bore down upon her. The *Merrimac* drew too much water to approach very near; her fire was not therefore particularly effective. The other steamers selected their positions, *fired with much accuracy, and caused considerable damage to the Minnesota."* Captain G. Van Brunt who commanded the *Minnesota* corroborates the above. Lieutenant Pendergrast who commanded the *Congress* in his report says: "After passing the *Congress*, she (the *Merrimac*) ran into and sank the United States sloop-of-war *Cumberland. The smaller vessels then attacked us killing and wounding many of our crew.* At 3.30 the *Merrimac* took a position astern of us at a distance of about 150 yards and raked us fore and aft with shells, *while one of the smaller steamers kept up a fire on our starboard quarter. In the meantime the Patrick Henry and Thomas Jefferson, rebel steamers, approached us from up the James river firing with precision and doing us great damage."*[2]

I think I have quoted enough to show that the wooden vessels bore an important part in this battle, and will only add that when Midshipman Mallory first boarded the *Congress*, Lieutenant Pendergrast asked him the name of my vessel and said that a shot from her went into the starboard quarter of the *Congress* and, traversing the whole length of the gun deck, went out of the port bow. We took from the *Congress* 16 navy revolvers, 8 Minie rifles, 20 Sharp's rifles, and 10 cutlasses, which I believe is about all that was saved from her by either side. And here I will stop to say that we made a mistake in not trying to get the *Congress* afloat and towing her up to Norfolk. I thought of doing it at the time the *Raleigh* came to me;

[2]*Report of the Secretary of the Navy* (December 1862). The passage quoted by Parker appears on p. 30. See also Lieutenant Austin Pendergrast to Welles, 9 March 1862. *O.R.N.*, I, 7:23–4.

but my orders to burn her were imperative and I did not feel at liberty to try it. She went on shore at half tide and I think could have been pulled off at the next high water.

We had to regret the loss of Jack Robinson, the captain of our gun. Poor fellow! he was faithful to the last. When I first sent my men on board the *Congress* to assist the wounded, I saw him standing, with his arms folded, at the breech of his gun, and demanded to know why he had not obeyed the order. "Why captain," said he, pointing to a gunboat nearby, "they can come and take you while we are gone." "Never mind that," said I, "I want your help here." He went, and I observed soon returned and took up his former position. He was killed at the first fire from the shore by a rifle ball passing through his body. In getting him below he suffered so much I had him taken to the cabin and laid upon my bed. We had no surgeon or medical stores, but that did not matter in his case as his wound was mortal. After the battle I went to see him and asked him what I could do for him. He said he would like a cup of tea and a pair of clean socks, which were given him. He died at 8 o'clock, quietly and resignedly; not the first sailor I have seen die in the same way.

Yet, though the worms gnaw his timbers and his vessel's a wreck,
When he hears the Last Whistle, he'll spring up on deck.

CHAPTER XXIV

The night of the 8th of March—the battle between the *Merrimac* and *Monitor*—remarks upon this battle—injuries of the *Merrimac*—what was expected of her north and south—what she could not have done—the case of Captain Smith and Lieutenant Pendergrast—what a white flag signifies—Lieutenant Jos. B. Smith—Commodore Tattnall relieves Admiral Buchanan in the command—his character—preparations for another battle

WHEN we retired the night of the 8th of March we hoped to accomplish a great day's work the following day. The *Minnesota* was aground, the *Roanoke* and *St. Lawrence* had retired below Old Point, and we knew the enemy was greatly demoralized. We did not know how much; no mortal man could have surmised what we afterwards knew; but we intended to destroy the *Minnesota* and then to see what we could do with the vessels below Old Point. But "the best laid plans of mice and men," etc. We had heard of the *Monitor;* though I believe our authorities did not know much about her, or how near she was to completion.

The *Monitor* and the *Merrimac*. Courtesy Beverley R. Robinson Collection, U.S. Naval Academy Museum.

Shortly after 8 A. M. on the 9th the squadron got underweigh and the *Merrimac* proceeded towards the *Minnesota*, closely attended by the *Patrick Henry*. The *Monitor* now made her appearance—some one said she looked like a cheese-box. She engaged the *Merrimac* for some time, the wooden vessels looking on. It was a naval duel, though the *Merrimac* occasionally fired at the *Minnesota* and received her shot in return. It appeared to be a battle between a giant and a pigmy; but it should be remembered that the *Merrimac* was very hard to manage and drew twenty-two feet of water, whereas the *Monitor* was readily handled, and drew but ten feet water. In point of fact, it was not necessary to manœuvre the *Monitor* at all; for as her turret revolved, all she had to do was to remain still. This indeed is one of the strong points of this class of vessels in fighting in rivers or shallow water. They can always bring a gun to bear as long as the turret will revolve.

After some time, the *Merrimac* succeeded in ramming the *Monitor*; but her prow had been broken off in ramming the *Cumberland* the day before, and she did her no harm. The *Monitor* in turn attempted to run close to the stern of the *Merrimac* in the hope of disabling her rudder, but was not successful. Towards 12 o'clock the *Monitor* steamed down towards Old Point, and the *Merrimac*, after waiting awhile, turned in the direction of Norfolk. The signal was made to follow her, and the squadron proceeded up to the Navy Yard, where we arrived at 2 P. M. and sent our wounded men to the Naval Hospital. The *Merrimac* went into dock at six o'clock the same day.

Much has been written and more said about this celebrated fight—the first encounter between iron-clads in the world's history. Viewing it as I did at a distance of more than a mile, I will state that my impression at the time was that, after hammering away at each other for three hours, and finding that the men were wearied out, without making much impression on either side, both vessels had simultaneously drawn off, and decided to consider it a drawn battle; that, in fact,

Each took off his several way.
Resolved to meet some other day.

A careful analysis of the testimony on both sides has since convinced me that the *Monitor* withdrew first, and ran into shoal water—she gave up the contest. It seems to me that Captain Van Brunt's testimony should be conclusive on this point. His vessel was on shore and her fate depended upon the result of the encounter—he must have closely noted it. He says (the italics are mine): "For some time after this the rebels concentrated their whole battery upon the tower and pilot-house of the Monitor, *and soon after the latter stood down for Fortress Monroe, and we thought it probable she had exhausted her supply of ammunition or sustained some injury.* Soon after the *Merrimac* and the two other steamers headed for my ship, *and I then felt to the fullest extent my condition.* I was hard and immovably aground, and they could take position under my stern and rake me. I had expended most of my solid shot; my ship was badly crippled, and my officers and men were worn out with fatigue: but even in this extreme dilemma, I determined never to give up the ship to the rebels, and, after consulting with my officers, I ordered every preparation to be made to destroy the ship, after all hope was gone of saving her. On ascending the poop-deck I observed that the enemy's vessels had changed their course and were heading for Craney Island."[1]

Why the *Merrimac* did not persist in destroying the *Minnesota* I never exactly understood. But the reasons were satisfactory to her commander and his officers, and to Captain Tucker; and no man who knew this group of highly-distinguished and gallant officers can doubt but that they were sufficient. Whatever the cause, candor compels me to say that the *Merrimac* failed to reap the fruits of her victory. She went out to destroy the *Minnesota*, and do what further damage to the enemy she could. The *Monitor* was there to save the *Minnesota*. The *Merrimac* did not accomplish her purpose. The *Monitor* did. She did it by resisting the *Merrimac* as long as she did, even if she did have to withdraw. The *Minnesota* was gotten afloat that night and towed below Old Point. I suspect the

[1]Report of Gersham J. Van Brunt, commanding officer of the *Minnesota*, to Welles, 10 March 1862. Printed in *O.R.N.*, I, 7:10–12.

Merrimac was making more water from the leak in her bow than her officers were willing to admit. She lost her prow in ramming the *Cumberland*. In reference to ramming the *Monitor*, Boatswain Hasker says in his account: "We drove our stem apron in when we struck the *Monitor*, which caused our ship to leak; which leak was stopped partially by shoving a bale of oakum against the stem apron;" and again: "in consequence of our stem being twisted, we were leaking badly, and only had time to steam to Norfolk and get into the dry-dock by high water."[2]

Captain Catesby ap R. Jones in a letter to the *Southern Historical Society Papers*, says: "The official report says our loss is 2 killed and 19 wounded: the stem is twisted, and the ship leaks; we have lost the prow, starboard anchor, and all the boats; the armor is somewhat damaged, the steam-pipe and smoke-stack both riddled; the muzzles of two of her guns shot away. None were killed or wounded in the fight with the *Monitor*. The only damage she did was to the armor. She fired 41 shots. We were enabled to receive most of them obliquely. The effect of a shot striking obliquely on the shield was to break all the iron and sometimes to displace several feet of the outside course; the wooden backing would not be broken through. When a shot struck directly at right angles the wood would also be broken through, but not displaced. The shield was never pierced. The ship was docked. A prow of steel and wrought-iron put on, and a course of 2-inch iron on the hull below the roof, extending in length 180 ft. Want of time and material prevented its completion. The damage to the armor was repaired; wrought-iron port-shutters were fitted, etc. The rifle guns were supplied with bolts of wrought and chilled iron. The ship was brought a foot deeper in the water, making her draft 23 feet."[3]

Upon our return to Norfolk, which was on Sunday, March 9th,

[2]Apparently Boatswain Charles H. Hasker, later commissioned a lieutenant in the Confederate Navy, wrote an account of the *Monitor* vs. *Merrimac* struggle. Parker quotes from this "narrative" frequently. An extensive search, however, has not turned up the original. Hasker served aboard the *Virginia* (*Merrimac*) in 1861–62.

[3]Jones, "Services of the *Virginia* (*Merrimac*)," pp. 72–73.

the whole city was alive with joy and excitement. Nothing was talked of but the *Merrimac* and what she had accomplished. As to what she could do in the future, no limit was set to her powers. The papers indulged in the wildest speculations, and everybody went mad, as usual. At the North the same fever prevailed. No battle that was ever fought caused as great a sensation throughout the civilized world. The moral effect at the North was most marvelous; and even now I can scarcely realize it. The people of New York and Washington were in hourly expectation of the *Merrimac's* appearance off those cities, and I suppose were ready to yield at the first summons. At the South it was expected that she would take Fortress Monroe when she again went out. I recollect trying to explain to a gentleman at the time how absurd it was to expect this of her. I told him that she might bombard Fortress Monroe all day without doing it any considerable damage; that she would get out of ammunition; that she carried but 350 men, and could not land a force even if her boats were not shot away, though they would be; that, in fine, I would be willing to take up my quarters in the casemates there and let the *Merrimac* hammer away for a month,— but all to no purpose; the impression had been made on him: a gun mounted on an iron-clad must be capable of doing more damage than one on a wooden vessel. An idea once fixed cannot be eradicated: just as we hear people say every day that Jackson at New Orleans defeated the veterans of Waterloo!

As to the *Merrimac* going to New York, she would have foundered as soon as she got outside of Cape Henry. She could not have lived in Hampton Roads in a moderate sea. She was just buoyant enough to float when she had a few days coal and water on board. A little more would have sent her to the bottom. When she rammed the *Cumberland* she dipped forward until the water nearly entered her bow port; had it done so she would have gone down. Perhaps it was fortunate for her that her prow did break off, otherwise she might not have extricated herself. I served afterward in the *Palmetto State*, a vessel of similar construction to the *Merrimac*, but much more buoyant; yet I have seen the time when we were glad to get under a lee even in Charleston harbor. The *Merrimac* with but a few days' stores on board drew 22½ feet water. She could not have gone to Baltimore or Washington without lightening her very much. This would have brought her unarmored hull out of the water and then she would no longer have been an iron-clad! I was not so much surprised at the extravagant expectations of the southern people who necessarily knew but little of such matters; but I must say I could not have imagined the extent of the demoralization which existed at Fortress Monroe and in the Federal fleet on the 8th and 9th of March. I have been told by an officer of high rank, who was present in the fort, that if the *Merrimac* had fired a shot at it on the 8th the general in command would have surrendered it; and, if I am not very much mistaken, I have seen a dispatch from that general to the effect that if the *Merrimac* passed Fortress Monroe it must necessarily fall! After this one can well understand what Napoleon has said in reference to the moral as compared to the physical effect in war.

Upon my reporting the facts in relation to Captain Smith and Lieutenant Pendergrast a question was raised as to whether they were not prisoners on parole. Questions of the kind were crudely treated by our navy department. The Secretary himself was ignorant of naval laws, customs and precedents; and his immediate advisers were in the same category. The older officers who had served in the war of 1812, and whose experience gave them a knowledge of such matters, were not consulted by him. Those about the Secretary were men who had not seen much service in war. It was held that Smith and Pendergrast had escaped, and should either deliver themselves up or refuse to serve until regularly exchanged. I, on the contrary, insisted that they were not bound to do so. They had been prisoners it is true—so had every officer and man of the *Congress* been; but I left them, and after the *Beaufort* left the side of the *Congress* they had no opportunity of getting back to her and they escaped to the shore as the others did. The officers and men of the Confederate man-of-war *Alabama* escaped, after her capture by the U. S. ship *Kearsarge*, under precisely the same circumstances—the enemy failed to take possession of them.[4]

Some time after, when Pendergrast was unfortunate enough to be captured in the *Water Witch*, a question was raised in Savannah, where he had been taken, as to his conduct in reference to the *Congress* affair. I immediately wrote to Commodore Tattnall, commanding the station, completely exonerating him from any unofficerlike or improper conduct on that occasion. I justified his action in every particular. Commodore Barron was a prisoner at the time and if I had held Captain Smith, could have been exchanged for him, but as I have said, I did not know it was Captain Smith; not expecting to see a senior officer to the lieutenant who said he commanded the ship. No one regretted more than I did that the result could not have been different; but I should have permitted him to return to the *Congress*, under the circumstances, if he had combined in himself the entire Smith family.

Conversing with an "official" afterwards, he said it was a pity I had not sent for pen, ink and paper at the time, and made them write out a written parole. Mark Twain, in describing a trip to Bermuda, says there was a young man on board known as the "Ass," and there was also on board an old man, whom he calls the "Ancient," who was returning to Bermuda after an absence of twenty-seven years. Upon their arrival a faded old gentleman stood up before the "Ancient," and asked him if he knew him. The "Ancient," after hesitating some time said: "There's something about you that's just as familiar to me as ———" "*Likely it might be his hat*," murmured the "Ass," with sympathetic interest. "The bearing of this remark lies in the application of it," said Jack Bunsby.

---

[4]Confederate Captain Raphael Semmes, commander of the raider *Alabama*, threw his sword over the side before plunging into the water himself after his vessel was overwhelmed by the U.S.S. *Kearsarge* on 19 June 1864. Semmes was picked up by the British yacht *Dearhound* and returned to serve the Confederacy in its last days. He was subsequently criticized for his act on the grounds that a gentleman ought not to have fled after capitulating.

The *Congress* did not haul her colors down, but hoisted a white flag. This is unusual in naval warfare. We had the right to continue to fire on her until she struck her colors, unless it had appeared that her colors were nailed to the mast and could not be lowered. A white flag does not necessarily imply a surrender; it signifies a parley. It is used by armies desiring to communicate and by fortresses preparatory to making terms; but ships at sea necessarily surrender unconditionally and they do so by lowering their colors. The historian of the French navy, *La Perouse de Bon Fils*, mentions an instance where a French line of battle ship hoisted a white flag and made terms. He says it is the only case on record, and I believe he is correct.[5]

Midshipman Mallory whom I first sent on board the *Congress* told me upon his return that he had seen the body of her commander, Lieutenant Joseph B. Smith, laid out on the main deck. Smith was a classmate of mine, and I had last met him in Rio when I was on my return home in the *Merrimac*. I spent the night with him on board the *Congress*. His character cannot be better illustrated than by the following incident: During the fight of the 8th the authorities in Washington were kept informed of the events as they occurred. Admiral Joseph B. Smith (the father of the lieutenant) was the chief of one of the departments. Upon being told that the *Congress* had surrendered, he replied: "Then Joe is dead!" Mallory showed me a sword he had taken from the *Congress*, and upon examining it I found "Jos. B. Smith" engraved on the blade. With Mallory's consent I gave it to Commodore Tattnall, who sent it with a kind letter to his old shipmate Admiral Smith.

Flag Officer Franklin Buchanan who was promoted to the grade of admiral for his great services in the *Merrimac* was too badly wounded to retain his command, and Flag Officer Josiah Tattnall was detailed to relieve him. Lieutenant J. Pembroke Jones was

[5]Jean François de Galaup La Pérouse (1741–1788) was a French naval officer and explorer. In 1785–88 he navigated the Alaskan and Siberian coasts, and explored the waters around China, the Philippines, and Samoa, but was killed when his ship was wrecked in the New Hebrides.

selected by Commodore Tattnall as his flag lieutenant to succeed Lieutenant Robert D. Minor who was also still suffering from his wounds. Commodore Tattnall entered the U. S. Navy in 1812; served in the U. S. frigate *Constitution* in the defence of Norfolk in that war, and distinguished himself while in command of the little steamer *Spitfire* during the Mexican war. Though opposed to secession, he promptly resigned his commission upon learning of the secession of his native State, Georgia. He was a striking-looking man, nearly six feet in height, with a florid complexion, deep-sunk blue eyes, and a protruding under lip. He was a chivalric gentleman, of pure character and untarnished reputation. No man stood higher in either the United States or Confederate Navy; and much was expected of him when he assumed the command, which he did on the 29th of March, 1862. His appointment gave great satisfaction to the entire squadron; and our damages being now repaired, we began to look forward to another trial of strength in Hampton Roads.

CHAPTER XXV

Our plan for boarding and smothering the *Monitor*—the *Merri-mac* challenges the *Monitor* to battle—we capture three vessels—operations in Hampton Roads on the 11th of April, 1862—remarks on—the *Merrimac* drives the vessels employed in bombarding Seawell's Point under the guns of Fort Monroe—the *Monitor* declines to fight the *Merrimac*—am ordered to command the *Dixie*—evacuation of Norfolk by the Confederates—Commodore John Rodgers—his attack on Drury's Bluff—blowing up of the *Merrimac*—Commodore Tattnall's report—reflections on the destruction of this ship—pilots

We now knew something of the *Monitor*'s construction, and it was determined that in the next engagement she should be boarded, and an attempt made to wedge the turret with iron wedges, to throw hand-grenades down the turret, and to cover her hatchways and ventilators in the hope of smothering out her crew. In order that the attempt should have every chance for success four gunboats, of which the *Beaufort* was one, were designated for it. Each vessel had her crew divided into the proper number of parties so that if even one got alongside, every point considered would receive proper attention. At a meeting of the captains the night before going down, it was resolved that in the case of a vessel's being sunk in trying to board, the others should not stop to pick up the survivors. Lieutenant Commanding J. H. Rochelle commanded one of these gunboats, and Lieutenant Commanding Hunter Davidson another—the other captain I cannot recall, unless it was [Joseph W.] Alexander of the *Raleigh*.

On the 11th of April, a little over a month after our first engagement, the squadron, consisting of the *Merrimac*, *Patrick Henry*, *Jamestown*, *Teaser*, *Beaufort*, and *Raleigh*,—with the *Harmony* and another tug-boat,—went down again to Hampton Roads. In Norfolk the same scenes were enacted as on the previous occasion—everybody who could get a conveyance went to see the fight. In the squadron we expected a desperate encounter. We knew the Federal fleet had been largely reinforced. The *Vanderbilt*, a powerful steamship fitted expressly to ram the *Merrimac*, we expected to see; and also the *Naugatuck*, a small iron-clad mounting one large rifle gun. Upon our arrival in the Roads we saw the fleet at anchor below Old Point, with the exception of the *Naugatuck*, which vessel was lying, I think, in Hampton Creek. There were present the *Minnesota*, bearing the flag of Flag Officer Goldsborough, the *Monitor*, several large frigates, and a large number of smaller vessels and transports. The *Vanderbilt* was not present in the morning, but arrived that afternoon. We took possession of the roads, but, to our extreme surprise, the enemy showed no intention of coming up to engage us; the vessels had steam up, but made no movement towards us.

Three merchant vessels caught unexpectedly in the Roads between Old Point and Newport's News were run on shore by their masters and partially abandoned. The *Jamestown* and *Raleigh* were sent to tow them off, which service was handsomely accomplished by Captains Barney and Alexander under the guns of the enemy. Their flags were hoisted Union down under the Confederate flag, to taunt their protectors and induce them to come up and endeavor to retake them. It produced no effect. An English and a French man-of-war were present in the Roads, and upon our arrival they slowly withdrew in the direction of Newport's News out of range, to witness the serious engagement which we, at least, anticipated. We passed and repassed them frequently during the day, as we steamed about the Roads between Newport's News and Fortress Monroe, and their crews waved their hats and handkerchiefs to us, and no doubt would have added their cheers if discipline had permitted.

It was our impression that torpedoes had been placed in the channel between Old Point and the Rip Raps to prevent the *Merrimac* from getting to York river, the base of General McClellan's operations against Richmond. It was said in Norfolk just before we went down that a French naval officer had given this information. This I do not for a moment believe; but it was reasonable to suppose they would be put down, and when we saw that Flag Officer Goldsborough did not advance, we thought his intention was to draw us down on his obstructions. I know that Commodore Tattnall was under the impression the channel was in some way obstructed; but even if it had not been, fighting the Federal fleet in the waters of Hampton Roads was one thing, and fighting it close under the guns of Fortress Monroe and the Rip Raps, with the additional danger from torpedoes, was another. He fairly offered the first, which he had every reason to suppose would be eagerly accepted. The gallant commodore made a short address to his men that morning, and concluded by saying: "Now you go to your stations, and I'll go to mine;" whereupon he coolly seated himself in an arm-chair on the upper deck. Had the enemy given battle he would have soon seen the difference between the shooting of *Mexican* and American sailors.

The squadron held possession of the Roads and defied the enemy to battle during the entire day (and for several days after in fact); but the Federal fleet declined it, and maintained its position under the guns of Fortress Monroe. The *Merrimac* passed the day in slowly steaming backwards and forwards between Newport's News and Old Point. She reminded me of a huge *centipede* crawling about. She certainly did not present an inviting appearance. A little before sunset as she was slowly turning in the channel for the last time that day she fired a single shot in the direction of Fortress Monroe. It was promptly replied to by the *Naugatuck*. I have reason to recollect this shot from the *Naugatuck* for it was the first of the long-range guns I had seen. I was talking to Hunter Davidson who was near me in his vessel when we heard the whistling of this shot which dropped in the water between us. Much surprised I sent for my chart and found the distance to be 3½ miles. Long range guns were then just coming into use, and caused Bill Arp afterwards to explain: "Blamed if they wasn't shooting at me before I knew they were in the county!"

At sunset the squadron went in under Seawell's Point. The *Merrimac* had permanent moorings placed there for her. Just before the signal was made to go in and anchor, John Downard who had succeeded Robinson as captain of our gun came to me on the part of the crew with the request that I would go to Newport's News and "give them a few rounds." "What for?" said I: "Why," he replied, "they killed Jack Robinson!" I should not have been sorry myself to give them a "few rounds" as he expressed it, but of course could not do so. As the *Monitor* did not come out we did not have the opportunity to board her with the gunboats. If her turret was not loop-holed for musketry, and I believe it was not, we would probably have captured her. Once on her deck the men could easily have avoided the fire of her two heavy guns by running around the turret, and a light sail thrown over it would have blinded her commander and helmsman. At all events we intended to try it. A few days after this the squadron returned to Norfolk; the *Merrimac* for repairs of which she stood in constant need either to her engines or hull. Captain Catesby Jones says "Commodore Tattnall commanded the *Virginia Merrimac* 45 days of which time there were only 13 days that she was not in dock or in the hands of the navy yard."[1]

On the 8th of May, only two days before we evacuated Norfolk, while the *Merrimac* was at the navy yard Flag Officer Goldsborough

---

[1]Jones, "Services of the *Virginia (Merrimac)*," p. 73.

took advantage of her absence to come above Old Point with the *Monitor* and a number of other vessels and bombard Seawell's Point. When the news was telegraphed to Norfolk the *Merrimac* cast off her fasts and steamed down the harbor. As soon as her smoke was seen the entire Federal fleet fled below Old Point again, and was pursued by the *Merrimac* until under the guns of Fortress Monroe. There is no doubt about the truth of this.

If, as Flag Officer Goldsborough said in his report of this affair: "she (the *Merrimac*) did not place herself where she could be assailed by his rams to advantage," what did she go down for? Where could a vessel drawing 23 feet, as the *Merrimac* did then, place herself so that "the *Baltimore*, an unarmed steamer of light draft," could not get at her? The flag officer says (the italics are mine): "The *Monitor* was kept well in advance, and so that the *Merrimac* could have engaged her without difficulty had she been so disposed; but she declined to do it, and *soon returned* and anchored under Seawell's Point."[2] Returned from where? How could she return and anchor under Seawell's Point, when the Federal fleet was bombarding Seawell's Point? Well may the German cynic exclaim:

When first on earth fair Truth was born,
She crept into a hunting-horn;
The hunter came, the horn was blown,
And where Truth went was never known!

From the facts I have stated, it is clear that after the battle of the 9th of March the *Monitor* several times declined to fight the *Merrimac*, and only ventured above Old Point when she knew the *Merrimac* was at Norfolk. Upon the appearance of the latter in Hampton Roads she would retire under the guns of Fortress Monroe. I can find nothing in the Federal reports in relation to what I have said of the occurrence in the roads on the 11th of April. If Flag Officer Goldsborough made a report it has been suppressed:

[2]Report of Flag Officer Louis M. Goldsborough to Secretary Welles, 12 May 1863. Printed in *O.R.N.*, I, 7:342–3.

but as to the truth of my statement, I am willing to abide by the log-book of the *Minnesota* for that day, and the testimony of the officers of the *Monitor*. It is not my intention to cast any imputations upon Flag Officer Goldsborough and his gallant officers. I have been told since the war that the Government had given positive orders that the *Monitor* should not fight the *Merrimac* unless forced to do so. I only mention what came under my own observation, not doubting that the orders issued by the Government were based upon good grounds.[3]

On the 12th of April I was detached from the *Beaufort* and ordered to command the *Dixie*, a new vessel just built at Graves' ship-yard in Norfolk, and fitting out at the Navy Yard. She was a pretty model and I think would have been fast. Her sister ship, which was about in the same state of preparation, was commanded by Captain John Rutledge.

We commenced early in May to hear something of the probable evacuation of Norfolk. The *Patrick Henry*, *Jamestown*, *Teaser*, *Beaufort* and *Raleigh* were sent up the James river to operate on the right flank of General Magruder's army, then falling back in the direction of Richmond. The *Nansemond* and *Hampton*, two gunboats built at the navy yard, were completed at this time and sent to Richmond. These vessels had saw-mill engines, and when they got underweigh there was such a wheezing and blowing that one would have supposed all hands had suddenly been attacked with the asthma or heaves. They ran by the batteries at Newport's News however without waking the sentinels up. Rutledge and I did our best to get our vessels ready so that we might follow their example; but the engines were not prepared and there was nothing left at the

---

[3]After the war a controversy erupted when John L. Worden, who commanded the *Monitor* in the battle, petitioned Congress for a million dollars in prize money for his "victory." Parker involved himself in the controversy by writing several public letters arguing that the *Merrimac* "remained for some days . . . offering battle and protecting the approaches to Norfolk and Richmond" and that the decision to destroy the ship was taken as a result of the advance of the Federal army on shore and not the presence of the *Monitor*. Reports of other eyewitnesses to the battle are printed in *O.R.N.*, volume 7.

yard to tow us up. While preparations were being made by the army to evacuate the city, the captain of a small steamer in the quartermaster's employ ran off with his vessel to Old Point and gave the information. This was on the 9th of May, and precipitated matters. I was staying on board the receiving ship *Germantown* at the time, and on the night of the 9th we heard firing. Some of the midshipmen went aloft into the main top and saw shells bursting in the direction of Willoughby's Point, about 7 miles distant. This was about 9 P. M., and I came to the conclusion that the enemy were shelling the beach preparatory to landing a force. I went to the house of Captain Sidney Smith Lee, then commanding the yard, to report the fact.[4] I found him about retiring. He said he did not think it probable; that he had heard nothing from General Huger, &c—he rather laughed at the idea. I left him about 11 o'clock, and so satisfied was I of a "call" that I threw myself on my bed without undressing. Sure enough at daybreak we were all called to the commandant's office and given our orders in reference to evacuating the navy yard. We set fire to the buildings and ships, and tried to blow up the dry dock; in fact destroyed everything we could. I set my vessel on fire with much regret; a few more days and she would have been ready to go to Richmond. We continued the work of destruction until we heard the Federal troops were in Norfolk, and then took our departure in the cars for Weldon where we arrived the same evening at 8 o'clock. I went to Henderson for a day or two, and then proceeded to Richmond, arriving there on the 15th—the day Commodore John Rodgers attacked the fort at Drury's bluff with the *Galena*, *Monitor*, *Naugatuck*, *Port Royal* and *Aroostook*, and was beaten off. The gallant commodore, who was noted for his fighting qualities, handled the *Galena* to perfection on this occasion, and I take pleasure in introducing a few extracts from the narrative of boatswain Hasker who commanded a gun at the fort:

"The attack upon Drury's Bluff (or Fort Darling, as the enemy called it,) was on the part of the *Galena*, I think one of the most

---

[4]Sidney Smith Lee was Robert E. Lee's older brother.

masterly pieces of seamanship of the whole war. She was brought into action in the coolest manner; indeed, she was brought to, and sprung across the channel in a much more masterly way than I have often seen at mere target practice. She steamed up to within seven or eight hundred yards of the bluff, let go her starboard anchor, ran out the chains, put her head in shore, backed astern, let go her stream anchor from the starboard quarter, hove ahead, and made ready for action before firing a gun. I could not but admire this manoeuvre although executed to bring death or wounds to so many of my brave comrades. A six-inch gun, 33 cwt. 32-pounder, [63 cwt. ?] which had been rifled and banded at the Gosport Navy Yard, did more damage to the *Galena* than all the rest of the guns on the bluff combined. This gun was manned by the crew from the *Jamestown*."

Considering the result of Rodgers' attack on Fort Darling, and the fact that Richmond did not fall till two years later, one cannot but be amused at reading the following extract from Flag Officer Goldsborough's letter to the Secretary of the Navy, under date from Hampton Roads, May 12, 1863:

"The *Monitor* and *Stevens* have both gone up the James river, with orders from me to reduce all the works of the enemy as they go along, spike all their guns, blow up all their magazines, and then get up to Richmond, all with the least possible delay, and shell the city to a surrender. With the above works reduced, I can keep our vessels supplied with coal, ordnance stores, provisions, etc., without difficulty."[5]

When David Copperfield gave a dinner, his landlady said "what she would recommend would be this: A pair of roast fowls—from the pastry-cook's; a dish of stewed beef—from the pastry-cook's; two little corner things—from the pastry-cook's; a tart and a shape of jelly—from the pastry-cook's." "This," Mrs. Crupp said, "would leave her at full liberty to concentrate her mind on the potatoes, and to serve up the cheese and celery as she could wish to see it done."

---

[5]Goldsborough to Welles, 12 May 1862. *O.R.N.*, I, 7:342–3.

Ay me! what perils do environ
The man that meddles with cold iron.

On the 10th of May, (the day we evacuated Norfolk) the
Merrimac was lying at her moorings off Seawell's Point, and
Commodore Tattnall who had not expected the evacuation so soon
was taken by surprise. Why he was not "signalled" I do not know.
Observing that the flag was not flying at Seawell's Point battery he
dispatched his Flag Lieutenant, Pembroke Jones, to Norfolk for
news. Lieutenant Jones returned at 7 P. M. with the information
that the city was in the possession of the enemy. In his report to the
Secretary of the Navy, dated Richmond, May 14, 1862, the
commodore, after mentioning this, goes on to say:

It was now 7 o'clock in the evening, and this unexpected
information rendered prompt measures necessary for the safety
of the *Virginia*. The pilots had assured me that they could take
the ship, with a draft of eighteen feet, to within forty miles of
Richmond. This, the chief pilot Mr. Parrish, and his chief
assistant, Mr. Wright, had asserted again and again; and on
the afternoon of the 7th, in my cabin, in the presence of Commodore Hollins and Captain Sterrett, in reply to a question of
mine, they both emphatically declared their ability do so.
Confiding in these assurances, and after consulting with the
First and Flag Lieutenants and learning that the officers generally thought it the most judicious course, I determined to
lighten the ship at once and run up the river for the protection
of Richmond. All hands having been called on deck, I stated
to them the condition of things, and my hope that by getting
up the river before the enemy could be made aware of our design we might capture his vessels which had ascended it, and
render efficient aid in the defence of Richmond; but that to
effect this would require all their energy in lightening the
ship. They replied with three cheers, and went to work at
once.

The pilots were on deck and heard this address to the crew.
Being quite unwell, I had retired to bed. Between one and
two o'clock in the morning the First Lieutenant reported to me
that after the crew had worked for five or six hours and lifted

the ship so as to render her unfit for action, the pilots had declared their inability to carry eighteen feet above the Jamestown flats, up to which point the shore on each side was occupied by the enemy. On demanding from the chief pilot, Mr. Parrish, an explanation of this palpable deception, he replied that eighteen feet could be carried after the prevalence of easterly winds, but that the wind for the last two days had been westerly. I had no time to lose. The ship was not in a condition for battle even with an enemy of equal force, and their force was overwhelming. I therefore determined with the concurrence of the First and Flag Lieutenants, to save the crew for future service by landing them at Craney Island, the only road for retreat open to us, and to destroy the ship to prevent her falling into the hands of the enemy. I may add that, although not formally consulted, the course was approved by every commissioned officer in the ship. There was no dissenting opinion. The ship was accordingly put on shore as near the main land in the vicinity of Craney Island as possible and the crew landed. She was then fired, and after burning fiercely fore and aft for upwards of an hour, blew up a little before five on the morning of the 11th. We marched for Suffolk, 22 miles, and reached it in the evening, and from thence came by railroad to this city.

It will be asked what motive the pilots could have had to deceive me. The only imaginable one is, that they wished to avoid going into battle. Had the ship not been *lifted*, so as to render her unfit for action, a desperate contest must have ensued with a force against us too great to justify much hope of success; and, as battle is not their occupation, they adopted this deceitful course to avoid it. I cannot imagine another motive, for I had seen no reason to distrust their good faith to the Confederacy.

My acknowledgments are due to the First Lieutenant, ap Catesby Jones for his untiring exertions, and for the aid he rendered me in all things. The details for firing the ship and landing the crew were left to him, and everything was conducted with the most perfect order. To the other officers of the ship, generally, I am also thankful for the great zeal they displayed throughout. The *Virginia* no longer exists, but three hundred brave and skillful officers and seamen are saved to the Confederacy.

I presume that a court of inquiry will be ordered to examine all the circumstances I have mentioned, and I earnestly solicit it. Public opinion will never be put right without it.

I am, sir, with great respect, your obedient servant,

JOSIAH TATTNALL,
Flag Officer Commanding.[6]

HON. S. R. MALLORY,
Secretary of the Navy.

The blowing up of the *Merrimac* caused a howl to go up from the whole Confederate States, and Commodore Tattnall had to bear the brunt of it. What the people expected her to do after the evacuation of Norfolk, God only knows; but her destruction dispirited our people from Virginia to Texas. Suppose the *Merrimac* had gone up the river to Harrison's bar, what could she have accomplished there? She certainly could not have prevented the enemy's ships from passing and repassing her at night. Our vessels used to run by the batteries at Newport's News without the least trouble, and they could bring many guns to bear, while the *Merrimac* had but five in broadside. The result so far as I can see would have been that in less than a month her boats would have been shot away by the enemy's ships at long range, and she would have found herself out of provisions; the banks of the river on both sides in possession of the enemy; iron-clads and gunboats above and below her; all communication cut off from Richmond,—she would have been in fact in the position of a besieged fortress. The alternative would then have been to surrender the ship, or blow her up with all hands on board. Some people said the latter should have been done; but I do not remember that we blew up any forts with their garrisons to prevent their falling into the hands of the enemy. The fact is the evacuation of Norfolk involved the ultimate loss of the *Merrimac*; because it cut her off from supplies of all kinds— ammunition as well as provisions. This point does not seem to have

[6]Tattnall to Mallory, 14 May 1862. *O.R.N.*, I, 7:335–8.

been properly appreciated by the Confederate authorities. It was only a question of time. Commodore Tattnall should have clearly presented this to the Secretary of the Navy, and made him assume the responsibility—perhaps he did represent it. The *Merrimac* might have gone to York river, and would doubtless have inflicted some damage there by destroying transports, &c.; but she had not men enough to attempt to land a force, and some cool head would soon have discovered that it was only necessary to knock away her boats and then keep out of her way and await the action of time.

This is the view I always took of this matter, and I remember when it was rumored Norfolk was to be evacuated I asked one of the commodore's advisers to suggest to him the propriety of his putting the question fairly to the Confederate Secretary of the Navy: "What am I to do with the *Merrimac*," and insisting upon a written reply. The crew of the *Merrimac* arrived at Drury's bluff in time to assist in the defence of Richmond on the 15th of May.

One important point I will allude to before closing this chapter, and that is that in our naval battles the commanding officers were in a measure in the hands of the pilots. On the ocean the captain handles his own ship and relies upon his own judgment; but it is far different when battles occur on sounds and rivers—there the pilot becomes and important agent. I suppose there was not a commander on either side who did not find himself crippled by his pilots at some time in his experience. When the *Minnesota* was aground the pilots could not place the *Merrimac* nearer than a mile from her. The *Minnesota*, too, drawing as much water as the *Merrimac*. Why if the *Minnesota* was a mile from the channel she must have been up among the sand hills on the main. When the *Minnesota*, *Roanoke* and *St. Lawrence* started to the assistance of their consorts they all three got aground. Who put them there? Immediately after the battle of Roanoke island where I had my first experience with pilots, I saw the necessity of taking some steps towards having an organized body of them attached to the navy. I called Mr. Mallory's attention to it, and proposed that pilots should be divided into two classes and given a commission if they desired it. Their pay was to be very large, and in the case of their being killed in action their widows were to receive a pension. We could hardly expect men who were receiving very moderate pay and for whose families no provision was made in case of their death to stand in the most exposed place in a ship in time of battle, as it was necessary for them to do if they did their duty well. My proposition was never acted upon. I do not mean to say that the pilots did not do good service in the war afterwards. They did. I saw many of them who performed their duties well and bravely, notwithstanding their small pay. What I mean to say is that the southern pilots, as a class, were not properly fostered and cared for by their government.

CHAPTER XXVI

Am ordered to command the gunboat *Drury*—the James River squadron—the seven days' fighting around Richmond—a board for the examination of midshipmen—am ordered to the iron-clad *Palmetto State* at Charleston—description of her—an incident—a fire at sea—Flag Officer Duncan L. Ingraham—battle off Charleston, January 31, 1863, between the Confederate iron-clads and the Federal fleet—surrender of the *Mercedita* and *Keystone State*—the other vessels driven off—proclamation of General Beauregard and Commodore Ingraham—remarks upon this engagement and its results

Upon my arrival in Richmond, May 15, 1862, I was placed in command of the gunboat *Drury*, then on the James river. She was a kind of an iron-clad, with no steam-power. She mounted one large rifle gun forward, protected by an iron shield in the form of a V. She was intended to fight bows on, and was fitted up very hastily to assist in the defence of Drury's Bluff, in the case of another attack by water. Her engines were put in a few months afterwards and the shield removed.

The river had been obstructed abreast of Drury's Bluff by sinking vessels, and cages loaded with stone. Among the vessels sunk was the steamer *Jamestown*, whose crew, under the brave Barney, had rendered such good service at the bluff on the 15th. The squadron at this time was commanded by Commodore French Forrest, and consisted of the *Richmond* (iron-clad), *Patrick Henry*, *Nansemond*, *Hampton*, *Beaufort*, *Raleigh* and *Drury*. The *Richmond* was just completed, and was a fine vessel built on the plan of the *Merrimac*. She was not so large, and her ends were not submerged. She carried a bow and stern pivot, and two guns in broadside. Drury's Bluff was strongly fortified, and garrisoned by marines under Captain Sims. The post was commanded by Captain Sidney Smith Lee, an elder brother of General Robert E. Lee. A few miles lower down, on the left bank of the river, at Chapin's Bluff, was another heavy battery commanded by Captain T. J. Page of the navy.

The enemy, under General McClellan, was advancing up the peninsula to attack Richmond; and the Confederacy was assembling all the troops possible to defend it. On the 31st of May was fought the indecisive battle of Seven Pines, or Fair Oaks as the Federals called it; and on the 25th of June the Confederates, under General Lee, made their first attack on General McClellan's forces at Mechanicsville. This was the beginning of the seven days' fighting around Richmond, which resulted in General McClellan's army being driven to Harrison's Landing, on the James river, and relieved Richmond from all danger. Shortly after these battles, General Lee advanced in the direction of Maryland, and the Federal troops were called to the defence of their own capital.[1]

Mr. Mallory, our Secretary of the Navy, ordered a Board for the examination and classification of the midshipmen in the Navy, and I was detailed as a member of it. Commodore George N. Hollins was the president, and the other members of it were Captains C.

[1] In fact, the decision to withdraw McClellan's army from the peninsula was made prior to Lee's northward movement, but McClellan was slow to execute his orders.

McBlair and Thorburn and Lieutenant Myers. We sat at first in Richmond for the examination of the midshipmen serving in the James river squadron and the different batteries, and then went to Charleston, Savannah and Mobile. We returned to Richmond and finished up our work. This Board did good work both for the Navy and the midshipmen. The secretary promoted all those who passed to the grade of passed midshipman, and it would have been better if some of these young gentlemen had been at once promoted to be lieutenants instead of those who were taken from civil life, and who did not know a ship when they saw one. While in Charleston on this duty I noticed two iron-clads building, which struck me favorably; and my friend John Rutledge telling me he was to have the command of one of them, I offered to give up my command on the James river and go with him as his executive officer. I did this as I saw there would be no fighting on the James river for some time to come, and I thought there was an opportunity to strike a blow at Charleston. There were then no iron-clads off that harbor. Rutledge held me to my word, and in the fall of 1862 I was detached from the *Drury* and ordered to report to Flag Officer Duncan L. Ingraham, at Charleston, for duty as executive officer of the iron-clad *Palmetto State*, Captain John Rutledge. The *Chicora*, her sister ship, was commanded by my comrade Captain John R. Tucker.

The *Palmetto State* was an iron-clad on the plan of the *Merrimac*, except that her ends were not submerged, and her side plating was turned down at the water's edge, making what we called a *knuckle*, and very strong. I think her plating was of four and a half inches of iron. Her roof, or upper deck, and her ends outside the shield were covered on top with two inches of iron, and her hatchways were covered with heavy iron gratings. Her pilot house, which was heavily armored, was abaft the smoke stack. Her armament consisted of an 80-pounder Brooke rifle gun forward, a 60-pounder rifle gun aft, and two 8-inch shell guns in broadside—four guns in all. Her engines always worked well, and under favorable circumstances she would go seven knots per hour, though her average speed was about six. She drew fourteen feet of water, and worked

The Confederate ironclad ram *Palmetto State*. Official U.S. Navy photograph.

and steered well. The *Chicora* was similar in all respects, except that she had but 4-inch iron, I think. These two vessels were built at private ship-yards in Charleston, and great rivalry existed between them as to which should turn out the best ship. Both were well-built, creditable vessels. All their arrangements were good, magazines, shell-rooms, quarters, etc., all admirably arranged.

When these two vessels had been in commission a short time, they were fine specimens of men-of-war and would have done credit to any navy. They were well officered and manned. Their drill at both great guns and small arms was excellent, and the discipline perfect. They were the cleanest iron-clads, I believe, that ever floated, and the men took great pride in keeping them so. Their fire drill was good, as I have reason to remember, for the *Palmetto State* caught fire one morning in the fore-hold, adjoining the magazine. I was dressing at the time, when I heard a running about, and immediately became conscious that "something was the matter." I hurried on my coat, and just then heard the cry: "There's fire in the magazine!" Thinks I to myself, "if that be the case we will very soon hear of it," as Lord Howe once said under similar circumstances. I sprang up on the deck and had the fire-bell rung, and every man and officer went promptly to his station. The fire-party went below, and discovered the place of fire, and in fifteen minutes it was suppressed.

Speaking of a fire so near the magazine, I was some years after this placed in a situation so very peculiar, that I may be pardoned for introducing it here. I doubt if ever a man found himself in the same situation: After the war I entered the service of the Pacific Mail Steamship Company, and for six years commanded one of their steamers running between San Francisco and Panama. July 1st, 1873, I left Panama for San Francisco in the steamship *Montana*, with about fifty cabin and four hundred steerage passengers, and a large freight. All went well until the evening of the seventh day, when I found myself 130 miles from Acapulco, Mexico, which place I expected to reach the next morning at 8. It was a dark night and raining at intervals, but there was not much wind. The ship was well clear of the Tartar Shoal and there was nothing to cause any uneasiness. I remained up, as was my custom, until midnight, and then gave the second mate, who had the mid-watch, the written orders for the night. I turned in, and was soon asleep. I was awakened by the officer of the deck calling me. Upon my replying, he said in a calm manner: "Captain Parker, the ship is on fire." "What time is it?" I asked. "Twenty minutes past three," he replied. I then asked where the ship was on fire, and he told me it was in the forward store-room, where I knew the oils and paints were kept. He asked if he should ring the fire-bell, but I told him no; I thought we might extinguish it without letting the passengers know anything about it. All this time I was rapidly dressing, as may well be imagined, and in a minute from the time I was called I was out on deck. As soon as I reached it I saw the smoke coming up the fore-hatch, and the steerage passengers rushing up in great alarm. I ordered the fire-bell rung, stopped the engine, and turned the ship so as to bring the wind aft. The men were well drilled and soon every man was at his station. The steerage passengers were all sent aft on the hurricane deck, and made to sit down flat on deck; officers were placed over them and they remained quietly so until the fire was extinguished. The cabin passengers remained in the saloon in charge of the purser and doctor. We soon had eight good streams of water forward, and I scuttled the deck in several places over the store-room, and put the pipes down. Two or three pipes were turned down the open hatchway, but the fumes arising from the burning paints were so stifling that the men could not remain more than a few minutes at a time. There was no flinching on their part, however,—quite the contrary; as soon as a man was hauled up, half-suffocated, others were eager to take his place. After working some fifteen minutes in this way, seeing that the flames were apparently getting the advantage of us, and knowing that if the hurricane deck caught fire we would burn up very rapidly, I sent for the second mate and boatswain and directed them to lower the boats near the water's edge, but to allow no one to get into them. We carried about one hundred pounds of powder in a copper tank, in the magazine, which was just under the store-room. It could be filled with water by turning a cock. Sending for the first officer I told him to drown the magazine. He replied in a low tone, that it was useless to do so, as the powder had not been returned to the magazine, but was in the store-room.

"Do you mean to say," said I, "*that it is in the fire?*" "Yes, sir," said he, "it is."

I reflected. If it became known that the powder was in the store-room there would be a stampede; if, on the other hand, it exploded and blew the bows of the ship out, there would necessarily be great loss of life. I stuck to my original resolution to put the fire out. I had always impressed it upon my crew that if my ship caught fire, it must be put out. I had no faith in the custom of putting on all steam and heading for the shore. I knew that that of itself caused a panic; that, moreover, the fire was fanned up and swept aft, endangering the lives of the cabin passengers; and that the boats could not be lowered with the ship running at full speed. My idea was that if the passengers had to be put in the boats, it could be better done eight miles from the shore than in the breakers after the ship grounded.

So I spoke but a few words to my men now. I said, "We are men enough to handle this fire, and we *must* do it." They wanted no encouragement, and at the end of an hour we had it under. As soon as a man could breathe in the store-room, the powder-tank was passed up to me. It was so hot you could not put your bare hand upon it. My first impulse was to order the mate to throw it overboard; but I thought for a moment, and then directed him to put it in his state-room. I knew it would not explode then, and as we had gotten so well out of the scrape, determined to take the matter coolly. The steerage passengers were now sent forward again, given a cup of coffee, and advised to turn in for a morning nap. We started the engine ahead at 5 o'clock, and at 9 made fast to our buoy at Acapulco. We poured an immense quantity of water into the ship during the fire, but as we kept the donkey-engine at work pumping it out as it ran aft, our cargo was not damaged.

On this occasion I had a Chinese crew, with a Chinese boatswain. The leading men, quarter-masters and firemen were white, and they showed the others the example. It shows what effect that will have,—for the Chinese were the only ones engaged in putting out the fire who knew the powder was in the store-room. Yet they stuck to their posts. The first officer, whose duty it was to see that the powder was kept in the magazine, had been very negligent of his duty. He would have been dismissed the service had it not been for his courageous conduct during the fire. I reported to the agent, that although he had neglected his duty in the case—probably through forgetfulness—yet he had exhibited during the fire the highest traits of an officer, and I thought he should be retained. As for the conduct of the passengers, I never knew which deserved the most credit—they or my crew. The cause of the fire was spontaneous combustion, probably from oiled rags in the paint-room.

To return to the *Palmetto State*. One drill I introduced on board her, to which I attached much importance. Every officer and man had his appointed port or hatch to escape by in case of the vessel's suddenly sinking—say by the explosion of a torpedo. The first men who reached the deck immediately took off the iron gratings, without waiting to be told. At the order, "clear the ship," all hands would assemble on the roof in less than a minute. We never went to general quarters that I did not try this; and as I say, in less than a minute, the men from the magazine, shell-room, fire-room, everywhere, would be out on deck. There were a good many sailor-men in our crew, and we managed to put them in uniform and keep them provided with clothing. Occasionally we got a man from the army,—and we kept a bathing arrangement on the wharf, where all recruits were bathed and their clothes well boiled before being allowed to come on board, for obvious reasons. Both vessels were painted a pale blue or bluish-grey, the blockade runners having demonstrated that it was the most difficult to be distinguished. Before going into action we greased the shield with slush, as the *Merrimac* had done at Hampton Roads. Our officers in the *Palmetto State* were: Captain John Rutledge; Lieutenants Parker, Porcher, Shryock and Bowen; Surgeon Lynah; Paymaster Banks; Engineer Campbell; Master Chew; Midshipmen Cary, Sevier and Hamilton. We had a good boatswain and gunner, and a crew of about 120 men.

The *Palmetto State* bore the flag of Commodore Duncan L. Ingraham, who commanded the station. He was known as the hero of the Koszta affair. Koszta was a Hungarian refugee, who, when in the United States in 1850, had declared his intention of becoming an American citizen, and went through the preliminary forms. June 21, 1853, being in Smyrna, he was seized by a boat's crew from the Austrian brig *Huzzar*. Captain Ingraham, who was present in the sloop-of-war *St. Louis*, of 20 guns, demanded his release by a certain time, and prepared to attack the *Huzzar* on the 2nd of July. Koszta was then given up, and he afterwards returned to the United States. Captain Ingraham was much commended by his Government for his prompt and decisive action. He entered the U. S. Navy in 1812, being then but nine years of age. He served in the frigate *Congress*, under Captain Smith. He told me that they were at sea 9 months without going into port. They made a few prizes, but were not fortunate enough to fall in with any of the British frigates. It was considered an unlucky cruise, and the *Congress* got the name of being an unlucky ship. Commodore Ingraham commanded the brig *Somers* until just before the war with Mexico. During the war he served for a time on Commodore

Conner's Staff. He was a delicate-looking man, of intelligence and culture, and bore the reputation of being a brave and good officer. He is still living.[2]

By January, 1863, the vessels being all ready, we commenced to think of making some demonstration, and it was decided to attack the fleet off Charleston on the night of the 30th. The enemy's fleet off the harbor on that night consisted of the *Housatonic*, *Mercedita*, *Keystone State*, *Quaker City*, *Augusta*, *Flag*, *Memphis*, *Stettin*, *Ottawa* and *Unadilla*. Of these, the *Housatonic*, *Ottawa* and *Unadilla* were, I think, the only regularly-built men-of-war; the others being converted merchant steamers,—some paddles, the others screws. Captain Taylor, of the *Housatonic*, was the senior officer of the blockading force. Admiral Dupont, who commanded the station, was at this time at Port Royal with the iron-clad *New Ironsides*, the frigate *Wabash* and the steamships *Susquehanna*, *Canandaigua* and some others.

About 10 P. M., January 30th, Commodore Ingraham came on board the *Palmetto State*, and at 11.30 the two vessels quietly cast off their fasts and got underweigh. There was no demonstration on shore, and I believe few of the citizens knew of the projected attack. Charleston was full of spies at this time, and everything was carried to the enemy. It was nearly calm, and a bright moonlight night,—the moon being 11 days old. We went down very slowly, wishing to reach the bar of the main ship channel, 11 miles from Charleston, about 4 in the morning, when it would be high water there. Commander Hartstene (an Arctic man who rescued Kane and his companions), was to have followed us with several unarmed steamers and 50 soldiers to take possession of the prizes; but, for some reason they did not cross the bar.[3] We

[2]Ingraham died on 16 October 1891.

[3]Dr. Elisha Kent Kane was the leading scientist on board the *Advance*, an arctic exploration vessel. He and the ship were iced in during the fall of 1853 and forced to winter over. The ice failed to clear in the spring of 1854, and they were forced to stay another winter. In the spring of 1855 they abandoned the *Advance* and struck out overland, reaching a Danish outpost in July where they met the American relief expedition commanded by Lieutenant Harry J. Hartstene. See Vincent Ponko, *Ships, Seas, and Scientists* (1974), pp. 181–98.

steamed slowly down the harbor and, knowing we had a long night before us, I ordered the hammocks piped down. The men declined to take them, and I found they had gotten up an impromptu Ethiopian entertainment. As there was no necessity for preserving quiet at this time the captain let them enjoy themselves in their own way. No men ever exhibited a better spirit before going into action; and the short, manly speech of our captain convinced us that we were to be well commanded under any circumstances. We passed between Forts Sumter and Moultrie—the former with its yellow sides looming up and reflecting the moon's rays—and turned down the channel along Morris Island. I presume all hands were up in the forts and batteries watching us, but no word was spoken. After midnight the men began to drop off by twos and threes, and in a short time the silence of death prevailed. I was much impressed with the appearance of the ship at this time. Visiting the lower deck, forward, I found it covered with men sleeping in their pea-jackets peacefully and calmly; on the gun-deck a few of the more thoughtful seamen were pacing quietly to and fro, with folded arms; in the pilot-house stood the Commodore and Captain, with the two pilots; the midshipmen were quiet in their quarters (for a wonder), and aft I found the lieutenants smoking their pipes, but not conversing. In the ward-room the surgeon was preparing his instruments on the large mess-table; and the paymaster was, as he told me, "lending him a hand."

As we approached the bar, about 4 A. M., we saw the steamer *Mercedita* lying at anchor a short distance outside it. I had no fear of her seeing our hull; but we were burning soft coal, and the night being very clear, with nearly a full moon, it did seem to me that our smoke, which trailed after us like a huge black serpent, *must* be visible several miles off. We went silently to quarters, and our main-deck then presented a scene that will always live in my memory. We went to quarters an hour before crossing the bar, and the men stood silently at their guns. The port-shutters were closed, not a light could be seen from the outside, and the few battle-lanterns lit cast a pale, weird light on the gun-deck. My friend Phil. Porcher, who commanded the bow-gun, was equipped with a pair of white kid gloves, and had in his mouth an unlighted cigar. As we stood at our stations, not even whispering, the silence became more and more intense. Just at my side I noticed the little powder-boy of the broadside guns sitting on a match-tub, with his powder-pouch slung over his shoulder, fast asleep, and he was in this condition when we rammed the *Mercedita*. We crossed the bar and steered directly for the *Mercedita*. They did not see us until we were very near. Her captain then hailed us, and ordered us to keep off or he would fire. We did not reply, and he called out, "You will be into me." Just then we struck him on the starboard quarter, and dropping the forward port-shutter, fired the bow gun. The shell from it, according to Captain [Henry S.] Stellwagen who commanded her, went through her diagonally, penetrating the starboard side, through the condenser, through the steam-drum of the port boiler, and exploded against the port side of the ship, blowing a hole in its exit four or five feet square. She did not fire a gun, and in a minute her commander hailed to say he surrendered. Captain Rutledge then directed him to send a boat alongside. When I saw the boat coming I went out on the after-deck to receive it. The men in it were half-dressed, and as they had neglected to put the plug in when it was lowered, it was half full of water. We gave them a boat-hook to supply the place of the plug, and helped to bail her out.

Lieutenant T. Abbott, the executive officer of the *Mercedita*, came in the boat. I conducted him through the port to the presence of Commodore Ingraham. He must have been impressed with the novel appearance of our gun deck; but his bearing was officer-like and cool. He reported the name of the ship and her captain, said she had 128 souls on board and that she was in a sinking condition. After some delay Commodore Ingraham required him to "give his word of honor, for his commander, officers and crew, that they would not serve against the Confederate States until regularly exchanged." This he did—it was a verbal parole. He then returned to his ship.

In the meantime the *Chicora*, under her dashing commander,

had passed us and had become warmly engaged, and we in the *Palmetto State* were most impatient to be off. We were ready to exclaim with Horace:

> E'en whilst we speak, the envious Time
>   Doth make swift haste away;
> Then seize the Present, use thy Prime,
>   Nor trust another Day.

We rammed the *Mercedita* at 4.30 A. M., and lost much valuable time while the commodore was deciding what to do with her officers and men. Our chance for making a great success lay in taking advantage of the darkness. We knew that when day came the enemy would see they were contending with iron-clads, and would refuse battle—and we with our inferior speed could not force it. We finally stood out to the eastward and engaged the *Quaker City*, *Memphis*, and some other vessels, as they came up, but they sheered off as soon as they felt the weight of our metal. When day broke I got a chance to get up on the spar-deck. I first looked astern for the *Mercedita*, and not seeing her, asked our pilot where she was. He said she must have sunk; and that was the general impression on board; but I knew she was not in deep water, and seeing no masts sticking up, "I had my doubts."

The fact is we did not ram her quite hard enough. The panic on board her caused by the shell from our bow-gun was at first so great that they thought she was sinking. One boiler being emptied caused her to heel over, I suppose; but as we stood out to engage the enemy to the eastward, they got matters to rights, and finally went off to Port Royal where she arrived safely. (But this we learned afterwards).

Tucker, in the *Chicora*, as we rammed the *Mercedita*, passed us to starboard and soon became warmly engaged with the *Keystone State*, which vessel came gallantly into action, with the intention to run the *Chicora* down. She soon received so much damage as to cause her to surrender by striking her colors.

As related to me by the officers of the *Chicora* the next day, the *Keystone State* struck her flag and they were about lowering a boat to take possession of her. Lieutenant Bier, the executive officer, observed that she was moving off by working her off wheel and called Captain Tucker's attention to it. The lieutenants begged the captain to renew the fire; but he not expecting any deception or treachery hesitated to fire on a ship with her colors down; and in a little while Captain [William E.] Leroy who commanded the *Keystone State* hoisted his colors again, renewed his fire and escaped. He was soon after taken in tow by the U. S. steamer *Memphis* and carried to Port Royal.

Captain Tucker in his official report, dated the same day, in relation to this matter says: "We then engaged a schooner-rigged propeller and a large side-wheel steamer, partially crippling both, and setting the latter on fire, causing her to strike her flag. At this time the latter vessel, supposed to be the *Keystone State*, was completely at my mercy, I having a raking position astern distant some 200 yards. I at once gave the order to cease firing upon her, and directed Lieutenant Bier, first lieutenant of the *Chicora*, to man a boat and take charge of the prize; if possible to save her, if that was not possible to rescue her crew. While the boat was in the act of being manned I discovered that she was in the act of endeavoring to escape by working her starboard wheel, the other being disabled. Her colors being down I at once started in pursuit and renewed the engagement. Owing to her superior steaming qualities she soon widened the distance to some two hundred yards. She then hoisted her flag and commenced firing her rifled gun; her commander by this faithless act placing himself beyond the pale of civilized and honorable warfare."[4]

In his official report to Admiral Dupont, dated same day, Captain Leroy does not mention the fact of his having struck his colors; but an extract from the log of his vessel says: "About 6. 17 A. M. a shell entering on the port side forward of the forward guard destroyed the steam chimneys, filling all the forward part of the ship with steam. The port boiler emptied of its contents, the ship gave a heel to starboard nearly down to the guard, and the

---

[4]Tucker's report is in *O.R.N.*, I, 13:619–20.

water from the boiler, and two shot holes under water led to the impression the ship was filling and sinking, a foot and a half water being reported in the hold. Owing to the steam men were unable to get supplies of ammunition from forward. Ordered all boats ready for lowering. Signal books thrown overboard, also some small arms. The ram being so near, and the ship helpless, and the men being slaughtered by almost every discharge of the enemy, I ordered the colors to be hauled down, but finding the enemy were still firing upon us directed the colors to be re-hoisted, and resume our fire from the after battery.">[5]

The vessels in our vicinity having put off under all steam to the southward, our two vessels stood to the northward and eastward to meet the vessels coming from that direction. We exchanged a few shots with the *Housatonic* at very long range, but she soon also withdrew. Commodore Ingraham in his report says: "I then stood to the northward and eastward, and soon after made another steamer getting underweigh. We stood for her and soon after fired several shots at her, but as we had to fight the vessel in a circle to bring the different guns to bear, she was soon out of our range. In this way we engaged several vessels, they keeping at long range, and steering to the southward. Just as the day broke we made a large steamer (supposed to be the *Powhatan*) on the starboard bow, with another steamer in company, which had just got underweigh. They stood to the southward under full steam, and opened their batteries upon the *Chicora*, which was some distance astern of us. I then turned and stood to the southward to support the *Chicora*, if necessary, but the enemy *kept on his course to the southward*." (The italics are mine.) "I then made signal to Commander Tucker to come to an anchor, and led the way to the entrance to Beach channel, where we anchored at 8.45 A. M., and had to remain seven hours for the tide, as the vessels cannot cross the bar except at high water."[6] The commodore took the *Housatonic* to be the *Powhatan*—the *Powhatan* was at Port Royal that day.

⁵The log entry is printed in *O.R.N.*, I, 13:582.
⁶Ingraham's report is in *O.R.N.*, I, 13:617–9.

We anchored off Sullivan's island, as the commodore says; the enemy's ships had all gone off to the eastward, and southward and eastward. It was useless to pursue with our inferior speed,—and they very wisely declined fighting iron-clads with wooden ships. The enemy's ships went off to the southward and eastward, and there they remained, hull down, for the remainder of the forenoon; their masts could be seen by using the spyglass. The *Housatonic* and some others some time during the afternoon took up a position more to the eastward, but remained a long distance off.

Soon after we anchored some of the foreign consuls were brought off to show them that the blockade had been raised, and General Beauregard and Commodore Ingraham issued a proclamation to that effect, I thought the "proclamation" ill-advised. The fact is that during the entire war the southern people attached too much importance to the recognition of the Confederacy by the English Government. Many thought that a recognition amounted to a declaration of war against the United States, and that England and France would become our allies. Entirely too much sentiment was wasted on this subject.

Admiral Dupont and his officers found fault with the proclamation and bitterly resented it. The captains of the vessels drew up a joint letter, denying pretty much everything,—but they confounded a newspaper statement with the terms of the proclamation. The proclamation said: "At about the hour of 5 o'clock this morning (January 31, 1863), the Confederate States naval forces on this station attacked the United States blockading fleet off the harbor of the city of Charleston and sunk, dispersed, or drove off and out of sight for the time the entire hostile fleet."[7]

Now as we supposed the *Mercedita* was sunk at the time this was written, and as the fleet was certainly dispersed and driven off, I cannot see what great objection there could be taken to the wording. The point in question was as to whether the fleet had been driven entirely out of sight. I have already given my recollec-

[7]See *O.R.N.*, I, 13:617.

tion of it. Captain Tucker in his report says: "We pursued them six or seven miles seaward;" and again: "At 7.30 a. m., in obedience to orders, we stood in shore leaving the partially crippled fleeing enemy about seven miles clear of the bar, standing to the southward and eastward."

While still outside the bar, and with the foreign consuls on board, Commodore Ingraham penned the following dispatch which was carried to Charleston by their boat and telegraphed to Richmond:

> On board the "Palmetto State,"
> January 31, 1863.

> I went out last night. This vessel struck the *Mercedita* when she sent a boat and surrendered. The officers and crew have been paroled. Captain Tucker thinks he sunk one vessel and set another on fire, when she struck her colors. The blockading fleet has gone to the southward and eastward out of sight.

> D. N. INGRAHAM.
> *Flag Officer Commanding.*[8]

Captain Wm. Rogers Taylor of the *Housatonic* was the senior officer of the blockading fleet, and the letter of the captains seems to have been based upon his report and the remarks in that vessel's log book.

Captain Taylor says (the italics are mine): "I now determined to go to my former station to pick up the anchor, *but was unable to get hold of any landmarks*, on account of the haze over the shore, until about 3 o'clock. *I would state that at no period from daylight up to that time had the land been anywhere distinctly visible.* On *approaching* my anchorage the two rams were seen lying in Maffit's channel, close to the shore, some distance to the northward and eastward of Fort Moultrie."

The *Housatonic*, however, did not anchor, as her log shows. Here are some extracts (italics mine):

[8]See *O.R.N.*, I, 13:589–90.

From 8 to meridian. At 8 A. M. secured the battery. *The two enemy's steamers out of sight towards Fort Sumter*; it being very hazy around the horizon, could not see into the harbor.

At 11 A. M. the haze cleared sufficiently to enable us to see Fort Sumter, but we could not see into the harbor.

Waiting for the haze to clear *to run in* and pick up our anchor. During the watch the following steamers communicated with us viz.; United States steamers *Quaker City*, *Augusta*, *Flag*, *Stettin* and *Unadilla*.

From meridian to 4 P. M. Ship lying off and on in five fathoms water.

From 4 to 6 P. M. Ship underweigh all the watch.

From 6 to 8 P. M. Ship underweigh, lying to; head east-southeast.[9]

I do not think the letter of Colonel Lechler helps the captains' case much in reference to the distance the vessels were driven off—he says: "By the aid of a glass a fort said to have been Sumter was visible!" The fact is the captains in their letter to Admiral Dupont attempted to prove too much. I do not think it necessary to insert it here. It can be found in the Secretary of the Navy's report for 1863, and I am willing to place their statement and my narrative in the hands of any unprejudiced man and abide by his decision in the case—"what we want," said Mr. Gradgrind, "are *facts*."[10] It will be observed that all the Federal officers speak of the haze; they say "a thick haze was prevailing;" Colonel Lechler says: "The morning was somewhat hazy." My recollection is that it was a very clear day, and the night was one of the brightest I ever remember. Still there may have been a haze over the land as seen from their vessels outside. An analysis of the reports on both sides, taken in connection with my own recollection, convinces me that the following were the facts: After day broke, the Federal vessels retreated to the southward and eastward and southward, until they were hull down as seen from the decks of our ships; the rams gave up the pursuit, their slow speed rendering it impossible to over-

---

[9]Abstract log of the *Housatonic*, O.R.N., I, 13:590.
[10]Another reference to Dickens's *Hard Times* (1854).

take the enemy; they anchored off Sullivan's island to await the afternoon's tide; during the afternoon the Federal vessels took up a position more to the northward, where they remained at a distance of eight or ten miles watching our movements—it being a case where "distance lent enchantment to the view," for no man can blame them for not fighting two heavily armored iron-clads with their wooden vessels.

It is rather singular that the reports of the captains of the *Quaker City*, *Augusta*, *Flag* and *Stettin* are not to be found in the Secretary of the Navy's report with the others. The Charleston papers said: "The British consul with the commander of the British war steamer *Petrel* had previously gone five miles beyond the usual anchorage of the blockaders and could see nothing of them with their glasses." I do not understand that General Beauregard and Flag Officer Ingraham endorsed this foolish statement in their proclamation. The *Petrel* was not there. In this engagement the Federals lost 4 killed and 3 wounded on the *Mercedita*, and 21 killed and 19 wounded on the *Keystone State*; total killed and wounded 47, and two of their vessels surrendered, but afterwards escaped to Port Royal. Our vessels were not even hit, and we had no casualties to report.

At 4 P. M. we got underweigh and returned to Charleston by the Beach channel, and were honored with salutes from Forts Moultrie, Beauregard and Sumter, and the acclamations of the citizens of Charleston: but I candidly confess I did not participate in the general joy. I thought we had not accomplished as much as we had a right to expect. As we entered the harbor, the Federal vessels closed in towards their old stations and resumed the blockade. It would not have been prudent for us to remain outside the bar during the night, as in case of a blow the vessels would have foundered. As to the proclamation in regard to the blockade being broken, I looked upon it as all bosh. No vessels went out or came in during the day, except our own river boats. Our only chance of any great success lay in a surprise under cover of the night. After ramming the *Mercedita*, we should have remained a little outside and near her with the *Chicora*; then, as the enemy's vessels came up in succession, we should have captured them: which it is reasonable to suppose we would have done. When a vessel struck, she should have been directed to run in and anchor near the *Mercedita*. By adopting this plan I think we would have retained the *Mercedita* and *Keystone State*, and probably have captured in addition the *Quaker City*, *Augusta* and *Memphis*. By that time daylight would have revealed to the other ships "what manner of men" they were contending against, and the fight would have ended. We could have sent our prizes in by the main ship channel, and returned ourselves in the afternoon by either channel. I am constrained to say that this was a badly managed affair on our part, and we did not make the best use of our opportunity.[11]

I think it was on the evening of the next day that the British steamer *Petrel* came in. Her executive officer came on board the *Palmetto State*, and told us of the safe arrival of the *Mercedita* at Port Royal. Our fellows said nothing; but, like the Irishman's parrot, "they kept up a devil of a thinking."

A question arose as to the *status* of Captain Stellwagen and the *Mercedita*. It was truly an exceptional case. We claimed that he paroled the ship with her crew; and that she should be given up to us. My opinion was, and is, that the officers and men, being paroled, could not be recaptured. They were in honor bound not to serve until regularly exchanged; and I have heard that Captain Stellwagen held the same opinion. With the vessel it was different; she had been captured, but not taken possession of; she could, therefore, be recaptured. Attempts were afterwards made by both governments to compare the case of Captain Stellwagen and his officers to that of the officers and men of the *Alabama* when captured by the *Kearsarge*. The cases were not at all similar. The

[11]"The *Princess Royal*, a captured blockade runner, was among the vessels off the harbor the morning we went out. Some stress is laid upon our not capturing her, in the various Federal accounts. I have a dim recollection of seeing this vessel scuttling away some time after sunrise, but cannot speak with certainty as to the hour. We did not capture her for the same reason we did not bring the *Housatonic* and other ships to close action—we could not catch her!" [Author's note]

Mercedita's officers and men were paroled prisoners. Those of the *Alabama* were captured, but not taken possession of. Their case was precisely similar to that of the officers and men of the *Congress*. When a general surrenders, all of his army escape who can; but a man once paroled and sent to the rear, cannot be recaptured.[12]

I will close this long chapter by saying that in the battle I have attempted to describe, the pilots of our vessels did their duty well and manfully. Mr. Gladden, our chief pilot, was highly commended by Commodore Ingraham.

[12]Union Secretary of the Navy Gideon Welles submitted this ticklish question to a board of officers headed by Rear Admiral William B. Shubrick. That board concluded that "the validity of the parole should be admitted." See *O.R.N.*, I, 13:614. In a footnote of his own, Parker wrote: "Since writing this chapter, my friend Admiral [Daniel] Ammen, U.S.N., writes me in reference to Captain Stellwagon, his officers and men: 'Their parole was observed, and they were regularly exchanged, I think, the following April.' I had not known this fact before, and am glad to have the opportunity to record it." [Author's note]

CHAPTER XXVII

Capture of the U. S. S. *Isaac Smith*—torpedoes—Charleston at this time—its defences—blockade runners—arrival of the U. S. iron-clad fleet off the harbor—attack on Fort Sumter by Admiral Dupont's fleet, April 7th, 1863—result of the attack—the *Keokuk* sunk—Admiral Dupont's captains—an intended torpedo expedition—the monitors leave Morris Island and go to the North Edisto River

The day before we attacked the vessels off the harbor (January 30th) the U. S. steamer *Isaac Smith* was captured on the Stono river by the light batteries of the army. She was turned over to the navy and put in commission under the name of the *Stono*. Captain Hartstene was placed in command of her. She was a vessel of 450 tons, and had originally been a "cattle" boat on the North river. She was propelled by a screw with a walking-beam engine; the walking-beam worked athwartship which gave her a very peculiar appearance. She carried a very heavy battery for a vessel of her size and construction; eight or ten 64-pounder shell guns in broadside and a rifle 30-pounder Parrot forward. We found her very useful.

Immediately after the battle of the 31st the fleet off Charleston was reinforced by the U. S. steamer *New Ironsides*—a heavily-armored frigate with a powerful battery. It was not considered advisable to send our vessels out to attack her. During the months of February and March we remained in a state of comparative inactivity; but kept our men in perfect drill. We put a torpedo on our bow at this time. The staff projected some 20 feet from the stem; it worked on a hinge or gooseneck, and by means of an iron davit the staff could be raised so as to carry the torpedo out of water—when ready for use it was lowered so as to bring the torpedo about six feet under water. The torpedo was loaded with 60 pounds of rifle powder, and had screwed in it in different positions near the head seven sensitive chemical fuses. We kept it in the water ready for use, and about every two weeks would bring it on board, take out the fuses and examine the powder to see that it was dry. As executive officer I always attended to this with the gunner, and it was no joke to do it. In the first place we had to go out in a boat and take the torpedo off the staff, and in rough weather it was hard to keep the boat from striking it. As a moderate blow was sufficient to break the glass phials inside the fuses and cause an explosion, this in itself was not a pleasant occupation. Upon getting it on board we would take it on the after "fantail," (as we denominated the ends outside the shield) behind a screen, and I have passed many a *mauvais quart d'heure* while the gunner unscrewed with a wrench, and took out, all the fuses. I think it was about the most unpleasant duty I ever had to perform.

Charleston was very gay about this time; parties and picnics were the order of the day, and all seemed inclined to follow the advice of the old poet who has written:

Gather ye rose-buds while ye may,
    Old time is still a-flying;
And this same flower that smiles to-day
    To-morrow will be dying.[1]

---

[1]From "To the Virgin: To Make Much of Time" by Robert Herrick (1591–1674).

General [P. G. T.] Beauregard was in command of the department, and General [Roswell] Ripley second in command. They were constantly engaged in strengthening the batteries, laying down torpedoes, and placing obstructions. I never knew much about the obstructions. There were some booms abreast of Fort Sumter with an opening close in to the fort, and piling abreast of Castle Pinckney; but I do not remember much about the obstructions or the torpedoes. Every now and then we would be cautioned in a public order against using certain channels; but I suspect much of this information was for the benefit of spies.

There was no doubt, though, about the strength of the different forts and batteries. They mounted very heavy guns, and were remarkably well manned. From personal inspection I can speak of the garrison of Fort Sumter. The regiment there, under the command of Colonel [Alfred] Rhett, bore more the appearance of "regulars" than any regiment I remember to have seen at the South.

We were enlivened by the occasional arrival of a blockade runner. They generally flew the British flag. One morning a steamer called the *Ariel* arrived, flying the Spanish flag, rather to our surprise. It seems she had intended going into Wilmington, but losing her reckoning, found herself off "a harbor," and was forced to run in or be captured. The captain did not know whether he was in Wilmington or not until he was told. She had a Spanish captain, and a drunken Englishman for a navigator. She took on board a cargo of cotton and as might have been expected was captured the night she went out. This vessel was schooner-rigged, and her masts worked on hinges at the spar-deck so that they could be lowered by swinging them back.

In March, 1863, Flag Officer Ingraham was relieved by Commodore Tucker, who assumed command of the vessels afloat, with his flag on board the *Chicora*; Commodore Ingraham retaining command of the station.[2]

[2]Commodore John R. ("Handsome Jack") Tucker (1812–1883) had entered the navy in 1826. He was to have one of the most eventful postwar careers of any

The Federals were now assembling a large number of monitors at Port Royal and the North Edisto river, and we knew that Charleston would soon be attacked by sea. The original *Monitor* foundered off Cape Hatteras on her way south, December 30, 1862. This class of iron-clads came to be called "monitors" from her name. Although we knew the monitors were now assembling at the North Edisto river, not many miles below Charleston, yet their appearance off the bar took us rather by surprise after all. It was on Saturday, April 5th, that as I was quietly smoking a cigar after the usual "muster" and "inspection," Lieutenant Macomb Mason—Commodore Tucker's flag lieutenant—came on board with the information that the iron-clad fleet was off the harbor. Our vessels were lying at their wharves at the time; but we immediately got underweigh and proceeded to our previously assigned stations off Fort Johnson. We were held as part of the inner circle of defence. I suppose one reason we did not go further out was that the Federals might not know there was an opening in the obstructions off Fort Sumter. The monitors and frigate *New Ironsides* crossed the bar on the 6th, and anchored off Morris island. That very night a blockade runner came in by the main ship channel and passed by them without being perceived. The captain of the blockade runner took them to be Confederate vessels, as they were at anchor inside the bar.

The U. S. iron-clad squadron consisted of the frigate *New Ironsides*, bearing the flag of Admiral [Samuel F.] Dupont, and the monitors *Passaic, Weehawken, Montauk, Patapsco, Catskill, Nantucket, Nahant* and *Keokuk*. The monitors were armed with one 15-in. and one 11-inch gun each, with the exception of the *Keokuk*, which I believe had two 11-in. guns. The *New Ironsides* mounted two 150-pounder Parrot rifle guns, and fourteen 11-in. Dahlgren

---

Confederate naval officer, accepting a commission as rear admiral in the Peruvian navy, in which he commanded the combined fleets of Peru and Chile in their last war with Spain (1866), and later, as president of the Peruvian Hydrographic Commission of the Amazon, exploring the upper reaches of that river (1873).

guns in broadside on her main deck, or casemate. She had on her spar-deck two 50-pounder Dahlgren rifle guns. There were also present a large number of wooden vessels of war, but they took no part in the subsequent engagement.

It was about 1 P. M. on the 7th of April, 1863, that we perceived the enemy to be underweigh, and advancing to the attack. Fort Sumter hoisted the Confederate and Palmetto flags, and the band, stationed on the parapet, played several patriotic airs. Our two vessels got underweigh and steamed slowly around in a circle during the entire bombardment. The monitors came up with the *Weehawken* in advance. She carried some kind of a false bow, designed by Ericson, to pick up torpedoes. The *New Ironsides* was in the centre of the line; but becoming unmanageable, the rear vessels were directed to pass her. She remained during the action about twelve hundred yards from Fort Sumter. The monitors fought at distances varying from five hundred to seven hundred yards. At 2.50 P. M. the first gun was fired from Fort Moultrie, and soon after Sumter opened, with Fort Beauregard and other batteries on Sullivan's and Morris islands.

It was the intention of Admiral Dupont to pass Fort Sumter, and attack its northwest face; but the leading monitor coming up to the obstruction and not liking the look of it, turned around. This threw their line into some confusion, but they kept up the fire on the northeast face and were under a terrific fire from Sumter. As the enemy did not pass the obstruction we had no opportunity of trying the effect of the torpedo on our bow, nor could we fire a gun. I do not know the number of guns our forts and batteries brought to play on the monitors, but it was very large, and I suppose no vessels were ever under so heavy a fire.

At 4.30 P. M. Admiral Dupont made the signal to his vessels to retire, and shortly after they withdrew to their former anchorage off Morris island. They were still inside the bar. We did not know, of course, what injuries his vessels had received in the encounter, and were inclined to consider the movement as a *reconnoissance* in force. In fact Admiral Dupont says in his report to the Secretary of the Navy:

"Finding no impression made upon the fort, I made signal to withdraw the ships, intending to renew the attack this morning." [April 8.]

"But the commanders of the monitors came on board and reported, verbally, the injuries to their vessels; when without hesitation or consultation, (for I never hold councils of war), I determined not to renew the attack; for in my judgment it would have converted a failure into a disaster; and I will only add that Charleston cannot be taken by a purely naval attack, and the army could give me no co-operation. Had I succeeded in entering the harbor I should have had twelve hundred men and thirty-two guns; but five of the eight iron-clads were wholly or partially disabled after a brief engagement."[3]

The next morning we observed that the *Keokuk* had sunk at her anchors, or while in tow of another vessel. She was not a regular monitor, but was constructed after a plan of Mr. Whitney of New York. Captain Rhind was ordered to give her a "good trial under fire," and he did! The captains of all the monitors did their duty manfully and gallantly. They were: Percival Drayton, John Rodgers, John L. Worden, Daniel Ammen, George W. Rodgers, D. McN. Fairfax, John Downes, and A. C. Rhind. Captain Thomas Turner commanded the *Ironsides*, and C. R. P. Rodgers was the fleet captain. Of this latter officer, Admiral Dupont says in his report: "No language could overstate his services to his country, to this fleet, and to myself as its Commander-in-chief." Certainly no commander, not even Nelson, was ever better supported by his captains than was Admiral Dupont. They concurred with him in the opinion that it was better not to make another attempt.

In this engagement the enemy fired at Forts Sumter and Moultrie 139 shots from 11-inch and 15-inch guns; of these—96 shells, 30 solid shot, and 13 coned shot. The *Keokuk* fired but three times. Captain George E. Belknap U. S. N. in a letter to the *United Service Magazine*, says: "The Confederates fired in this engagement two

[3]Du Pont's report is in *O.R.N.*, I, 14:3.

thousand two hundred and nine shot, shell, and rifle-balls of heavy calibre."

The Federal loss was one killed and a few wounded. On our side the casualties were: One man killed and five wounded in Fort Sumter; and one killed at Moultrie.

Fort Sumter was not materially damaged. Some casemates were battered in, and a brick traverse knocked down. The damages were immediately repaired with sand-bags. It was said in Charleston at the time, that in this action the *New Ironsides* was anchored over a torpedo containing 1200 pounds of powder, and that the electrician could not explode it. It was made of an iron boiler or tank, and was supposed to have leaked. I cannot vouch for this, but I think it was true.

The failure of Admiral Dupont to take Charleston by a *coup de main* gave great offence to the authorities at Washington. Not knowing anything about the difficulties in the way, they expected him to repeat Admiral Farragut's performance at New Orleans. The Secretary of the Navy in his report for 1863 says in reference to this affair: "But comparatively slight injury was sustained by the turreted vessels, and only one life was lost in this remarkable contest."[4] It resulted in Admiral Dupont being relieved, at his own request, on the 6th of July by Admiral John A. Dahlgren; and whether he was correct or not in the opinion that the vessels could not have passed Fort Sumter on the 7th of April and taken Charleston, certain it is that they never did so afterward! Fort Sumter, though finally battered to a heap of ruins, was never captured. It was evacuated, with the city, in February 1865.

Some weeks before this attack upon Fort Sumter Lieutenant [William A.] Webb came to Charleston with orders from the Secretary of the Navy to organize a fleet of small torpedo boats—the idea being that they were to attack the monitors in case they should succeed in entering the harbor. It seems that a board of officers had been assembled in Richmond to devise plans of action

[4]*Report of the Secretary of the Navy* (1863). The passage quoted by Parker is on p. v.

in such an event. An old and distinguished commodore proposed that they should have hawsers with large hooks in the ends laid along the streets. "Then," said this old sea-dog, "let a boat go out, hook on to a monitor, clap on two or three hundred soldiers, and haul her, by G—d, right into the wharf." "But commodore," said one, "she would fire her gun and rake down the entire party!" "By G—d, I never thought of that," he replied. Webb had great difficulty in finding boats; but finally succeeded in collecting a lot of skiffs and canoes with a few serviceable cutters. These boats were fitted with poles 20 feet long on their stems, with 60 pound torpedoes on their ends. Webb had some thirty officers and men, and he hired a warehouse for their accommodation and a depot for the torpedoes. It was not at all uncommon to see a sailor rolling down to his boat, when they were called for exercise, with a quid of tobacco in his cheek and a 60 pound torpedo slung over his back; and when it is recollected that these torpedoes had seven sensitive fuses which a tap with a stick or a blow with a stone was sufficient to explode and blow half the street down, it can readily be believed that we gave him a wide berth.

When the monitors appeared off the harbor on the 5th a detachment of sailors was sent on from Wilmington under my old friend Johnson. They were assigned to the torpedo boats under Webb, and never having had anything to do with torpedoes had much to learn. The iron-clads remained at anchor off Morris island, and we were expecting another and perhaps more desperate attack. On the morning of the 10th a signal was made by the flag ship *Chicora* requiring me to repair on board. Upon getting alongside I found Commodore Tucker pacing the "fantail," and I joined him. "What," said he, "is your opinion as to making an attack on the three upper monitors to-night with six torpedo boats?" "I think well of it," I answered. "Will you take the command of them," said the commodore. "Yes, sir," I replied, and the thing was settled. He gave me an order on Webb for the boats which I was to select, and the attempt was to be made that night. Now I had never had any fancy for this kind of service; in fact it was repugnant to me; but this was a case of *noblesse oblige*. I went immediately to work to get everything ready. I went on shore and selected six pretty good cutters with their officers and crews, and after directing them to come out singly I returned to the *Chicora* where I had the use of the cabin to draw up my plan of attack, &c. While about it, Webb came off and said General Beauregard thought it would be better to take all the torpedo boats and attack the entire fleet of monitors.

Commodore Tucker called a council of war, and submitted the proposal. It was decided that it should be attempted; and as the council broke up, the commodore directed me to retain the command. The boats were ordered to come off singly, or in pairs, so as not to attract the attention of the enemy; and to rendezvous alongside the *Stono*. This vessel had a large cabin, and I used it to collect the commanders together so that I might explain my method of attack, once for all. It was growing towards sunset, and time was pressing. I intended to drop down with the ebb tide, close along Morris island, and to attack the monitors at the beginning of the flood tide, which would be about midnight; and my written orders required that every commander should explode his torpedo against one of the enemy's ships before returning to Charleston. We intended to "double bank" the monitors. The moon was 23 days old, and would not rise until about 1 A. M.

We had about fifteen boats in all; and as I looked at them lying alongside the *Stono*, some of them half full of water, and with inexperienced crews, my heart sank. I could see no possible chance of success under the circumstances. After explaining my plan of attack, I broke up the conference and directed the captains to have their boats ready to move as soon as it became dark. My old friend Johnson came to me for further instructions. He had never seen a torpedo-boat, and had some doubts in relation to them. "It seems to me, captain," he said, "that when I explode the torpedo, the reaction will knock the bow of my boat in." This, to tell the truth, was *my* private opinion also; but of course I could not express it. I tried to explain to him why it might not happen. "Well," he said, "I'll explode my torpedo against a monitor; but that's the way it looks to me!" I shall never forget his earnest expression at the time, and I felt sure that whatever his "doubts" might be, I could rely upon him to the death.

When nearly ready to start, the officer of the deck reported to me that Commodore Tucker was coming on board. I thought he had come to bid us Godspeed; but he said as soon as he reached the deck: "Parker, you have lost your chance—the monitors are leaving—they can be seen crossing the bar." I thought for a moment, and then replied: "I am glad of it." "Why!" said the commodore, much surprised. For answer I took him to the side of the vessel and pointed to the group of half-swamped canoes and skiffs! Why the *Stono* was not blown up, or why they did not blow each other up, is more than I can account for. The commodore agreed with me that it would have been a forlorn hope. We had not known when it was decided to send the boats down how entirely unfitted they were for the service.

I think it was on the 12th that the last of the monitors left the offing; and soon after we heard of their arrival in the North Edisto river. The *New Ironsides* remained on the blockade.

CHAPTER XXVIII

Reconnaissance of the monitors in the North Edisto River—I organize a torpedo expedition to attack them—arrival at Rockville—a deserter—skilful and original flank movement—return to Charleston—Commander W. T. Glassell's attack on the *New Ironsides*—Admiral Daniel Ammen—I am ordered to Richmond

The monitors went to the mouth of the North Edisto river, where they remained undergoing repairs. Commodore Tucker and I now had torpedo "on the brain," and I was sent down to the Edisto by land to reconnoitre. The monitors lay near the mouth of a creek, and could be plainly observed from the little village of Rockville, on the southern end of Wardmelaw island. Rockville had been built by the planters of the neighboring islands as a summer resort; it was deserted. Our pickets occupied the church steeple which overlooked the decks of the monitors; but now

The sound of its church-going bell
   These valleys and rocks never heard;
Never sighed at the sound of a knell,
   Or smiled when a Sabbath appeared.[1]

At the time of my visit the pickets told me that the enemy would occasionally land in Rockville, and then our pickets would fall back from their posts until they left. I believe this was a tacit understanding between them and they did not fire on each other. Having carefully observed the position of affairs, I made up my mind that a small number of boats could go up Bohicket creek, abreast the monitors, and there await a dark and rainy night; then with their torpedoes ready they could make a dash at the monitors, which would be taken by surprise, and the boats having but a short distance to row the chances were that some at least of the vessels would be destroyed. I returned to Charleston and reported the result of my observations to Commodore Tucker, and was directed to organize an expedition of six boats for the attempt. I took four of the best of Webb's boats, and one from the *Chicora* and *Palmetto State* each. The boats were well officered and manned by volunteers, and we took great pains in preparing them. The torpedo staffs were not fastened to the stems; but were carried about six feet below the keels of the boats. When rowing, the staff could be brought close up to the keel of the boat, and it could be raised and lowered at pleasure. By removing keys at the stem and stern posts it could be let go altogether. The boats made slow headway with the staff lowered, or indeed with it pulled up against the keel; but after exploding the torpedo the whole affair was to be detached to give the boat a chance to escape. I drilled the boats well before starting on this expedition, and satisfied myself that everything was in good working order, and that every officer and man understood what he was expected to do. We kept our plans to ourselves so that spies might not carry the news to the enemy. Our route was

---

[1]The lines are from "Alexander Selkirk" by William Cowper (1782), lines 29–32.

to be up the Ashley river to Wappoo creek; through Wappoo creek into the Stono river; up the Stono to Church flats; by Church flats to the Wardmelaw river; and down the Wardmelaw to the North Edisto river. The Wardmelaw empties into the Edisto about seven miles from its mouth. On the 10th day of May, 1863, we started from Charleston with six boats, in tow of an army tug which was to take us as far as Church flats. Lieutenant W. T. Glassell was my second in command. All hands were in fine spirits. Upon being cast off by the tug we took to our oars and pulled down the Wardmelaw river into the Edisto, which we reached about sunset. We landed at White Point, and hauling our boats up out of sight went into camp for the night. The Federal gunboats patrolled the river up to and beyond this point, and all the plantations were abandoned on both sides of the river.

The next day General Hagood (since Governor of South Carolina), came to my quarters for consultation. It was agreed that if we were successful in sinking the monitors that he would make an attack on the troops on shore in the neighborhood. He also agreed to have a company of infantry, a company of artillery, and a company of cavalry at the place on Bohicket creek, where I expected to land. The first two companies to protect us in case we were chased up the creek, and the last to act as scouts. All the day we remained quietly at White Point, keeping ourselves out of view of the enemy's vessels, which we could see very distinctly anchored near the mouth of the creek, in the vicinity of Rockville, distant five or six miles. About 10 o'clock that night we started down the river with muffled oars. Our object was to get up Bohicket creek without being discovered, and there await our opportunity. The night was clear, but there was no moon. The torpedoes were taken off the staffs and carried in the stern-sheets, and the staffs were carried over all,—so there was nothing to impede our headway.

We went down the river in line ahead, Lieutenant Glassell with an experienced pilot leading, and the boats closed up to boat-length intervals. The men were armed with cutlasses, and the officers in charge had orders to board and carry any boat we came across, if we were seen by it. We pursued our way, not even whispering to each other,—passed the monitors without being discovered, and went up the creek. Here we found the companies anxiously awaiting our arrival. There was a deserted mansion here which we determined to use as our headquarters; so, hauling the boats close in under the banks, and stowing the torpedoes in an empty room, we all turned in for a nap, it being then about two o'clock in the morning.

Glassell and I had a field-bed in a room together; and shortly after daybreak I saw his coxswain come in and call him. After a few whispered words they went out together. I feared something was wrong, and got up; and while making a hasty toilet Glassell returned and reported that one of his very best men could not be found, and he feared he had deserted to the enemy. Glassell had been out several times during the winter trying to blow up one of the vessels off Charleston, and this man had always accompanied him; consequently he knew all about our torpedo arrangements. I immediately sent the cavalry to scout the country in the hope of picking him up, and posted the artillery and infantry on the banks of the creek to be prepared to resist an attack by boats. Soon after this, one of the monitors got underweigh and anchored off the mouth of the creek, and a gunboat went up the river and shelled White Point, where we had bivouacked the night before. "Quoth Hudibras, 'I smell a rat.'"

A picket soon came in who had been occupying the church-steeple at Rockville during the night. He said that shortly after daylight he saw a boat from one of the monitors pull in to the marsh and take a *stake* from it. He said he remarked to his companion that he wondered at their doing so, as the stake must be wet and would not burn. That "stake" was our man. He had made a straight wake for the fleet, waded through the marsh to the water's edge, and waved his hat for a boat to take him on board. I sent Glassell up the creek with the boats, and told him to go up as far as he could, and awaited further developments. During the day the monitor fired some shell at our position, as well as I recollect; but I am not sure of this. I recollect the bank of the creek was high and we had only to keep under it to be perfectly protected, and I know that no one was hurt. In the afternoon General Hagood came down and we agreed that the expedition must be given up. Our hope of success lay in a surprise, and that was no longer possible. The point now was to save the boats and men; the loss of the latter would seriously impair the efficiency of our two iron clads at Charleston. To return by the way we came was obviously out of the question; so after some thought, I asked the general to send six army wagons, with their teams, to meet me at the head of the creek next morning. This he promised to do. About sunset Glassell sent a boat down to see what had become of me, and I went back in it to rejoin my command. I found the party at a deserted mansion on Wardmelaw island. The furniture (much abused of course) was still in the house; the garden with its orange and lemon-trees, etc., was overgrown with weeds. All bore the imprint of cruel war. I cannot say I gave way to much sentiment myself upon the occasion. I think I had a pretty keen perception of what was to come when war was declared between the states, and I had made up my mind to bear up philosophically under all circumstances. Though disappointed at the result of our expedition, and somewhat anxious as to the saving of my men I remember to have enjoyed a cigar among the orange groves very much that night, after a hearty supper of hard-tack and salt pork.

The next morning, bright and early, six wagons, each drawn by four mules, made their appearance. We took the bodies off, hauled the fore and hind wheels farther apart, substituted the torpedo staffs for fore-and-aft pieces, and mounted the boats gallantly on top. The road was across a champaign country, through very high marsh grass, and the mules moved off so freely that some of the men sat in the boats and rode there. With flags flying, we formed line ahead, and struck out for the Stono—thus turning the Edisto and Wardmelaw rivers. Some of our soldiers who were at batteries on the opposite side of the river, said afterwards, that our appearance caused the greatest astonishment. The grass being very high, the mules could not be seen, nor the men walking alongside. To them the appearance was that of six boats, manned and with colors flying, sailing over the land in some mysterious manner. Macbeth was not more astounded when he saw "great Birnam wood approaching the walls of Dunsinane." But for making out our colors they would have given us a shot or two. We launched our boats in the Stono river and returned to Charleston, *via* Wappoo creek, as before. That night at midnight I awakened Commodore Tucker, and informed him of the nonsuccess of our expedition.

That was my last torpedo service; but Glassell who had been an enthusiastic "torpedoist" from the beginning, afterwards made a daring attempt to destroy the *New Ironsides*. He went down Charleston harbor in a steam torpedo boat on the night of October 5, 1863. He had with him a pilot, an engineer and two men. Applying the rule I have given in chapter 13 of this book I find that on that night the moon was 24 days old, and consequently would not rise until about 3 o'clock in the morning. The *Ironsides* was lying off Morris island at anchor, and about 9.15 P. M. Glassell struck her with his torpedo, and as he did so he fired with a rifle and killed the officer of the deck, Acting Ensign Howard. The explosion of the torpedo threw up a column of water which swamped the boat. Glassell and one man jumped overboard and swam to a coal schooner near by and were made prisoners. The engineer, Mr. Tombs, and the pilot and another man clung to the boat, and as she drifted up the harbor with the flood tide they succeeded in getting into her and raising steam again. They got back safely to Charleston. Glassell was sent to Fort Warren, and was exchanged in 1864. He was promoted for his services in the *Ironsides* affair. After the war I met him in California, where he died about 1875. He was a zealous officer and a gentleman born and bred. The *New Ironsides* was not materially damaged by the explosion of the torpedo.

At the time I went down to the Edisto to attack the monitors my old friend and shipmate, Rear Admiral Daniel Ammen, was the senior officer in command of them. After the war, when I was commanding the Pacific Mail Steamship Company's steamship *Colorado* running between San Francisco and Panama, he took passage with me to Panama being then on his return home from China. In a trip of fourteen days we naturally fought our battles o'er again. He told me all about my deserter, and said he had given him very accurate information, as I supposed he would do.[2]

Upon my return to Charleston I received a letter from Mr. Mallory, our Secretary of the Navy, directing me to make out an estimate for books, apparatus, &c., necessary for the establishment of a naval school. I accordingly did so, and sent it as instructed to the house of Fraser & Trenholm who were to direct their agent to purchase the articles required in England. Soon after this I received orders to report in person at the Navy Department in Richmond. I parted with my shipmates in the *Palmetto State* with much regret. Lieutenant Philip Porcher succeeded me as her executive officer. These two fine iron-clads, the *Chicora* and *Palmetto State*, assisted in the defence of Charleston until it was evacuated by the Confederates, February 18th, 1865. They were then set on fire by their captains and blown up.

[2]Ammen's report to Welles is dated 12 May 1863 and is printed in *O.R.N.*, I, 14:188–9.

CHAPTER XXIX

Organization of the Confederate Naval Academy—the
schoolship *Patrick Henry*—capture of the U. S. S. *Underwriter*—the iron-clads *Virginia*, *Richmond* and *Fredericksburg*—
the defence of James River by torpedoes—Captain Hunter
Davidson—his attack on the U. S. S. *Minnesota*—opening of
the campaign of 1864—General Butler's lost opportunity—
battle of Drury's Bluff—I am ordered to command the iron-
clad *Richmond*—Trent's reach

I was not unwilling to leave Charleston for the James river,
because I thought the enemy would not make another attempt
there for some time, and I thought there would be a better
opportunity to see service on the James river; but hardly had I
reported to the Secretary in Richmond when we got news that the
iron-clads had reappeared off Charleston, July 10th, 1863.

This was in fact the beginning of the combined operations of
General [Quincy Adams] Gilmore and Admiral [John A.] Dahl-
gren on Morris island, which finally led to the evacuation of Fort
Wagner. This was about all that General Gilmore and Admiral

Dahlgren did do towards taking Charleston. The evacuation of Fort Wagner was most skilfully performed; and Captain William Henry Ward, of the *Palmetto State*, superintended the handling of the boats on that occasion; though I believe he has never received credit for it.

Upon hearing the news of the arrival of the monitors off Charleston, I was inclined to insist upon returning to the *Palmetto State*; but the Secretary declaring that he particularly wished me to remain on the James river, I gave it up. It was now determined that the steamship *Patrick Henry* should be converted into a school-ship—this was a pet scheme of Mr. Mallory's and he should be entitled to reap the credit of the results, which I will show hereafter were much greater than were at that time anticipated. The ship was to be kept fully manned and armed, and to remain at anchor off Drury's Bluff to assist in the defence of the river when necessary. We made some alterations in her quarters, to enable her to accommodate the large number of midshipmen we expected; and in the fall of 1863, the First Session of the Confederate States Naval Academy opened with a full and very efficient corps of professors and about 50 midshipmen.

I have no notes; but I think the Academic Staff at this time was as follows:

Captain William H. Parker,	Superintendent.
Lieut. B. P. Loyall,	Commandant of Midshipmen.
" W. B. Hall,	Professor of Astronomy, Navigation and Surveying.
Lieut. Davies,	Assistant.
" Graves,	Instructor in Seamanship.
" Billups,	Assistant.
" Comstock,	Instructor in Gunnery.
Professor George W. Peek,	Mathematics.
" Armstead,	Physics.
" Huck,	English Literature.
" Péple,	French and German.
" Sanxey,	Infantry Tactics.

There were some changes among the lieutenants at different times, but the professors—all of whom had served in the army up to this time—remained until we broke up, which was not until the end of the war. The exercises of the school went on regularly through the exciting times of 1864–5, only interrupted by details of officers and men for the several cutting-out expeditions. A foremast with a complete set of yards and sails, was put in the ship; and the midshipmen were given as much instruction in practical seamanship as the circumstances would admit of. The senior classes were regularly graduated as Passed Midshipmen, and sent to the various vessels in commission, where they rendered good service as ordnance and drill officers. They were all also skilful in the handling of boats. These young gentlemen were, at first, very loth to come to the ship and take up their books; but when they found that it resulted in their returning to their ships as passed midshipmen, eligible to promotion to the grade of lieutenant, they became reconciled to it. I need not say that we felt very much the want of educated junior officers in the Confederate Navy. The

The Confederate States Naval Academy school-ship *Patrick Henry*. Official U.S. Navy photograph.

Volunteer Navy contained many lieutenants who had never been to sea—men who did not know a ship from a brig—who wrote in their logs such remarks as: "the moon was over the port bow, and the wind was hard a-starboard." These gentlemen were officers of the navy without being naval officers, a distinction which does not seem to be properly appreciated even at the present day.

The secretary of the navy took much interest in the School, as I have said, and our annual examinations were largely attended. We had an exceptionally good corps of professors; they were men before they became teachers. All who attended our examinations spoke highly of the school, and the graduates were much prized by their commanding officers. For my own part it has since very often been a subject of—I was going to say pride, but I only had a share in it—but I will say gratulation that the Naval School was established and carried on as well as it was under the almost insuperable difficulties in the way. It has often occurred to me that in all the losses of the war, here at least, was something saved in the education, partial though it was, of the Confederate midshipmen. After the war many of them went to sea and some rose to important commands, to which their school-ship education materially helped them. Only the other day one of them told me that immediately after the war he shipped before the mast in a vessel bound to Liverpool from Baltimore. Ambitious and determined to rise, he carried with him a sextant as part of his outfit. When the ship got to sea he went up to "take the sun;" and at the sight of this unusual proceeding of a foremost-hand the captain sent for him to make some inquiries. My young friend told him he had never been to sea, but had learned some navigation on board the school-ship *Patrick Henry*. "Well" said this old salt, "you may know something about it *theodically*, but you don't know a d——d thing about it practically. This was true enough at the time; but he soon did know something of it practically, and in a few years had a much better command than his captain. During my service in the Pacific Mail Steamship Company, from 1865 to 1874, I met many of my former pupils in the Pacific, and all were doing well. Among them I may mention young Jeff Howell who commanded a steamer on the northern coast. He was drowned by his steamer being run down; but was as fine a seaman for his years as I have ever seen. Of my own knowledge I can name quite a number of our midshipmen who are now ministers, lawyers, merchants, etc. So, as I have said, *something* was saved from the Confederacy, and I had a share in saving it.

The ship lying with the other vessels of the squadron abreast Drury's Bluff, just above our obstructions in the river, made the officers and men feel that they were not withdrawn from active service. It was not like being shut up in a bomb-proof, for their vessel was performing the same duty as the others. A detail from the ship under the executive officer, Lieutenant Benjamin P. Loyall, went with Commander John T. Wood and assisted at the capture of the U. S. steamer *Underwriter*, Februrary 2, 1864. The *Underwriter* was lying in the Neuse river above the town of New-bern, N. C. She was boarded by our party in boats and captured. As she could not be carried up the river she was burned. Palmer Saunders, one of our midshipmen, was killed in this affair. He was a mere boy, but a gallant one. The seaman who killed him—a petty officer of the *Underwriter*, and fine fellow himself—told a friend of mine after the battle that he very much regretted having to do so, seeing his youth; but Saunders and another midshipman attacked him with such impetuosity that he was forced to cut him down in self-defence. Lieutenant Loyall for his gallantry upon this occasion was made a commander, and a few months later was sent to Kingston on the Neuse river to superintend the building of an iron-clad there. The vessel was built, and when about ready had to be burned to prevent her falling into the hands of the enemy. This was not Captain Loyall's fault; but somehow during the war it was the fate of a good many of the vessels built by our secretary. It would surprise even the Confederates if a list could be made out showing the large number of vessels we built in out-of-the-way places during the war. They were mostly burned. They were always finished just too late. The most noted case was that of the iron-clad ram *Mississippi* built at New Orleans and *nearly* ready when Farragut captured the city. She was the most powerful vessel built at the south during the war, and it is supposed would have been able to destroy Farragut's entire fleet; but she was not *quite* ready and was burned. Treason was said to be at the bottom of this affair; but I knew nothing about it myself. We felt the loss of Captain Loyall very much. A highly accomplished officer, a good disciplinarian, and much beloved by all, but especially by the midshipmen, he left us with our earnest prayers for his future success. They have been fulfilled, for the man who would grace the quarter deck of a vessel in any navy lives now in Norfolk a successful merchant and an honored citizen.

During the winter of 1864 we remained quietly attending to our duties; the monotony only being broken by the affair of the *Underwriter*. The squadron on the river at this time consisted of the iron-clads *Virginia*, *Richmond* and *Fredericksburg*, and the gunboats *Nansemond*, *Hampton*, *Drury*, *Roanoke*, *Beaufort* and *Raleigh*. The *Virginia* was a very powerful vessel. She, like the others, was after the plan of the *Merrimac* with the exception of the submerged ends. I think the *Virginia* had 6 inches of iron on her sides and 8 inches on her ends. The *Fredericksburg* was the lightest and weakest vessel of the three. She had, perhaps, 4 inches iron. Each of these iron-clads carried four heavy Brooke rifle guns as well as I recollect. The squadron was commanded by Flag Officer French Forrest; an officer who had a fine record in the Mexican war. He was a man of undoubted courage and would have distinguished himself in this war had he had the opportunity. During the spring of 1864, as the winter broke up, we had fearful freshets in the river; and much as I had seen of the sea I do not know that anything ever impressed me with the power of water more than these freshets. Our ships made some narrow escapes of being wrecked on the obstructions by the floating masses of timber getting across their bows; but by hauling in close to the bank at Drury's Bluff we managed to hold on. Drury's Bluff is about six miles below Richmond on the right bank of the river; and a few miles below on the other side was a fort at Chapin's Bluff. Below these two fortifications the approaches were guarded by torpedoes. These torpedoes constituted the most formidable defence of the city of Richmond on the water side.

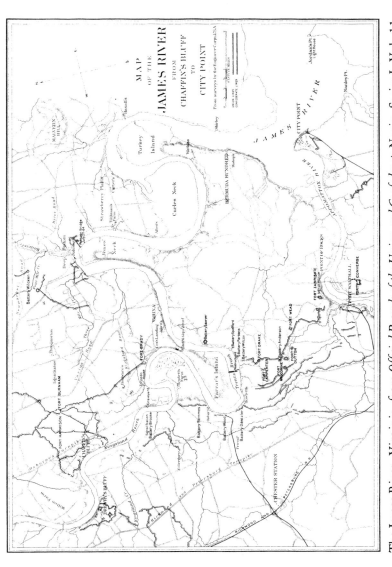

The James River, Virginia, from *Official Records of the Union and Confederate Navies*, Series I, Vol. 11.

Lieutenant Hunter Davidson had been in charge of this important branch of defence for about a year; he found it in an embryo state, and by his energy and perseverance he brought it to perfection. To him should be given much credit for the defence of the river in the summer of 1864. He had a small steamer in which he visited his batteries (for his torpedoes were exploded by electricity), and being a man of much ingenuity as well as untiring energy he kept everything in his department in perfect order; he had under him a small corps of intelligent and courageous men. During the winter he had had built in Richmond a small boat propelled by steam. She was a screw and was fitted with a torpedo. She was about 25 feet long and 4 wide, and carried four men, who were protected against musketry by a steel shield. The torpedo staff was about 15 feet long and was fitted to the stem; it could be triced up and lowered at pleasure. The engine was built in Richmond. I made several trips in this little boat, and when she was running at about half or three-quarter speed the engine made absolutely no noise. Her speed was ten miles per hour.

In this boat Davidson went down the river, and on the night of April 9, 1864, he rammed the U. S. frigate *Minnesota*, lying off Newport's News. He struck her just abaft the port mainchains, and exploded the torpedo. The frigate was not much damaged, but when it is considered that Davidson was more than one hundred miles outside of our lines, and that the *Minnesota* was guarded by tug-boats, having one towing astern at the time in fact, the boldness of the act will be appreciated. He was made a Commander for it. The little boat did not suffer at all from the shock; and the torpedo staff was not even splintered.

Speaking of torpedoes reminds me of a laughable incident. Our river steamers went down to City Point occasionally with prisoners to exchange. As we had torpedoes in the river anywhere from Drury's Bluff to Trent's reach, and below, their captains ran great risks. On one occasion two of our boats were returning from City Point, fortunately with no passengers, when one of them struck a torpedo and immediately went down. A boat went from the other steamer and found the captain struggling in the water, with a

Webster's Unabridged Dictionary in his arms. As he was pulled into the boat he said: "I did not have time to get it on." He thought he had seized a life-preserver!

The campaign of 1864 opened with the battles in the Wilderness between General Lee and his new opponent, General Grant.[1] Drury's Bluff was at this time commanded by Captain Sidney Smith Lee, a brother of the General, and I spent many evenings with him talking over the news from the battle fields. I confess that I did not like the look of things from the beginning: it seemed to me that if it had been McClellan, Burnside, or any of the other generals who had been in command of the Federal Army, that the two or three first battles would have ended the campaign for that year—such having been my observations of the previous ones—but when I found General Grant holding on with bulldog tenacity, in spite of his heavy losses, knowing as I did his powerful supports and reinforcements; and knowing equally that we had given General Lee pretty much all the men we had, I began to fear for the safety of the capital. Many others did also, I presume; but we never acknowledged it to each other—all preserved a cheerful countenance.

On the 5th of May, 1864, Major Frank Smith, temporarily commanding the post at Drury's Bluff in the absence of Colonel Terrett, came on board the *Patrick Henry*, about 2 o'clock in the afternoon. Captain Robert Pegram happening to be in Richmond, I was the senior officer on the river. Walking into my cabin, the major showed me several dispatches from the signal officers on the river below City Point to the effect that a "large number of gunboats and transports were coming up the river." Whilst I was reading the dispatches a messenger came off from the shore with another, saying the enemy were landing at Bermuda Hundred.

[1]Grant's army crossed the Rapidan River on 4 May 1864. The next day Lee struck the Federals in a huge forested area known as "the Wilderness." For the next five weeks the two armies remained locked in nearly constant combat as they worked their way in a southeasterly direction, until Lee was forced within his defensive lines around Richmond and Petersburg.

We saw at once that Drury's Bluff was threatened, and we had hardly any troops there. I went on shore with all the sailors we could spare from the squadron, and we manned the inner line of the defences. We had not men enough to attempt to hold the outer lines.

We soon knew that a large force was landed at Bermuda Hundred, only twelve miles below us, and with a good road to Drury's Bluff and Richmond, we expected to see the head of their column at any moment. [2] As our signal officers had now fallen back from their stations at Bermuda Hundred, we had to rely upon our scouts for information; and as these were men who had been long in garrison their work was imperfectly done, and our dispatches became very unreliable. We could get no authentic information as to the number of the enemy and their movements. Dispatches were sent to Richmond and to General Lee stating our situation and asking for reinforcements. We remained all night in this condition, expecting an attack at any moment, and knowing we had not men enough to resist it. Drury's Bluff overlooks the river, and our vessels lying under it could render us no assistance as they could not elevate their guns sufficiently to bear.

About daylight we were very much relieved by the arrival of General Bushrod Johnson, with his fine brigade of Tennesseeans. He assumed the command; but at 10 o'clock the same morning he received orders to move off in the direction of our right flank; and although this left us again exposed to an attack by the river-road, he did not feel at liberty to remain, and at noon he moved out. Captain Pegram and Colonel Terrett had by this time arrived and resumed their commands. I had gone on board my ship to dinner when a messenger came in hot haste from Captain Pegram requesting my return to the Bluff. In answer to my question he informed me that the enemy were close at hand, and that our troops had abandoned the attempt to hold the intrenchments and were assembling inside Fort Drury, an enclosed earthwork that commanded

[2]The Federal army was the newly created "Army of the James," some 30,000 men under Major General Benjamin F. Butler.

the river principally, though there were some guns pointing landward. Upon getting on shore I found such to be the case, and I went into the fort with my crew intending to share the fate of the garrison. Provisions and ammunition were hastily put in. Captain Pegram made arrangements by which we could communicate with the vessels and be supplied with provisions in the case of an investment. He himself returned to his ship as he did not think it proper that he should run the risk of being cut off from the squadron—nor did I.

We waited for some hours but the enemy did not appear. General Butler lost his opportunity. Had he advanced immediately upon landing, or even the next day, Richmond would have been in his possession by the afternoon of the 6th of May. We had no troops to oppose the movement successfully, and although the iron-clads and gunboats might have operated on his flank and annoyed it considerably, they could not have prevented his advance. I know it now, and I knew it then. Twenty-four hours after the landing at Bermuda Hundred the Federal army could have been in Richmond. With Drury's Bluff and fortifications in the hands of the enemy we could not have prevented their fleet from raising and passing the obstructions. Our iron-clads could not resist the 15-inch shot, as I have good reason to know, and would have been overpowered and captured. The Federal fleet would soon have been off the city. But all this was not to be. During the night of the 6th troops came pouring in, and by the next day we felt able to hold Fort Drury and all the fortifications in connection with it.

While Butler's troops were landing at Bermuda Hundred, Admiral S. P. Lee, who was in command of the Federal fleet on the river, sent his small steamers up above City Point to drag for torpedoes. While engaged in this work the steamer *Commodore Jones* was blown up by one of them near Four mile creek. It was discharged from the shore by electricity. This made the enemy very cautious in their advance by the river. Admiral Lee in a dispatch to the Secretary of the Navy, dated May 13th, says: "General Butler asks for monitors above Trent's reach. Torpedoes, commanded by rebels on the left bank, which commands our decks, and shoal water, by chart several feet less than the monitors draw, make difficult the advance which I shall push to-morrow morning."[3] This goes to corroborate what I have before said in regard to the efficiency of Captain Davidson's work; though if, as the admiral says, there was less water by several feet in the river than the monitors drew, the torpedoes might as well have been anywhere else. General Butler having failed to avail himself of his grand opportunity now advanced to invest Fort Drury; but General Beauregard was in command there, and had collected men enough not only to hold the fort but to justify an advance. He accordingly attacked General Butler on the 16th of May and drove him back in the direction of City Point again. The failure of a column from Petersburg to co-operate prevented General Beauregard from gaining the great victory he would otherwise have done. As it was he took many prisoners and drove Butler back until his right rested on the river at Howlets on Trent's reach, and there it remained till the close of the war.[4] Our forces threw up a battery at Howlets to command Trent's reach, and held it until Richmond was evacuated. While this fight between Beauregard and Butler was going on our vessels remained inactive on the river, not being able to render any assistance. I recollect being very much astonished at the noise made by the musketry firing on this occasion. I had never witnessed a great battle on shore before, and it seemed to me that a million of men could not have made more noise. The prisoners sent in to the Bluff were Germans. I think we captured the whole of Blenker's brigade. It was hard to find a man in it who could speak English.[5]

The James river squadron was now re-organized. Flag Officer John K. Mitchell was placed in command of it. Captain R. B. Pegram was placed in command of the *Virginia*; Captain T. M.

[3]Admiral Lee's report to General Butler is dated 13 May 1864 and printed in *O.R.N.*, I, 10:51–52.

[4]Howlett's was a local farm. Beauregard's entrenchments came to be called the Howlett Line.

[5]Parker's reference is to the division of Brigadier General Louis Blenker, whose command was largely German-speaking.

Rootes of the *Fredericksburg*; and I was given the command of the *Richmond*. The *Patrick Henry* was left in charge of the executive officer, as the secretary intended that I should resume the command of her at the close of the summer's campaign. Captain Rootes was an old shipmate of mine; he was the executive officer of the *Yorktown* when she was wrecked September 5, 1850. Captain Pegram who was assigned to the *Virginia* was a gallant officer. He distinguished himself in China in 1855 in an attack on Chinese pirates, in conjunction with a British force under Captain Fellowes R. N. Lieutenant Pegram, with two boats and 120 men, and Captain Fellowes, with three boats and 60 men, attacked a large number of junks carrying, it was supposed, 100 guns and over a thousand men. They captured or destroyed most of them. For this service Captain Fellowes was promptly promoted by his government. Our Secretary of the Navy rewarded Pegram by writing him that the correspondence between Admiral Sterling, R. N., and himself in reference to the affair, "should be put on file." The State of Virginia, with a better appreciation of his conduct, presented him with a sword. Pegram, with a party under his command saved all the powder in the Norfolk magazine for the confederacy. He afterwards made a run to England and back in the Confederate cruiser *Nashville*. In the British Channel he burned the American ship *Harvey Birch*.[6]

All of our vessels on the James river, iron-clads and gunboats, had torpedoes attached to their bows this summer. We used occasionally to have exercises under steam, somewhat after the style of the "Georgia Theatricals," to show how we could have "fout!" The first time we tried it two of the gunboats collided and punched holes in each other; fortunately, the torpedoes were not loaded. It must be remembered that the river was very narrow, and this calls to mind what I have previously said concerning the monitor class of vessels. Their not having to manœuvre gives them

[6]Parker's chronology is flawed. Pegram, in command of the *Nashville*, captured and burned the Union clipper ship *Harvey Birch* on 19 November 1861.

great advantage in narrow channels. The monitor, in fact, is a movable fort, and is specially valuable for harbor defence.[7]

It was now decided to remove the obstructions sufficiently to permit the passage of our vessels; and at the end of May the entire squadron went through and anchored off Chapin's Bluff. Our vessels should have been sent below some time before this. The enemy were dragging the river above Trent's reach for torpedoes with their tugs and small boats; and our gunboats should have been on hand to prevent it. They all had long-range guns, and could have rendered good service in this way. But the fact is, the authorities were very reluctant to remove the obstructions.

We were very much surprised to find on the 15th of June that the enemy himself had obstructed the river at Trent's reach, abreast of General Butler's right flank. There were several monitors anchored in the reach at the time. It reminded me of a circumstance I had read of in the war of 1812: After the capture of Washington by the British under General Ross, our forces retreated across the great bridge into Virginia; and we broke down our end of the bridge so that the British should not cross in pursuit; and they broke down their end so that the Americans should not return to attack them. The Federal naval officers were mortified at this act, as they thought it had the appearance of their not being willing to meet our iron-clads. I believe General Grant himself insisted upon its being done, as he felt the necessity of absolute security to his base of supplies at City Point.

There was much "fencing" between Admiral Lee and General Butler as to which should bear the responsibility of closing the river. The correspondence between these two officers on this point is very curious reading. Admiral Lee, in a letter to the Secretary of the Navy, June 7, 1864, says: "The navy is not accustomed to putting down obstructions before it, and the act might be con-

[7]During the 1870s and 80s when Parker wrote these "recollections," the U.S. Navy depended heavily on monitors, many of them Civil War relics, for coastal defense. Within a very few years, a new class of ocean-going warships was begun, sparking the American naval renaissance of the 1890s.

strued as implying an admission of superiority of resources on the part of the enemy. The object of the operation would be to make the river more secure against the attempts of the enemy upon our vessels by fire and explosive rafts, followed by torpedoes and iron-clad vessels and boats. Of course, myself and officers desire the opportunity of encountering the enemy, and feel reluctant to discourage his approach. But the point of embarrassment with me is the consequences that would follow a failure of the campaign, should the novel plans of the enemy succeed in crippling the monitor force."[8]

All of which reads as though it were a case of:

He can and he can't, he will and he won't;
He'll be d——d if he does, and he'll be d——d if he don't.

These obstructions in Trent's reach remained until the end of the war, and the monitors never went above them until that time.

---

[8]Admiral Lee to Welles, 7 June 1864. *O.R.N.*, I, 10:129.

CHAPTER XXX

Curious target practice—attack on the monitors in Trent's reach, June 21, 1864—the Confederate iron-clad *Albemarle* and her engagements—Captain James B. Cooke—Lieutenant W. B. Cushing—the *Alabama* and the *Kearsarge*—the *Florida* and the *Wachusett*—attempt to get our iron-clads to City Point—its failure—blowing up of the gunboat *Drury*—General Joseph E. Johnston and President Davis—Vice President Stephens—the Confederate government—state of affairs in Richmond and on James River in March, 1865

About this time I accompanied Commodore Mitchell several times to General Beauregard's headquarters. The commodore was in constant communication with the general; but I am unable to say what their plans were. On the 19th of June our squadron got underweigh from the anchorage at Chapin's Bluff and proceeded down the river. At 2 P. M. we anchored off upper Howlets, which I suppose is in an air line two miles from lower Howlets; but by the river much farther. A reference to the map will show that the James river pursues a very circuituous course between City Point and Richmond. It is indicated by the names, such as Curl's Neck, Turkey Bend, Dutch Gap, &c. In some cases a distance by land of a mile requires eight or ten to accomplish by water. From our anchorage at upper Howlets nothing could be seen of the monitors in Trent's reach—in fact we were anchored under a bluff on the right bank of the river. General Butler had erected a tower of wood at Trent's reach perhaps 120 feet high, as a post of observation. It gave him a very good one. Our artillery officers were prevented from trying to destroy it by the scarcity of ammunition. We could see the top of this tower from our anchorage, and of course the masts of our gunboats were visible from it, but not the hulls. We had been at anchor an hour or two not expecting a movement of any kind—indeed I was sitting in an arm-chair on the shield of the *Richmond* reading—when a shell was fired from one of the monitors in our direction. It exploded just at the river bank and scattered the pieces about the forward deck of the *Virginia*, wounding three men. Whilst we were wondering at this, another shell came and exploded just after it had passed over us, and again another. As we could not return the fire, and there was no necessity to remain and be made a target of, we got underweigh and went back to Chapin's Bluff. As the guns had to be pointed by directions from those in the tower I have mentioned, I thought this the most remarkable shooting I had ever seen or heard of; but happening to mention this circumstance after the war to a naval officer present at the time on board one of the monitors he informed me that they were not shooting at us at all. He said that some officials had come from Washington on a visit, and they wishing to see a large gun fired, the monitors had obliged them. In those days they were not particular as to where they fired, and the result was as I have mentioned. A curious incident certainly, but the facts were precisely as I have stated them.

The authorities in Richmond now became very anxious that the navy should make some demonstration on the river in order to relieve the great pressure on the army. Commodore Mitchell held a council of war; and it was decided to attack the monitors lying in Trent's reach, at long range, in connection with the heavy guns we had by this time mounted at Howlets. Our vessels could not go fairly up to the obstructions and face the monitors, for we knew that the *Richmond* and *Fredericksburg* could not stand the 15-inch shot. We thought then that the *Virginia* could, but were afterward undeceived.

On the 21st of June the vessels got underweigh, and stood down. The *Fredericksburg* was to take a station in a bend in the river, about two miles (in an air line) from the monitors, and the *Virginia* and *Richmond*, with the gunboats, were to anchor on the north side of Dutch gap, about a mile and a half above them. In getting underweigh my vessel, the *Richmond*, parted a wheel-rope and it got wound up round the shaft and disabled her. We got a gunboat to tow us down, but did not get to the *Virginia* until the afternoon. We only fired a few shots. The whole affair, however, was a *fiasco*. We could not see the monitors, and they could not see us. They were not hit once during the day by us, and the reports speak of the firing of our vessels as extremely wild. How could it be otherwise under the circumstances? The battery at Howlet's struck the monitors but once. The fact is we were wrong in yielding to the clamor of the army to "do something." We knew that we could do nothing with the monitors at long range, even if we could see to hit them; we knew equally well that we could not stand the effect of their guns at close quarters. We might have gotten our gunboats through the obstructions, and made a dash at them with torpedoes; but it must be remembered that the enemy had a battery on shore to cover the obstructions. Our army anticipated a great naval engagement that day, and we were expected to accomplish wonders. The soldiers were all on the lookout; they looked to see us run over the obstructions like smoke, and destroy the monitors in no time. The result being so much of a disappointment to them, we were much ridiculed. The whole affair was a mortification to us of the navy. From this time until the close of the summer campaign we remained below Chapin's Bluff, shelling the batteries put up by the enemy on the left bank of the river occasionally, and assisting the army so far as we could. The enemy made no advance on the right bank of the river, but advanced on the north side. On the

19th of September, 1864, the Federals captured Fort Harrison, near Chapin's Bluff.

We were on pretty short rations in the squadron this summer—the allowance was half-a-pound of salt pork and three biscuits per man a day. A permanent bridge was built across the James river about two miles below the city, and just above Drury's bluff was a pontoon bridge. General Lee had occasion to cross his men from one side to the other frequently during the fall and winter—so I very often saw portions of his army. I well remember the appearance of the poor fellows, half-starved and badly clothed as they were. They were full of fight, though, and showed no signs of giving up. General Grant had crossed to the south side of the James river on the 14th of June, after his bloody repulse at Cold Harbor, June 1st, and had settled down to the siege of Petersburg. All eyes were consequently turned in that direction.

In the squadron we were gladdened by the success of our iron-clad ram *Albemarle*, which vessel, under Captain James B. Cooke, had (after overcoming innumerable difficulties) succeeded in descending the Roanoke river, April 19th, and dispersing the Federal squadron off Plymouth, N. C. She sunk the steamer *Southfield*, and drove the other vessels off; and her presence led to the recapture of Plymouth by the Confederates.

On the 5th of May the *Albemarle* started from Plymouth with the small steamer *Bombshell* in company, on what was called a secret expedition. I think it probable the intention was to destroy the wooden men-of-war in the sounds, and then tow troops in barges to Hatteras and retake it. If this could have been done the *Albemarle* would have had it all her own way, and Roanoke island, Newbern and other places would again have fallen into the hands of the Confederates. Shortly after leaving Plymouth the *Albemarle* fell in with the Federal squadron, consisting of the steamers *Mattabesett*, *Sassacus*, *Wyalusing*, *Whitehead*, *Miami*, *Ceres*, *Commodore Hull* and *Seymour*—all under the command of Captain Melancton Smith, and after a desperate combat was forced to return to Plymouth. Here Captain Cook had to leave her, as his health was much broken by his hard work and previous wounds.

The *Albemarle* was sunk by a torpedo-boat under Lieutenant W. B. Cushing, U. S. N., on the night of the 27th of October, 1864—one of the most dashing acts on the part of Lieutenant Cushing ever recorded in the history of war. Immediately after the *Albemarle* was sunk Plymouth again fell into the hands of the enemy. I had not known Captain Cook in the old navy, but I saw enough of him at Roanoke island and Elizabeth City to know that he was a hard fighter. Few men could have accomplished what he did in taking the *Albemarle* down the river with the carpenters still at work upon her. It was only done by his energy and persistence. He was deservedly promoted for his services.

Young Cushing had been a pupil of mine at the Naval Academy in 1861. He was rather a delicate-looking youth; fair, with regular, clear-cut features, and a clear, greyish-blue eye. He stood low in his classes. He was first brought to my notice during the war by my happening to get hold of his report of the loss of the U. S. steamer *Ellis*, under his command, at New River inlet, Nov. 24, 1862. I was impressed with this part of his official report (the italics are mine): "and the only alternatives left were a surrender or a pull of one and a half miles under their fire in my small boat. The first of these was not, *of course*, to be thought of." Knowing him to be at that time but 19 years old, I comprehended his heroic qualities and was not at all surprised to hear more of him. Immediately after the war I went to San Francisco, and my first visitor was Cushing. He was the hero of the hour, and the citizens made much of him. Under the circumstances I thought he conducted himself with much modesty. He died in 1874.

But if we were gladdened by the success of the *Albemarle* we were depressed by the news of the capture of the *Alabama* by the *Kearsarge* June 19, 1864. This action has been described by the two commanders, and by English and French spectators, so that we now know all about it; but the Hon. Secretary of the Navy in his report for 1864 says in relation to Captain Semmes and his surrender: "when beaten and compelled to surrender he threw overboard the sword that was no longer his own." "Having surrendered, he cannot relieve himself of his obligations as a prisoner of war until he shall be regularly exchanged."[1] As the captain of the frigate *Congress* acted precisely in the same manner, and as he served without being regularly exchanged one might consider this a little strained. But the Hon. Secretary was a tremendous fellow with his pen, as we shall see in his account of the capture of the *Florida*:

> He could distinguish and divide
> A hair 'twixt south and south-west side.[2]

Captain Semmes in his report of the combat finds fault with Captain Winslow of the *Kearsarge* for "faking" his chain cables up and down his ship's sides so as to protect the machinery and boilers. I can see no reason in his complaint. He might as well have objected to his slinging his yards in chains, or making any other preparation for battle. We are told that at the battle of Fontenoy there was some altercation between the commanders of the English and French "guards" as to which should take the liberty of "firing first;" *mais nous avons changé tout cela!*[3] Captain Winslow was fortunate in having for his executive officer Lieutenant Commander James S. Thornton; a fighting man every inch of him. I could never understand why he was not made a commander for his great services on this occasion.

Not very long after the loss of the *Alabama* we heard of the capture of the Confederate man-of-war *Florida* by the U. S. steamer *Wachusett*, October 7, 1864. The circumstances as is well known were these: The *Florida*, Captain Charles M. Morris,

[1]*Report of the Secretary of the Navy* (1864). The passage quoted by Parker is on p. xxi.

[2]Lines from "Hubridas" by Samuel Butler (1793), part I, canto I, lines 67–68.

[3]At the Battle of Fontenoy on 11 May 1745, during the War of Austrian Succession, a French army under Marshal Maurice de Saxe defeated a British-Hanoverian army under the Duke of Cumberland in an engagement often characterized as the archetype of formal land battles. As a chivalrous gesture, each commander offered the other the opportunity to fire first. The French is: but we have changed all that.

entered the port of Bahia, Brazil, and found there the *Wachusett*, Captain Napoleon B. Collins. Being in a neutral port Captain Morris took no more precautions against an attack than he would have done if commanding a vessel in time of peace. He gave his men liberty, a watch at a time, and kept on watch only the usual harbor sentinels. On the night of October 7, he himself with many of his officers and half his crew being on shore, and the crew on board being in the usual condition of men who have just returned from liberty, his vessel was unexpectedly attacked by the *Wachusett*, and after a slight resistance captured. The *Florida* was taken to Hampton Roads, and upon a demand being made for her delivery by the Brazilian Government, she was designedly run into by a vessel appointed for the purpose and sunk. I have heard an account of this whole affair from Captain Morris, his executive officer Porter (who was on board at the time she was captured), and from an officer who was on board the *Wachusett*. I have reason to believe that Captain Collins' action, and the subsequent course of the U. S. authorities, were not generally approved of by the officers of the U. S. Navy. It is understood that Captain Collins' course was prompted by the American Consul at Bahia. He probably lived to regret it.[4]

The following is the account given of this affair by the Hon. Secretary of the U.S. Navy, in his report for 1864. As it is not to be found in Disraeli's *Curiosities of Literature*, I must give it a place here: "Subsequently, entering the Bay of San Salvador, she (the *Florida*) encountered the steamer *Wachusett*, commanded by Commander Collins, to whom she surrendered, and by whom she was brought in a leaky and dilapidated condition to Hampton Roads. Here, while at anchor, an army transport came in collision with

---

[4]Thomas Wilson, the American consul at Bahia, gave his promise to the Brazilian government that no attack on the Confederate visitor would be made in Brazilian waters. Collins attacked anyway and was subsequently found guilty by a court-martial for his act, but Secretary Welles restored him to command. After the war the United States apologized to Brazil, and an American warship fired a 21-gun salute in Bahia harbor.

the shattered vessel, which sunk a few days after near the wreck of the *Cumberland.*[5]

Shade of Sir Percie Shafton![6]

But the spot for sinking her was ill-chosen. Could the noble men who lay coffined in that gallant craft (the *Cumberland*) have risen from the dead and spoken they would have protested against the act as a shameful violation of the laws of honorable warfare.

In the fall of 1864 I was ordered back to the *Patrick Henry*, and the exercises of the school were continued during all the exciting scenes of the winter. Captain James H. Rochelle, an officer of high professional standing, and who had served with distinction during the entire war, joined us as Commandant of Midshipmen and executive officer.

I think it was on the night of the 23d of January, 1865, that an attempt was made to get the iron-clads down the river, the object being to destroy General Grant's transports and stores at City Point. Had this succeeded it would have made a very great difference in the result of the next campaign. City Point was the base of General Grant's supplies, and if they had been destroyed, and we had resumed the control of the river, it is difficult to say what would have become of his army. It might have led to his surrender, and in any event would have seriously crippled him.

The affair was wisely planned. There was but one monitor, the *Onondaga*, on the river, and the design was to push boldly through the obstructions at night and strike for City Point. The gunboats were to go down under the lee of the iron-clads, and sink the captured transports at Harrison's bar, below *City Point*, to prevent any more vessels being sent to Grant's assistance. Upon approaching the obstructions the leading vessel, the iron-clad

---

[5]*Report of the Secretary of the Navy* (1864). The passage quoted by Parker is on p. xxii.

[6]Sir Percie Shafton, a character in Walter Scott's *The Monastery*, is a pedantic and ridiculous caricature of an Elizabethan courtier.

Fredericksburg, Captain Frank Sheppard, passed through safely; but the next vessel, the *Virginia*, got aground and barred the way for the others. The monitor, which had been lying in Trent's reach, retired down the river, but the battery at Howlets opened a heavy fire. Finding it impossible to get the *Virginia* off, Commodore Mitchell pulled down to the *Fredericksburg* in an open boat, and finally recalled her, and the attempt was abandoned. The next morning the monitor returned and opened fire on the *Virginia*, still aground. We here saw the effect of the 15-inch shot upon the strongest of our iron-clads. One of them struck the *Virginia*'s shield, bow on, and shattered it very much. We had no vessels in the Confederate Navy that could withstand the 15-inch shot. This was very evident. Fortunately the *Virginia* succeeded in getting off and out of range, otherwise she would have been destroyed. The gunboat *Drury* was also aground. A shot from Howlet's battery passed through her magazine, and she blew up. Providentially the officers and men had been removed to the *Virginia*.

So ended this affair. It was thought by some that if the *Fredericksburg* had been permitted to go alone to City Point she might have accomplished our purpose, as she had a torpedo on her bow for the single monitor. Her commander [Thomas R. Rootes] was a dashing officer and would have accomplished as much as it lay in the power of any one man to do. I must add in justice to the captain of the monitor *Onondaga* [William A. Parker, no relation to W.H.P.] that he explained that he retired down the river so as to have more room to manœuvre; he said he had no intention of retreating below City Point. Certain it is that, finding he was not pursued, he returned to the seat of action, and opened fire upon the *Virginia*, with the effect I have described. He was, however, relieved of his command and placed on the retired list. General Grant was very much annoyed at his retreating below Trent's reach; and to show the importance the Federal authorities attached to this movement of ours, Admiral D. Farragut was immediately placed in command of the James river squadron, in the absence of Admiral Porter, who was at this time at Wilmington with most of his vessels. Admiral Farragut, however, did not assume it.

After General Joseph E. Johnston had fallen back to Atlanta in the summer of 1864 he was relieved of his command, and General Hood appointed to succeed him. This was a fatal mistake—we all see it now. President Davis has been much blamed for this; but I happen to know that great pressure was brought upon him to relieve General Johnston by the citizens of the south-western states. Many of these gentlemen were very quiet about it afterwards and are now; but when they found General Johnston continually falling back, and even the President could get no satisfactory information from him as to how far he intended to retreat (for Johnston is not the most communicative of men) a clamor was raised to relieve him. General Hood had been a successful colonel, brigadier general, major general and lietenant general, so that it was reasonable to suppose he would do well in command of an army. Suppose he had captured Nashville as he could have done had he advanced upon it immediately after the battle of Franklin, how then. I yield to no man in my admiration for General Johnston. I know him to be a soldier born, and his friendship I value. We know now that his campaign of 1864 was a model of tactics and strategy—Moreau's retreat through the black forest did not equal it—but the general belief that President Davis relieved him of his command entirely of his own motion I know to be a misapprehension, and the Southern papers of that day prove it.[7]

February 3d, 1865, Vice President Stephens accompanied by two commissioners went to Hampton Roads and met President Lincoln and Secretary of State Seward in the hope of arranging terms on which to make peace. Here again President Davis has been most unjustly criticised since the war. It has been said that we could have made better terms than we finally got. I suppose we could; but what I mean to say is that the majority of the army and navy would not have been satisfied with any terms that Mr.

[7]General Jean Moreau (1763–1813), commander of the French Army of the Rhine and Moselle, conducted a skillful retreat through the Black Forest in 1795 and even brought back 5,000 Austrian prisoners of war despite being hard pressed by a numerically superior Austrian army.

368 RECOLLECTIONS OF A NAVAL OFFICER

Lincoln was prepared to offer us at that time. Nothing would have convinced them that the cause was hopeless but exactly what happened. I speak for myself, and it is reasonable to suppose that thousands felt as I did, and say that my wish was to fight it out to the bitter end. It has been also said that President Davis and the Confederate government were harsh and intolerant. There was never a greater mistake. Treason stalked triumphant o'er the land, and many a man was spared who should have had his neck streched. While every man had a right to his opinion before the war, yet after war was actually declared every man should have been made to stand by the Confederacy or leave the country. Perhaps if we had had something like Mr. Seward's "little bell" it would have been all the better for us.[8] The Confederacy had "set its life upon a cast." I think our statesmen failed to fully appreciate this fact. War is an unequal thing at best; but why some men should have been expected to give up everything for the "cause," and others permitted to reap money by the war, is something I fail to understand. My observation during the war was that the generals in the field did not have that strong support from the government which was so necessary to them. It is a singular fact that while the war produced many generals it produced absolutely no orators or statesmen.

Charleston was evacuated February 18, and Wilmington was captured February 22, 1865. The naval officers and sailors arriving in Richmond from these and other places were organized as a naval brigade under Commodore Tucker, and sent to man the various batteries below and in the neighborhood of Drury's Bluff. Admiral Raphael Semmes, who had returned from Europe, landed in Texas and made his way to Richmond, was put in command of the James river squadron February 18, 1865.

During the winter we were visited in the squadron by the Secretary of the Navy and the naval committees of the two Houses

[8]Secretary of State William H. Seward supervised the arrest and detention of disloyal persons in the North. More than once he demonstrated his willingness to ignore constitutional guarantees when he believed the public safety was at stake.

several times. I remember that on the occasion of one of these visits the chairman of the Naval Committee in the House fell to me to escort. While ascending the hill at Drury's Bluff I expatiated upon the value of the ram and torpedo as defensive weapons. I said that even if the Confederate Navy had done nothing else but to develop these two great weapons, it would have immortalized itself, etc., etc. At the lunch which Mr. Mallory gave on the bluff that day, this gentleman upon being called for a speech, "stole my thunder;" but as I am not much given to public speaking myself perhaps it did not very much matter.

Affairs were looking very badly for us about this time—the winter of 1865. Men were deserting in large numbers from General Lee's army and from the James river squadron. The cause of the large desertion in the army was the march of General Sherman through Georgia and South Carolina. The letters received by the soldiers from their wives and families describing their sufferings, maddened these poor fellows, and they could not resist their appeals to return for their protection. In the squadron, where very few of the men were "to the manner born," the scanty ration was the principal cause of their leaving. A man shut up in an iron-clad with nothing to do after the morning drill, broods over his hunger—it is not like being on shore, where a man can move about and forage a little. Still the sailors, with all their sufferings, were better off than General Lee's soldiers, inasmuch as they were well-clothed and had always a dry hammock at night.

One of my officers, who was remarkably neat in his dress, told me that coming on from Charleston he had a seat alongside a soldier who was returning to his regiment in the field. The soldier was very badly clad and looked haggard and careworn. Eyeing my friend critically and earnestly, he asked him a number of questions: 'If he was a general?" (we wore silver stars on our straps, as the brigadier-generals did); "if he was returning to his regiment;" 'where it was stationed," etc., etc. My friend finally told him that 'he belonged to the navy." After some reflection, the soldier said confidentially: "I tell you what it is, if things don't soon look better, I'll be dogged if I don't try to navy it a little too."

We knew in February, if not before, that everything depended upon General Lee's being able to hold his lines about Petersburg. I was in constant and confidential communication with the Secretary of the Navy, and knew, how very anxious our authorities were. It was strange how Mr. Mallory clung to the idea of keeping up the Naval School, even if Richmond had to be abandoned. By his direction I sent Lieutenant Graves into North Carolina and Georgia to select buildings, with a view to our leaving Richmond and establishing ourselves inland. Graves made two or more trips for this purpose, but we could not settle upon any locality. What with Sherman and Wilson to the south, and Stoneman to the west—to say nothing of other commands—it was difficult to hit upon a quiet spot. What we wanted was "a pleasant cot, in a tranquil spot, with a distant view of the changing sea;" but it was hard to find. I did not take much interest in this search myself, having long before considered our success hopeless; and I felt sure that the loss of Richmond involved the fall of the Confederacy.

After the capture of Fort Harrison by the Federal troops, the *Patrick Henry* was ordered up to protect the bridge above Wilton. The enemy were making demonstrations on the north side of the river the entire winter, and not a day passed that we did not hear the booming of great guns and the rattling of musketry; yet the midshipmen pursued their daily routine. We had at this time sixty midshipmen, and these with their officers constituted a force of about seventy men, armed with rifles and extremely well disciplined and drilled. We had among them representatives of the best families of the South. I need not say that, under the circumstances, the care of these young gentlemen gave me many anxious moments.

Towards the end of March the *Patrick Henry* was moved up the river near Rocketts, and I was directed to prepare her for sinking in the obstructions. I commenced getting her ready, and rented a warehouse on shore to which to remove the midshipmen and stores. Many families were now leaving Richmond, among them the President's and Mr. Mallory's. The squadron under Admiral

Semmes was at anchor between Chapin and Drury's bluff, and the naval brigade under Commodore Tucker was distributed among the batteries near by, as I have before said. Such was the position of affairs on the river on the evening of April 1st, 1865.

CHAPTER XXXI

The evacuation of Richmond—ordered to take charge of the Confederate treasure—the corps of midshipmen—the night of April 2d—scenes at the depot—departure of the president and cabinet—arrival at Danville—go on to Charlotte, N.C.—General Stoneman at Salisbury—resolve to carry the treasure farther south—Mrs. President Davis and family—leave Charlotte—pass through Chester, Newberry, Abbeville and Washington—arrival at Augusta, Georgia—the armistice between Generals Johnston and Sherman—determine to retrace my steps—leave Augusta for Washington, Georgia

On the afternoon of Saturday, April 1st, 1865, I went up to Richmond—not having left the ship for some little time before—intending to pass the night there. Wishing to learn the latest news I drove direct to Mr. Mallory's house. It was then near sunset. I found Mr. Mallory walking to and fro on the pavement in front of his house, with a revolver in his hand. I presumed he had been perhaps shooting at a mark, though I did not ask him. In reply to my question Mr. Mallory informed me that the news that day from General Lee was good, and that affairs about Petersburg looked promising. I told him I had proposed spending the night in the city, if nothing was likely to happen in the river requiring my presence on board the *Patrick Henry*. He said he knew of nothing to prevent, and after some further conversation I left him. I passed the night in the city. If I recollect aright our Home Guards were out on the Brooke turnpike to repel a threatened raid in that direction—but the night passed quietly.

The next morning I walked down to Rocketts [Landing], and went on board my ship. We had the customary Sunday muster and inspection, and as we piped down I observed a company of Home Guards going out in the direction of Wilton, and I wondered at it. Shortly after I received a dispatch from the Secretary of the Navy which read as follows: "Have the corps of midshipmen, with the proper officers, at the Danville depot to-day at 6 P. M., the commanding officer to report to the Quartermaster General of the Army."[1]

Sending for Captain Rochelle I directed him to carry out the order and to have three days provisions cooked to carry. He asked me if I would go myself. I told him no; that he would go in command and I would remain and take care of the ship; that he would probably be back in a few days. While preparations were being made, it struck me that it would be as well to go to the Navy Department myself and obtain more definite information. I landed, and as I passed Rocketts (the landing-place of our river steamboats) I met a large number of prisoners on their way to the boats to be sent down to be exchanged. It passed through my mind at the instant that in the case of the evacuation of Richmond this was just what would be previously done, and it had not been the custom to send them off in the middle of the day—they were always sent off at daylight. However I pursued my way up Main street and in a few moments met a clerk who inquired of me how he could get down to Drury's Bluff. I told him, and observing him to be excited inquired if there were any news. "Why don't you

[1] Not found.

know," said he with his eyes starting out of his head, *"Richmond is to be evacuated this evening!"* I at once returned to the *Patrick Henry* and gave orders for all hands to be at the Danville depot at 6 o'clock with the exception of Lieutenant Billups and ten men whom I left to burn the ship. I then went to the Navy Department and saw Mr. Mallory. He told me the news. The city was to be evacuated that evening, and my command was to take charge of the Confederate treasure and convey it to Danville. Everything was being packed up for carrying off about the departments, though a good many things had been sent away in March in anticipation of this event. In the city those who had anything to do were at work at it, and yet in the midst of all the excitement there was a peculiar quiet— a solemnity—I have never ceased to remember; perhaps the pale, sad faces of the ladies aided to bring it about—they knew it was impossible for them to leave, and they prepared to share the fate of their beloved city with the same heroism they had exhibited during the past four years. The provost marshal had given orders to his men to seize and destroy all the liquor they could find in the stores, and they did so—a wise precaution. I went to the depot at 6 o'clock and found the treasure packed in the cars, and the midshipmen under Captain Rochelle in charge of it. So far as I know there was about half a million of dollars in gold, silver and bullion; at least that is what the senior teller told me, as well as I recollect. I saw the boxes containing it many times in the weary thirty days I had it under my protection, but I never saw the coin. The teller and his assistant clerks had charge of the money, and the corps of midshipmen guarded and eventually saved it. In addition to the Confederate money, there was also some belonging to the Richmond banks. It was in charge of their officers, and travelled with us for safety. I had nothing to do with it; but, of course, gave it our protection.

At the depot, the scene I find hard to describe. The President's train was to precede mine, which was expected to be the last out of the city; both trains were packed—not only inside, but on top, on the platforms, on the engine,—*everywhere*, in fact, where standing-room could be found; and those who could not get that "hung on by their eyelids." I placed sentinels at the doors of the depot finally, and would not let another soul enter.

And here I must pay a tribute to the midshipmen who stood by me for so many anxious days; their training and discipline showed itself conspicuously during that time—the best sentinels in the world—cool and decided in their replies, prompt in action, and brave in danger,—their conduct always merited my approbation and excited my admiration. During the march across South Carolina, foot-sore and ragged as they had become by that time, no murmur escaped them, and they never faltered. On the 2d day of May they were disbanded in Abbeville, South Carolina, far from their homes. They were staunch to the last, and verified the adage that "blood will tell." Their officers I cannot say too much for. Our professors, as I have before said, had all seen service in the army, and they resumed their campaigning with alacrity. From the time we left Richmond until we disbanded, they set the example to the corps to obey orders, with the watchword: "guard the treasure." I am sure that Mr. Davis, and Mr. Mallory if he were alive, would testify to the fact that when they saw the corps in Abbeville, wayworn and weary after its long march, it presented the same undaunted front as when it left Richmond, and that it handed over the treasure, which had been confided to it thirty days before, intact; and that, in my opinion, is what no other organization at that time could have done.

While waiting in the depot I had an opportunity of seeing the President and his Cabinet as they went to the cars. Mr. Davis preserved his usual calm and dignified manner, and General Breckenridge (the Secretary of War), who had determined to go out on horseback, was as cool and gallant as ever—but the others, I thought, had the air (as the French say) of wishing to be off. General Breckenridge stayed with me some time after the President's train had gone, and I had occasion to admire his bearing under the circumstances. The President's train got off about 8 p. m.; but there was much delay with mine. Hour after hour passed and we did not move.

The scenes about the depot were a harbinger of what was to

come that night. The whiskey, which had been "started" by the Provost guard, was running in the gutters, and men were getting drunk upon it. As is the case under such circumstances (I noticed it, too, at the evacuation of Norfolk), large numbers of ruffians suddenly sprung into existence—I suppose thieves, deserters, etc., who had been in hiding. These were the men who were now breaking into stores and searching for liquor. To add to the horror of the moment (I say horror, for we all had friends who had to be left behind), we now heard the explosions of the vessels and magazines, and this, with the screams and yells of the drunken demons in the streets, and the fires which were now breaking out in every direction, made it seem as though hell itself had broken loose. Towards midnight, hearing the rumbling of artillery crossing the bridge below us, I sent an officer to see what it was. He returned with the information that it was *Lightfoot's* battery and the rear guard of the army. I thought the name suggestive. Shortly after, to our relief, our train started and crossed the bridges; and after a short delay in Manchester we steamed away at the rate of some ten miles an hour.

I must pause here to say that the Federal troops under General Ord, upon their entrance into the city about daylight next morning, soon put an end to all disorder, and conducted themselves with much moderation and propriety towards the citizens of Richmond.

We went along at a slow rate of speed, stopping at Amelia Court House and other places, and arrived at Danville on the afternoon of April 3d. We found the Cabinet here; and President Davis issued a short and stirring proclamation. During the night, Admiral Semmes arrived in a train with the officers and men of the James river squadron. It seems he had but scanty notice of the evacuation; but he blew up the vessels, seized upon a train, and made his way to Danville under great difficulties. He was commissioned a Brigadier-General, and his force organized as a brigade. He was put in command of some batteries around Danville.

The sailors in the batteries below Drury's Bluff, under Commodore Tucker, had also very scanty notice of the evacuation, if any; but they got away together, and formed part of the rear guard of the army in General Custis Lee's division. They were in the battle of Sailor's creek [on 6 April 1865] and fought desperately. After the brigades on either side of them had surrendered, Tucker still continued to fight. The general in command could get no word to him to surrender; and the Federals, not understanding why that particular body of men held out were massing a large number of guns upon it, when a staff officer finally made his way to Tucker with the order to give up. The commodore told me afterwards he had never been in a land battle before, and he had supposed that "everything was going on well." The Federal troops cheered the sailors after their surrender. The creek was not named for the sailors engaged in this fight, as some have supposed. It bore the name Sailor before—rather a singular coincidence; though, as Mark Twain says, every man must take this "at his own risk."

Lieutenant Billups faithfully carried out my orders, and burned the *Patrick Henry*. He then attempted to join me, but by the time he got to Charlotte, N. C., I was down in Georgia, and the war was over. I did not meet him until 1878. Happening to be in Barnum's hotel, in Baltimore, a gentleman accosted me. Seeing that I failed to recognize him, he exclaimed: "I am Lieutenant Billups of the rear guard." Said I: "report," and he did so accordingly. I am glad to say he is doing well in the merchant marine, and is recognised as a trustworthy officer and most estimable man.

We did not unpack the treasure from the cars at Danville, except that taken for the use of the Government at the time. How much was taken, or for whom it was taken, I never knew—it was not my business to inquire. The midshipmen bivouacked near the railroad station. We were very anxious to hear from General Lee's army as may well be imagined, and for some days had fears for General Breckenridge's safety, but he finally rode in with his staff. We remained in Danville several days, and I was then ordered to convey the treasure to Charlotte, N. C., to deposit it in the mint there, and then await further orders. I here requested Mr. Mallory to see the secretary of the treasury (Mr. Trenholm) in reference to the Confederate treasurer and assistant treasurer accompanying the treasure as its appointed custodians. It was their duty to be with it at this time. I did not think it right that it should be left with a Teller as the senior civil officer. This was a source of annoyance to me from that time forward; not that I had anything against the Teller, (I did not know him) but I thought it was a time when every man should be made to do his duty. It was not a time to be falling sick by the wayside, as some high officials were beginning to do. I thought so then, and am of the same opinion now.

We left Danville about the 6th of April and went to Greensboro where we remained for a day, and then continued on to Charlotte. As we approached Salisbury we saw cavalry descending the hills in the vicinity and we stopped to reconnoitre—for the times were troublous; but it turned out to be some of our men and we passed on. We reached Charlotte about the 8th, and I deposited the money in the mint as directed, and left it in the custody of its proper officers. I thought I was rid of it forever. We remained here several days, and upon going to the telegraph office at the end of that time to telegraph the Secretary of the Navy I found the wires had been cut by General Stoneman who was then in possession of Salisbury, with his command. It was supposed he would obtain information there concerning the treasure, and that he would soon make his appearance in Charlotte where there were no troops to oppose him. I was the senior naval officer present on duty in Charlotte, and had to decide as to the necessary steps to preserve the treasure. After consultation with the treasury officers I determined to remove it farther south—probably to Macon, Georgia. Mrs. President Davis and family were in town, and I called to offer her the protection of my command. After some demur she decided to accompany us. I rather pressed the point as I feared she would be captured, and I could not bear the idea of that. We found in the naval storehouse here large quantities of sugar, coffee, bacon and flour, and I took enough to support my command several months. It was a most fortunate proceeding on my part as the result will show. The storekeeper rather objected to it; he wanted requisitions approved by the Secretary of the Navy, &c.; but I told him it was no time for red tape, and that moreover I had the force and intended to have it—"Tom Collins whether or no." He gracefully acquiesced and rendered us all the assistance in his power in selecting the best of the stores. A company of uniformed men from the navy yard, under Captain Tabb, volunteered to accompany us. These men were principally from Portsmouth, Va., and they remained with me to the end. A better set of men I never served with. During the entire march I always found them cheerful and ready for any duty. They left me finally at Abbeville, S. C., after all was over, and I have a distinct recollection of their marching off in gallant array, with their field music playing Dixie, on their return to Charlotte. Just before they started a keg of cents was presented to them to be divided out—they indignantly refused to accept it—who authorized this magnificent donation I do not know.

We left Charlotte in the cars on or about the 11th of April, and arrived at Chester, S. C., the next morning. We here packed the money and papers in wagons and formed a train, having to cross the country to Newberry, S. C. We were not ready to start till late in the afternoon; but I thought it better to get out of town and organize, and accordingly marched out about five miles, and went into camp near a "meeting-house," which afforded shelter for the ladies accompanying the party. I here published orders regulating our march, declared martial law, and made every man carry a musket. I had about 150 fighting men under my command, and expected, if attacked, that we could give a good account of ourselves.

Mrs. Davis came out in an ambulance and took up quarters in the church with the other ladies. I slept in the pulpit myself, being the head of the party. The next morning early we took up the line of march, with the Charlotte company in advance, and during the rest of the march the midshipmen led the advance one day and the Charlotte company the next. All hands were on foot, myself included, and I gave strict orders that no man should ride, unless sick.

The first night in camp I heard the midshipmen discussing the prospects of a long march, and the probability of "Old Parker's" breaking down; but I had walked too many midwatches to have

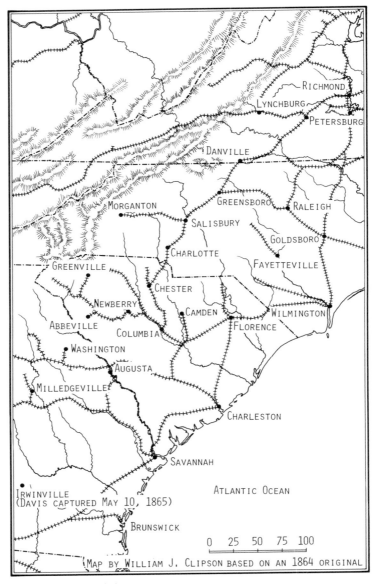

The eastern Confederacy.

any fears of it. I had an idea that naval officers should be good walkers. It was so in my case, at least; for, upon our arrival at Washington, Georgia, I was almost the only officer who had not, at some time during the march, ridden in an ambulance or wagon. I did not have a blister on my feet during the whole time, and found I could make my three miles an hour with great regularity and without discomfort. One day we marched 30 miles, between our camp at Means' and Newberry; and, as I had to be sometimes with the rear guard and at others in advance, I did more walking than anyone else.

About sunset of the first day's march we went into camp, and I was arranging a place for the ladies to pass the night, when a gentleman came from a neighboring house; I found it was Mr. Edward C. Means, who had been a midshipman with me in the U. S. S. *Yorktown*, and who was then a Lieutenant in the Confederate Navy. He had lately had command of a gunboat on the James river. Means took all the ladies to his house and made them comfortable for the night. His plantation had fortunately escaped the ravages of General Sherman's army. Sherman's left wing had just cleared it; but he told me he had only to go a few miles to see the ruins of many houses burned by Sherman's troops, and most of them had been owned by his relatives. He was a descendant of Governor Means. He showed me that night a trap-door under his dining-room table, where a pit had been dug in which to conceal the family silver, etc.

We started very early the next morning, and about noon crossed the Broad river on a pontoon bridge. I was surprised to see so beautiful a sheet of water. It reminded me of something I had read of General Sumter or Marion in the revolutionary war. That afternoon we arrived at Newberry, after a march of twelve hours' duration. We had marched rapidly, as we supposed General Stoneman to be in pursuit with his cavalry. I left rear guards at every bridge we crossed, to be ready to burn it if necessary to check a pursuit. I am not sure now whether General Stoneman (the present Governor of California) was after us or not; but we thought at the time he would get news of the treasure at Charlotte and follow us.[2]

During the march I never allowed any one to pass us on the road, and yet the coming of the treasure was known at every village we passed through. How this should be was beyond my comprehension. I leave it to metaphysicians to solve, as also the fact that when an army meets with a disaster, mysterious rumors are circulated concerning it before one would suppose sufficient time had elapsed for the news to travel the distance. I had sent a courier on ahead to Newberry asking the quartermaster to have a train of cars ready to take us on to Abbeville, S. C., distant some 45 miles, and upon our arrival we transferred the treasure to the cars and left the same evening at sunset. We arrived at Abbeville at midnight and passed the remainder of the night in the cars. Mrs. Davis and family here left me and went to the house of the Hon. Mr. Burt, a former member of the U. S. Congress. We formed a wagon train again here and set off across the country for Washington, Georgia. The news we got at different places along the route was bad: "unmerciful disaster followed fast and followed faster." We "lightened ship" as we went along—throwing away books, stationery and even, as we heard the worst news, Confederate money. One could have traced us by these marks and formed an idea of the character of the news we were in receipt of. From Abbeville to Washington is about 40 miles, and we made a two days march of it. The first day after leaving Abbeville we crossed the Savannah river on a pontoon about 4 P. M., and went into camp for the night. We arrived at Washington the next day, and here I heard that General Wilson, U. S. A. had captured Macon, and was on his way farther north, so I resolved to halt for a time, to deliberate. We transferred the money to a house and put a strong guard over it. The ladies were accommodated with rooms at the tavern. There were no meals served there; but we had an abundance of provisions. Our coffee and sugar was as good as gold, and by trading it for eggs, butter,

[2]General George Stoneman retired from the army in 1871 and served two terms as governor of California (1883–1887).

poultry and milk we managed to keep up an excellent mess. All the men, teamsters and all, were allowed plenty of bacon, coffee and sugar, and if they were ragged they were at all events "fat and saucy." After a day's deliberation and a consultation with some of the citizens of Washington I resolved to go to Augusta. I knew there was a general in command there, and also a naval officer senior to myself, and I thought I would at least have the benefit of their advice. We left the ladies behind at the tavern in Washington for we expected now a fight at any time. Affairs were looking very threatening. We left Washington on the cars for Augusta on the 18th of April, I think. We were on a branch road, and when we arrived at the junction with the main road across Georgia— running from Augusta westward to Atlanta—we fell in with the train from Atlanta and stopped to allow it to pass.

Captain Rochelle went to inquire for news, and he soon returned with information that General Lee had surrendered on the 9th of April. To show how completely isolated we had been, it never entered my head that the news could be telegraphed *via* Nashville and Atlanta. Our lines I knew were down, and as I was the last to arrive from Danville, I supposed I had the latest news. I thought that some speculator on his way to Augusta was circulating this news for his own purposes, and I directed Captain Rochelle to take a guard and arrest him. Fortunately for him, and for me too, I suppose, the man could not be found. We followed on after the mail train, and I really did not believe the report until it was confirmed to me upon our arrival at Augusta that night.

We did not unpack the money from the cars in Augusta. The midshipmen bivouacked near by. I called upon General Fry who commanded the post, and upon Commodore William Hunter, senior naval officer present. There was a gunboat or two in the river, which had escaped from Savannah. General Fry said he could offer us no hope of protection, that he had but few troops, and that the place must fall when attacked, which would be very soon. However, Generals Johnston and Sherman had just entered upon a convention, and I decided to take advantage of the armistice existing to look about me.

I found in Augusta one of the Confederate Treasury officers. I called upon him and requested him to take charge of the treasure and remain with it. This he seemed disinclined to do, but I insisted that he should do so for the reasons I have before assigned. I finally called upon him in company with General Fry and Commodore Hunter, and finding that they took the same view of the matter that I did, he consented to do so; with the *proviso* that I would continue to guard it. This I readily consented to do. I had no idea of giving up my control of it to any other command, even if there had been one to assume it, which there was not. In a letter to the *Southern Historical Society Papers*, my paymaster, Mr. Wheliss, says that upon the return of the corps to Abbeville and the arrival there of the President: "Captain Parker, feeling the great responsibility of his position and satisfied that his command was wholly inadequate to the protection of the treasure, earnestly requested to be relieved."[3] He is mistaken. He did not understand. I was anxious to be relieved of the *moral* responsibility of being the custodian of the money; but I considered my command the best protectors of it to be found at the South, and I never requested to be relieved, as I shall show. Paymaster Wheliss, (the present General Wheliss of Nashville, and a very gallant officer), of course only meant to describe the matter as he understood it. His account of our march, etc., is very accurate, and his views I most cordially agree with as to the final disposition of the Confederate treasure, so far as I know anything about it.

The simple fact is that I had made up my mind to hand that treasure over to President Davis, if it were in the power of one man to do so. I sought no advice on that point. The money had been confided to my keeping, and I determined to hold it as long as the war lasted. The war was not over, as some in Augusta would have had me to believe. So long as an army remained in the field the war to me existed. I knew that it must be soon over; but what I mean to express is, that until I knew that General Johnston, under whose command I now considered myself, had surrendered, my duty was

---

[3]John F. Wheliss, "The Confederate Treasure," *Southern Historical Society Papers* (1882), pp. 137–41. The quotation appears on p. 140.

plain to me. If any man supposes that his opinion, or advice, had anything to do with governing my action in the case, let him disabuse his mind of it now and forever.

Whilst in Augusta, and afterwards, I was advised by certain persons to divide the money out, as the war was over, and it would otherwise fall into the hands of the Federal troops. I was told that we would be attacked by our own men, and might, at the very end of the war, fall by the hands of our friends. To this I made but one reply: The treasure had been put in my keeping, and I would hold it until I met President Davis; and that, if necessary, the command would be killed in the defence of it. My officers and men stood firmly by me in this, and all advances were met by a quiet reply to this effect.

The armistice continuing, I took up my quarters at the hotel, and there met, for the last time, the gallant veteran Commodore Tattnall. He was not on duty at this time, and during the few days I was in Augusta I was much with him. The Commodore preserved his cheerfulness, and I remember his telling me many incidents connected with his early naval career. One I recall: He said that in 1833 he was in Key West, Florida, and was taken ill with the cholera. His medical attendant was Dr. Bailey Washington, a character in his way. Becoming more and more ill, the doctor finally gave him up, and so informed him. He said: "Now, Tattnall, I have told you all; I can do nothing more for you—if there is anything you would like to eat or drink, take it; it can do you no harm." Tattnall replied: "Well, I believe I will take a mint julep." "You shall have it," said Dr. Bailey; "and I'll take one with you." The *julep* was probably just what was wanted to save Tattnall's life.

While waiting in Augusta I received a telegraphic dispatch from Mr. Mallory, directing me to disband my command,—but, under the circumstances, I declined to do so. At this time we heard of the assassination of President Lincoln; an event which gave much pain to all with whom I conversed, and which cast a gloom over all thinking men. It was universally condemned at the South; but "that goes without saying."

On the 20th General Fry notified me that the armistice would end the next day, and he advised me to "move on." I decided to go back, and try to meet President Davis in his retreat. I knew he would cross the Savannah river at one of two points—between Abbeville and Washington, or lower down. After much reflection, I determined to retrace my steps, in the hope of intercepting him at some point on the former route. Accordingly we left Augusta on the 23rd in the cars for Washington, Georgia, again.

CHAPTER XXXII

Return to Abbeville—an alarm—arrival of President Davis and cabinet—I transfer the treasure to General Basil Duke, and disband my command—interview with President Davis—his departure from Abbeville—General Jos. E. Johnston's surrender—am paroled—leave Abbeville on my return home—bad traveling—a day at Burksville—arrival at Norfolk, Virginia

We formed a wagon train again at Washington, picked up our ladies, and started for Abbeville. On the way we met Mrs. President Davis and family, escorted by Mr. Burton Harrison, the President's private secretary. They could give me no news as to the whereabouts of the President. I have forgotten where they told me they intended to go. They had a comfortable ambulance, and two very fine led horses, which I thought they would very likely lose. In crossing the Savannah river I remember saying to Captain Rochelle that if the money were mine I would throw it overboard rather than be longer burdened with it. I had had it nearly thirty days; the midshipmen were suffering for shoes, hats and clothing, and the care and responsibility weighed upon me.

We arrived at Abbeville about the 28th, and here I stored the treasure in a warehouse on the public square, and placed a guard over it as before. I also kept a strong patrol in the town, which was now full of General Lee's paroled soldiers on their way to their homes. Threats were frequently made by these men to seize the money, but they always received the same reply.

Abbeville was on the direct route south, and all the trans-Mississippi troops passed through it, as well as others. The citizens had known but little of the sufferings of war. They were very kind and hospitable to us. On the night of the 1st of May, I was invited to a May-party, which I attended more to find out what was going on in the town than anything else. While there a paroled officer of General McGowan's brigade approached me and said he had information that the paroled men intended to attack the treasure that night, and he thought it his duty to tell me. I thanked him and went to my quarters, where I issued orders to double the guard and patrol. I had given directions as soon as I arrived in Abbeville that a train and engine should be held ready for me, with steam up, at all hours of the day and night. My intention was, if threatened by the enemy, to run by steam to Newberry, and then take to the dirt road again. Everything seemed to be in a state of quietude, I retired about midnight: leaving directions with the officer-of-the-guard to call me if anything occurred. I had quarters in a private house, and slept on the floor of the parlor where I could be easily aroused.

About 3 o'clock in the morning Lieutenant Peek the officer of the guard tapped at my window. I can hear him now: "Captain," said he in a low voice, "the Yankees are coming." Upon inquiry I learned that a detachment of Federal cavalry had captured two gentlemen at Anderson about thirty miles distant the evening before. One of the gentlemen had escaped and brought the news to Abbeville, and as Mr. Peek told me, "thought the Federals would arrive about daylight." I immediately called all hands and packed the money in the cars, and by daybreak had everybody on the train in readiness to move. I walked the platform in thought—for I had not quite decided to run. About sunrise we saw a company of cavalry winding down the hills in the distance, and I sent out two scouts who shortly returned with the information that it was the advance guard of President Davis' escort. So I had judged rightly in returning to Abbeville. About 10 A. M. President Davis and his Cabinet rode into town and were well received by the population of Abbeville. It was a sad enough sight to me, I know. It reminded me of scenes I had witnessed in Central American revolutions! By order of Secretary Mallory I transferred the treasure to the acting Secretary of the Treasury, and by him was instructed to deliver it to the care of General Basil Duke, which I did at the railroad station. By Mr. Mallory's order I then immediately disbanded my command, and the Charlotte company marched off for home before I left the depot. The midshipmen left in detached parties, and an hour after President Davis' arrival the organization was one of the things of the past. And yet to show how unwilling we were to acknowledge that the Confederacy was broken—how hard we died, in fact—I present here a copy of the letter I furnished every midshipman under my command, when I bid them farewell:

ABBEVILLE, S. C., May 2, 1865.

SIR: You are hereby detached from the naval school, and leave is granted you to visit your home. You will report by letter to the Hon. Secretary of the Navy as soon as practicable. Paymaster Wheliss will issue you ten days rations, and all quartermasters are requested to furnish you transportation.

Respectfully your obedient servant,

WM. H. PARKER, commanding.

Midshipman ——————————C. S. Navy.

We had about thirty colored servants in the command, and they started for Richmond in a body. They went off in high spirits, singing a song in chorus, and all walking lame in the left leg as it is the habit of the colored population to do. I gave them all as much bacon, sugar and coffee as they could carry; and did the same to the midshipmen and the Charlotte company. The remainder was then divided into equal parts and distributed among the officers who remained with me.

Mr. Davis had with him four skeleton brigades of cavalry, viz.: Duke's, Dibbrell's, Ferguson's and Vaughn's. Many of the men traveled with him, I believe, to get their rations. Some of them were throwing away or selling their arms, as they looked upon the war as over. There were many noble spirits among them who were ready, and anxious, to follow and defend the President to the death: but the force taken as an organization was demoralized.

President Davis went to the house of the Hon. Mr. Burt. After finishing my duties in regard to transferring the treasure, and disbanding my command, I called upon him. I never saw the President appear to better advantage than during these last hours of the Confederacy. He was captured eight days after this, near Irwinsville, Georgia, about 175 miles from Abbeville. His personal appearance has been often described. I remember him as a slender man, of about 5 feet 10 inches in height, and with a grey eye as his most marked feature. His deportment was singularly quiet and dignified. At this time he showed no signs of despondency. His air was resolute; and he looked, as he is, a born leader of men. His cabinet officers, with the exception of General Breckenridge and Mr. Reagan, stood, I thought, rather in awe of him.

General Breckenridge presented his usual bold cavalier manner; but Mr. Mallory, Secretary of the Navy, and Mr. Benjamin, Secretary of State, were much depressed and showed it. I do not recall Mr. Reagan—he was the Postmaster-General, and acting Secretary of the Treasury. Mr. Trenholm, Secretary of the Treasury, and Mr. Davis, Attorney General, had been taken ill by the way and were not with the party.

In addition to the four brigades of cavalry the President had in company more Brigadier-Generals than I thought were in the army. Many of them had ambulances and wagons, and the train must have been several miles long. It seemed to me that it was half a day coming in. Referring to the Federal cavalry I have alluded to, it was said that it was marching on Abbeville, when it met Mr. Davis' escort and turned back. I never knew the truth of this report.[1]

---

[1]Basil Duke's cavalry brigade fought a drawn battle near Marion, Virginia, prior to joining Davis's escort, but the escort itself fought no battles after leaving Virginia.

After shaking hands with President Davis, whom I found alone, I first gave him an account of my taking his family from Charlotte, and told him of my having met Mrs. Davis a few days before. He thanked me, and then inquired after my command. I told him I had disbanded it. He said: "Captain, I am very sorry to hear that," and repeated it several times. I told him I had but obeyed Mr. Mallory's order; that my command had been on the march for thirty days, and was without shoes and proper clothing. The President seemed to be in deep thought for a few moments, and I, wishing him clearly to appreciate my position, said: "Mr. President, I must beg you to understand that I acted upon the peremptory order of the Secretary of the Navy." He then replied: "Captain, I have no fault to find with you, but I am very sorry Mr. Mallory gave you the order." After seeing the escort, I understood Mr. Davis' regret. I told the President of my trip to Augusta, and of General Wilson's movements, and asked him what he proposed to do. He said he should remain four days in Abbeville. I then mentioned the affair of the previous night, and said I looked upon his capture as inevitable if he prolonged his stay. He replied that he would never desert the Southern people; that he had been elected by them to the office he held, and would stand by them. He gave me to understand that he would not take any step which might be construed into an inglorious flight. He was most impressive on this point. The mere idea that he might be looked upon as fleeing, seemed to arouse him. He got up and paced the floor, and repeated several times that he would never abandon his people. I stuck to my text; said I: "Mr. President, if you remain here you will be captured. You have about you only a few demoralized soldiers, and a train of camp followers three miles long. You will be captured, and you know how we will all feel that. It is your duty to the Southern people not to allow yourself to be made a prisoner. Leave now with a few followers and cross the Mississippi, as you express a desire to do eventually, and there again raise the standard."

The interview lasted an hour, and I used every argument I could think of to induce him to leave Abbeville; but it was in vain. He insisted that he would remain four days. Upon leaving the President I found Messrs. Mallory and Benjamin awaiting me. The latter very nervous and impatient to continue the retreat. Mr. Mallory was more phlegmatic, but was of my opinion, that they would all be captured if they remained.

During the afternoon the soldiers packed the treasure in the wagons again, preparatory to moving. After it was taken away from Abbeville, which was on that night, I have no further personal knowledge of it. The admirable letter of Captain M. H. Clark published in the *Southern Historical Society Papers* December, 1881, gives the best account of it I have seen.[2] A day after the party left I yielded to the solicitations of my officers and sent Paymaster Wheliss to Washington, Georgia, to see if he could not secure money enough from Mr. Reagan to enable us to get back to our homes. We were paid fifteen hundred dollars, which was divided *pro rata*. It gave us each about twenty days pay. A reference to Captain Clark's letter shows that several of the President's aids received each as much as my entire command. But everything was in confusion, and no justice was to be expected. I think the President took as little account of the money as I did myself, and I cannot say more than that. As to the charge that he took an undue portion of it, I scorn to notice it.

I asked Mr. Mallory to come to my quarters to tea that evening, and about 8 o'clock Mr. Benjamin came in. He begged me to see the President again, and to urge him to leave. After some demur I consented to do so. I found Mr. Davis alone as before, and apologizing for my intrusion, said my intense anxiety for his safety must excuse it. I remained some time, and saw that he had a better appreciation of the condition of affairs in Georgia than when I had seen him in the morning. I proposed to him that he should leave Abbeville with four naval officers, (of whom I was to be one) and escape to the east coast of Florida. The object of taking naval officers was that they might seize a vessel of some kind and get to Cuba or the Bahamas; but this he rejected.

---

[2]Captain M. H. Clark, "The Last Days of the Confederate Treasury and What Became of its Specie," *Southern Historical Society Papers* (1881), pp. 542–56.

I left the President at 9 o'clock, and as I went out he sent one of his Aids to call the Cabinet together. I went to my quarters, and not long after received a note from Mr. Mallory saying they would leave that night, and he notified me so that I might accompany them if I desired. As they were all mounted and I was on foot and could not get a horse, I was obliged to decline. About 11 o'clock the President and his escort left Abbeville for Washington, Ga. If I have given undue prominence to myself in relating the occurrences of this day at Abbeville it is only because I had just returned from Georgia, and was supposed to have a better knowledge of the condition of affairs there than any one else about the President. *C'est tout.*

A few days after this a passing soldier told me General Johnston had surrendered, and showed me his parole. I called together the few officers still with me, and told them that as we were in General Johnston's command we must accept the conditions—and now after the four years war, in which I certainly never desired to figure as a prisoner, I did wish to be captured so that I might obtain my parole: without it I did not like to set out upon my return to Virginia.

We had several alarms that the Federals were coming, and upon such occasions the officers would assemble at my quarters, where we would await our fate like the Roman senators, but they came not, and finally hearing that a troop of cavalry was in Washington, Ga., I sent a Lieutenant there with a letter to the commanding officer explaining my condition and enclosing a list of my officers. He very kindly spared us the trip to Washington by sending us paroles, only requiring the officer I had sent over to swear us in, which he accordingly did.

Our party now consisted of Captain Rochelle, Professor McGuire and wife, my wife and myself, and being "far away from home," we began to cast about for means to get back to Virginia. We went in the cars to Newberry, S. C., where I fell in with Surgeon Lynah, who had been a messmate of mine in the *Palmetto State;* and he kindly found quarters for us whilst we were detained there. We hired a wagon for our baggage, and an ambulance for the ladies—paying for them in sugar and coffee—to take us to Chester. On the way there we passed a night with my old friend Means, and were most hospitably entertained. The trip across the country passed without incident, except the stalling of our wagon the morning we left Means'. We would never have left that spot, I believe, had it not been for the superhuman energy of Professor McGuire, who with a small sized tree finally persuaded the mules to pull together. We stayed a day or two in Chester, and then took the cars for Charlotte, N. C., where we first fell in with the Federal troops. It seemed strange to see them walking around, and no one shooting at them!

From Charlotte we went to Danville by easy stages. The roads were out of repair and the cars went very slowly, getting off the track every few hours. We slept in the cars, which were always crowded. All the negroes in the country were making for Richmond, with their "things." They did not feel free until they had left the plantations; a very natural feeling. We clung to our seats day and night, determined not to "let go our hold" until we reached Burksville, where we intended to take the south-side railroad for City Point, on the James River.

I really do not remember how many days we were in going from Charlotte to Burksville; but we got there at last, one day about four o'clock in the afternoon. The first news we got was that there would not be a train to City Point until the next afternoon. Twenty-four hours to remain in Burksville. Ye gods and little fishes! Our previous sufferings sank into insignificance in comparison to it—and to make matters worse it was raining. I went out to find quarters for the night. If there was a tavern it was full. I believe I went to every house in town to inquire for rooms, but they were all full. I explained that I only wanted accommodations for two ladies, but all my entreaties were in vain—not a room could I get. Nothing better offering, we determined to remain in the cars; so Rochelle and I made the coffee as usual, and after supper we went about making the ladies comfortable for the night. The rain had driven the negroes and soldiers into the cars,—and, to make matters worse, some of them were drunk. While we were making our preparations, a Federal surgeon passed through the cars, and, noticing the state of affairs, very kindly told me I could have a room at the hospital. He said it was a poor enough place, but, he thought, better than the cars. We were glad to accept his offer, and accompanied him to the hospital. It was a frame building, and the room had neither windows nor doors. We pinned up blankets as substitutes, and, leaving McGuire to sleep across the doorway as a guard, Rochelle and I went to the railway station, where we made a delightful bed of sacks, full of shelled corn, and passed the night *al fresco*. I never slept better. The next morning early I called at the hospital to see how the ladies were getting on, and found that, for the first time, they had broken down. They had bivouacked by the wayside, slept in the cars, and undergone hardships of every description; but *Burksville* was entirely too much for them.

In despair I set out again to look for quarters: although I was assured it was useless to do so. I determined to try the country, and walked up the road intending to continue on until I found a house. I had not gone a mile before I came to a deserted mansion. The window frames and doors were gone, and the house was much torn to pieces; it evidently had been a well-kept, pretty place.

"A jolly place," said he, "in times of old! But something ails
it now: the spot is cursed."[3]

While looking over the fence, pondering, a negro woman came to the door of the kitchen, and as soon as I caught sight of the *bandanna* handkerchief on her head I knew she was the cook. She told me the family had "done run away," a long time before. She said she would gladly cook our provisions for us; that the rooms had no furniture in them, but there was plenty of fresh water, etc.

I returned in triumph to Burksville and brought back my entire party. We enjoyed the luxury of a bath and as we had an abundance of provisions we soon had a smoking breakfast on the table. I had kept three servants with me, so there was no lack of attendance. I

[3]These lines are from "Hart-Leap Well" by William Wordsworth (1800), part ii, lines 123–24.

passed here one of the most pleasant days of my life. We made a sort of a pic-nic of it, and enjoyed it beyond measure. We were "far from the madding sword," and had for the time at least no cares.

About 4 P. M. we packed up and went to the train, which soon after left for City Point. We arrived within a mile of the Point at dark, and here the engine left us and the conductor coolly informed us that the cars would be taken down the next day. But we did not mind; the cars were not crowded. We got out to cook our supper, and we sat around our camp-fire that night for the last time.

From the time of our leaving Charlotte until we got to City Point we were constantly thrown with the Federal soldiers as well as our own, and I do not remember in that time hearing an unpleasant word spoken on either side. The fighting men on both sides were the most tolerant.

In the morning the engine took us to City Point, where we were to take the boat to Norfolk. Professor and Mrs. McGuire left us here, and I discharged my last servants and sent them to their homes. At 10 o'clock the boat arrived from Richmond, and we went on board. It seemed strange to find myself on board with nothing to do. I could hardly realize it. About 4 we arrived in Norfolk and were at home again—just three years after our evacuation of it in 1862. So ended my career as a Naval Officer. "Farewell! Othello's occupation's gone."

Index

ABOUT THE EDITOR

Craig L. Symonds is an Associate Professor of History at the United States Naval Academy. Born in Long Beach, California, he graduated from U.C.L.A. in 1967 and received his Ph.D. from the University of Florida in 1976. He served four years in the U.S. Navy and spent three years on the faculty of the U.S. Naval War College at Newport, R.I. He is the author of *Charleston Blockade* (1976), *Navalists and Antinavalists* (1980), and *A Battlefield Atlas of the Civil War* (1983).